Freud, Race, and Gender

Freud, Race, and Gender

Sander L. Gilman

PRINCETON UNIVERSITY PRESS

PRINCETON, NEW JERSEY

Copyright © 1993 by Princeton University Press
Published by Princeton University Press, 41 William Street,
Princeton, New Jersey 08540
In the United Kingdom: Princeton University Press,
Chichester, West Sussex

Library of Congress Cataloging-in-Publication Data

Gilman, Sander L.
Freud, race, and gender / Sander L. Gilman.
p. cm.
Includes bibliographical references and index.
ISBN 0-691-03245-9 (CL : alk. paper)
1. Freud, Sigmund, 1856–1939—Religion.   2. Judaism and
psychoanalysis.   3. Antisemitism—Psychological aspects—
History.   4. Medicine—Austria—Vienna—History.
5. Jewish men—Psychology—History.   I. Title.
[DNLM: 1. Ethnopsychology.   2. Freudian Theory.   3. Gender
Identity.   4. Race Relations.   GN 502 G474f]
BF109.F74G554   1993
150.19′52—dc20
DNLM/DLC
for Library of Congress   92-48252   CIP

This book has been composed in Adobe Sabon

Princeton University Press books are printed
on acid-free paper and meet the guidelines for
permanence and durability of the Committee on
Production Guidelines for Book Longevity
of the Council on Library Resources

Printed in the United States of America

3   5   7   9   10   8   6   4   2

For Judith Dieckmann

———————————

JEW: Now, look at this hand of mine?
See if I am sick or healthy!
ISAIAH: You have the felon's disease,
From which you will never be cured!
JEW: Am I really sick then?
ISAIAH: Yes, sick with error!
—*Jeu d'Adam*, ll. 898–903

SHYLOCK: I am a Jew. Hath not a Jew eyes? Hath
not a Jew hands, organs, dimensions, senses,
affections, passions? fed with the same food, hurt
with the same weapons, subject to the same
diseases, healed by the same means . . . as a
Christian is?
—Shakespeare, *Merchant of Venice* 3.1.64ff.

The human body is always treated as an image of
society and . . . there can be no natural way of
considering the body that does not involve at the
same time a social dimension. Interest in its
apertures depends on the preoccupation with
social exits and entrances, escape routes and
invasions. If there is no concern to preserve social
boundaries, I would not expect to find concern
with bodily boundaries.
—Mary Douglas, *Natural Symbols*

CONTENTS

List of Illustrations   xi

Preface   xiii

INTRODUCTION
Freud's Jewish Identity and Its Interpretation   3

CHAPTER ONE
Sigmund Freud and the Epistemology of Race   12

Freud and Race   12
The Mind of the Jew   23
*The Transmutation of the Rhetoric of Race into the
    Construction of Gender*   36

CHAPTER TWO
The Construction of the Male Jew   49

The Indelibility of Circumcision   49
Reading the Meaning of Circumcision   56
Circumcision and Disease   60
Freud and Circumcision   70

CHAPTER THREE
Jewish Madness and Gender   93

The Predisposition of Jews to Specific Forms of Mental Illness   93
Trauma and Trains: The Testing Ground of Masculinity   113
*Reading Insanity: Male Homosexuality and the Rhetoric
    of Race*   132

CONCLUSION
Systemic Diseases: Cancer and Anti-Semitism   169

*Whose Cancer Is It, Anyway? Freud's Male Body as the
    Locus of Disease*   169
*The Circumcised Body as the Precipitating Factor for a Social
    Disease: Males and Anti-Semitism*   179

Notes   201

Index   267

ILLUSTRATIONS

Figure 1. The male Jew and the male African are seen as equivalent dangers to the "white" races in the anti-Semitic literature of the late nineteenth century. From Eduard Schwechten's parody of Schiller's "Song of the Bell," *Das Lied vom Levi* (1895), drawings by Siegfried Horn (reprint; Düsseldorf: Knippenberg, 1933). (*Source*: Private collection, Ithaca, N.Y.)   19

Figure 2. A ritual circumcision as depicted in volume 1 of *Jüdisches Lexikon*, ed. Georg Herlitz and Bruno Kirschner (Berlin: Jüdischer Verlag, 1927). (*Source*: Olin Library, Cornell University, Ithaca, N.Y.)   50

Figure 3. Francis Galton's original photographs of Jewish students at a London school. Galton then superimposed the photographs to produce a form of multiple exposure and created an image of the "essence" of the Jew. From the *Photographic News* 29 (April 17 and 24, 1885). (*Source*: Private collection, Ithaca, N.Y.)   73

Figure 4. The physiognomy of the male hysteric as beardless degenerate. From Wilhelm Weygandt, *Atlas und Grundriss der Psychiatrie* (Munich: Lehmann, 1902). (*Source*: National Library of Medicine, Bethesda, Md.)   114

Figure 5. Images of the Hungarian Jew Klein with his limping leg from the *Poliklinische Vorträge von Prof. J. M. Charcot*, trans. Sigmund Freud and Max Kahane, 2 vols. (Leipzig: Deuticke, 1892–95). (*Source*: National Library of Medicine, Bethesda, Md.)   118

Figure 6. The Jewish hysteric as represented by a chart from Hermann Strauss, "Erkrankungen durch Alkohol und Syphilis bei den Juden," *Zeitschrift für Demographie und Statistik der Juden*, n.s. 4 (1927): 33–39; chart on p. 35. (*Source*: National Library of Medicine, Bethesda, Md.)   119

Figure 7. The comparatively higher rate of mental illness (among 60,630 Jews) in the United States in a special census of 1889. From John Shaw Billings, *Vital Statistics of the Jews in the United States*, Census Bulletin no. 19, December 30, 1890. (*Source*: National Library of Medicine, Bethesda, Md.)   121

Figure 8. Images of the physiognomy of congenital syphilis, with the hidden destruction of the palate revealed. From Byrom Bramwell, *Atlas of Clinical Medicine* (Edinburgh: Constable, 1892–96). (*Source*: National Library of Medicine, Bethesda, Md.) 174

PREFACE

WRITING ON Sigmund Freud almost a century after the creation of psychoanalysis means acknowledging the extraordinary debt I have to the legions of scholars and critics who have previously written on virtually every aspect of Freud's life and thought. The biographers have constructed, reconstructed, and deconstructed his daily life; the psychoanalysts have given meaning to his errors and shifts of opinion; the historians have framed his life and works in contexts ranging from the history of culture to the history of the family; the literary critics have provided complex analyses of Freud's language, his rhetoric, and his theories. From all of these I have benefited. My own reading combines aspects of each of these approaches. The claim for this study is that it provides a new reading of the meaning of "race" and its relationship to constructions of ideas of "gender" at the turn of the century. Writing as I do at the turn of the millennium, I find this relationship an important one for my own culture and for my own self-definition. I have discovered in my study of Freud that the meanings of "race" and "gender" have varied greatly from his age to mine and that one must work at reconstructing the relationship between the two in an age that seems to be simultaneously so close and so distant. Each aspect of this book addresses the question of the relationship between these two constructions. From the initial consideration of Freud's internalization of models of race as a reflex of the medical culture in which he was trained, and his resistance to it, to the latent meaning of gender present in the discussions of the illness from which he eventually died, I explore how "race" and "gender" were linked in the medical culture of Freud's time and in his responses to that culture. This volume builds on earlier studies, especially my own work on Freud, which has now spanned more than two decades.

This book originated as a lecture series during my stay in the fall of 1988 as the Visiting Senior Fellow of the Council of the Humanities and the Old Dominion Foundation Fellow in English at Princeton University. I am indebted to Elaine Showalter of Princeton, whose scholarly work, friendship, and intellectual rigor helped shape this volume.

The lecture series became a graduate seminar held during my tenure in the spring of 1989 as the Northrop Frye Visiting Professor of Literary Theory at the University of Toronto. My presence there was made possible by J. Edward Chamberlin, with whom I have written on topics closely related to this book and for whose intensive criticism and intelligent comments I am always grateful.

The lectures were then given during the academic year 1989–90 as an undergraduate course held under the auspices of the departments of German studies, psychology, and comparative literature and the program in biology and society at Cornell University, and as a graduate seminar in the departments of psychology, history, English, and religious studies during my tenure as the B. G. Rudolph Visiting Professor of Jewish Studies at Syracuse University in the fall of 1991. I was substantially aided in my research by the students in all these classes at all these institutions. I am grateful for their attentive questions and their contributions.

The final draft of the book was written while I was the visiting historical scholar at the National Library of Medicine, National Institutes of Health, Bethesda, Maryland, during 1990–91 and the director of a National Endowment for the Humanities Seminar on "Freud and the Culture of His Time" at the Freud Museum in London in the summer of 1991. Funding for the overall project was provided by the Lucius Littauer Foundation and the National Endowment for the Humanities. I am grateful to the director of the Freud Museum, Erica Davies, and its former director, Richard Wells, for their help.

I am grateful to William Griffiths at Toronto and Marjorie Howes at Princeton, and at Cornell to Heather Munro, Chandak Seengoopta, John Davidson, and Catherine Gelbin for the work they put into the preparation of the book. Jane Lincoln Taylor's editing turned my prose into readable English, and Jane Marsh Dieckmann helped make the volume more useful through her index.

At the National Library of Medicine, the Library of Congress, and the Library of the University of Maryland (College Park) I was able to examine all the materials that Freud cites in his references. At the Rare Book Room of the College of Physicians and Surgeons, Columbia University, and the Library of Congress, I was able to examine books from Freud's library (as well as the other books included in the sale of books from Freud's library in 1938). At the Freud Museum I was able to examine the bulk of Freud's library.

The question of what volumes actually belonged to Freud remains a complicated one. Nolan D. C. Lewis and Carney Landis ("Freud's Library," *Psychoanalytic Review* 44 [1957]: 327–28, and the catalogue, 28 pp.) provide a reprint of the bookseller's catalogue for the volumes purchased in 1938 for the Psychiatric Institute (which are now at Columbia). David Bakan ("The Authenticity of the Freud Memorial Collection," *Journal of the History of the Behavioral Sciences* 11 [1975]: 365–67) draws the attribution of some of these titles into question, showing that a number of them had simply been added by the bookseller to those books purchased by him from Freud. K. R. Eissler ("Bericht über die sich

in den Vereinigten Staaten befindenen Bücher aus Sigmund Freuds Bibliothek," *Jahrbuch der Psychoanalyse* 9 [1977]: 10–50) provides further in-
formation about the origin of some of the volumes now at the Columbia
Medical College, and reproduces the bookseller's catalogue. Eissler also
lists those titles now at the Library of Congress. Further comments on
Freud's books in New York are found in the work of Ernest Harms, "A
Fragment of Freud's Library," *Psychoanalytic Quarterly* 40 (1971): 491–
95, and, concerning the small number of books in the Freud Museum
in Vienna, the essay by Hans Lobner ("Some Additional Remarks on
Freud's Library," *Sigmund Freud House Bulletin* 1 [1975]: 18–29). The
library Freud retained, which is now housed at the Freud Museum, 20
Maresfield Gardens, London, was first catalogued by Harry Trosman
and Roger Dennis Simmons ("The Freud Library," *Journal of the American Psychoanalytic Association* 21 [1973]: 646–87). A more complete
catalogue is now available at the museum, compiled by Keith Davies. My
notes on the volumes in these collections are reflected in the documentation for each chapter. Only those titles in the New York collection that
were clearly not part of Freud's library have been ignored. It is clear that
Freud did not read all the books in his possession; some of them are uncut
dedication copies.

In addition I want to thank the staff at the Olin Library, Cornell University; the Wellcome Institute for the History of Medicine; the Library of
the Royal Society of Medicine; and the British Library, for their help in
locating materials. The visual sources are from a number of collections, as
noted in the list of illustrations. I wish to thank the owners for giving me
permission to reproduce them.

This book is dedicated to Judith Dieckmann, as I promised long ago,
in thanks for her friendship and in memory of her father, a righteous
Christian who decided to leave Hitler's Germany even though he could
have remained.

All quotations from Freud's works in this study, unless otherwise
noted, are from Sigmund Freud, *Standard Edition of the Complete Psychological Works of Sigmund Freud*, ed. and trans. J. Strachey, A. Freud,
A. Strachey, and A. Tyson, 24 vols. (London: Hogarth Press, 1955–74)
(referred to in the notes as SE). I have compared each quotation with the
original as it appears in Sigmund Freud, *Gesammelte Werke: Chronologisch Geordnet*, 19 vols. (Frankfurt a. M.: Fischer, 1952–87) (referred to
in the notes as GW). Changes in the translations are recorded in the notes.
While I have critiqued the existing English translation, it is the most
widely available one and is the format in which Freud is best known in the
English-speaking world. See "Reading Freud in English: Problems, Para-
doxes, and a Solution," *International Review of Psychoanalysis* 18

[1991]: 331–44.) Unless I cite translations in my notes, all translations in this study are mine. Where possible I have tried to use contemporary English translations.

Some of my original work on Freud, especially that found in *Difference and Pathology: Stereotypes of Sexuality, Race, and Madness* (Ithaca, N.Y.: Cornell University Press, 1985) and *The Jew's Body* (New York: Routledge, 1991), as well as essays in *American Imago* and *Descant*, is reflected in the present volume; all of it has been reworked here. Another of my books, a closely related study on medicine and identity at the turn of the century, will be published by Johns Hopkins University Press.

Freud, Race, and Gender

FREUD'S JEWISH IDENTITY
AND ITS INTERPRETATION

THIS BOOK intends to question many of the assumptions scholars have made about Sigmund Freud's Jewish identity. Freud's Jewish identity has long been a topic for scholarly exegesis.[1] Recently Harold Bloom asked:

> What is most Jewish about Freud's work? I am not much impressed by the answers to this question that follow the pattern: from Oedipus to Moses, and thus center themselves upon Freud's own Oedipal relation to his father Jakob. Such answers only tell me that Freud had a Jewish father, and doubtless books and essays yet will be written hypothesizing Freud's relation to his indubitably Jewish mother. Nor am I persuaded by any attempts to relate Freud to esoteric Jewish traditions. As a speculator, Freud may be said to have founded a kind of Gnosis, but there are no Gnostic elements in the Freudian dualism. Nor am I convinced by any of the attempts to connect Freud's Dream Book to supposed Talmudic antecedents. And yet the center of Freud's work, his concept of repression, as I've remarked, does seem to me profoundly Jewish, and in its patterns even normatively Jewish. Freudian memory and Freudian forgetting are a very Jewish memory and a very Jewish forgetting. It is their reliance upon a version of Jewish memory, a parody-version if you will, that makes Freud's writings profoundly and yet all too originally Jewish.[2]

My answer to Bloom's question is only a partial one. For Sigmund Freud, an acculturated Jewish medical scientist of late-nineteenth-century Vienna, one of the definitions of the Jew that he would have internalized was a racial one, and it was a definition that, whether he consciously sought it or not, shaped the argument of psychoanalysis. Being a male scientist-physician and being a Jew were linked at the turn of the century in many complex ways. One of the most salient for any investigation of Freud's understanding of the meaning of his own Jewishness is the powerful association between Jews and disease made in fin de siècle racial biology. The assumption of the predisposition of the Jew to specific diseases (and the related role of the Jew as physician) presented an epistemological pitfall for the turn-of-the-century Jewish physician.[3] How could he both be at risk for certain diseases, especially specific forms of psychopathology, and simultaneously study and treat these illnesses? How could he (and here gender *is* important) be both the neutral scientist-physician demanded by fin de siècle assumptions about the positivistic nature of science and the individual at risk?

Given Freud's analysis of many of his dreams, the latent or manifest content of which reflects on the problem of being Jewish in a violently anti-Semitic world, the question of the racial identity ascribed to the Jew seems to have been raised first by Freud himself.[4] I endorse Peter Homans's model of Freud's response to the idea of "Jewishness" as analogous to the relationship of "a key to its wax impression or a statue to a plaster cast of the statue—psychoanalysis emerged as the negative image, so to speak, of its Jewish surroundings."[5] Homans sees the deidealization of Jewish men to whom Freud had attached himself as the key to the rise of this movement; I see this deidealization as, in part, the result of Freud's struggle with the very definition of science that became central to his primary-group orientation.[6]

Biological science at the turn of the century had a strong racial component, and Jews served as the major examples in the discussion of the role of racial difference in the predisposition to or immunity from specific diseases. Freud's apparent fixation on a biological explanation for psychological phenomena, a fixation that has greatly stirred the interest of historians over the past two decades, must be tied to his contemporary understanding of science as a domain in which debates about his Jewish identity were carried out.

Such an approach means neither reducing all of psychoanalytic theory to debates about Freud's Jewish identity nor seeing it solely as his way of coping with ideas of race and difference. It would be simplistic to argue that because Jewish sexuality was at the center of the fin de siècle image of the Jew, Freud's fascination with the sexual directly resulted from the internalization of this image. One can argue, however, that the form taken by the sexual in Freud's argument, and the rhetoric used, were shaped by a number of factors, including the discourse about Jewish sexual anatomy and sexual identity, and that this discourse was found within as well as outside the medical establishment of the time. I wish to measure, using Homans's paradigm, how this discourse impressed itself on Freud's language and thought, to what degree he was conscious of it and reacted to it, and to what degree he unconsciously incorporated it into his own manner of seeing (and therefore representing) the world. Some of what I will describe, such as the discourse about racial inferiority, is overt, and Freud deals with it as such; some of it, such as the nature of disease and Jewish risk or immunity, is incorporated in a more complex manner within Freud's texts.

Inherent in Freud's world, or at least in those scientific aspects of the world to which he early gave great value, were racial models of the Jew.

These models are found not only in the "crackpot" pamphlet literature of the time; they are present in virtually all discussions of pathology published from 1880 to 1930. It is in the "serious" medical literature, the literature Freud knew (and accepted or rejected), that these ideas of Jewish difference appear. Freud had to confront these models of the Jew hidden in himself in order to function in his world. And what was his world? It was the world of science into which Freud entered as a student, within which he formulated the basic structures of psychoanalysis, from which he attempted to escape in the 1920s with his advocacy of lay analysis, and from which his later "historical" studies stemmed. The biological scientist (and Freud was a biological scientist) and the physician of the nineteenth century absorbed the ideology of race as part of the "truth" of science. It belonged to the "high" culture of science, and was never completely questioned, even by Jewish scientists, who were seen in this world as being more limited in their mental construction than their Aryan counterparts. It is precisely the ubiquitousness of race in the "high" medical and biological science of the late nineteenth and early twentieth centuries that provides the context that can help one understand Freud's Jewish identity. His was a reaction formation that saw new value in the category of difference generated.

In this book I examine closely the German-language (and related foreign) medical literature on aspects of the special nature of the Jew, a literature Freud would have known, either directly (as it was cited by him in his scholarly work or was in his library or was written by his colleagues, friends, and teachers) or indirectly (because it was part of the culture of medicine in his time). After documenting in detail Freud's use of this discourse in his informal comments and letters as well as his rare, overt answers to it in his published writing, I read some of the texts and problems in Freud's work as more complex, qualified responses to this medicalization of the idea of race. My goal is not to portray Freud as a Jew responding only to racial science, but to show the effect of the paradigms of racial science on his sense of self as a Jew and as a medical scientist. I then show that the paradigm of science present in Freud's writing (especially in his appropriation of the language of "high" science, such as his use of evolutionary metaphors) is influenced by its overt use in the discourse of race.

Frank J. Sulloway wrote the basic book on nineteenth-century biological science as reflected in the works of Sigmund Freud without mentioning these arguments.[7] Sulloway focused on what he considered the "serious" science of Freud's day. This is a late-twentieth-century view that separates the "serious" science of biology from the biology of "race."[8] But this was not the case in the medical and scientific discourse of the nineteenth and early twentieth centuries. There was a seamlessness

to all aspects of the biology of Freud's day that made the biology of
"race" a vital part of the arguments of biological and medical science.
Had Sulloway looked at other Jewish scientists during that age of self-
consciously "international" science (such as Cesare Lombroso or Rafael
Becker), he would have found ample evidence to suggest that this was a
(if not the) central problem for the Viennese physician-scientist Sigmund
Freud. Thus I have brought parallel examples from the work of Freud's
contemporaries to present alternative readings of the meaning of Jewish
difference. Freud's powerful readings dominated those of his contemporaries during the early decades of psychoanalysis but did not expunge
their alternative understanding of the differences attributed to the Jew. As
virtually all of Freud's early disciples were Jews, the lure of psychoanalysis for them may well have been its claims for a universalization of human
experience and an active exclusion of the importance of race from its
theoretical framework. This was especially true since the heavy "Jewish"
representation among the early psychoanalysts was in fact an Eastern
European Jewish presence. In addition to Freud, Josef Breuer, Hanns
Sachs, Isidor Sadger, Viktor Tausk, Sabina Spielrein, Theodor Reik, Ludwig Jekels, Hans Kelsen, Sándor Ferenczi, and Abraham Aron Brill were
all either born in the East or were the children of Eastern European Jews
who had moved to Vienna. Such individuals would have had a sense
of displacement that would have been exacerbated by the intense anti-
Semitism of fin de siècle Vienna.

Unlike Frank Sulloway, Peter Gay does deal with this topic in his
work.[9] According to the title of one of Gay's books, Freud was a "godless
Jew." The juxtaposition (taken from a letter from Freud to Oskar Pfister)
is intended to startle. Jew and atheist—these concepts cheek by jowl in a
title must jar! However, such a juxtaposition only startles if the definition
of the "Jew" is primarily a religious one. For Freud, as we shall see, the
definition of the Jew had a further dimension. Being Jewish meant being
a member of a race. The argument in Gay's subsequent biography about
the structure of Freud's sense of self also ignores this aspect. Indeed, Gay's
primary discussion of the ideology of race comes almost at the end of the
volume, evoked by the rise of Nazism in Germany and the potential of the
Anschluss. Race is rarely mentioned in Gay's earlier study *A Godless Jew:
Freud, Atheism, and the Making of Psychoanalysis*. This is the major
difference between the image of Freud in Gay's later biography and in his
previous work on Freud's Jewish identity, and it is an important one. In
acknowledging the role of race in defining the anxieties of Jews in the
1930s, Gay points backward in his biography to his earlier discussion of
cultural anti-Semitism, implying that phenomenon also may well have
had something to do with race. But race remains an amorphous category,
placed in the streets and not in the classroom, in the graffiti scribbled on

the walls of the Viennese university and not in the textbooks taught within its walls. The importance placed on the rhetoric of race in the science of Freud's time is a quality missing in Gay's biography.

It has been assumed that if Freud did not explicitly counter the biology of race in his work, it played no real role. I have argued in earlier studies, as well as here, that there are other models for resistance to the language of biological determinism. Freud's works on the origin of humor, on the meaning of creativity, on the interpretation of childhood and sexuality, and on the construction of hysteria all fit into the models of "universalization" of attributes and "projection" of these attributes onto other categories of difference.[10] Central to my own work has been Freud's covert construction of the relationship between categories of difference, such as the constructed categories of "race" and "gender."[11]

Most recent discussions of Freud's gender politics have concentrated on his definition of the feminine.[12] These discussions have generally not included an analysis of the relationship between stereotypical representations of race and those of gender in Freud's work and times. Freud has often been accused of having a fundamentally negative image of the female. Where the analysis of race has taken place in this literature, it has always been in the shadow of this presupposition. Judith Van Herik, in her discussion of the relationship between Freud's understanding of the feminine and his Jewish identity, sees Freud identifying with Judaism as the ideal of masculinity and its power.[13] The view that Freud saw Jewish identity as imbued with patriarchal power not only creates a false image of Judaism as a purely religious practice, but assumes that Freud, who systematically rejected all religious values, could not abandon this one. Estelle Roith evokes an equally problematic stereotype of Eastern European "rabbinic sexual doctrines" and the family structure of the shtetl in explaining Freud's construction of the feminine.[14] She stresses the centrality of the mother's position in the "traditional Jewish family" and the concomitant need for the son to emphasize paternal authority. For her Freud was an Eastern European Jew rather than a highly acculturated Western Jewish physician-scientist with Eastern Jewish roots whose knowledge of the Eastern European rabbinic tradition was probably limited to what he read in the German-language journals of his day. Indeed, the complex questions that Freud's new science of psychoanalysis proposed in regard to human sexuality certainly had more to do with Freud's understanding of science than with rabbinic lore. While Roith's reconstruction of the social context of Freud's Vienna is sensitive to the multiple identities of Jews in this context, there is no sense that there might be a link between the scientific and the Jewish aspects of this world.

Both these studies are flawed in that they seek to localize Freud's discussion of the feminine without much attention to his construction of images of masculinity. The "masculine" at the turn of the century was associated with other realms besides that of religion. Indeed, during this period in which the institutions of science were only slowly opening to women, the "masculinity" of science was overt and intense. The emphasis on the power of science in late-nineteenth- and early twentieth-century Germany and Austria became closely tied to masculine self-identification, especially in those groups of marginal men, such as Eastern European Jewish men, who could enter into this identity through the institutions of science. Feminist critics also have made the unwarranted assumption that Freud's "Jewishness" is a vestigial psychic remnant of a monolithic religious or social practice. What I have tried to do for Freud is to "deconstruct the monolithic phallus," as Lesley A. Hall has undertaken to do for early-twentieth-century Britain, and to understand the social complexity of constructing a male identity as an acculturated Eastern Jew in the world of fin de siècle Viennese science.[15]

To understand the complex issue of what Jewishness meant to Freud, it is necessary to examine the implications of the stereotype of the Jewish male, especially the Eastern Jewish male, in the science of his time. (The very term "Jew" is as much a category of gender, masculine, as it is of race.) The relationship between the stereotype of the Jew and that of the woman (as parallel categories to the Christian and the male) became a central element in the structuring of Jewish identity. Neither image reflected an unmediated conceptual category. Each was constructed to present a means of influencing aspects of a world thought to be out of control. These two stereotypes were not equivalent, even though they underwent certain similar shifts at the close of the nineteenth century. The feminine was primarily an inclusionary stereotype. Woman was not the opposite of man, but rather was reduced to his complement; in the eye of the male, without women there could be no reproduction, and thus women must belong to a protected category. The stereotype was that women are weak and intuitive, while men are strong and intelligent. It is only in the work of a few individuals of the time, such as Arthur Schopenhauer and Paul Julius Möbius, who either did not wish to or could not sustain relationships with women, that women became totally expendable.

By the nineteenth century, the fixed relationships of the empowered male to the stereotype of the woman (as a conceptual category) had indeed become strained. This category could no longer be perceived as purely inclusionary; threatening aspects of it were reconceptualized as marginal. Thus the intellectual woman, failing to meet the reproductive expectations of the male, was viewed as sterile; the prostitute, seen as a threat to the male because of his anxiety about the spread of sexually transmitted disease, was viewed as destructive, as criminal. But these conceptual categories, the extension of the image of the introjected "bad"

Other, were always linked to the image of the "good" (m)Other. Here is where the inclusionary image of the woman was most powerful.

Jews, on the other hand, had been historically classified as an inclusionary stereotypical category with a status analogous to that of women. As long as Christians saw themselves in some way the extension and fulfillment of Jews, they needed Jews in their conceptual framework. Jews were that historical element against which they could define themselves; Jews were what the Christians had been and were no longer. The Synagogue was thus old, while the Church was young. However, with the secularization of the stereotype of the Jew (now the antithesis of the Aryan) there was no longer any need for the parallelism of the Jew to the Christian. The Jew became an exclusionary category. The Jew defined what the Aryan was *not*. It was that which the Aryan neither was nor ever would be. The Jew became the projection of all the anxieties about control present within the Aryan. There was no need to "protect" aspects of this image, because no necessary link remained between the Jew and the Aryan like the one between the male and the female.

Indeed, even as the "prostitute" and the "bluestocking" became representatives of those aspects of the feminine that provoked anxiety, the circumcised Jew became the representative of the anxiety-provoking masculine. The Jew became inherently "bad" as the image of those projected aspects of a world out of control and threatening to the integrity of the Aryan. As a result, the difference of the Jewish body and mind from that of the Aryan became absolute in the Western tradition. One can observe how the very body of the (male) Jew became the image of the anxiety generated by the potential sense of the loss of control, a loss of control that replicates and evokes the initial construction of the division between the "bad" and the "good" Other.

For male Jews the equation of the "Jew" (read: Jewish male) with the "feminine" was both highly problematic and potentially beneficial. It was problematic because it drew into question the status of the male Jew's masculinity. The male Jew became different from the male Aryan and, therefore, less than he was, much as the female was different from and less than the male. It was beneficial because it promised potentially to place him into an inclusionary category rather than into an exclusionary one. He could thus see himself (like the woman) as essential to the world in which he lived, even if he were viewed as dangerous within it. In his own fantasy, he became like the "bluestocking" or the "prostitute," negative aspects of an inclusionary category. But such a movement was possible only if another exclusionary category was constructed within his system of psychic organization of difference. This excluded Other within the psychic world of acculturated Western European Jewish culture took the form of the Eastern European Jew (perhaps because it evoked the all-too-recent past of this thought-collective, as well as the image of the Jew as physically and psychologically different). Such a realignment took place only in the fantasy of the male Jew. For the Aryan, the male Jew was a unified category and remained essentially different and excluded. The antithetical figures of the Jew and the woman became foregrounded during the late nineteenth century as both groups made substantial claims in the political world on the power held by the Aryan male. What is not immediately apparent is that each of these categories made a different claim on its relationship to the primary group in power, the Aryan male.

These demands collided in the world of science in the nineteenth and early twentieth centuries. In acquiring the professional mantle of the scientist, the Jew became "masculine." The scientist as defined in the age of positivism did not permit any role for the Jew but that of the "neutral" (male) observer. Thus the exclusionary category of the Jew was abrogated and the Jew became, in his own estimation, a scientist equivalent to every other scientist. It is precisely in the equation of scientist = male that the question of racial identity was suspended, at least in the perception of the Jewish scientist. The tension between the perceived common goals of the feminist and Jewish agendas in the acquisition of full civil emancipation and the "male" role that Jewish men had acquired in the world of science led to remarkable contrasts. It is not surprising that Jews, including some members of the Vienna Psychoanalytic Society, such as Fritz Wittels, could vociferously condemn the "absurdity" of women studying medicine, while at the same time Freud invited women, such as Margarete Hilferding, to join the all-male society.[16]

Stanley Rosenman notes the need of the Jewish social scientist to "analyze the psychosocial conditions that encouraged or inhibited resistance [within the world of the Jewish scientist]" while keeping in mind that such an "on-going Jewish discourse on Jewish survivorship [has not been] sufficiently seasoned by critiques of Jewish behavior."[17] I shall undertake to see both aspects of the question from my own standpoint as a Jewish scholar intensely confronted with the role of "being Jewish" within another Diaspora academic setting, that of the United States at the turn of another century. My cultural position is not identical to that of Freud; the sense of difference inherent in the image of the Jew in Western culture is presented with dissimilar rhetoric in varying times and places. It is necessary to understand that Freud on one level of his self-definition as Jew and scientist accepted the centrality of race as an epistemological category, while constantly needing to draw it into question.[18] Freud's frame within which he understood the Jew is different from mine. Yet we each have frames that reflect to some greater or lesser degree those definitions that dominate the cultures in which we live. Freud spent his life defining and redefining his sense of the Jew. This process of definition is our opening to an understanding of a conflicted and complex element in the dynamic formation of his identity. This study will examine three interrelated aspects of the image of the Jew as mirrored in the medical and cultural debates from 1850 to 1938: the body of the Jew and its meaning (in the discussion of circumcision); the psyche of the Jew; and the diseases associated with the Jew. These topics are closely interrelated—each is reflected in the formulation of the others. My task will be to show how these topics are countered in the rhetoric of psychoanalysis through the construction of specific concepts of gender onto which the anxiety about the Jew's body and mind (and, directly, Freud's own body and mind) are displaced.

Chapter One

SIGMUND FREUD AND
THE EPISTEMOLOGY OF RACE

FREUD AND RACE

Sigmund Freud, like any other Jewish scientist at the turn of the century, was faced with the double bind of the Jewish medical scientist: both physician and prospective patient, both scientist and Jew, both the observer and the observed. It is important to remember that Freud's life spanned the rise and the most intense period of anti-Semitic activity in Europe, culminating in the Shoah. Following a period of relatively reduced public anti-Semitism, the negative rhetoric increased during the period from 1870 to 1930. The implications of the term "Jew" altered in configuration and intensity from the 1870s to the late 1930s, along with the changes in the political and cultural climate. It was a period in which being Jewish meant being marked as different. There was no arena of public life in which this intensity was absent, including that of medical science. Not only did anti-Semitism exist in the institutions in which medicine (and its related disciplines, such as biology and anthropology) was taught and practiced, but anti-Semitic views became a staple of the substance of medicine itself.[1] Older theological models that described and explained the difference between Jews and Christians came to be secularized in terms of the biology of race. As Peter Winch has noted, "our idea of what belongs to the realm of reality is given for us in the language that we use."[2] And the language of Freud's Vienna, especially in the discourse of medicine as practiced in Vienna (and elsewhere in Europe), incorporated the notion of the special status of the Jews.

For Jews, it was an age of intense insecurity, of anxiety about themselves and their world that was a response to the level of public defamation. This anxiety haunted Sigmund Freud's dreams. In response to seeing Theodor Herzl's drama *The New Ghetto*, he dreamed about "the Jewish question, the worry about the future of one's children, whom one could not give a homeland."[3] But even these worries were cast in the language of exactly that late-nineteenth-century discourse of national identity in which Jews were presented as the antithesis of the Germans and the French because of their lack of a real homeland. The Jews were eternal wanderers, according to the legend of the Wandering Jew, which had a remarkable efflorescence during this period, because of their denial of

Christ, a denial caused by their "blindness." Translated into racial par-
lance, they were marginalized in European society because of their innate
biological and psychological differences. Freud's sense of the reality of
anti-Semitism cannot be doubted; that he, like Viennese contemporaries
of his such as Theodor Herzl, internalized a racialist model of the Jew is
also evident.

Freud's earliest references to Jews entirely fit the model of the Western,
acculturated Jew seeing himself as different from and better than the
Eastern Jew (*Ostjude*). All the stereotypical images of the Jew that were
present in an undifferentiated manner in Central Europe, and that were
applied to all Jews, Eastern and Western alike, came to be applied by
acculturated Western Jews to Eastern European Jews. The Western Jew
saw himself or herself as a German or Austrian nationalist, culturally
German, as well as commanding German, the language of high culture.
This image can be traced in Freud's early description of the Jewish accent
(the *Mauscheln*) of two Eastern Jewish males in a letter to his friend
Emil Fluss on the return trip from Freiburg to Vienna on September 18,
1872:

> Now this Jew talked the same way as I had heard thousands of others talk
> before, even in Freiburg. His face seemed familiar—he was typical. So was
> the boy with whom he discussed religion. He was cut from the cloth from
> which fate makes swindlers when the time is ripe: cunning, mendacious,
> kept by his adoring relatives in the belief that he is a great talent, but unprin-
> cipled and without character. A cook from Bohemia with the most perfect
> pug-face I have ever seen put the lid on it. I have enough of this lot. In the
> course of the conversation I learned that Madame Jewess and family hailed
> from Meseritsch: the proper compost-heap for this sort of weed.[4]

The distance between his own language and the language of the Jew also
separated his appearance from that of the Jew. Language, especially the
use of an identifiable Jewish accent, was seen in the medical literature of
the ages a reflection of a different muscular construction. Jews speak differently because the "muscles that are used for speaking and laughing are
used inherently differently from those of Christians and this use can be
traced . . . to the great difference in their nose and chin."[5] It is important
to note that by the 1880s at least Western European Jews were well
enough integrated into the linguistic communities in which they lived that
they spoke the regional dialects. Yet in popular images of Jewish difference, such as picture postcards, one of the most salient markers of this
difference remained the innate linguistic incompetence of the Jew in the
use of the indigenous language of the state. Acculturated Jews translated
this charge into a perceived advantage—they wrote about the "inborn
capacity of Jews for language-learning."[6]

All aspects of the human being are linked, as Freud himself remarked in the same letter: "People are not as different as they look and they can be easily divided into definable categories by the way they think and act. This is only natural, for similar circumstances always result in similar products." Freud saw the difference of the Jew in terms of the difference of the Eastern Jew, and he defined this difference in terms of race—not race in the global sense, for that would have implicated his own sense of self too greatly, but using the model of geographic influence and appropriateness. The standard definition of "race" was the sum of all the "physical characteristics and psychological qualities" of a people.[7] This would and did indeed include the predisposition of a race to specific forms of illness. Freud related the Jewishness of one young woman to an image of disease. When Freud joined the family described above, he was repulsed by the "poor soul, her face terribly disfigured by boils. I tried to force myself to stay in order not to hurt the poor girl, but my plight became more and more unbearable, and when to top it all she started to speak and lift her head-scarf, repulsion won out over the forbearance I owed a suffering human being. We left the compartment." Language and illness, especially illnesses written on the skin, were, as I shall discuss, attributed to the Jew as factors of the Jew's nature. It was the Eastern Jew who embodied the difference in race for the young Freud.

Freud was, of course, exactly such an Eastern Jew, a fact he could articulate in public only in the 1920s. He introduced his short autobiography written in 1925 as a contribution to a series on the contemporary history of medicine that was widely circulated among fellow professionals with this statement: "I was born on May 6th 1856, at Freiburg in Moravia, a small town in what is now Czechoslovakia. My parents were Jews, I have remained a Jew myself. I have reason to believe that my father's family were settled for a long time on the Rhine (at Cologne), that, as a result of persecution of the Jews during the fourteenth or fifteenth century, they fled eastwards, and that, they migrated back from Lithuania through Galicia into German Austria."[8] Freud acknowledges in his autobiography that he is not only a Jew, but a specific subspecies of Jew, an Eastern Jew, out of his appropriate place (and class) and living now in the center of Austrian culture, Vienna.[9] And yet, according to this account, he is not truly an Eastern Jew. Just as Theodor Herzl imagined his ancestors coming from an idealized medieval Spain, so too Freud saw his family moving from one cultural landscape (Germany) through the barbaric East and returning eventually to another cultural sphere (Austria). This tension between the perception of belonging and not belonging to any given culture mirrors the position of the acculturated Jew in late-nineteenth-century Europe.

Freud's birthplace, Freiburg (now Príbor), in Moravia, was a town with 4,600 inhabitants, of whom 342 (7.2 percent) were Germans and 137 of these "Germans" were Jews (2.9 percent).[10] Didier Anzieu stated the complexity of Freud's ethnic identity elegantly:

> Freud's first misfortune—premature exile at the age of about three and a half—turned out in fact to be yet another boon: a person creates not by continuing to mourn for what he has lost, and what he knows to be irretrievable, but by replacing it with a work of the kind that enables him, in the process of constructing it, to reconstruct himself. His second misfortune was also a blessing. From the end of his fourth year he lived in Vienna, where he experienced poverty and constant house-moving in an urban milieu: he came to resent the city, which intensified his masochism and, by way of reaction, his determination to succeed [in the field of medical science]. In Vienna, he learned to write a language that existed in two forms of characters (Roman and Gothic), a language of reference by which his parents set great store, and a code that arranged, but did not destroy, previously existing structures. He read the Bible in an illustrated translation, then Shakespeare in the original. He studied classics with great success. He attended one of the oldest universities in the world, where he acquired scientific exactitude. . . . In other words Vienna was an ideal medium for his conquering identifications.[11]

And, one might add, the most anti-Semitic city in Europe.[12] It was in this setting that "Freud consciously became a Jewish child, although not a religious one."[13]

Vienna was the city in which Eastern Jews, speaking German with a Yiddish accent, residing in the second district, were seen by "Viennese" Jews in other districts of the city as being figuratively on an island in their midst, the "Island of the Matzohs."[14] These Eastern Jews desired, as Josef Breuer commented about his father, to "replace Jewish jargon by literate German and the slovenliness of the ghetto by the cultured custom of the Western world, to win for themselves a place in the literature, poetry, and philosophy of the German people. [Science and medicine go unmentioned in Breuer's account.] All this required the highest degree of mental effort in observation of the environment, in a sympathetic striving for union with it, and in study which received almost no encouragement."[15] Freud needed to see his language as different from that of other Eastern Jews in Vienna, Eastern Jews such as Josef Breuer and Breuer's father.[16] He "never learned or spoke Yiddish," but he certainly was aware of the implications of the traces of that tongue in the image of the Eastern European Jew.[17] This quality was thought to be especially masculine, as it was the male Jew who had daily interactions with the public world, precisely the space that defined the difference of the Jew by his command of the language.

For Freud, the self-described displaced Eastern Jew in Vienna, it was the East itself that deformed the Jew into an ill-spoken and ill-featured caricature. The language of the Eastern Jew trying to attain "higher" culture reveals the impossibility of acculturation and acceptance. It is written on the tongue as well as on the face. The biological model that saw geography as a determining factor provided a boundary between Freud, the putative "Western" Jew, and the diseased, corrupt Jews of the East. In a letter to Eduard Silberstein he commented on having met Nahum Sokolow in the summer of 1875. Sokolow impressed him with his intellectual abilities and his knowledge of German culture. Freud dismissed him "as undoubtedly brilliant, but unfortunately a Polish Jew."[18] Likewise he derided his fellow student Josef Bettelheim by calling him a "coarse Jew" in *Mauscheln* ("grobber Jüd," a version of the Yiddish phrase for vulgarian, "grobber yung"), noting that Bettelheim spent his time mocking a handicapped woman.[19] The language of Bettelheim, the coarse male as Eastern Jew, was a sign of the Jew's pathology and was parallel to the pockmarked face of the diseased woman Freud saw on the train. For both, their physiognomy revealed their character. The male Jew was clever without being profound. This theme reappears in a sublimated manner in much of Freud's later scientific work. Indeed, in 1937, when he discussed the American psychoanalyst Smiley Blanton's patient Mr. R., who was bright and aggressive, Freud said: "Yes—some of these Eastern Jews are very bright." Blanton, a Christian, "went on to say how irritating this arguing was and asked Freud if he was ever irritated with patients. He laughed. 'Sometimes,' he said."[20]

For the young Freud, then, being Jewish meant being seen as different, as diseased, as culturally incomplete. The category of race had a real meaning for Freud throughout his life, and it was closely associated with the field of science. But the initial impetus for the construction of these categories antedated Freud's formal studies at the University of Vienna. Freud was made to realize this attitude as early as his high school years. He noted that "in the higher classes I began to understand for the first time what it meant to belong to an alien race, and anti-Semitic feelings among the other boys warned me that I must take up a definite position."[21] As he told the nationalistic German-American journalist George Sylvester Viereck in 1926: "My language . . . is German, my culture, my attainments are German. I considered myself German intellectually, until I noticed the growth of anti-Semitic prejudices in Germany and German Austria. Since that time, I prefer to call myself a Jew."[22] (Viereck's comment was that he was "somewhat disappointed" by this remark.) The language of race within science underlies the rhetoric and structure of Freud's discourse about difference. Especially in the medical faculty, he found himself "expected to feel . . . inferior and an alien because I was a

Jew."[23] Freud noted that the newly coined idea of the Jews as a "race" was then (in 1873) being used to label Jews as different.

Even in contexts where the talk was of Judaism as a religion, Freud used the rhetoric of race. In 1882 Freud wrote a long and often-cited letter to his fiancée, Minna Bernays, about meeting a student of her grandfather, the renowned rabbi Isaac Bernays.[24] The description of the old man and his evocation of Judaism as a religious force is permeated with biological language that echoes the discussion of race. For example, he writes of Martha's piety as a sign of the "stock not having deteriorated."[25] At the same time he chronicles the "hereditary" or "neuropathological taint" of mental illnesses such as neurasthenia, epilepsy, and feeblemindedness in his own family as "stories which are very common in Jewish families."[26] The vocabulary of racial science is part of the stock of concepts Freud brought with him to the university and found reified there in the classroom.

As early in his career as 1889, in a critical review of a study by the Swiss psychiatrist Auguste Forel (whose radical views on racial purity and eugenics were widely known), Freud attacked the widespread assumption that "nationality, race and geographical latitude" of a scientist attested to the truth or falsity of his or her science.[27] Freud was referring to the status of French science, and specifically the debate about hypnosis, in the German-speaking lands, but his statement would also reflect the perception that a "Jewish" scientist could never quite become an "Aryan" scientist. And those labeled as different are, according to Freud, hated because of this constructed idea of difference: "We are no longer astonished that greater differences would lead to an almost insuperable repugnance, such as the Gallic people feel for the German, the Aryan for the Semite, and the white races for the colored."[28]

Freud placed the conflict between Jew and Aryan centrally on his list of the racial conflicts in science. One must remember the debate in the 1840s between von Rosas and Mannheimer about the role of the Jewish physician. As early as 1842, the conservative ophthalmologist Anton Edler von Rosas had lamented, in a long piece published in one of the major medical journals in Austria, the decay of the medical establishment in Vienna because of the "annually greater increase of Israelites into the study of medicine."[29] (He wrote that in 1842 there were seventy-one Christians and nineteen Jews studying medicine in Vienna; that is, a full quarter of the students were Jews.) For von Rosas these Jews were ill fit to practice medicine because they were "so identified with the spirit of capitalism" and because they had a "much greater tendency to be quacks."[30] That Jewish physicians were quacks, that they practiced within a medical tradition that ran counter to the prevailing one in the German-speaking lands, and that they used their secret Jewish treatments as a means of hurting rather than helping their Christian patients were commonplaces of the medical literature from at least the sixteenth century.[31]

Von Rosas's cure was to exclude them "as long as they continue exclusively to trade and as long as they remain subservient to the laws of Moses."[32] Isaac Noah Mannheimer, the rabbi of the Seitenstettengasse synagogue and the de facto "chief rabbi" of Vienna (although this title did not officially exist), offered a long rebuttal of von Rosas's comments in another medical journal.[33] He contradicted all of von Rosas's claims but also made it clear to his medical public that the purpose of training Jewish physicians was to serve the Jewish population of the empire.[34] These Jewish physicians would not be competing with his Christian readers for patients. Von Rosas's rejoinder to Mannheimer also agreed with his assumptions.[35] Jewish physicians service Jews.

One of the most prominent members of the medical faculty at the University of Vienna, the brilliant and innovative surgeon Theodor Billroth, restated it most clearly when he wrote in 1876 that Vienna was being overrun with Jewish medical students, who, "even if they speak and think more beautifully and better in the German language than many Teutons of the purest water . . . can no more become a German any more than a Persian, a Frenchman, or New Zealander, or African."[36] The Jews are a race apart. They are inferior (in Billroth's 1876 view) as potential medical scientists because of their race. Billroth's argument had long been familiar in Vienna. But in the 1840s von Rosas and Mannheimer saw the definition of the Jew clearly as a religious one (conversion was at least a possibility for von Rosas); for Billroth, the basis of the definition of the Jew had shifted. By the end of the nineteenth century the term "Jew" (even in the phrase "Jewish physician") was redolent with the implications of race. The result of Billroth's views was that on December 10, 1876, as soon as the volume had circulated among the students at the University of Vienna, violent anti-Semitic activities took place in the medical faculty. Fistfights broke out between Jewish and non-Jewish students, and groups of Jewish students were physically removed from the school of medicine.

Sigmund Freud's argument about science and race in his review of Forel is cast specifically in terms of late-nineteenth-century images of race. These ideas of the relationship between race and nationalism were debated in the Reading Circle of the German Students in Vienna, of which Freud was a member (and to whose faculty Billroth belonged).[37] It illuminates the complexity of his understanding of the idea of race, as he came to see himself as a member of a race different than that of the dominant scientific culture. The antithesis between the Celt and the German, a subset of the antithesis between the greater categories of "Aryan" and "Semite," was resolved in Freud's rhetoric in the most overarching antithesis, between "white" and "colored."

Figure 1. The male Jew and the male African are seen as equivalent dangers to the
"white" races in the anti-Semitic literature of the late nineteenth century.
From Eduard Schwechten's parody of Schiller's "Song of the Bell,"
Das Lied vom Levi (1895), drawings by Siegfried Horn.

But are Jews really "white"? Freud certainly wanted to believe so, since
he had been labeled a "black" Jew. A story is ascribed to him in which he
was confronted with the question whether he was "all red" (a Socialist)
or "all black" (an Austro-fascist). He answered that "it was enough if a
man were flesh-colored."[38] While this seems simply to be a version of an
old joke (which has been attributed to a number of prominent twentieth-
century figures, such as the French conductor Pierre Monteux), it is important to understand that this was not merely taken as a metaphor in the
world of the "royal and imperial" monarchy and its successor states. In
1923, Joseph Roth, perhaps the most important Jewish novelist in German, whose origin was in the Yiddish-speaking areas of Eastern Europe,
writing in the Viennese *Workers' News*, described his central Jewish char-

acter as "black."[39] In writing to Milena Jesenská in 1920, Franz Kafka
commented that "naturally for your father there's no difference between
your husband and myself; there's no doubt about it, to the European we
both have the same Negro face."[40] When the non-Jewish writer Jesenská
herself turned, in 1938, to write about the persecution of the Jews and
other minority peoples of Central Europe by the Germans, she wrote
about them metaphorically as "the Negroes of Europe."[41]

The general consensus in the ethnological literature of the late nineteenth century was that Jews had "black" skin, or were at least "swarthy."
As early as the staged debates between Jews and Christians during the
Spanish High Middle Ages, Jews accepted that they were "dark and ugly"
while "most Gentiles [are] fair-skinned and handsome."[42] The rationale
provided by one Jewish source is that Jews at birth "are pure of menstrual
blood so that there is no initial redness" while Gentiles "have sexual relations during menstruation." This immoral and unhealthy redness "becomes lighter," as an apple does, while the Jews begin "white" and grow
black, like plums. Another, equally powerful argument for the skin color
of the Jew is that "Gentiles are incontinent and have sexual relations
during the day, at a time when they see the faces on attractive pictures."
The Jewish prohibition of images eliminates such an influence. The arguments, which are all reversals of internalized arguments about Jewish difference, center on the image of the Jew as "healthier." Indeed, the author
asserts that Christians (not Jews) are much more subject to diseases of the
skin, diseases that were generally understood as being the cause of the
blackness of the Jew's skin.[43]

The "liberal" Bavarian writer Johann Pezzl, who traveled to Vienna in
the 1780s, described typical Viennese Jews of his time. He saw them as
"covered from foot to head in filth, dirt, and rags, in a type of black sack
. . . their necks exposed, the color of a black, their faces covered up to the
eyes with a beard, which would have given the High Priest in the Temple
chills, their hair turned and knotted as if they all suffered from the *plica
polonica*."[44] Western medical science of the period also attributed the
Judenkratze, the fabled skin and hair disease associated with the Viennese
Jew, known in Yiddish as the *parech*, to all the non-Germanic peoples of
Central Europe.[45] The skin color of the Jews was an inherent quality, but
it was as much a sign of their illness as was their hair.

The Jews' disease is written on the skin. The appearance, the skin
color, the external manifestations of Jews mark them as different. They
have the skin color of "Kaffers," of blacks. But black skin also had medical significance. The Enlightenment Jewish physician Elcan Isaac Wolf
saw the "black-yellow" skin color of the Jew as a pathognomonic sign of
disease. [46] By the close of the nineteenth century this image of the black
skin of the Jews as a sign of their inherent illness came to be associated

with their inherent "racial" character. According to Houston Stewart Chamberlain, Jews are a "mongrel" (rather than a healthy "mixed") race, who interbred with Africans during the period of the Alexandrian exile.[47] Jews bear the sign of the black, "the African character of the Jew, his muzzle-shaped mouth and face removing him from certain other races, and bringing out strongly with age the two grand qualities—disproportion, and a display of the anatomy," as Robert Knox noted.[48] The blackness of the Jews is a key to their nature written on their bodies.

The image of the mixed race appears when Freud later compares the unconscious with the preconscious. He evokes the image of the *Mischling* or "half-breed": "We may compare them with individuals of mixed race [*Mischlingen menschlicher Rassen*] who, taken all round, resemble whites, but who betray their colored descent by some striking feature or other, and on that account are excluded from society and enjoy none of the privileges of white people."[49] The inability to "pass" is central here. This image of individuals who attempt to cross racial lines but who inevitably reveal their difference is at the center of Freud's concern. One can convert, but one cannot hide.[50] Indeed, in turn-of-the-century Vienna this sense of difference was felt unto the fourth generation. In 1893, the nineteen-year-old Viennese poet Hugo von Hofmannsthal, whose paternal great-grandfather had been Jewish, recognized in a diary entry the struggle of his Jewish with his Aryan ancestry: "If my entire internal development and struggles were only the stirrings of my inherited blood, the revolt of the Jewish blood . . . against my Germanic and Roman blood, and the responses to these revolts."[51] For Hofmannsthal there was a permanent sense of only "resembling" the true Aryan rather than being one. But what is this "striking feature" (*auffälliger Zug*) that marks these "half-breeds" to which Freud points? Is it not what Freud came to call the "narcissism of minor differences?"[52] What marks the Jew as only marginally different, but as so visible? Is it not the salient sign of Judaism, the marking of the male body through circumcision? By the end of the nineteenth century the body of the Jew came to be the body of the male Jew, and it was the immutability of this sign of masculine difference that was inscribed on the psyche of the Jew. The fantasy of the difference of the male genitalia was displaced upward—onto the visible parts of the body, onto the face and the hands where it marked the skin with its blackness.

But what does "visibility" mean in fin de siècle science? If the Germans (Aryans) are a "pure" race—and that is for turn-of-the-century science a positive quality—then the Jews cannot be a "pure" race. Their status as a mixed race was exemplified in the icon of the *Mischling*. The Jewishness of the *Mischling*, to use the term from racial science, "undoubtedly signifies a degeneration: degeneration of the Jew, whose character is much too alien, firm, and strong to be quickened and ennobled by Teutonic blood, degeneration of the European who can naturally only lose by crossing with an 'inferior type.' "[53] These people can have "Jewish-Negroid" features.[54] And their physiognomy is associated with their facile use of language, "the use of innumerable foreign words and newly created words to enrich the German language in sharp contrast to the necessary simplicity of the language of Germanic students."[55] Language, and therefore thought processes, reflect the racial origin of the "black" Jew. And this "taint" can appear among families "into which there has been an infusion of Jewish blood. . . . [It] tends to appear in a marked and intensely Jewish cast of features and expression."[56] Is this not precisely the anxiety that lies behind the young poet Hugo von Hofmannsthal's sense of himself as a *Mischling*? In the "mixed" breed, these "negative" qualities associated with the "blackness" of the Jew are most evident. The purity of the (Jewish) race became for Freud, as we shall see, an important medical factor in mental health. Indeed, in 1911 he joined the International Society for the Protection of Mothers and Sexual Reform (along with many other prominent Jewish and non-Jewish figures of the day), which advocated, among other things, "racial health and selective breeding."[57]

Such "minor differences in people who are otherwise alike . . . form the basis of feelings of strangeness and hostility between them."[58] Freud gave this phenomenon the clinical label "the narcissism of minor differences." But are these differences "minor" from the perspective of either those labeling or those labeled? By reducing this sense of the difference between "people who are otherwise alike" Freud drew on the Enlightenment claim of the universality of human rights, but he evoked the Christian underpinnings of this claim, for this "narcissism" fights "successfully against feelings of fellowship and overpower[s] the commandment that all men should love one another." Freud evoked the Christian claim to universal brotherly love in claiming that the differences between his body and the body of the Aryan were trivial. Freud comprehended the special place the Jew played in the demonic universe of the Aryan psyche. But he marginalized the Jew's function to that of "an agent of economic discharge . . . in the world of the Aryan ideal" rather than seeing it as one of the central aspects in the science of his time, the world he saw defining himself.[59] By asserting the claim of the tangential importance of race over and over, from his first articulation of it in 1918 to its final promulgation in *Civilization and Its Discontents* (1930), Freud pointed out quite the opposite— that the difference projected into the body and mind of the Jew came to have as great a meaning for the Jew as it did for the Aryan.

Thus Freud saw himself as a Jew, as a "completely godless Jew,"[60] as he wrote to the Lutheran pastor Oskar Pfister in 1918, or an "infidel Jew,"[61] using the colonial phrase in English in 1928, but as a Jew. Being a Jew had little or nothing to do with God. It was a racial category. Freud wrote to Israel Cohen in 1938 that he was "a good Jew, who had never repudiated Judaism," but also that he had a "completely negative view of all religion, including the Jewish religion."[62] And Freud "objected strongly to the idea of [the Jews] being unpopular or in any way inferior."[63] Yet that sense of inferiority was not dismissed from Freud's system, but rather transferred to another object, the woman.

THE MIND OF THE JEW

For Sigmund Freud in the 1870s the idea of race was confining and limiting, as it implied a biological, immutable pattern of development. After the turn of the century, it came to acquire a more positive valence as a sign of the special status of the Jewish way of seeing the world. It moved from a purely biological category to a purely psychological one. In 1886, about the time Freud was studying with Jean-Martin Charcot in Paris, Gustave Le Bon, the anti-Semitic French sociologist, published his overt discussion of the inheritance of the psychological attributes of race, which he ascribed as much to biology as to social environment.[64] (The American–Eastern Jewish psychiatrist A. A. Roback much later still accused Freud of putting Roback "to the test in piecing me together out of my environment ['Americanism'] and antecedents [Jewish 'Chuzpah'].")[65] Le Bon's views of the nature of the crowd were central to Freud's later work on the psychology of mass movements, which contains his unstated analyses of anti-Semitism. Freud's experience in Paris was as intensely anti-Semitic as that in his native Vienna had been.[66] Freud wanted to reject Le Bon's biological view of race as "the innumerable common characteristics handed down from generation to generation, which constitute the genius of a race."[67] For Le Bon, race stood in the "first rank" of those factors that help shape the underlying attitudes of the crowd. Racial character "possesses, as the result of the laws of heredity, such power that its beliefs, institutions, and arts—in a word, all the elements of its civilization—are merely outward expressions of its genius."[68] And yet for the older Freud it was within the psyche, not the body, that the difference between Jew and Aryan existed.

Anthropologists such as Richard Andree evoked the unknowable essence of the Jew. Andree observed, concerning the conservative nature of the Jewish body and soul: "No other race but the Jews can be traced with such certainty backward for thousands of years, and no other race displays such a constancy of form, none resisted to such an extent the effects of time, as the Jews. Even when he adopts the language, dress, habits, and customs of the people among whom he lives, he still remains everywhere the same. All he adopts is but a cloak, under which the eternal Hebrew survives; he is the same in his facial features, in the structure of his body, his temperament, his character."[69] Or, as a patient of the Viennese psychoanalyst Theodor Reik commented, "Once a Jew, always a Jew."[70] The body of the Jew is the sign of this immutability. Unlike Andree, Freud gave this essence a positive valence.

In 1926, Freud stated in an address to the B'nai B'rith on the occasion of his seventieth birthday that being Jewish meant sharing "many obscure emotional forces [*viele dunkle Gefühlsmächte*], which were the more powerful the less they could be expressed in words, as well as a clear consciousness of inner identity, the safe privacy of a common mental construction [*die Heimleichkeit der gleichen seelischen Identität*]."[71] His contemporaries, such as Theodor Reik (along with Freud and Eduard Hintschmann, the only psychoanalysts to be members of the B'nai B'rith), "were especially struck" by these words as the central definition of the Jew.[72]

Freud's version of the ethnopsychology of the Jew twisted Le Bon's claims concerning the biology of race. It evoked the Lamarckianism of William James's view of the transmission of "the same emotional propensities, the same habits, the same instincts, perpetuated without variation from one generation to another."[73] The uncanny nature of the known but repressed aspects of the mental life of an individual—about which Freud wrote in his essay on the uncanny—haunts Freud's image of the internal mental life defining the Jew. (Here it is the "uncanny" [*unheimlich*] that domesticates the "canny" [*heimlich*] nature of Jewish identity.) One of Freud's models is that of the ethnopsychology of the Jew—that there is a racial memory that exists in each generation. He observes (concerning "the uncanny associated with the omnipotence of thoughts") that "we— or our primitive forefathers—once believed that these possibilities were realities, and were convinced that they actually happened. . . . As soon as something actually happens in our lives which seems to confirm the old, discarded beliefs we get a feeling of the uncanny."[74] The affirmation through daily events—such as the exposure to anti-Semitism—revivifies the group memory, confirming the "common mental construction" of the Jew. This does not take place on the level of rationality, but within the unconscious. As he wrote to his Viennese Jewish "double," Arthur Schnitzler: "Judaism continues to mean much to me on an emotional level."[75] The return of the repressed—not the ancient traditions of religious identity, but the suppressed discourse of anti-Semitism, expressed by Freud within the model of racial memory—haunted Freud. He articulated this discourse of the difference of the Jew within the phylogenetic model of the inheritance of racial memory.

The debate about the meaning of what Philip Rieff sees as the Victorian and Edwardian generalities about the "persistent character of the Jews" must be understood as part of the quest of scientific psychology in the late nineteenth century.[76] For Freud this sense of the psyche of the Jew had to do not only with the mental construction of the Jew but also with the Jew's emotional construction. Here he would have found substantial support in the work of William McDougall, whose study *The Group Mind* (1920) played a central role in shaping Freud's own argument about the psychology of the masses.[77] McDougall sees the fusing of the Hebrew tribes into a nation as having "played a vital part in its consolidation, implanted and fostered as it was by a succession of great teachers, the prophets. . . . The national self-consciousness thus formed has continued to be not only one factor, but almost the only factor or condition, of the continued existence of the Jewish people as a people, or at any rate the one fundamental condition on which all the others are founded—their exclusive religion, their objection to intermarriage with outsiders, their hope of a future restoration of the fortunes of the nation, and so forth."[78] Jewish self-consciousness leads to the establishment of institutions that preserve this "common mental construction." And these institutions reflect the emotional bonds of the Jews. For McDougall, but not necessarily for Freud, this sense of common purpose within the sphere of the political defines the Jew. Central, however, is that all aspects of the Jewish mind—including all the affective components—have their roots in this "common mental construction."

When Freud commented to his "brothers" in the B'nai B'rith about their "common mental construction," he was also specifically evoking the Jewish body. Freud's major association with Jews in the 1870s and 1880s was in joining (and helping form) a new lodge of the B'nai B'rith in Vienna.[79] "B'nai B'rith" means "sons of the Covenant." While the name was selected as a replacement for "Bundes-Brüder"—a German-Jewish lodge founded in New York in 1843—it evoked, for fin de siècle Viennese Jews, the image of circumcision. As Theodor Reik noted in 1915: "The bond which the primordial fathers of the Jews concluded with their god is represented . . . as a glorified and emended account of an initiation ceremony. The connection of the *B'rith* with circumcision is just as little an accident as the covenant meal in which the worshippers of Jahve identified themselves with him; and the giving of the law—*B'rith* can also signify law—which stands in such an intimate relationship to the concluding of the covenant (Sinai) should be set side by side with the procedures of the puberty rites."[80] The sense of "common mental construction" is associated closely with the special form of the Jew's body and the ritual bonding it signifies. Central to this is the act of circumcision and its resulting "feminization" of the male body.

There was a general assumption in Europe at the time that there was a "Jewish mind" that transcended conversion or adaptation.[81] This was usually understood as a fault. Ludwig Wittgenstein commented about Jews such as Freud that "even the greatest of Jewish thinkers is no more than talented. (Myself, for instance.) I think there is some truth to my idea that I really only think reproductively. . . . Can one take the case of Freud and Breuer as an example of Jewish reproductiveness?"[82] The Jewish mind has no true originality. The Jewish mind is prosaic, as Freud wrote to Emil Fluss in the 1870s: "How well I can imagine your feelings. To leave the native soil, dearly-beloved relatives,—the most beautiful surroundings—ruins close by—I must stop or I'll be as sad as you—and you yourself know best what you are leaving behind. . . . Oh Emil why are you a prosaic Jew? Journeymen imbued with Christian-Germanic fervor have composed beautiful lyrical poetry in similar circumstances."[83] This view echoes the negative interpretation of the "common mental construction" of the Jew as expressed in anthropological and cultural debates in the late nineteenth century. The "intellectual attributes of the Jews," whether in the desert or in the banks of Europe, "have remained constant for thousands of years."[84] The qualities of the Jewish mind, of the "common mental construction" that defined the Jew, usually were understood in fin de siècle culture as negative and destructive.[85] The Jews "possess no imagination. . . . All who have any claim at all to speak, testify unanimously that lack—or let us say poverty—of imagination is a fundamental trait of the Semite."[86] The "Jewish mind does not have the power to produce even the tiniest flower or blade of grass that has grown in the soil of another's mind and to put it into a comprehensive picture."[87] "Hence the Jewish people, despite all apparent intellectual qualities, is without any true culture, and especially without any culture of its own. For what sham culture the Jew today possesses is the property of other peoples, and for the most part it is ruined in his hands."[88]

Such views of the Jews are statements about their psychopathology. Freud concurred with the notion that the Jewish mind-set is pathological. In his lecture on anxiety (1917) he evoked the Lamarckian model of the inheritance of acquired characteristics in order to argue that the "core" of anxiety "is the repetition of some particular significant experience. This experience could only be a very early impression of a very general nature, placed in the prehistory not of the individual but of the species."[89] Or, one might add, in the prehistory of the race. Freud went on to note that this "affective state . . . [is] constructed in the same way as a hysterical attack and, like it, would be the precipitate of a reminiscence."[90] The anxiety of the Jew is analogous to but not identical with the suffering of the hysteric. As I shall argue in chapter 3, the male Eastern Jew is the quintessential psychopath for fin de siècle medical science. The psychopathology of the Jew is impressed through the experience of the collective on the individual.

The roots of this view lie deep in the theories of ethnopsychology as formulated by two Jews, the psychologist Moritz Lazarus and his brother-in-law, the philologist Heymann Steinthal, in the 1860s. In the opening issue of their journal for ethnopsychology and linguistics, *Zeitschrift für Völkerpsychologie und Sprachwissenschaft* (note the link between mind and language), they outlined assumptions about the knowability of the mind.[91] Lazarus and Steinthal's object of study was the "psychology of human beings in groups [*Gemeinschaft*]." Unlike in other fields of psychology at the time, where laboratory and clinical work were demanded to define the arena of study, ethnopsychology depended on historical and cultural-ethnological data. Their work was highly medicalized: Lazarus had studied physiology with the materialist Johannes Müller and cofounded the Medical-Psychological Society with the Berlin neurologist Wilhelm Griesinger in 1867. While they wished to separate their psychology from materialistic physiology, they were bound by the scientific rhetoric of the materialistic arguments about inheritance. They subscribed to a Lamarckian theory of mnemonic inheritance in the construction of the mind. The great laboratory psychologist Wilhelm Wundt remained the major proponent of their views of "universal mental creations" well into the twentieth century.[92] And Freud made extensive use of Wundt's explication of these views in his *Psychopathology of Everyday Life* (1901) and *Totem and Taboo* (1913).[93] The psychology of the individual, as one of Freud's other sources, the Princeton psychologist James Mark Baldwin, commented, recapitulates the history of the "race experience." One can expect "general analogies to hold between nervous development and mental development, one of which is the deduction of race history epoches from individual history epoches through the repetition of phylogenesis in ontogenesis, called in biology 'Recapitulation.' "[94] The history of the human race was to be found in the development of the individual. But "racial memory" has a very different connotation for a Jewish reader of Wundt and Baldwin.

Freud, like the ethnopsychologists, needed to separate the idea of the psyche from the body; he needed to eliminate the image of a fixed, immutable racial composition that determines all thoughts and actions. For these thinkers, the psyche was separate from, and yet still part of, the body. It seemed impossible, even given the need of such thinkers to avoid the pitfalls of race, truly to separate the mind from the body.

Freud dismissed the Germanic weltanschauung as a "specifically German concept, the translation of which into foreign languages might well raise difficulties." It was not the rigid paradigm of knowing that appealed to Freud, but rather the acceptance of the "scientific" model, which, while it allows the "uniformity of explanation of the universe," only "does so as a programme, the fulfillment of which is relegated to the future."[95] The scientific mode of seeing the world is not too Germanic; it allows the Jew to see the world as a scientist does.[96] By the mid-1930s Freud could shrug his shoulders at the Nazi burning of his books, sensing that this action represented the German response to his own "common mental construction": " 'They told me,' he said, 'that psychoanalysis is alien to their *Weltanschauung*, and I suppose it is.' He said this with no emotion and little interest, as though talking about the affairs of some complete stranger."[97] Freud the positivist dominated in his comprehension of the mind-set of the Jews.

Lazarus and Steinthal call these groups "peoples" (*Völker*) but they stress that these groups are constituted by the individuals they comprise and are not fixed biological "races."[98] "Human beings," Lazarus observes, "are the creation of history; everything in us, about us, is the result of history; we do not speak a word, we do not think an idea, there is neither feeling nor emotion, that is not in a complicated manner dependent on historical determinants."[99] The standards for definition of a people are fluid and change from group to group; the standards for being French are different than those for being German.[100] Even though a "people is a purely subjective construction" it reflects itself in "a common consciousness of many with the consciousness of the group."[101] This "common consciousness" exists initially because of the "same origin" and the "proximity of the dwellings" of the members of the group.[102] And "with the relationship through birth, the similarity of physiognomy, especially the form of the body, is present."[103] For them this "objective" fact of biological similarity lays the groundwork for the "subjective" nature of the mental construction of a people.[104] But the biological underpinnings of this argument are clear: the Irish eat potatoes as a reflex of being in Ireland, which makes them Irish, and they are Irish because they eat potatoes.[105] Could one not argue that Jews are Jews because they circumcise their male infants and they circumcise their male infants because they are Jews? The place where these acquired characteristics are localized is not the body, but within the language of the *Volk*. For Lazarus and Steinthal, group identification is rooted in what is for them an observable and demonstrable relationship, but they self-consciously build on this basic identity a sense of group cohesion. This is an answer to the argument about "race" constructing the mentality of the group. Here, the constitution of the group is based on the biological accidents of birth and dwelling, not the inborn identity of blood. And yet it is the observable that structures their argument.

Freud sees the construction of the mentality of a group as a reflex of biology tempered by the social context of the individual. But this mentality need not be empirically based. It may indeed be based on fantasies about others. The Jew forms for Freud the touchstone of difference.

Thus, anti-Semitism is not wrong, an "error," but rather is an illusion of Aryans, the mental claim of their own superiority. In *The Future of an Illusion* (1927), Freud argued that the belief "of a former generation of doctors that *tabes dorsalis* [syphilis] is the result of sexual excess" was an outright error, as it was not based in fact. (This is an oblique reference to the common medical association of Jews, syphilis, and sexual excess.) But the belief that "the Indo-German race is the only one capable of civilization" is an illusion "derived from human wishes" rather than a misapprehension.[106] Freud here introduces the notion that there may be a "kernel of truth" in the origin of the Aryan view. The fantasy about the superiority of the Aryan, which provides the roots of anti-Semitism, is isolated in his construction of history from Freud's sense of the meaning of the active persecution of the Jews that resulted from the fantasies of the "Indo-German race."

In *Civilization and Its Discontents* (1930), Freud commented on the subjectivity of happiness: "No matter how much we may shrink with horror from certain situations—of a galley-slave in antiquity, of a peasant during the Thirty Years' War, of a victim of the Holy Inquisition, of a Jew awaiting a pogrom—it is nevertheless impossible for us to feel our way into such people—to divine the changes which original obtuseness of mind, a gradual stupefying process, the cessation of expectations, and cruder or more refined methods of narcotization have produced upon their receptivity to sensations of pleasure and unpleasure."[107] Freud separates himself and the reader (the "us") from the victim of the illusion of the persecutor.[108] This works in terms of the historical images he uses from antiquity, the seventeenth century, and the sixteenth century, but the image of the pogrom, while obliquely "historical" in that the term refers to the persecution of Russian Jewry at the end of the century, was also quite immediate to Freud, as "pogrom" was a term evoked in the Jew-baiting riots in Vienna and Berlin. In his narrative he displaces what was occurring in his own experience, even while he wrote *Civilization and Its Discontents*, into a "distant" past from which "he" and "we" stand apart as observers.

But officially and publicly (at least with non-Jews), as in his earlier review of Forel, Freud rejected traditional definitions of "race" as an operative category in science. During his analysis of Smiley Blanton, he commented: "My background as a Jew helped me to stand being criticized, being isolated, working alone. . . . All this was of help to me in discovering analysis. But that psychoanalysis itself is a Jewish product seems to me nonsense. As a scientific work, it is neither Jewish nor Catholic nor Gentile."[109] He wrote in a birthday greeting to Ernest Jones in 1929: "The first piece of work that it fell to psychoanalysis to perform was the discovery of the instincts that are common to all men living today—and not only to those living today but to those of ancient and of prehistoric times. It called for no great effort, therefore, for psychoanalysis to ignore the differences that arise among the inhabitants of the earth owing to the multiplicity of races, languages, and countries."[110] Yet this was written to an individual about whom he felt a "racial strangeness" (*Rassenfremdheit*) upon their first meeting in 1908.[111] Jones reported that Freud had said, during this meeting, that "from the shape of my [Jones's] head I could not be English and must be Welsh. It astonished me, first because it is uncommon for anyone on the Continent to know of the existence of my native country, and then because I had suspected my dolichocephalic skull might as well be Teutonic as Celtic."[112] Even Jones's response to Freud's remark is couched in the language of racial biology. Yet there was always the possibility that this view could erupt in anti-Semitic utterances. While Jones deplored the common discourse of anti-Semitism, when angered by the Viennese Jew Otto Rank in 1923 he lashed out at him as a "swindling Jew."[113]

The Viennese-Jewish psychoanalyst Hanns Sachs, writing in the mid-1940s, was much more attuned to the implications of "seeing" race as written on the face: "I remember now, not without a note of sadness, that Freud, who had no trace of any 'racial' predilection one way or the other, in showing us [the pioneer hypnotist Ambroise Auguste] Liébeault's photograph pointed out how un-Latin (today the word would be 'Nordic') his face was and how well this was suited to his name which evidently was a variant of the Germanic *Luitpold*."[114] Likewise, when Freud sat for the sculptor Oscar Nemon in 1931 he described him in a letter to his Jewish colleague Max Eitingon as "from his appearance a Slavic Eastern Jew, Khazar or Kalmuck or something like that."[115] The use of these categories was at the time in no way questioned.

The apparent contradiction of his public claim of the neutrality of science in his letters to his Jewish colleagues is evidence of Freud's complicated resistance to and restructuring of the idea of a group mentality. His conviction of the compatibility of neutral science and ethnocentric perception is found in a letter written on June 8, 1913, to one of his most trusted Jewish followers, the Hungarian-Jewish psychoanalyst Sándor Ferenczi: "Certainly there are great differences between the Jewish and the Aryan spirit. We can observe that every day. Hence, there would assuredly be here and there differences in outlook on art and life. But there should not be such a thing as Aryan or Jewish science. Results in science must be identical, though the presentation of them may vary."[116] This difference in "spirit" is present and yet undefined. Many opponents of political anti-Semitism at the time acknowledged that there were "indeed, many scientific Jews, but I see nowhere a Jewish science," to quote Anatole Leroy-Beaulieu.[117] Yet it was clear that Freud understood that his own identification as a Jew provided the "ground" for the new science of psychoanalysis as well as limiting the access of this new field to the claims of a "neutral science." In 1910 he had confronted his Viennese colleagues at the second Psychoanalytic Congress and stated the case bluntly: "Most of you are Jews, and therefore you are incompetent to win friends for the new teaching. Jews must be content with the modest role of preparing the ground. It is absolutely essential that I should form ties in the world of general science. . . . The Swiss will save us."[118]

But the Swiss, at least Carl Gustav Jung, came to see psychoanalysis in Freud's formulation as a "Jewish" science. Jung noted the differences between a Jewish and an Aryan psychology as early as 1918. He stressed the rootlessness of the Jew, that "he is badly at a loss for that quality in man which roots him to the earth and draws new strength from below."[119] This view made the Jew's creativity, especially in the sphere of psychology, of value only for the Jew: "thus it is a quite unpardonable mistake to accept the conclusions of a Jewish psychology as generally valid."[120] This statement, made in 1927, was repeated virtually verbatim in 1934, at which point he noted that it was "no deprecation of Semitic psychology, any more than it is a deprecation of the Chinese to speak of the peculiar psychology of the Oriental."[121] He further qualified his view of the psychology of the Jew (and the very meaning of a Semitic psychology) by paraphrasing Ernest Renan; he wrote of the "Jew who is something of a nomad, has never yet created a cultural form of his own and as far as we can see never will, since all his instincts and talents require a more or less civilized nation to act as a host for their development."[122] Jung's private condemnation of the "essentially corrosive nature" of the "Jewish gospel" of Freud and Alfred Adler in a 1934 letter reflected his general view of the lack of value of the "Jewish points of view" that dominate Freudian psychoanalysis.[123] Jung based his thinking on a theory of racial memory that was part of early psychoanalysis, but he presented this view of racial memory within a clearly anti-Semitic discourse.

Jung also articulated one aspect of racial theory that came to have central importance for Freud and for many Jewish physicians dealing with the biology and psychology of human beings. For Jung, male Jews are feminized. They "have this peculiarity in common with women; being physically weaker they have to aim at the chinks in the armor of their adversary, and thanks to this technique which has been forced on them through the centuries, the Jews themselves are best protected where others are most vulnerable."[124] He does not mean that male Jews are women, only that they share certain characteristics with women. They are thus neither entirely masculine nor entirely feminine. It is this compensatory and feminized psyche of the Jews that generated psychoanalysis:

> In my opinion it has been a grave error in medical psychology up till now to apply Jewish categories—which are not even binding on all Jews—indiscriminately to Germanic and Slavic Christendom. Because of this the most precious secret of the Germanic peoples—their creative and intuitive depth of soul—has been explained as a morass of banal infantilism, while my own warning voice has for decades been suspected of anti-Semitism. This suspicion emanated from Freud. He did not understand the Germanic psyche any more than did his Germanic followers. Has the formidable phenomenon of National Socialism, on which the whole world gazes with astonished eyes, taught them better?[125]

Jewish males are "gender-benders"; they exist between the conventional categories of "normal" (and normative) sexuality, just as they exist between the categories of European national identity and ethnopsychology.

Jung's views were stated in the light of his understanding of the relationship between the Jewish body (weak like the body of his essential woman) and the Jewish mind. The entire field of Freudian psychoanalysis was merely a further representation of the weakness, of the sexualized disease of soul, that dismissed the Teutonic psyche as a "morass of banal infantilism." (Jung's reversal of the traditional anti-Semitic charges about the nature of the Jew's psyche is striking.) Jung's categories reflect the complex relationship between the structure of gender and that of race. No wonder the Jews desire to become but cannot become Christian Aryans: "Just as every Jew has a Christ complex, so every Negro has a white complex. . . . As a rule the colored man would give anything to change his skin, and the white man hates to admit that he has been touched by a black."[126] And the Jew cannot shed his Jewishness even though, to follow Jung's argument, he desperately desires to do so and the Aryan cringes at any contact with the Jew.

Freud's anger at Jung at the time of the rupture of their friendship (or, at least, of Jung's discipleship) was cast by him in racial terms. In 1913, when he learned of her pregnancy, he wrote to Sabina Spielrein, who had been Jung's mistress as well as his patient, that he "would like to take it that if the child turns out to be a boy, he will develop into a stalwart Zionist."[127] Freud commented that he was "cured of the last predilection for the Aryan cause. . . . He or it [the expected child] must be dark in any case, no more towheads. Let us banish all these will-o'-the-wisps!" In the next letter, following her announcement that the infant was a girl, Freud commented: "It is far better that the child should be a 'she.' Now we can think again about the blond Siegfried and perhaps smash that idol before his time comes." Freud's discourse about blond Aryans such as

Jung and their eternal opposition to the "dark" Jews framed his conflict with Jung. It also simply reverses the rhetoric of race applied to him by Jung. But Freud did not articulate the difference in terms of gender—the imagined Jewish "boy" can become a Zionist, a Jewish nationalist, and the Jewish "girl" (Spielrein's daughter Renate) "will speak for herself." Jews, male and female, have a "common mental construction" as "dark" Jews.

Freud's romanticization of "darkness" is an acknowledgment of the "blackness" of the Jews and its glorification. But the image of the "dark" Jew is always linked to that of the "diseased" Jew. "Darkness" becomes a sign of the predisposition of the Jew to disease and the disqualification of the Jew as a physician, a neutral observer. Here one can return to the Hippocratic demand that the physician must appear healthy. Hippocrates opens *The Physician* with the observation that "the dignity of a physician requires that he should look healthy, and as plump as nature intended him to be; for the common crowd consider those who are not of excellent bodily condition to be unable to take care of others."[128] This tradition dominates even the modern view of the physician in which the doctor must have "a sound constitution and a healthy look, which indeed seem as necessary qualifications for a physician as a good life and virtuous behavior for a divine."[129] The dark Jew in turn-of-the-century Vienna would not fulfill this requirement and would be disqualified from becoming a true physician. Freud's romanticization of the "dark" Jew as the idealized Jew of the future also placed this "dark" Jew, male or female, in opposition to the claims of racial science about the intellectual and moral capacities of the Jew.

Freud was aware of the anti-Semitic association of the products of Jewish scientists with the nature of the Jewish mind. This tendency in the medical science of his day was evident when he commented to Smiley Blanton in 1930 that he had tried to place Jung at the head of the psychoanalytic movement because "there was a danger that people would consider psychoanalysis as primarily Jewish."[130] He said to Abraham Kardiner that he hated the idea that "psychoanalysis would founder because it would go down in history as a 'Jewish' science."[131] Psychoanalysis had to be freed from the perception that it was a "Jewish science," but it could not be freed from the Jewish mind, which, at least in Freud's view, constructed it.

In a 1936 letter (written in English) on the death of his friend and early British supporter Montague David Eder, Freud evoked the "common mental construction" that sets the Jew apart: "We were both Jews and knew of each other that we carried that miraculous thing in common, which—inaccessible to any analysis so far—makes the Jew."[132] A similar phrase ("a consciousness of numerous inner similarities") reappears to characterize his relationship with a fellow Jewish physician (and his own doctor) in his obituary of the Viennese Jewish cardiologist Leopold Braun published in a journal for Jewish physicians in the same year as his comment about Eder.[133]

Freud used this rhetoric often in his exchanges with Jews. He wrote to Karl Abraham on May 3, 1908, of their common "racial kinship" (*Rassenverwandtschaft*) as opposed to the "Aryan" views of C. G. Jung.[134] Freud's letter reflects his anxiety about the labeling of psychoanalysis as a "Jewish national affair."[135] As he later wrote to Jones, science should be beyond such designations, but evidently is not. Both Freud and Abraham saw a grain of truth in this charge, a truth rooted in the way Jews were assumed to see the world. Abraham wrote to Freud: "I find it easier to go along with you rather than with Jung. I, too, have always felt this intellectual kinship. After all, our Talmudic way of thinking cannot disappear just like that. Some days ago a small paragraph in *Jokes* strangely attracted me. When I looked at it more closely, I found that, in the technique of apposition and in its whole structure, it was completely Talmudic."[136] Freud's response did not deny this but rather placed this "shared mental construction" in the following terms: "May I say that it is consanguineous Jewish traits [*verwandte, jüdische Züge*] that attract me to you? We understand each other."[137] Abraham's claim was that the Jews in psychoanalysis have a common discourse and he evoked, in a positive manner, the traditionally negative label "Talmudic" for this approach. (This negative association was part of a long-standing Christian image of the Talmud as the source of Jewish error, which became part of the discourse of the Jewish Enlightenment in the late eighteenth century.) Abraham and Freud both accepted (and gave a positive value to) the charge that the Jews possessed a secret or hidden language, which was manifested in the manner in which Jews used (or rather, abused) language. The charge was that Jews *Mauscheln*, that they speak (and therefore think) differently from others.

In 1912, when the break with Jung was clear, Freud in a letter to Ferenczi despaired of yoking "Jews and *goyim* in the service of psychoanalysis" for "they separate themselves like oil and water."[138] How Freud experienced the "goyim"—that is, Jung—can be seen in a letter to Otto Rank a month later when the "Jews and *goyim*" became "Jews and anti-Semites."[139] In writing to Sabina Spielrein in August 1913, Freud commented, "We are and remain Jews. The others will only exploit us and will never understand or appreciate us."[140] His response in 1914 to Theodor Reik's critique of the Lutheran pastor-psychoanalyst Oskar Pfister's theological understanding of psychoanalysis was that Reik's comment was "too good for those *goyim*."[141] Not only are Jews different in mentality from Aryans, but this is an unbridgeable difference. Jews are unknowable to Aryans.

In Freud's comments on the "resistances to psychoanalysis," he wrote in 1926 that "the question may be raised whether the personality of the present writer as a Jew who has never sought to disguise the fact that he is a Jew may not have had a share in provoking the antipathy of his environment to psychoanalysis. . . . Nor is it perhaps entirely a matter of chance that the first advocate of psychoanalysis was a Jew. To profess belief in this new theory called for a certain degree of readiness to accept a situation of solitary opposition—a situation with which no one is more familiar than a Jew."[142] Even though Freud expressed both pride and fear that psychoanalysis would become identified as a Jewish undertaking, he also wrote to the Italian psychiatrist Enrico Morselli[143] in 1926 that, "while he does not know whether his thesis that psychoanalysis is a direct product of the Jewish mind is correct, I would however not be ashamed if it were. Although long alienated from the religion of my ancestors, I have a feeling of solidarity with my people [*Volk*] and think with pleasure of the fact that you are a student of a man of my race [*Stammesgenossen*], the great Lombroso."[144]

The irony is that by 1938 Freud had come to see that his anxiety about psychoanalysis being understood as a product of the Jewish spirit was a reflex of the culture in which he lived and had little or nothing to do with him. Anything that was seen as negative, whether created by Jews or by Aryans, came to be labeled "Jewish" and "corrupting" by the Nazis. When Freud disbanded the Vienna Psychoanalytic Society on March 13, 1938, he evokes the model of Rabbi Jochanan ben Zakkai after Titus's destruction of the Temple, who fled into the provinces and began a school of Torah studies, continuing unbroken the chain of Jewish learning.[145] Vienna was thus finally understood as Jerusalem, psychoanalysis as firmly anchored in the "common mental construction" of the Jew who formulated and shaped it.

It was not Judaism as a religion (which was "of great significance to me as a subject of scientific interest") with which Freud identified in a public letter in 1925, but rather the "strong feeling of solidarity with my fellow-people [*mit meinem Volk*]."[146] In his response to the greetings of the chief rabbi of Vienna on the occasion of Freud's seventy-fifth birthday, Freud stressed the communal, psychological identity of the Jew: "Your words aroused a special echo in me, which I do not need to explain to you. In some place in my soul, in a very hidden corner, I am a fanatical Jew. I am very much astonished to discover myself as such in spite of all efforts to be unprejudiced and impartial. What can I do against my age?"[147] Indeed, the 1934 preface to the Hebrew edition of *Totem and Taboo* stated the case for a secular, racial (or at least ethnopsychological) definition of the Jew quite clearly:

> No reader of [the Hebrew version of] this book will find it easy to put himself in the emotional position of an author who is ignorant of the language of holy writ, who is completely estranged from the religion of his fathers—as well as from every other religion—and who cannot take a share in nationalist ideals, but who has yet never repudiated his people, who feels that he is in his essential nature [*Eigenart*] a Jew and who has no desire to alter that nature. If the question were put to him: "Since you have abandoned all these common characteristics [*Gemeinsamkeiten*] of your countrymen [*Volksgenossen*], what is left to you that is Jewish?" he would reply: "A very great deal, and probably its very essence." He could not express that essence in words; but some day, no doubt, it will become accessible to the scientific mind.[148]

But it is not only the Jew who is unknowable within the pantheon of Freud's scientific world.

THE TRANSMUTATION OF THE RHETORIC OF RACE INTO THE CONSTRUCTION OF GENDER

Freud's comments on the unknowability of the Jew parallel his claims about the unknowability of the feminine. We have seen Jung's facile association of Jewish racial difference with the feminization of the Jewish male. Jung "knows" what Jews and women are. For Freud, the positive unknowability of the (male) Jew is transmuted into the imponderability of the feminine. The "neutral" scientist can know neither the essence of the Jew nor the essence of female sexuality, even its developmental structure: "Unfortunately we can describe this state of things only as it affects the male child; the corresponding processes in the little girl are not known to us."[149] Freud wrote this in 1923. It was part of a trope, echoed by fin de siècle sexologists, such as Paul Näcke, that "a man can never penetrate [*eindringen*] into the psychology of the female and vice versa."[150] But, unlike Näcke, Freud stressed the unknowability of the female by the "neutral" scientist; it was only the feminine that could not be known. Näcke stated that everyone in the system was influenced by his or her gender and unable truly to understand the Other. Freud understood the epistemology of science as a neutral act of observation in which the observer is not affected by his own role in the process.

Freud's comments on the unknowability of the feminine echo his earlier view, in *Three Essays on the Theory of Sexuality* (1905), that "the significance of the factor of sexual overvaluation can best be studied in men, for their erotic life alone has become accessible to research. That of women—partly owing to the stunting effect of civilized conditions [*Kulturverkümmerung*] and partly owing to their conventional secretiveness [*konventionelle Verschwiegenheit*] and insincerity [*Unaufrichigkeit*]—is still veiled in an impenetrable obscurity [*undurchdringliches Dunkel*]."[151] Here it is clear why Freud needs to construct the neutral scientific observer. The pejorative tone of this description parallels the anti-Semitic rhetoric of the hidden nature of the Jew and the Jew's mentality widely circulated, even in the medical literature, at the turn of the century. Jews are the victims of civilization and modern life, which makes them mentally and physically ill; they engage in hidden practices and conspiracies; they lie as a natural reflex of their character. Even though similar anti-feminist rhetoric is also present in the medical literature of the day on the nature of women (as in the work of P. J. Möbius, which Freud clearly knew and rejected) as well as the (male) Jew, in Freud's scientific writing this set of images was transferred exclusively to the image of women.

The rhetoric of race was excised from Freud's scientific writing and appeared only in his construction of gender. But this construction of gender was clearly two-edged. Not only did Freud construct a specific image of the feminine onto which the qualities of the male Jew were projected (which reified the image of the female found in the popular and medical literature of his age), but this construction was the result of Freud's assumption of the persona of male scientist. In addition to what George Mosse has described as "the idealization of masculinity as the foundation of the nation and society," one can say that it played a major role in the foundation of science, or at least in the creation of the image of the scientist, in the late nineteenth century.[152] It is precisely the construction of masculinity (and its variations, as in Freud's discussions of the [male] homosexual and the [male] anti-Semite) that will be the centerpiece of the present analysis of gender in Freud. For it was through the assumption of the neutrality of the definition of the (male) scientist that Freud was able in his scientific writing to efface his own anxiety (which he expressed in private) about the limitations ascribed to the mind and character of the Jewish male. Thus the fabrication of the image of the female was a reflex of the central construction of masculinity in Freud's writing.

The language Freud used about the scientific unknowability of the core of what makes a Jewish male a male Jew was parallel to that which he used concerning the essence of the feminine.[153] The rhetoric Freud employed in all these categories was taken from the biology of race, with its evocation of hidden essences and unknown forces shaping the actions of an individual. Only the nature of the self can be known: "In consequence of unfavorable circumstances, both of an external and an internal nature, the following observations apply chiefly to the sexual development of one sex only—that is, of males."[154] But is the Jewish male truly a male, or has

Freud constructed a definition of gender, here the male, that would include himself in a category from which Jewish males are excluded? The assumption of the knowability of the self, as one can glean from Freud's own remarks, is not extended to the essence of the Jew, only to the essence of the male. The unknowability of the Jew, the hidden nature of the Jewish mind, replicates the discourse about the Jewish body and its diseased and different nature.

The problem of the knowability of the Other and the self provides the rhetoric at the heart of one of the most complex and debated aspects of Freudian theory, Freud's reading of the meanings of male and female anatomy.[155] In 1926, Freud (in his essay on lay analysis) referred (in English) to female sexuality as the "dark continent" of the human psyche, the sphere less accessible to science: "The sexual life of adult women is a 'dark continent' for psychology. But we have learnt that girls feel deeply their lack of a sexual organ that is equal in value to the male one; they regard themselves on that account as inferior, and this 'envy for the penis' is the origin of a whole number of characteristic feminine reactions."[156] In this phrase, Freud translates the complicated, pejorative discourse about the "dark" Jew with its suggestion of disease and difference into a discourse about the "blackness" (the unknowability) of the woman. The "Jewish" body (which in Freud's discourse is the body of the male Jew) becomes the body of the woman. (Elsewhere I have sketched the implications of this phrase in terms of the medicalization of the black female body during the nineteenth century.)[157]

In the passage about the "dark continent," we should note Freud's language concerning the sense of inferiority attributed to the woman because of her "envy for the penis." The question of the woman's attribution of meaning to the female genitalia, and specifically the clitoris, is raised by Freud in this context: "Women possess as part of their genitals a small organ similar to the male one; and this small organ, the clitoris, actually plays the same part in childhood and during the years before sexual intercourse as the large organ in men."[158] The view that the clitoris is a "truncated penis" is generally rejected in contemporary psychoanalytic theory. To date the only explanation for Freud's view has been found in the arguments about homologous structures of the genitalia.[159] But little attention has been given to what Freud could have understood about the powerful model of homologous structures, which argued that the male and female genitalia were absolutely parallel, that every structure in the genitalia of the female had an analogy in the genitalia of the male.

Thus the clitoris was seen as a "truncated penis." Within the turn-of-the-century understanding of sexual homology, this truncated penis was seen as an analogy not to the body of the idealized male, with his large, intact penis, but to the circumcised ("truncated") penis of the Jewish male. This is reflected in the popular fin de siècle Viennese view of the relationship between the body of the male Jew and the body of the woman. The clitoris was known in the Viennese slang of the time simply as the "Jew" (*Jud*).[160] The phrase for female masturbation was "playing with the Jew." The "small organ" of the woman became the *pars par toto* for the Jew with his circumcised organ. This pejorative synthesis of both bodies because of their "defective" sexual organs reflected the fin de siècle Viennese definition of the essential male as the antithesis of the female and the Jewish male. (This feminization of the Jewish male continues into the present. In 1987, circumcision was attacked as the "rape of the phallus," a choice of language that reflects the sense of the feminization of the procedure.)[161]

But the clitoris, the "Jew," became a sign of masculinity for Freud. In his *Three Essays on the Theory of Sexuality* Freud stressed that the "assumption that all human beings have the same (male) form of the genital" is the primary fantasy of all children (male and female) about the structure of the body.[162] According to this view, all children believe that they have a penis and may lose it (male) or had a penis and lost it (female). The clitoris, the "truncated penis," becomes the sign of the missing (castrated) penis. In Freud's theory the unitary fantasy of a "male" penis is transmuted into the image of the clitoris as parallel to the penis (at least in terms of masturbatory activity). In the genital stage the little boy and the little girl masturbate using the "penis/clitoris." It is a unitary male penis that unites all the fantasies of the genitalia.

For Freud, the power of the homology of the genitalia introduced a basic confusion between the glans and the clitoris. Freud wrote in *Three Essays* concerning infantile masturbation that "in both male and female children it [genital sexuality] is brought into connection with micturition (in the glans and clitoris) and in the former is enclosed in a pouch of mucous membrane, so that there can be no lack of stimulation of it by secretions which may give an early start to sexual excitation."[163] The anatomically correct image of the glans covered by the preputium penis (the prepuce or foreskin) transforms the image of the preputium clitoridis, the fold formed by the labia minora anterior with the clitoris, bringing both "into connection with micturition." It was the glans, eternally exposed to sexual excitement through the accumulation of sexually stimulating fluids under the foreskin, that in the late nineteenth century justified the medical practice of circumcision as a treatment (or punishment) for masturbation. Here the "Jew," the clitoris, stands in relation to the intact male. In an extraordinary reversal of the stereotype of the hypersexual Jew, circumcised Jewish males are revealed as not excessively sexually stimulated (unlike uncircumcised males or females). Indeed, one of the oldest sourcebooks on human sexuality in Freud's private library revealed the true rationale for circumcision to be prophylactic, for under the "hot sun of the desert many evils can befall the male sexual organ."[164] Among these unspoken evils most certainly would have been the stimulation to masturbate. From his own studies, Freud knew that the clitoris does not stand in the same anatomical relationship to the urethra muliebris as does the glans to the urethra masculina,[165] yet he makes them analogous. The intact penis becomes the clitoris; the sign of the intact male becomes the "little penis" of the female.

Everyone, male and female, seems to relate to this male organ. The woman must transcend her own fantasy of castration and her penis envy. She must not remain fixated at the level of masculine sexuality but must move to the higher level of vaginal (reproductive) sexuality. As late as 1931, Freud stressed the need for female sexuality to develop from the early masturbatory emphasis on the masculine genital zone, the clitoris, to the adult sexuality of vaginal intercourse. The clitoris, the "Jew," is the sign of the masculine that must be abandoned if and when the female is to mature into an adult woman.[166] The "Jew" is the male hidden within the body of the female for Freud. The "Jewish" nature of "castrated" female sexuality is replaced by the universal "male" nature of the child's fantasy of the human body. This masculine aspect of the woman must be transcended if she is to define herself antithetically to the male. But with which male is she to identify? For the body of the Jewish male is not identical to that of the Aryan. The Jew's penis is different, and visibly so. The Aryan is the "healthy," "normal" baseline that determines the pathological difference of the male Jew. In Freud's discussion of the nature of the female body, the distinction between male Aryan and male Jew is repressed, to be inscribed on the body of the woman.

The analogy of the body and mind of the Jew to the body and mind of the woman was a natural one for the turn of the century. Within German high culture this image of the nature of the woman was already present. The entire medical vocabulary applied to the body of the female stressed her physical and mental inferiority to the male. And the terms used were precisely parallel to those used in the discourse about Jews. Thus like the Jew, the female, as Elaine Showalter has so brilliantly shown, was thought to be at great risk for mental illness.[167] But the pathologies of the mind are marked by the innate differences of the body. The female, like the Jew, is marked by her smell. The female, like the Jew, is atavistic in her body and her mind. Cesare Lombroso, the founder of modern forensic anthropology and himself an Italian Jew, provided a reading of the origin of the sense of shame in the "primitive." He remarked that in the Romance languages the term for shame is taken from the root *putere*, which he interpreted as indicating that the origin of the sense of shame lies in disgust for body smells. This he "proved" by observing that prostitutes show a "primitive pseudo-shame," a fear of being repulsive to the male, since they are loath to have their genitalia inspected when they are menstruating. But the association between odor and difference also points quite directly to the image of the source of pollution. The smell of the menses is equated with the stench of ordure, both human and animal, in the public-health model of disease that still clung to the popular understanding of illness during the late nineteenth century. Edwin Chadwick, the greatest of the early Victorian crusaders for public sanitation (who built on the theoretical work of German writers such as E.B.C. Heberstreit), perceived disease as the result of putrefaction of effluvia. In Chadwick's view, "all smell is disease."[168] The link between public sanitation and the image of the corrupting female (and her excreta) was the agency of smell. As much as was said about the nature of the female, about her body, the claim was still made that science can never truly capture her essence, which is beyond the understanding of the male. In the later philosophical works of Arthur Schopenhauer as well as in their medicalization in the work of Freud's contemporary, P. J. Möbius, the rhetoric of female inferiority was coupled with the charge of unknowability.[169] The ultimate distance between the "neutral" scientific observer and the object observed was the claim that the object could not share in the same perceptual strategies as the observer. Whether the object was a Jew or a woman was not germane; the central concern was the difference in the object's ability to comprehend the world.

In the course of his work on the centrality of human sexuality, Sigmund Freud redefined the subject so as to diminish the stress on sexual anatomy, on the association with the "normal adult." While sexuality came to be defined against the idea of the degenerate, it no longer was possible to recognize the "male" or the "female" at first glance. Sexuality was now part of the mental structure of all human beings. And their bisexual nature destroyed any specificity about the meaning of sexual anatomy. Each person reflected qualities of mind on the spectrum from the purely "masculine" to the purely "feminine":

> In the first place sexuality is divorced from its too close connection with the genitals and is regarded as a more comprehensive bodily function, having pleasure as its goal and only secondarily coming to serve the ends of reproduction. In the second place the sexual impulses are regarded as including all of those merely affectionate and friendly impulses to which usage applies the exceedingly ambiguous word "love." I do not, however, consider that these extensions are innovations but rather restorations; they signify the removal of inexpedient limitations of the concept into which we had allowed ourselves to be led. The detaching of sexuality from the genitals has the advan-

tage of allowing us to bring the sexual activities of children and of perverts into the same scope as those of normal adults. The sexual activities of children have hitherto been entirely neglected, and though those of perverts have been recognized, it has been with moral indignation and without understanding. [170]

By eliminating reproduction as the goal of the sexual, Freud destroyed the argument that Jewish sexual practices (circumcision or endogamous marriage) were at the root of the pathology of the Jews. But if we were to substitute the word "Jew" for the word "pervert" in this passage, we would find a restatement of the need to incorporate the liminal into the universal. "Jews" and "perverts" were virtually interchangeable categories at the turn of the century.

This phantasm of knowing on the part of the "neutral" observer is also attributed to the unknowability of the Jew. At about the same time Freud commented on the unknowability of the Jew, he also complained to his friend and analysand Marie Bonaparte, princess of Greece, that he did not know what women wanted.[171] These comments point to the unknowability of the female body as that "object" (in a Freudian sense) that is different from the self. It also places the "Jew"—in its slang sense as the clitoris—into the body of the female. But the essence of the Jewish body is too well known to be hidden and too well hidden to be known. It is "canny" and "uncanny" simultaneously.

Freud's contradictions about the meaning and function of race and racial identity and his assumption that race is a category vitiated by the new science of psychoanalysis are central themes of the present book.[172] The idea of the Jew in the science that formed Freud and other Jewish physicians at the turn of the century is present in the images, metaphors, and deep structures of his own theory. Jung's overt statement about the feminization of the male Jew was an accepted view of racial and gender politics in nineteenth- and early-twentieth-century science. The image of the male Jew was "feminized" even in the work of Jewish scientists of the period. Indeed, accepting the view that the Jews are a single race in 1904, the Jewish physician Heinrich Singer commented that "in general it is clear in examining the body of the Jew, that the Jew most approaches the body type of the female."[173] Hans Gross, the famed Jewish criminologist from Prague (and father of the psychoanalyst Otto Gross), commented about the "little, feminine hand of the Jew."[174] It is the pathology of the Jew, the Jew's "feebleness," that "often gives him a somewhat unmanly appearance."[175] These medical views echoed older anthropological views, such as that of the Jewish ethnologist Adolf Jellinek, who stated quite directly, "In the examination of the various races it is clear that some are more masculine, others more feminine. Among the latter the Jews belong, as one of those tribes that are both more feminine and have come to represent [*repräsentieren*] the feminine among other peoples. A juxtaposition of the Jew and the woman will persuade the reader of the truth of the ethnographic thesis." Jellinek's physiological proof is the Jew's voice: "Even though I disavow any physiological comparison, let me note that bass voices are much rarer than baritone voices among the Jews."[176] The association of the image of the Jew (read: male Jew) with that of the woman (including the Jewish woman) is one of the most powerful images embedded in the arguments about race.

The association of gender and race can be found quite directly in the attacks on Freud and psychoanalysis prior to Jung's comments. In responding to Felix von Luschan's attack on the new science of psychoanalysis in 1916, coming from one of the greatest "experts" on the nature of the Jew, Freud expressed himself in racial terms in a letter to Sándor Ferenczi: "an old Jew is tougher than a noble Prussian Teuton."[177] Luschan's attack on Freud, Wilhelm Fliess, and Hermann Swoboda saw them as a pseudoreligious collectivity parallel to Christian Science. He employed a phrase coined by Konrad Rieger for such pseudoscientific undertakings: "Old Woman-Psychology" (*Altweiber-Psychologie*).[178] Not only are Jewish scientists feminized, but their very claim to doing science is rejected as feminine. Jung's view simply recapitulated the more general charge that Jewish males were a "third sex" (to use the fin de siècle Jewish sexologist Magnus Hirschfeld's term for homosexual) as well as the specific charge that psychoanalysis was a product of this thought-collective.

When we turn to Sigmund Freud's internalization of the image of his own difference, we see that it is the relationship between ideas of race and ideas of gender that frames Freud's answer. On the one hand, Freud counters the charge of the special nature of the Jews by illustrating (using an ethnopsychological model) how the Jews, as a group, underwent the same Oedipal struggles as any other collective could have experienced. This view (reflected in Freud's anthropological writings) places the origin of Jewish difference in the past and understands it in terms of a universal model of experience. On the other hand, Freud explodes the charge of the inherent difference of the Jews by subsuming the qualities ascribed to the Jew and the Aryan into the female and the male. It is through the analysis of the theory in terms of its own critical presuppositions that the repression and projection of the image of the Jew can be found in psychoanalytic theory—not in a theory of race (as in the work of C. G. Jung) but in Freud's representation of the image of gender.

Drawing on earlier work published in 1925 and 1931, Freud wrote about the role of the scientist in resolving the question of gender in his comprehensive *New Introductory Lectures on Psychoanalysis* (1933 [1932]):

To-day's lecture, too, should have no place in an introduction; but it may serve to give you an example of a detailed piece of analytic work, and I can say two things to recommend it. It brings forward nothing but observed facts, almost without any speculative additions, and it deals with a subject which has a claim on your interest second almost to no other. Throughout history people have knocked their heads against the riddle of the nature of femininity—

> Häupter in Hieroglyphenmützen,
> Häupter in Turban und schwarzem Barett,
> Perückenhäupter und tausend andre
> Arme, schwitzende Menschenhäupter . . .

> [Heads in hieroglyphic bonnets,
> Heads in turbans and black birettas,
> Heads in wigs and thousand other
> Wretched, sweating heads of humans . . .]

Nor will you have escaped worrying over this problem—those of you who are men; to those of you who are women this will not apply—you are yourselves the problem. When you meet a human being, the first distinction you make is "male or female?" and you are accustomed to make the distinction with unhesitating certainty. Anatomical science shares your certainty at one point and not much further.[179]

This argument can be read as part of a rhetoric of race. First, let me translate this problem, which Freud articulates within the rhetoric of gender science, into the rhetoric of racial science: "There is an inherent biological difference between Jews and Aryans, and this has a central role in defining you (my listener) and your culture." The "you" whom the "I" is addressing is clearly the Aryan reader, for the Jewish reader is understood as part of the problem. The Aryan is the observer, the Jew the observed. Upon seeing someone on the street the first distinction "we" (the speaker and his listener as Aryans) make is "Jew or Aryan?" and that distinction can be made with certainty based on inherent assumptions about differences in anatomy. Indeed, according to a contemporary guidebook, in Vienna the first question one asks about any person one sees on the street is: "Is he a Jew?"[180]

This biological distinction can be clearly and easily "seen" even through the mask of clothing or the veneer of civilization. The young American-Jewish psychoanalyst Abraham Kardiner recounted his rejection by a young woman he met at a masked ball in Vienna once they unmasked and she saw that he was a Jew.[181] The violence associated with being seen as a Jew, being "marked" with the sign of Jewishness, is reflected in a case presented by Alfred Adler to the Vienna Psychoanalytic

Society in 1907. Adler told of a Russian-Jewish student at the University of Vienna who, having attended a violently anti-Semitic high school, had developed a "Jewish complex." The analysand commented that it was common practice in Russia to bathe nude and there were often people who covered their genitalia with their hands. He too did this. When asked why, he replied: "Perhaps because I am a Jew."[182] Adler's patient associated a culturally determined sense of shame as evident in the entire culture with the form of his circumcised penis.

But it was not merely social rejection or the internalization of shame that could follow. The threat of what it meant to be seen as a Jew was also articulated on the streets of Vienna. Violence against Jews was a common, daily occurrence from the time Freud was at the university and bands of anti-Semitic toughs would drag Jewish students out of classrooms and beat them. Jews, both male and female, responded to their own sense of increased vulnerability and their heightened visibility. Martin Freud, Sigmund Freud's eldest son, remembered "walking with Dolfi [his aunt Adolfine Freud, his father's youngest sister, who died in 1942 in Theresienstadt] one day in Vienna when we passed an ordinary kind of man, probably a Gentile, who, as far as I knew, had taken no notice of us. I put it down to a pathological phobia, of Dolfi's stupidity, when she gripped my arm in terror and whispered: 'Did you hear what that man said? He called me a dirty stinking Jewess and said it was time we were all killed.' "[183] The Jew is "dirty" and "stinking," the Jew is unhygienic and diseased. And the male Jew is the essential image of the Jew in this system. The only real cure for this disease is the extirpation of the Jew.

The clear construction in Freud's lecture on femininity is that the uniformity of the identity of all "males," as opposed to all "females," can be made in terms of the form of their genitalia. Freud continues his argument to show that this physiological determinant is central to any discussion of the nature of sexual difference. He identifies himself as a male in this text, quoting a male author, Heinrich Heine, who represented the Jew as the diseased feminine in fin de siècle culture, in the context of the impossibility of "knowing" the truth about the "dark continent" of the feminine.[184] For the anti-Semitic "Aryan" reader Heine's references would evoke quite a different set of associations than they had in the original text. Heine was (and remains) the primary Jewish writer in the German cultural sphere. Readers attuned to Heine's Jewishness would have associated the oriental turbans, the Egyptian hieroglyphs, the sweat of ghetto poverty, the wigs of the shaved heads of Orthodox Jewish brides as hidden signs of racial, not merely sexual, difference. Here is a Jew (Freud) citing a Jew (Heine) about an essentially Jewish focus, human sexuality. Freud can short-circuit this association only by constructing an image of the "male" to which he, Heine, and his male Aryan listeners can all belong. In his lecture on femininity, Freud's argument continues—he challenges the seeming dichotomy between the "male" and the "female" and constructs a universal continuum between these two poles. The distinction between "male" and "female," like the biological distinction between "Jew" and "Aryan," is dissolved as the seemingly fixed borders are shown to be movable. Freud's desire to abandon such rigid distinctions in a biology of gender mirrors the acculturated Jew's desire to abandon them in a biology of race.

The voice in Freud's text is that of a neutral male and a participant in the central discourse about gender in the scientific thought-collective. In my racial rereading, the voice would become that of the Aryan and part of the Aryan thought-collective. The fantasy of Freud's identification with the aggressor in my retelling of this passage as one about race seems to be vitiated when Freud transforms the problem of the relationship between the subject and the object into a question of sexual identity. The "male" is the "worrier" (read: subject) and the "female" is the "problem" (read: object). But this assumes that Freud's definition of the male body as uniform and constant is the norm in his fin de siècle scientific thought-collective. The Jewish male body is different, is marked, by the act of ritual circumcision and in many other ways. It is not that the anatomy of the genitalia creates two independent (and antagonistic) categories, but that there were three such categories—the male Jew's genitalia were understood as a marker of difference. Freud's need to distance the challenges to the special nature of the Jew's body through his creation of a universal "male" body transmutes categories of race into categories of gender. The power of these constructs is such that their reaction-formation nature is obscured, and they are accepted as the basis for the discussion of ideas of masculine and feminine gender as primary categories in Freud's system.

The exclusionary and inclusionary stereotypes discussed in the Introduction present themselves within Freud's construction of the categories of masculine and feminine. The image of the Jew, itself feminized, becomes the projected image of the woman. Thus the excluded Other (the Jew) becomes the included Other (the woman). The power of this fantasy of the necessary inclusiveness of the Jew can be seen in Freud's discussion of narcissism (especially in his 1914 essay on the topic). Here Freud constructs the desired love object as the mirror of one's own body. The memory of what one was, and the fantasy of what was, are what is reborn in the act of love. The "ego-libido," the emotional investment in oneself, is replaced through the process of civilization with the "ego ideal," the internalized sense of what society demands one become. But what if the sense of one's own body is deformed by the pressure of the "ego ideal"? How can one understand the sense of one's own body as damaged, as incomplete?

Freud ties the image of the narcissist to that of the woman. Women are idealized by society (read: men). "Especially if they grow up with good looks, [they] develop a certain self-contentment which compensates them for the social restrictions that are imposed upon them in their choice of object. . . . Such women have the greatest fascination for men, not only for aesthetic reasons, since as a rule they are beautiful, but also because of a combination of interesting psychological factors. For it seems very evident that another person's narcissism has a great attraction for those who have renounced part of their own narcissism and are in search of a love-object."[185] The social restrictions placed on the choice of object are equally great for Jews and for women. But Jews are never considered beautiful, with their "black hair and eyes or slightly prognathous face."[186]

Freud realized that his charge that women are substantially more narcissistic than men might well be understood as a "tendentious desire on my part to deprecate women." In acknowledging that his rhetoric could be understood as pejorative, taken as it was from the rhetoric of race, he also defended himself against this charge. He countered that "apart from the fact that tendentiousness is quite alien to me, I know that these different lines of development correspond to the differentiation of functions in a highly complicated biological whole; further, I am ready to admit that there are women who love according to the masculine type and who also develop the sexual overvaluation proper to that type."[187] The image Freud wished to evoke was that of a closed system, with each part playing its assigned and necessary role. Using the model of bisexuality, he stressed that either element in this system could shift, but the reciprocal parts remain fused in a necessary relationship. The image of bisexuality necessarily excludes any "third sex." This is clearly an answer to Magnus Hirschfeld's view (which follows a major tradition of nineteenth-century defenses of homosexuality) that there are fixed sexual identities that are neither masculine nor feminine. But, on a deeper level, it extirpates the position of the male Jew as a "third sex," neither truly male nor truly female.

What Freud constructed in his image of the feminine was the absolute counterimage of the Jew: beautiful rather than ugly, and intensely narcissistic. It was the Jew whom Freud saw as the favored target for the narcissistic aggression of other groups. The Jew was the target of this "narcissism of minor differences." But it was the Jew, at the turn of the century, who was considered to be the great narcissist, whose "character is weaker than his intellect." The Jew is "the most self-willed and the most yielding of men, the most stubborn and the most tractable." Jews "possess a strength of will, a doggedness, rarely found in the Occidentals."[188] Freud cryptically acknowledged this in passing, for he saw women not only as narcissists but also as "great criminals and humorists, as they are represented in literature." The exemplary criminals and humorists in fin de siècle culture were Jews. In linking the Jew with the image of the woman, Freud provided a place where the Jew could be made to disappear and still find a safe haven. This contradiction of the presence and absence of the Jew would haunt Freud's resistance to the power of race in his own time.

The movement Freud undertook in converting the image of the Jew, understood by his culture as intensely involuted and self-absorbed, into that of the woman is the translation of an image of exclusion into one of inclusion. The woman, no matter how intense (or because of the intensity of her narcissism), becomes the sought-after love object of the man. This fantasy of the exclusionary Other becoming an inclusionary Other is replicated in the popular Viennese-Jewish author Hugo Bettauer's extraordinary novel *The City without Jews* (1922).[189] The plot of the novel is straightforward. The Viennese city council finally acts on its anti-Semitic program and banishes all Jews from the city. We are shown how all the "best" aspects of the city—its culture, its economy, its health care—run down and finally collapse. The Jews are then begged to return to the city, which they do. This intense fantasy of being needed, being as necessary to the life of the city as the female is necessary to the life of the species, is an equally powerful retelling of Freud's translation of the narcissistic Jew into the narcissistic woman. The woman is not simply a substitute for the Jew; she is a needed and desired object no matter how complicated her image within turn-of-the-century thought. This tension mirrors the anxiety about the nature of the Jew, and specifically about the male Jew's body, that dominated the rhetoric of race in fin de siècle culture. The question of the definition of the Jewish male in the scientific literature of the time can be highly localized in the discourse about infant male circumcision as a cultural reification of the special nature of the Jewish body. This discourse frames the transmutation of images of race into images of gender, especially that of masculinity, within the creation of psychoanalysis.

Chapter Two

THE CONSTRUCTION OF THE MALE JEW

THE INDELIBILITY OF CIRCUMCISION

The core of the definition of the Jew for medical science during the latter half of the nineteenth century was also the most salient popular image of the Jew's body: the practice of infant male circumcision. "In the folk-mind scarcely anything was more important than circumcision. Circumcision *made* the Jew," as the American historian Jacob R. Marcus cogently observed.[1] Speaking of the late nineteenth century, the German anthropologist Richard Andree noted that in "Yiddish the very term 'to make into a Jew' [*judischen*] means to circumcise."[2] Circumcision marked the Jewish body as unequal to that of the Aryan, and the male Jew as the exemplary Jew. What would circumcision have meant to a Jewish scientist who had internalized the negative associations with the practice? As the anti-Semite Ezra Pound once remarked to his friend Charles Olsen: "There was a Jew, in London, Obermeyer, a doctor . . . of the endocrines, and I used to ask him what is the effect of circumcision. That's the question that gets them sore . . . that sends them right up the pole. Try it, don't take my word, try it. . . . It must do something, after all these years and years, where the most sensitive nerves in the body are, rubbing them off, over and over again."[3] The rub was a social as well as a scientific rub, as we shall see.

The centrality of the act of circumcision in defining what a Jew is made the very term "Jew" in the nineteenth century come to mean the male Jew. Thus there was an immediate dichotomy—all Jews, male and female, are different from the "neutral" scientific observer (who is male and Aryan in his ideology), but male Jews are uncanny, in that they superficially appear to be males but are not because of the altered form of the genitalia. (Jewish women are different too—different in a manner other than that in which Aryan women are different from Aryan men.) The anti-Semitic British explorer and author Richard Burton commented that "Christendom practically holds circumcision in horror."[4] The supposedly neutral male, Aryan scientific gaze became the means of defining the healthy perspective. Jewish scientists, their bodies marked by the act of circumcision, cannot share in this sense of community.

The circumcised penis was not in itself the most unusual biological feature of the anthropological image of the male Jew in nineteenth-cen-

Figure 2. A ritual circumcision as depicted in volume 1 of *Jüdisches Lexikon*, ed. Georg Herlitz and Bruno Kirschner (Berlin: Jüdischer Verlag, 1927). This reference work is in Freud's library. This image reproduces an older image from 1756. Also illustrated are the instruments used in the ritual, including the wineglass from which the *mohel* drinks before he performs the act of *metsitsah*.

tury science; indeed, debates about the specificity of all the physiological and psychological markers of difference invented by eighteenth- and nineteenth-century ethnology, from skull capacity, size, and shape (cephalic index) to skin and hair color, were employed to document the difference of the Jews from all other races.[5] But it was in the arena of this ritual practice that the pathological nature of the Jews was thought to manifest itself most clearly. The *brit milah*, the practice of infant male circumcision, became, for thinkers of the late nineteenth century, the major sign of Jewish difference.[6] And all the controversies over circumcision in the medical literature were colored by its centrality as the means of distinguishing between the healthy and the diseased, between the Aryan and the Jew. As an anonymous author stated in the leading German pediatric journal in 1872: "The circumcision of Jewish children has been widely discussed in the medical press as is warranted with topics of such importance. But it is usually discussed without the necessary attention to details and the neutrality that it deserves. Indeed, it has not been free of fanatic anti-Semitism."[7] This association continued strongly even as circumcision became widely practiced (in countries such as the United States and Great Britain). Indeed, as late as 1920 the *British Medical Journal* printed the following comment on circumcision: "This injurious procedure, like that of keeping women in bed after childbirth, we owe to the Jews, and we have nothing to thank them for as regards these two of their religious rituals."[8] There is a constant tendency to blame the Jews for the dangers perceived as inherent in this procedure present in most of the anticircumcision literature through the present.[9] Circumcision marks the Jew as damaged and as potentially damaging. Even after the Shoah, the sign of circumcision marked a group fantasy about the hidden nature of the male Jew's body, even when the body in question was uncircumcised in German popular culture in the 1980s.[10] For German Jews, the internalization of the sense of their bodies' difference cannot be underestimated.[11]

The social significance of reliance on circumcision as the marker of Jewish difference in European medicine in the late nineteenth century can be seen when one realizes that Western European Jews by that time had become indistinguishable from other Western Europeans in language, dress, occupation, the location of their dwellings, and the cut of their hair. Indeed, if Rudolf Virchow's extensive study of over ten thousand German schoolchildren, published in 1886, was accurate, they were also indistinguishable in skin, hair, and eye color from the greater masses of those who lived in Germany.[12] Virchow's statistics sought to show that where a greater percentage of the overall population had lighter skin or bluer eyes or blonder hair, a greater percentage of Jews had lighter skin or bluer eyes or blonder hair. Later, this tendency was explained by Felix von Luschan as a social phenomenon, rather than as one of adaptation or biological mimicry. He suggested that Jews select mates who mirror the ideal types present in the societies in which they live. Thus they select for precisely those qualities that would make them most like the majority culture.[13] Unlike skin or hair or eye color, the circumcision of the male Jew was a marker of difference. The debates about the meaning of circumcision in the nineteenth century must be understood in the context of this specifically European recognition of circumcision as the most evident sign of the racial difference of the Jew.[14]

But race was perceived as immutable (or at least virtually so). How then could circumcision, a ritual practice, be a permanent sign of Jewish difference? The assumption as early as the seventeenth century was that acquired characteristics, such as circumcision, could be and were inherited. If circumcision were so central in defining the body of the Jew as a damaged male, it logically could not remain an incidental social practice, a practice imposed from without, for then it could cease and, in the next generation, the male Jew would truly look like everyone else. What was "real" in the biological science of the nineteenth century was what was of the body, not what was inscribed on the body—whether circumcision or any related practice. Thus nineteenth- and twentieth-century science grappled with the enigma of congenital circumcision, which would seem to continue to mark the Jew's male body even if Jews ceased to circumcise their male young.

There was a long history of describing the male Jew as having been born circumcised. In the work of Johann Jakob Schudt, at the beginning of the eighteenth century, there is an account of the Talmudic debate during the first century between the stringent Shammai and the more lenient Hillel about whether a child born without a prepuce needs to have a symbolic drop of blood drawn from the penis in lieu of circumcision.[15] (The school of Shammai dominated, which is rarely the case in Talmudic argument, and the symbolic drop of blood was and is demanded.)

Johann David Michaelis, the noted orientalist of the German Enlightenment, added a long excursus to Schudt's discussion of the Talmudic injunctions concerning Jews who are born circumcised. According to Michaelis, it is true that the Jew, like the ape, can be born circumcised. But Michaelis interpreted this anomaly in no way as a sign of the higher status of the Jew. What would give circumcision higher status for Michaelis would be if such a condition gave a specific advantage to those born with it. For Michaelis, living in a world that firmly believed masturbation was the origin of myriad physical and psychological ailments, circumcision had no curative powers to reverse or prevent illnesses caused by masturbation. Circumcision, he states, is not a cure for masturbation. Those born without a prepuce are no better off than anyone else. Nature would have made the act of masturbation, which is a sin as well as a source of illness, completely impossible rather than deal with it in this manner.[16] The Jew, Michaelis notes, following Philo, takes those born circumcised to be especially holy men since they have a diminished sexual urge, but we, he implies, know better.[17]

Between Schudt and Michaelis there was a shift in the theological meaning ascribed to congenital circumcision. It illustrates the presence of a debate in the general culture of the eighteenth century about the inherent nature of the Jew. The Jew can be born circumcised—that is, born with the signs of his Jewishness impressed on his skin—and the truth of this "fact" can be adduced from the Jews' own text, the Talmud. (According to the general view of Christian theologians of the time, it is only in such internal documents that Jews ever reveal truths about themselves.) Schudt and Michaelis were in the business of revealing the truth about Jews to their German readers, with one central purpose in mind—to enable their readers to "see" the reality of the Jew and protect themselves against him. Michaelis was in no way opposed to the existence of the Jews in Western society, as was Schudt, but both acknowledged the inherent difference of the Jew as inscribed on the Jew's body. Neither found it necessary to rebut the implication that being born circumcised provides any benefits to the Jew. It was merely one more overt proof of the innate, immutable difference of the Jew.

Johann David Michaelis's rebuttal bridges the seeming abyss between the new "rational" science of the Enlightenment and the more conservative theology of the late eighteenth century. His argument is as much medical as it is theological. Congenital circumcision came to have value in the biological sciences in the late eighteenth century as a proof of the inheritability of acquired characteristics. Michaelis's contemporary, the liberal anthropologist Johann Friedrich Blumenbach, so interpreted congenital circumcision in his study of the sexual drive (1781). It is important to note that Blumenbach was a strong opponent of the polygenetic theory of the races, which saw as inherently different. (However, he believed that Jews—or at least their skulls—were immediately and incontrovertibly identifiable as distinct.) But he was also a strong advocate (as were most of his contemporaries) of the view that acquired characteristics could be inherited. If Jews (and others) circumcised their children, it would be reasonable to expect that some "boys in the orient are born circumcised." His scientific authority for this is Michaelis.[18]

The view that the male Jew's body was marked as different through inherited circumcision was a cultural commonplace in the late eighteenth century. The revolutionary physician and poet Friedrich Schiller ironically showed the duplicity of his "Jewish" character Moritz Spiegelberg in his first play, *The Robbers* (1782), by having Spiegelberg deny his Jewish identity. He is made to refer to himself as having been "miraculously born circumcised."[19] Schiller's use of this medical "fact" ironically emphasized Spiegelberg's Jewish identity to his audience, for they would have known that anything Spiegelberg said was by nature duplicitous (as all statements by Jews to non-Jews were self-serving). In a later draft of this speech Schiller altered the basis for Spiegelberg's claim that he was not Jewish even though he was circumcised. He had Spiegelberg state that he needed a Hebrew grammar to learn the Jew's language.[20] This was an absurdity, for Jews, just as they are born circumcised, are also born knowing Hebrew, the hidden language of the Jews. Schiller's medical training may well have exposed him to the argument about the inheritance of the congenital sign of Jewishness among male Jews, but it was also commonplace in Western culture.

Not all the medical scientists of the eighteenth century accepted the dominant view. Johann Heinrich Ferdinand von Autenrieth, a renowned professor of medicine at the University of Tübingen, felt himself constrained by Blumenbach's argument concerning hereditary circumcision.[21] As Autenrieth argued, not only the male children of circumcised Jews are born circumcised; even Christian boys can be born without a prepuce ("where the women certainly did not have any contact with a Jew"). He cites the seventeenth-century descriptions of Melchior Fribe[22] and Salomon Reisel[23] on birth defects of the penis, which do not evoke any mention of race. Autenrieth's voice was virtually alone in the nineteenth-century discussions of congenital circumcision.

Most of the literature in the second half of the nineteenth century saw congenital circumcision as an inherent problem that has a higher frequency among Jews and other people who circumcise their male young. Gideon Brecher, a Jewish physician in Prossnitz, included in his presentation of the practice of circumcision in 1845 the question of what must be done to circumcise such children.[24] Even the liberal Berlin pathologist Rudolf Virchow postulated that this defect was inherited.[25] In Vienna, C. Lederer simply claimed (in 1871) that Jewish males were more frequently born without a prepuce than non-Jewish males.[26]

But in the field of evolutionary biology, the question of the inheritance (and meaning) of congenital circumcision was raised most clearly. Charles Darwin had left the question open in his 1868 study, *The Variation of Animals and Plants under Domestication.* In asking whether mutilations or injuries can be acquired, he observed: "With respect to Jews, I have been assured by three medical men of the Jewish faith that circumcision, which has been practiced for so many ages, has produced no inherited effect; Blumenbach, on the other hand, asserts that in Germany Jews are often born in a condition rendering circumcision difficult, so that a name is there applied to them signifying 'born circumcised.' "[27] The question of the Jew's body became a touchstone for the debate about inheritance (and, therefore, the adaptability of the body).

August Weismann, certainly one of the most important German biologists of the nineteenth century,[28] denied at the sixty-first annual Meeting
of German Natural Scientists and Physicians (in 1888) the incidental
transmission of acquired characteristics. He used congenital circumcision
as his prime example of the impossibility of such transmission in human
beings. Weismann had proposed (in the early 1880s) that inheritance lay
solely in the molecular substance of the cell, and thus rejected any notion
of the inheritance of acquired characteristics. For Weismann the "germ
track" was separate from the soma in its very structure. He discussed the
argument about inheritance of circumcision after his presentation of
lower mammals (such as cats). One substantial manner of proving this
was to show how alterations in body structure, such as amputation, did
not influence the form of the body. The belief was that each body part
sent "gemmules" to the germ cells. If that body part was amputated over
generations, it should eventually be reduced in size in the offspring. This
issue was the major proof for his contemporaries of the transmission of
acquired characteristics in human beings. He began by discussing "those
cases of habitual mutilation which have been continually repeated for
numerous generations of men, and have not produced any hereditary
consequences. . . . Furthermore, the mutilations of certain parts of the
human body, as practised by different nations from times immemorial,
have, in not a single instance, led to the malformation or reduction of the
parts in question. Such hereditary effects have been produced neither by
circumcision, nor the removal of the front teeth, nor the boring of holes
in the lips or nose, nor the extraordinary artificial crushing and crippling
of the feet of Chinese women."[29] But only to the question of circumcision
does Weismann add a footnote: "It is certainly true that among nations
which practise circumcision as a ritual, children are sometimes born with
a rudimentary prepuce, but this does not occur more frequently than in
other nations in which circumcision is not performed. Rather extensive
statistical investigations have led to this result." Weismann's language
stresses the universal nature of this occurrence. It is a potential reflex of
the germ plasm in all human beings, not an acquired characteristic of a
specific group.

Weismann used this example in his standard argument against the supposed inheritance of mutilations. The importance of this example for the
science of the late nineteenth century cannot be underestimated. Weismann was one of the most widely read and hotly debated thinkers on the
question of the nature of inheritance. His dismissal of this view indicated
that it was central to the debate about the inheritance of human characteristics, about what makes certain individuals different from others. It
was an important enough part of the argument of science that even Jewish
scientists of the period accepted it. A Dr. Levy in Stettin, who identified
himself as a Jew, anecdotally answered Weismann, noting that he and his

four brothers were all born circumcised and that their father fulfilled the
rabbinic law and drew a drop of blood with a needle in lieu of circumcision.[30] He assumed that Jews have a higher incidence of congenital circumcision because of their ritual practice. And, in a study of the inheritance of signs of degeneracy published in 1898, Eugene Talbot of the
Women's Medical College in Chicago addressed the question of whether
Jews have a higher rate of such births than other groups by citing a much
higher incidence of congenital circumcision among Jews in the United
States.[31] Talbot and Levy answered Weismann directly, citing his work as
the basis of their rebuttal. The Viennese-Jewish anthropologist Ignaz
Zollschan, in a fin de siècle volume on the ethnology of the Jews carefully
read by Sigmund Freud, accepted Weismann's dismissal of the inheritance of acquired characteristics, repeating Weismann's litany of precisely those cultural phenomena, such as circumcision, that are not inherited. This seems to be an important point in Zollschan's summary of the
contemporary theories of biological inheritance. Yet it is precisely on the
point of the inheritance of circumcision that he is captured by the complexity of the argument. He provides a footnote: "While it is true that in
general Weismann is correct, it is not absolutely certain. For example, it
is the case that congenital circumcision does occur among Jews, if rarely
(3 percent). There is [among the Jews] the more frequent occurrence of an
underdevelopment [of the prepuce]. This fact indicates that this may be
the case with other such malformations of the body; but as of now there
is no irrefutable study."[32] Zollschan's ambivalence reflects his view of the
uniform nature of the Jews as a race and his evident association of this
view with the model that tied specific physical characteristics to the definition of race.

In 1904, in his detailed survey of the "diseases of the Jews," Heinrich
Singer reported that one of the results of the "removal of the prepuce over
the span of generations" is its reduction or disappearance. Here, he comments, rebutting Weismann, "the otherwise often contradicted inheritance of acquired characteristics finds to a certain degree its substan-
tiation."[33] Likewise, Moses Julius Gutmann, one of the most prolific
authors on the special diseases that afflict the Jews, cites the greater number of cases of congenital circumcision among the Jews in 1920.[34] This
view has not disappeared. As late as 1971, medical literature still stated
that groups who circumcise their young have more cases of congenital
circumcision.[35]

READING THE MEANING OF CIRCUMCISION

But to say that it was assumed that male Jews bore the stigmata of circumcision as signs of their difference is much too vague. There has been a
wide range of meanings associated with the act of circumcision in the

West. Circumcision has been read as a sign of everything from sexual hygiene, to cosmetic appearance, to tribal identity or a mark of adulthood, to diminishment or enhancement of sexual desire, to increased or decreased fertility, to patriarchal subjugation, to enhanced purity, to the improvement of sexual endurance, to a form of attenuated castration, to menstrual envy, to a substitute for human sacrifice. But there are four "traditional" views of the "meaning" of circumcision in connection with the Jews that have dominated Western thought since the rise of Christianity.[36] Following the writings of Paul, the first saw circumcision as inherently symbolic and, therefore, no longer valid after the rise of Christianity. This view was espoused by the church fathers, Eusebius and Origen, and continued through the Renaissance (Erasmus) and through the Reformation (Luther). It formed the theological basis for the distinction Christians were able to make between their bodies and the bodies of the Jews.[37]

The second view saw circumcision as a sign of a political or group identity. The rhetoric in which the accepted science of the late nineteenth century clothed its rejection of circumcision is important. It was intense and virulent, as has been remarked, and never free from negative judgments. One central example should suffice. The liberal Italian physician Paolo Mantegazza (1831–1901), one of the standard "ethnological" sources in the late nineteenth century for the nature of human sexuality, decried the "mutilation of the genitals" among "savage tribes," including the Jews.[38] (Mantegazza's importance for Freud cannot be underestimated. Mantegazza was the most widely read popular "expert" on human sexuality at the turn of the century. His work appears as the "dirty book" Dora is accused of having read, which illustrates her lack of sexual naïveté to both her accuser and Freud.)[39] Indeed, it is only in Mantegazza's discussion of the Jews that the text turns from a titillating account of "unnatural practices" into a polemic (echoing Spinoza's often cited comments on the centrality of circumcision for the definition of the feminized Jewish male)[40] against the perverse practices of those people out of their correct "space" and "time"—the Jews:

> Circumcision is a shame and an infamy; and I, who am not in the least anti-Semitic, who indeed have much esteem for the Israelites, I who demand of no living soul a profession of religious faith, insisting only upon the brotherhood of soap and water and of honesty, I shout and shall continue to shout at the Hebrews, until my last breath: Cease mutilating yourselves: cease imprinting upon your flesh an odious brand to distinguish you from other men; until you do this, you cannot pretend to be our equal. As it is, you, of your own accord, with the branding iron, from the first days of your lives, proceed to proclaim yourselves a race apart, one that cannot, and does not care to, mix with ours.[41]

This was not his view alone. Edvard Westermarck, one of Freud's major sources for the history of human groups, simply labeled circumcision "the mutilation of the sexual organ."[42]

Mantegazza notes that "the hygienic value of circumcision has been exaggerated by the historians of Judaism. It is true enough that the circumcised are a little less disposed to masturbation and to venereal infection; but every day, we do have Jewish masturbators and Jewish syphilitics. Circumcision is a mark of racial distinction; . . . it is a sanguinary protest against universal brotherhood; and if it be true that Christ was circumcised, it is likewise true that he protested on the cross against any symbol which would tend to part men asunder."[43] This view is clearly antithetical to the view of such scholars as the sociologist Edvard Westermarck and the sexologist Auguste Forel, who link "the intention of exciting the sexual appetite" through circumcision with "the hygienic advantage of circumcision [that] took a part in its transformation into a rite."[44] "We may go to Moses for instruction in some of the best methods in hygiene," according to William Osler in 1914, even though the Jew is less adept in the world of "intellect and science."[45] And one of Freud's sources, Ernest Crawley's study of marriage, reported that the "Jews considered circumcision as a 'cleansing.' "[46] Mantegazza's rhetoric sets the Jew apart and makes out of his body a sign that he is a pariah.

The third reading of circumcision saw it as a remnant of the early Jewish idol or phallus worship. Thus J.H.F. von Autenrieth saw circumcision as a primitive act practiced by culturally inferior peoples such as Jews and African blacks. Autenrieth, by 1829 the chancellor of the University of Tübingen, entered the discussion of the meaning of circumcision with a public lecture on its history. For him, as for others, circumcision was a surrogate for human sacrifice.[47] Freud would have found this view supported in the anthropological literature with which he was familiar. John Lubbock saw the rite of sacrifice as a "stage through which, in any natural process of development, religion must pass."[48] But the Jews also sacrificed their animals at the Temple as "symbols of human sacrifice . . . [which] were at one time habitual among the Jews."[49] Circumcision was a sign of "the inherent barbarism of this people," a view seconded by a Dr. Hacker in a medical journal in 1843.[50] Here again, the medical discussion of a social practice became contaminated by the racial context in which it was placed. Indeed, this view dominated the discussion of the ethnopsychologists in the late nineteenth and early twentieth centuries about circumcision as a semantic sign. The experimentalist Wilhelm Wundt saw circumcision as "of the nature of sacrifice. Along with the offering of hair in the cult of the dead and with the pouring out of blood in connection with deity worship, it belongs to that form of sacrifice in which the sacrificial object gains its unique value by virtue of its being the vehicle of the soul. Thus, the object of sacrifice, in the case of circumcision, may perhaps be interpreted as a substitute for such internal organs as the kidneys or testicles, which are particularly prized as vehicles of the soul but which can either not be offered at all, on the part of the living, or whose sacrifice involves serious difficulties."[51] For Wundt, politically a liberal in his time, Judaism was "but one of those vanquished cults which struggled for supremacy in the pre-Constantinian period of the Roman World Empire."[52] And the practice of this substitute for ritual sacrifice was a sign of the barbarism and marginality of the Jew.

The fourth reading of circumcision saw it as a form of medical prophylaxis. This seems to be first claimed by Philo, who was writing in a strongly Hellenistic culture that found any mutilation of the body abhorrent.[53] He claimed that it was a prophylactic against diseases of the penis, but that it also promoted the well-being of the individual and assured fertility. The hygienic rationale was also evoked, as we have seen, in the work of Johann David Michaelis, the central German commentator on this practice in the eighteenth century. It was only in the middle of the nineteenth century that the debate about the medical meaning of circumcision affected the Jewish community in Central Europe. Prior to this, discussions of the meaning of circumcision in the Christian community remained separate from Jewish concerns in Europe. While the image of the circumcised Jew was raised as a central metaphor for Jewish difference in Great Britain with the presentation of the Jewish Naturalization Act in 1753,[54] it only became important with the gradual acculturation of the Jews in Germany and Austria toward the middle of the nineteenth century. The debates within and outside the Jewish communities concerning the nature and implications of circumcision surfaced in Germany during the 1840s. German Jews had become acculturated to German middle-class values and had come to question the quasi-sacramental requirement of circumcision as a prerequisite of their Jewish identity.

On July 15, 1843, a position paper by the "Friends of Reform" was published in the *Frankfurter Journal* in which the platform for a new, "reformed" Judaism was put forth. The abolition of circumcision was one of the key elements of that program. Led by the radical reform rabbi Samuel Holdheim, it responded not only to a Christian (both Catholic and Protestant) tradition that denigrated circumcision as a sign of inferiority, but also to the growing charge that it was an "unhealthy" practice.[55] Holdheim held that circumcision was a ritual that was not binding on Jews, any more than was the observation of rabbinic laws concerning many other rituals.[56] Holdheim saw circumcision as having a purely religious function as a sign of membership in the community. The sign of the covenant was understood symbolically and internally rather than incised on the body. He did not see it as a necessity any more than was the abandoned sacrifice of the paschal lamb. Holdheim's position was the most radical in the Jewish community of his day. While Holdheim did not address the medical opposition to circumcision, it was already quite widespread in Germany.

In 1844 a Berlin physician, J. Bergson, a Jewish advocate of circumcision, responded to Holdheim's call for the abolition of infant male circumcision by promoting medical reforms that would enable the procedure to become safer.[57] He shifted the debate from its religious necessity to its medical implications. Already in 1825 a Dr. Wolfers, a physician and "male midwife" from Lemförde, had argued that circumcision was a dangerous procedure and should be placed under the supervision of the "medical police."[58] He discussed their poor preparation of the ritual circumcisers, the *mohelim*, and the destructive results of their incompetence. Beginning in 1819 the Berlin Jewish community had insisted on a medical presence at the *brit* (ritual circumcision).[59] This remained a concern well into the middle of the century. A Dr. Klein in Ratibor suggested in 1853 that this was in no way a violation of freedom of religious practice, but solely a public-health issue.[60] This view became one of the leading proposals that formed the background to Holdheim's suggestion. If the procedure was dangerous, then it must be abolished. But the political implications of abolition were not clear to Holdheim. Under Prussian and Austrian state law, at least, if a child were not circumcised, he had to be baptized. Indeed, in a case in Brunswick in 1847, the parents, after refusing to have their child circumcised for medical reasons, were ordered to have him either circumcised or baptized within fourteen days.[61] Here the echo of the discussion of the inheritability of the act of circumcision is heard. Can Jews truly abandon circumcision as a sign of their religious identity? Or is that as useless as trying to abandon their racial identity? The choice between circumcision or baptism meant, given the marginal status of baptized Jews in German culture, in practice remaining a Jew, baptized or not. The inner sign of circumcision remained, and could be spontaneously written on the body through the somatic inheritance of acquired characteristics.

CIRCUMCISION AND DISEASE

In the medical discourse of the nineteenth century, circumcision was as evil as it was inescapable for the Jew because it led to specific diseases that corrupted the individual and eventually the body politic. These are diseases that could transcend the boundary between Jew and Christian, between the circumcised and the uncircumcised. The danger to the body and to society (through the weakening of the offspring) in the eighteenth century resided in masturbation; syphilis and its potential social ramifications gave nightmares to physicians in the nineteenth century.[62] Sigmund Freud's practical experience in the area of syphilology came during the period from October to December 1883, when he worked in the Second Division for Syphilis in the Viennese General Hospital. Both masturbation and syphilis were associated in the medical as well as in the popular mind with the power of sexuality. The linked dangers of sexuality, syphilis, and madness were constantly associated with the figure of the male Jew. The Jew, who had become identified with his circumcised state, came to personify this threat. Central to the definition of the Jew was the image of the male Jew's circumcised penis as impaired, damaged, or incomplete, and therefore threatening to the wholeness and health of the male Aryan. The damaged penis represented the potential ravages of sexually transmitted disease.

Syphilis had been associated with the Jews from the first appearance in Europe of the disease in the fifteenth century.[63] Indeed, it was "commonly called the Peste of the Marranos," according to the Genovese ambassador to Charles VIII in 1492.[64] Its association with Jews was a continuation of the ancient view that the Jews were infected with leprosy (a view as old as the ancient Egyptian historian Manetho). Leprosy, like syphilis, was closely associated with sexuality and the genitalia, and this association stressed the unclean and impure nature of the Jew. The literature on syphilis in the nineteenth century contains a substantial discussion of the special relationship of Jews to the transmission and meaning of syphilis. This association was made not only with the act of circumcision, but with the fear that the Jews carried syphilis and that the disease would undermine the strength of the body politic. Jewishness was the central category of "racial" difference for German readers and writers at the turn of the century. The need to "see" and "label" the Jew at a time when Jews were becoming more and more "invisible" in Germany made the association with socially stigmatizing diseases that bore specific visible "signs and symptoms" especially appropriate. Mantegazza's view linked the act of "seeing" the Jew sexually with the defamed practice of circumcision. In the German Empire of the late nineteenth century, all the arguments placed the Jew in a "special" relationship to syphilis and, therefore, in a special relationship to the "healthy" body politic that needed to make the Jew visible. (The central medical paradigm for the establishment of the healthy state was the public-health model that evolved specifically to combat the "evils" of sexually transmitted disease through social control.) Western Jews had been completely acculturated by the end of the nineteenth century and thus bore no external signs of difference (unique clothing, group language, group-specific hair or beard style). They had to bear the stigma of their diseased nature literally on the skin, where it could be seen, not only on the penis, where (because of social practice) it could be "seen" only in the sexual act—and then, because of the gradual abandonment of circumcision, be "seen" not to exist at all!

In European science and popular thought, the Jew was closely related to the incidence and spread of syphilis. Such views had two readings. The first model saw the Jews as the carriers of sexually transmitted diseases who infected the rest of the world. In his dissertation in 1897, Armand-Louis-Joseph Béraud noted that Jews needed to circumcise their young males because of their inherently unhygienic nature but also because the "climate in which they dwelt" otherwise encouraged the transmission of syphilis.[65] The Jew in the Diaspora was out of time (having forgotten to vanish like the other ancient peoples); he was out of his correct space (where circumcision had validity). His Jewishness (as well as his disease) was inscribed on his penis. Here the link between the idea of the Jew as city dweller, as a disease lurking in the urban environment, became manifest. The source of the "hysteria" of the city was the diseased sexuality of the Jew. Indeed, even the Jewish physician Heinrich Singer, in his standard overview of the diseases of the Jews, argued that Jews evidenced especially destructive forms of syphilis.[66] Other medical scientists argued that Jews in mental institutions in Great Britain evidenced a rate of "general paresis," the neurological presentation of tertiary syphilis, as high as 21 percent.[67] In Vienna the official view was identical. Alexander Pilcz, Freud's colleague in the Department of Psychiatry at the University of Vienna, argued that there was a substantially higher rate of syphilitic infection of the nervous system among Jews.[68] So did Joseph Adolf Hirschl, Julius Wagner-Jauregg's assistant, who later was instrumental in linking specific psychoses (such as general paresis and general paralysis of the insane) with syphilitic infection.[69] The association of Jews, syphilis, and madness demanded an interpretation that stressed the inherent corruption of the Jews. This view is found in Adolf Hitler's discussion of syphilis in fin de siècle Vienna in *My Struggle* (1925). Like his Viennese compatriot Bertha Pappenheim, the original of Josef Breuer's patient Anna O.,[70] but with a very different intent, he links it to the Jew, the prostitute, and the power of money: "Particularly with regard to syphilis, the attitude of the nation and the state can only be designated as total capitulation. . . . The invention of a remedy of questionable character and its commercial exploitation can no longer help much against this plague. . . . The cause lies, primarily, in our prostitution of love. . . . This Jewification of our spiritual life and mammonization of our mating instinct will sooner or later destroy our entire offspring."[71] Hitler also linked Jews with prostitutes and the spread of infection. Jews were the "arch-pimps"; Jews ran the brothels; Jews infected their prostitutes and caused the weakening of the German national fiber.[72] Jews were also associated with the false promise of a "medical" cure separate from the social "cures" Hitler wished to see imposed—isolation and separation of the syphilitic from the body politic. Hitler believed that the fields of dermatology and syphilology were especially dominated by Jews, who used their medical status to sell quack cures.

The second model associating Jews and syphilis seemed to postulate exactly the opposite—that Jews had a statistically lower rate of syphilitic infection—either because of their religious practices (such as infant circumcision) or because they had become immune to it through centuries of exposure. This view can be traced to the beginning of the modern appearance of the disease. Isaac Abravanel, the great Spanish Talmudist, observed at the start of the sixteenth century that "it appears that this is the sickness which has arisen anew in these times for formerly wise physicians never saw it nor knew of it. It is called the French disease which is similar to leprosy and it occurs only among Gentiles and is not found among Jews."[73] In a study undertaken by the British surgeon Jonathan Hutchinson in 1854, the incidence of syphilis among London Jews was one-fifteenth that found in the general community. He posited that this was not a reflex of a higher moral stance (as the gonorrhea rate was the same in both groups), but assumed that it was the result of a more general immunity.[74] Hutchinson's views echo the common assumption of the time that "Jews escape the great epidemics more readily than the other races with whom they live."[75] In a debate about the nature of Jewish immunity to disease, Rabbi Isaac Wise, one of the founders of Reform Judaism in the United States, observed that few Jewish "fathers are sick of syphilis."[76]

In the medical literature of the period, reaching across European medicine, it was assumed that Jews had a notably lower rate of infection. In a survey of the incidence of tertiary lues, the final stage of syphilis, in the Crimea undertaken between 1904 and 1929, Jews had the lowest consistent rate of infection.[77] P. J. Möbius argued for the overall immunity of the Jews in the East to syphilitic infection, in a source cited by Sigmund Freud in a paper on the clinical symptomology of anxiety.[78] In an eighteen-year longitudinal study, H. Budul demonstrated the extraordinarily low rate of tertiary lues among Jews in Estonia during the prewar period.[79] All these studies assumed that the biological and social differences of the Jews were at the root of their apparent "immunity." Jewish scientists of the period, such as the Zurich-trained psychoanalyst A. A. Brill, gave a different explanation. Eastern Jews were seen as having a different rate of infection because of "the fact that in Russia the Orthodox Jews are in the majority and owing to their rigid religious tenets and early marriages they lead a pure sexual life."[80] Repressive religious practices have a beneficial side effect: they lessen the rate of syphilitic infection.

Jewish scientists also had to explain the "statistical" fact of their immunity to syphilis. In a study of the rate of tertiary lues undertaken during World War I, the Jewish physician Max Sichel considered the general view that the relatively lower incidence of infection among Jews resulted from the sexual difference of the Jews.[81] He responded—out of necessity—with a social argument. The Jews, according to Sichel, show the lower incidence because of their early marriages and the patriarchal structure of the Jewish family, but also because of their much lower rate of alcoholism. They were, according to the implicit argument, more rarely exposed to the infection of prostitutes whose attractiveness was always associated with the greater loss of sexual control attributed to inebriation. The relationship between these two "social" diseases is made into a cause for the higher incidence among other Europeans. The Jews, because they are less likely to drink heavily, are less likely to be exposed to the debilitating effects of alcohol (which increase the risk for tertiary lues) or to the occasion for infection. This view was widely cited and supported by German-Jewish physicians of the period, such as Hugo Hoppe.[82] This reflects the importance of Jewish abstinence in the anti-Semitic literature of the period.

Sexual control is at the heart of an elaboration of this view found earlier in the nineteenth century. Ephraim M. Epstein, a Russian-Jewish physician practicing in Cincinnati in the 1870s, noted: "In common with others . . . I once believed that circumcision affords a protection against venereal [diseases], but my practice in Vienna, Austria, and in this country, since 1862, persuaded me fully to the contrary. The apparent immunity which the Jews of Russian and European Turkey, whom I know best, seem to enjoy from venereal diseases, arises from their greater chastity and the practice of early marriage."[83] It is not just that Jews "say no," but that they are in greater control of their drives. This is aided by their social practices, at least from the perspective of the Jewish physician. Early marriage, precisely the cause attributed to the widest range of illnesses in the eighteenth century, came to be seen as a prophylactic against sexually transmitted disease in the nineteenth century.

In 1927 Hermann Strauss, who died in 1944 in Theresienstadt, looked at the incidence of syphilitic infection in the Jewish Hospital in Berlin, where he was director of the Department of Internal Medicine. He explored this problem in order to determine whether the Jews had a lower incidence but also to see whether they had "milder" forms of the disease because of their life-styles or background.[84] (This question was analogous to the one that lay behind the infamous Tuskegee experiments among African Americans.)[85] He found that Jews indeed had a much lower incidence of syphilis (while having an extraordinarily higher rate of hysteria) than the non-Jewish control group. He proposed that the disease might well follow a different course in Jews than in non-Jews. The unevoked yet implied sign for such a view of the heightened susceptibility or resistance to syphilis is the circumcised penis.

Medical theorists of the period thus saw circumcision either as a source of disease or as a prophylactic against disease. In either case it remained associated with the particular characteristics of the Jews. If the diseased nature of the Jew was represented by the act of circumcision, then the disease from which the Jew suffered was sexually transmitted. Moritz Mombert, in 1828, argued that venereal diseases were much less frequent among male Jews "because of their practice of circumcision" and because Jewish females only had intercourse with circumcised males.[86] A Dr. Niemann in Magdeburg argued that circumcision was in no way a prophylactic against sexually transmitted disease, "as I have seen Jews with gonorrhea and syphilitic lesions."[87] The opposing view of circumcision in the scientific literature of the time saw it as a mode of prevention that precluded the spread of sexually transmitted diseases because of the increased capacity for "cleanliness." Dr. S. N. Kutna from Przemysl argued that it provided ample protection against gonorrhea and syphilis.[88] Both the Jewish male and the Jewish female were less exposed to the ravages of syphilis because of their ritual practices and, therefore, the Jewish male was less at risk: "The Jew has . . . two avenues of infection from syphilis cut off—the lesser liability due to his circumcision and the chastity of the woman."[89] It is classified as an aspect of "hygiene,"[90] the favorite word to critique or support the practice, even though Herbert Spencer was at pains to point out that circumcision did not exist among the "most cleanly" races in the world, while being common among the "most uncleanly."[91] But Freud's younger colleague A. J. Storfer reminded his readers in the 1920s that the "hygienic advantages of circumcision . . . still did not explain the ethnopsychological occurrence of this practice."[92] Circumcision, no matter what the overt rationale for it, held hidden, often contradictory implications.

This view is closely associated with the therapeutic use of circumcision throughout the nineteenth century as a means of "curing" the diseases caused by masturbation, with, of course, a similar split in the idea of efficacy: circumcision was either a cure for masturbation, as it eliminated the stimulation of the prepuce and deadened the sensitivity of the penis, or it was the source of Jewish male hypersexuality.[93] Hermann Rohleder, one of the most important sexologists of the late nineteenth century, advocated a form of particularly painful negative reinforcement as a treatment for male masturbation—the removal of the prepuce without anesthesia. This was parallel to his treatment of female masturbators, the "painful—but safe" removal of the clitoris through the application of acid.[94] Circumcisions and clitoridectomies were seen as analogous medical procedures.

Syphilis and circumcision were linked, as both were seen in some way to be related to sexuality and its dangers. It is not surprising that the key to the greater risk adult Jewish males ran (or did not run) in regard to their exposure to syphilis lay in the danger of subsequent infection of the circumcised area, according to J. Bergson.[95] Indeed, as early as 1818 the Prussian state authorities had mandated that the *mohel*, the ritual circumciser, be of "good character."[96] The "good character" of the *mohel* was a guarantee of his being free from sexually transmitted diseases. This view was repeated in a statement by the Prussian Minister of the Interior on May 31, 1865.[97]

There is a detailed medical literature that links the act of circumcision to the transmission of syphilis. Rather than being a prophylactic, circumcision becomes the source of infection. The literature that discusses the transmission of syphilis to newly circumcised infants through the ritual of *metsitsah*, the sucking on the penis by the *mohel*, is extensive and detailed. The pattern assumed is that the immorality of adult Jews, especially of religious figures such as the *mohel*, made possible the infection of Jewish male infants. In 1845 Gideon Brecher argued for the abolition of the act based on the risk of syphilitic infection: "Often children are born, who, through contact with their mother's diseased sexual organ during the birth process, are thoroughly covered with venereal ulcers a few days after birth. What are the results of sucking on the infected organ of shame for the *mohel*? . . . On the other hand, ritual circumcisers, who have venereal ulcers in their mouths, can transmit this poison to the newborn infant."[98] This mirrored the image of congenital circumcision. Just as the diseased image of the adult Jew's body (whether male or female) is found again in the spontaneously circumcised (and, therefore, Jewish) body of the male infant, so too is the diseased nature of the adult Jew's body mirrored in the diseased body of the infant. The disease that is transmitted from adult Jew to Jewish child is Jewishness, hidden under the disguise of the debate about circumcision and sexually transmitted diseases.

The literature on this topic is extensive (and never neutral). Dr. Niemann in Magdeburg stressed that through the ritual of *metsitsah*, disease, specifically syphilis, is spread to the child, or by the child, infected at birth, to the *mohel*.[99] An article in a leading American medical journal presented masses of evidence about the transmission of syphilis through the act of circumcision.[100] Indeed, an anonymous author in 1872 stressed the risk run by children who are circumcised being infected with syphilis by the *mohel*.[101] In 1874 an Austro-Hungarian Jewish physician, Dr. Levit in Horic, published a blistering attack on the ritual of circumcision as a central medical problem, an attack provoked by the death of his infant son from an infection stemming from his circumcision.[102] This attack, which emphasized the medical risks, including the transmission of disease, from the procedure caused a furor in Vienna.[103] Levit stressed the origin of the ritual in the need to bring young men into pubescence much earlier than was "natural" in order to facilitate early marriage (as practiced, he noted, among Polish Jews.)[104] At the November 11, 1874, meeting of the Viennese Medical Society, Prof. Emil Kohn (and a number of his colleagues) supported Levit's view that there was a substantial risk to infants of the transmission of syphilis either by the contamination of ritual instruments by the blood of infants with congenital syphilis or through the act of *metsitsah*. As a result, he noted, more and more Jews were refusing to have their children circumcised.[105] There was general agreement with his presentation. In Berlin a similar argument was made by a Dr. Lewin in the opening volume of the journal of the major public hospital, the Charité.[106]

The association between circumcision and disease remained even after the introduction of antisepsis, as Julius Jaffé noted in 1886.[107] In the standard medical handbook on syphilis, written by Jonathan Hutchinson in 1887 (and quickly translated into German), the argument moved away from the *mohel*'s direct transmission of syphilis through *metsitsah* (which, however, Hutchinson acknowledged as a potential problem).[108] He described other practices that transmit syphilis from one Jewish male to another without the intervention of a female. Newly circumcised infants are exposed to the blood of infected infants through the *mohel* storing the amputated prepuce in the same container as the lint used to stanch the bleeding.[109] He later commented that such infections can also be iatrogenic, stemming from the instruments surgeons use to circumcise.[110] This view appears repeatedly at the close of the century, with its only rebuttal the evidence supplied by the Viennese professor Zeissl, in what remains the standard turn-of-the-century Jewish defense of circumcision: that there was no higher incidence of syphilis in circumcised than in uncircumcised infants.[111] This view is contradicted by Heinrich Singer, in his overview of the diseases of the Jews in 1904.[112]

Metsitsah was condemned by the medical establishment of the nineteenth century as the cause of the transmission of specific, stigmatizing diseases between adult Jewish males and Jewish male infants. This practice colored the intense debate about the retention of circumcision as a ritual practice that was carried on in Jewish communities in Europe from the middle of the century. The debate was over whether circumcision was ritually necessary and whether it was safe. This debate raged in Vienna during the mid-nineteenth century as vociferously as anywhere else in Europe. The leading Reform rabbi in Vienna, Isaac Noah Mannheimer, who presided at the marriage of Freud's parents, opposed the position taken by the most radical theologians, such as Samuel Holdheim, in favor of the abolition of circumcision. Mannheimer's position was more conservative. He supported the use of Hebrew in the liturgy (even though he had preached in Danish during his tenure in Copenhagen), and opposed mixed marriages and the abolition of circumcision. No compromise was found on the first two issues (Hebrew was maintained as the language of the liturgy and mixed marriages were not authorized), but an alternative was found in the third case during the 1850s.[113]

The arguments against the practice of *metsitsah* were labeled "hygienic" rather than theological and were separated from the ritual meaning of the act of circumcision. Together with Rabbi Lazar Horowitz, the spiritual leader of the Orthodox community in Vienna, Mannheimer abolished the practice of *metsitsah*. (It had already been abolished elsewhere in Europe for "hygienic" reasons, including the spread of syphilis. It ceased in 1844 in France, through the enactment of a legislative act, as well as in Brunswick.)[114] Although Horowitz was a follower of the ultra-Orthodox Pressburg Rabbi Moses Sofer, the abolition of *metsitsah* became a dividing line between the practices of Viennese Jewry and the tradition of Eastern Jewry, such as the Jews of Pressburg and Freiburg. By the close of the nineteenth century, the practice of *metsitsah* had been either abandoned or, in those Orthodox communities that insisted on its retention, modified by the introduction of a glass tube over the penis through which the *mohel* could draw blood, which was filtered before it reached his mouth. The initial purpose of the procedure, the stanching of the blood, was abandoned but the form of the ritual remained. By 1911, Franz Kafka could record in his diary the view that *metsitsah* had become a relic of Eastern Jewry, where the half-drunken *mohel* with his red nose and stinking breath sucked on the bloody penis. Kafka contrasted this with the boring but not unhygienic practices of Western Jewry that he had just witnessed, seeing his nephew circumcised.[115]

In analyzing the risks associated with circumcision, the discourse about this practice returned the debate to its function as a preventative of disease. Following the trend toward seeing circumcision as a purely medical convention, Carl Alexander addressed the Reform congregation in Breslau on April 15, 1902, on the "hygienic implications of circumcision." This signified the ultimate acceptance of the idea that infant male circumcision was good for the Jewish body: it prevented masturbation (and its results) and thus it had no symbolic significance. It was not a form of repressed human sacrifice. But even Alexander came out strongly against *metsitsah* on the grounds of its risk to the health of the child. It is only where this practice was still pursued, in the benighted lands of "Russia, Poland, Galicia, and Algeria," that disease was still a problem.[116] Debates about the hygienic or unhygienic practice of circumcision continue in the twentieth century. In Germany through the 1930s, they were connected with the quality of the Jew's body, with the inherent diseased nature the Jew's body represented.[117]

In the debates, the meaning of *metsitsah* as part of the discourse about Jews and hygiene is clear. A male Jew can infect another male Jew with a sexually transmitted disease (which can cause, among other things, madness). Thus no male Jew is free from the risk of becoming infected with syphilis as part of his becoming a Jew. This is quite different from the conventional model of infection that haunted this syphilophobic age. In the exemplary novel on the theme, Emile Zola's *Nana* (1879–80), the woman infects the man and makes him unable to fulfill his role as a man. It makes him unable to fight and to generate children. (For Zola, this was the explanation for why the Germans conquered the French during the Franco-Prussian War!) *Metsitsah* was associated with the feminization of the male Jew and his absolute position as one at risk for a sexually transmitted disease. The male Jew's presence in emancipated European society presented another source of infection and pollution, a source independent of the presence of women.

It is no wonder that male Jews, in Vienna as elsewhere in German-speaking Europe, looked on their own bodies as the objects about which the debates over the meaning and source of health and disease were held. The primary way of avoiding these confrontations was to understate the meaning of circumcision. This avoidance was also reflected in the debates about the need for circumcision among acculturated Jews in Vienna. The extraordinary, anonymous tale of "Herr Moriz Deutschösterreicher," written in the mid-1940s, begins with an argument between the father and the mother of "Mr. Average Austrian Jew":

> Moriz Deutschösterreicher was born on June 2, 1891, in Vienna. His mother did not want him to be circumcised: "It's crazy, Sandor, to purposely violate my child, think about when he goes into the army and they all have to bathe naked together, or what if he marries a Christian, how embarrassing. . . . If you are dumb enough and don't have him baptized, don't do this to him. Does one have to send such a poor worm with such a handicap into the world?" She cried day and night. But it didn't help a bit. Sandor agreed with his old mother—by himself he would have perhaps hesitatingly agreed, because he did not place much store in such things.[118]

Circumcision has no positive meaning in this context, except as a means of pleasing someone of an older generation. At the end of the century the internalization of the debates about circumcision, especially among the Jews of Central Europe, provided a heightened sense of their vulnerability because of their visibility.

FREUD AND CIRCUMCISION

On a biographical level the facts seem rather straightforward. Sigmund Freud's parents, Kallamon Jacob Freud and Amalia Nathanson, were married on July 29, 1855, by Isaac Noah Mannheimer. Their oldest son, Sigismund Schlomo, was born on May 6, 1856, and circumcised a week later, on May 13, 1856. But, of course, nothing is quite that simple. Questions have arisen about the implication of his parents having been married in the Seitenstetten synagogue and about the very date of Sigmund Freud's birth—never mind that he was given the name Sigismund, one of the essential Jewish names in the comic literature of the period. What we do know is that he was circumcised and that he was exposed to the older, unreformed ritual of *metsitsah* in his Moravian hometown of Freiburg. Freud was thus part of the system that both practiced *metsitsah* and was aware of the dangers of syphilitic infection attributed to it.

What did circumcision come to mean for Freud? To what degree did he incorporate the prevailing views of the male Jewish body into his discussion of the "meaning" of circumcision, and where did he locate the nexus? In *An Outline of Psychoanalysis*, which occupied the final months of his life, Freud returns to the "meaning" of psychoanalysis in an extended footnote concerning the anxiety the young boy feels when threatened with castration by his mother, a castration that is to be implemented by the father because of the child's masturbatory activity:

> Castration has a place too in the Oedipus legend, for the blinding with which Oedipus punishes himself after the discovery of his crime is, by the evidence of dreams, a symbolic substitute for castration. The possibility cannot be excluded that a phylogenetic memory-trace may contribute to the extraordinary terrifying effect of the threat—a memory trace from the pre-history of the primal family, when the jealous father actually robbed his son of his genitals if the latter became troublesome to him as a rival with a woman. The primeval custom of circumcision, another symbolic substitute for castration, can only be understood as an expression of submission to the father's will. (Cf. the puberty rites of primitive peoples.) No investigation has yet been made of the form taken by the events described above among peoples and in civilizations which do not suppress masturbation in children.[119]

Two factors enter into this discussion: first, the theme of the unknown, here the unknown world of an unrepressed sexuality, and second, the universal claims of the phylogenetic model.[120] This model dominated Freud's biological thinking (as it did that of most of his contemporaries). Linked to this was the general acceptance (until Weismann) of the view that acquired characteristics were inherited (the Lamarckian model). Indeed, Freud's outlook was standard for most late-nineteenth-century biological scientists and physicians. The double model was applicable not only to the realm of the physical development of the genotype, but also to the construction of the psychology of the group. It is in the real, phylogenetic experience of earlier generations that the psyche is formed, and it is in such a group experience that the psychic development of each of us is mirrored.

The discussion about the nature of the Jew's body as inherently different rested on the nineteenth-century idea of the inheritance of acquired characteristics that is generally associated with Jean Baptiste Pierre Antoine de Monet de Lamarck.[121] However, virtually all the major Darwinian biologists, including Charles Darwin himself, believed that somehow changes in the soma would appear in future generations. Sigmund Freud's lifelong acceptance of this model has been well documented.[122] This view and his view of recapitulation—that the development of the individual mirrors the development of the species—are linked. We retain our overall evolutionary model within our bodies and psyches because our genetic makeup is accretive. This view is best known in Ernst Haeckel's reformulation of 1868: "ontogeny recapitulates phylogeny." But it is an older, pre-Darwinian view well established with the German Romantic biologists such as Lorenz Oken, who in the 1820s first stated that "a human foetus is a whole animal kingdom."[123] These models are at the root of all theories of racial difference in the late nineteenth century, as they are at the root of all medical science of the age. When biologists such as August Weismann attacked this thesis at the close of the nineteenth century and separated the development of individual and group from past events, this was a radical break; Freud, trained in the scientific laboratories of Vienna during the 1870s, was no more influenced by these alternative views than most other scientists of his generation.

Freud's initial studies in biological science at the University of Vienna from 1873 to 1882 were done under the tutelage of Carl Claus, Ernst Wilhelm Brücke, and Theodore H. Meynert, all individuals who generally subscribed to the standard Darwinian model of inheritance and for whom inheritance meant predisposition. (There are slight variations among the views of the three on topics such as instinct and inherited learning. But all agreed to the basic premise of inheritance through use and disuse.) For Freud, in his last discussion of circumcision, predisposition to neurosis still meant the creation of a tradition (circumcision) that served as a substitute for a castration, an image evoked by the repression of a forbidden form of sexuality, masturbation. Circumcision was seen as a "cure" for the diseases associated with masturbation; it was also seen as a sign of the sexual disease of the Jewish male.

Freud thought that actually seeing female genitalia was a necessary precondition that defined for the male child the potential of his own cas-

tration: "there is another condition [that must be] fulfilled before or afterwards. In itself it seems too inconceivable to the boy that such a thing
could happen. But if at the time of the threat he can recall the appearance
of the female genitals or if shortly afterwards he has a sight of them—of
genitals, that is to say, which really lack this supremely valued part, then
he takes what he has heard seriously and, coming under the influence of
the castration complex, experiences the severest trauma of his young
life." The threat comes from the mother ("she threatens to take away
from him the thing he is defying her with")[124] and is reinforced by the
sight of the mother's body. Géza Róheim commented that the Jewish
male child's loss of the foreskin and the separation from the mother occur
simultaneously, so that the Jew potentially undergoes a double loss.[125]
But it is the mimetic gaze at the real body of the mother on which Freud
(and Róheim) insist. Given Freud's early abandonment of mimetic memory and its replacement by remembered fantasies, this stress on the actual
event is analogous to Freud's insistence on the reality of the phylogenetic
memory or "common mental construction" of the race. If we push
Róheim's reading further, we can argue that the circumcised child becomes aware of the difference of his own body (as does Little Hans, the
Jewish child in Freud's 1909 case) and projects that difference into the
body of the mother. The reality of the child's genitalia and their association with pain and loss become the child's fantasy of the mother's body.
    The nature of this frightening and threatening body seen by the male
child becomes a leitmotif in Freud's work. There is no question but that
the act of seeing here is not neutral, is not distanced, is real and frightening. It is precisely the constructed opposite of the scientific gaze: Francis
Galton gazing at the Jew. Francis Galton, Charles Darwin's cousin and
the founder of modern eugenics, tried to capture this "Jewish physiognomy" in his composite photographs of "boys in the Jews' Free School,
Bell Lane."[126] Galton claimed that he was able to generate a type that was
representative of the psychological as well as the physiological essence of
the Jews. Responding to two papers to be given before the Anthropological Institute "on the race characteristics of the Jews," Galton believed he
had captured the "typical features of the modern Jewish face." Galton's
trip to the Bell Lane school confronted him with the "children of poor
parents, dirty little fellows individually, but wonderfully beautiful, as I
think, in these composites." There, and in the adjacent "Jewish Quarter,"
he saw the "cold, scanning gaze of man, woman, and child" of the Jew as
the sign of their difference, of their potential pathology, of their inherent
nature: "There was no sign of diffidence in any of their looks, nor of
surprise at the unwonted intrusion. I felt, rightly or wrongly, that every
one of them was coolly appraising me at market value, without the slight-
est interest of any other kind."[127] It is in the Jews' gazes that the pathology

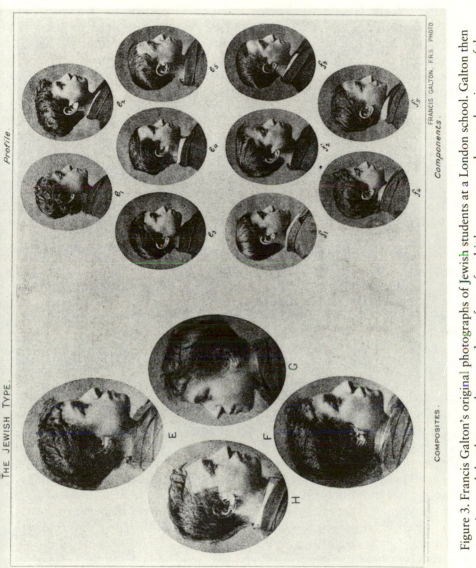

Figure 3. Francis Galton's original photographs of Jewish students at a London school. Galton then superimposed the photographs to produce a form of multiple exposure and created an image of the "essence" of the Jew. From the *Photographic News* 29 (April 17 and 24, 1885).

of their souls can be found.[128] At the turn of the century, Sigmund Freud read this view of the "vivacity of the eye" as a sign of the "remarkable persistence" of Jewish physiognomy.[129] Using Galton's photographs, the anthropologist Hans F. K. Günther attempted to describe the "sensual," "threatening," and "crafty" gaze of the Jew as a direct result of the physiology of the Jewish face, reflecting the essence of the Jewish soul.[130] This view is at least as old as Robert Burton's *Anatomy of Melancholy*, where Burton writes of the "goggle eyes" of the Jews, as well as "their voice, pace, gesture, [and] looks" as signs of "their conditions and infirmities."[131]

But it is not merely that Jews "look Jewish," but that this marks them as inferior: "Who has not heard people characterize such and such a man or woman they see in the streets as Jewish without in the least knowing anything about them? The street arab who calls out 'Jew' as some child hurries on to school is unconsciously giving the best and most disinterested proof that there is a reality in the Jewish expression."[132] The gaze of the non-Jew seeing the Jew is immediately translated into action. For Freud, Galton's photographs became central models for visualizing how the unseen processes of the psyche work.[133] Freud was well aware of the use of such composite photographs by Houston Stewart Chamberlain as a salient proof of the immutability of race.[134] This context haunted Freud for his entire career. With these images, the Jew suddenly becomes aware of his own physical difference and sees that difference, his circumcision, projected into the body of the female, with its hidden "Jew," its castrated penis.

But what sort of body did the young Freud examine in his initial training as a biologist? In 1875 Freud went to Trieste to undertake fieldwork. Carl Claus had assigned to him the study of eel gonads.[135] The reproductive ability of the hermaphroditic female eel had been understood by the 1870s, but the male's reproductive organs were not. Indeed, they had only recently been discovered. Freud was able to distinguish between the females (*Weibchen*) and those with masculine gonads (*solche mit Lappenorgane*). This distinction between the feminine and the Other, the ambiguity of grasping the disguised signs of masculine sexuality, led Freud to pursue an "anthropological" measurement of the male eels. He needed to see whether other factors—the length of the head, the diameter of the eye—were influenced by this hidden masculinity. He examined the primitive body of the eel, looking for its male sexuality. Here the model of the race is present in its essence—not because Freud looked into the eel and saw the hidden masculinity of the Jew, but because the science of the time absolutely linked disguised motivating factors with external observable signs.

The gonads of the eel are a hidden sign of masculinity much as the hidden, but omnipresent, sign of circumcision (present even when the Jew is uncircumcised!) marks the Jewish male as different. Like the congenital circumcision of the Jew, the gonads are present even when they cannot be seen. (Freud's knowledge about congenital circumcision does not rest only on his awareness of the scientific debate, but also on his intensive knowledge of Schiller's *Robbers*, passages from which he [like all other high-school students of his day] learned by heart.)[136] But such potentials for illness are present in the male Jew and are only triggered by the presence of the female. Freud's perspective in these early biological papers is "purely" scientific. He observes his specimens with total neutrality. Indeed, this distance shapes his relationship to the sexuality hidden within.

The biology (with its "scientific" distance) that Freud studied in Carl Claus's laboratories was not, however, limited to the study of the lower vertebrates. Claus's work encompassed the discussion of the biological implications of race. He argued for the gradual changes that established the barriers between "species or races." He outlined the distinction between "natural" races, those tied to geographic location, and "artificial" races, those bred by human beings.[137] The origin of the natural races "is hidden in the deepest darkness, never to be revealed by the light of science."[138] The unknowability of the race places it beyond science. Freud totally disavowed his work with Carl Claus. He mentioned him only once later, when applying for a professorship at the University of Vienna, where Claus's reputation as a scientist would have carried some weight. The account of his disavowal usually cited is the one he gave to Ernest Jones. According to Jones, Freud "gave such a disparaging version of this piece of work as almost to insinuate that it had been a futile and pointless one. . . . In the circumstances no one could well have done better, but Freud was much more dissatisfied with his inconclusive results than was his chief. An ambitious youth must have hoped for a task where some brilliant and original discovery would be made."[139] The discovery Freud made in Claus's laboratory and in Trieste was that biology and inheritance predisposed some creatures to having certain qualities, such as hermaphrodism, that could be seen, if only by the scientific eye. What Freud learned in Claus's classroom was that race was a real category that had to be taken into consideration when understanding sexuality and reproduction. Sexuality was an object of the science of the time, perceived as both the force for reproduction of the individual and the formative force of the extended group.

Within Freud's theory the meaning of circumcision is linked, as we see in his last work, to the cultural context given to sexuality at the beginning of human activity. It is the meaning of circumcision in Freud's own sense that is important. The phylogenetic inheritance shapes the mind, but circumcision is an even more significant factor in determining the attitude of the Christian toward the Jew. In the case of the Wolf Man (1914), a

Russian nobleman (the very image of anxiety for Eastern European Jews) is associated with "the sacred story [of] . . . the ritual circumcision of Christ and of the Jews in general."[140] Indeed, the sign of circumcision would have been a sign of the "prehistory [in which] it was unquestionably the father who practiced castration as a punishment and who later softened it down into circumcision."[141] But it was also a sign of contemporary Jewish history, with the "Little Father"—a popular name for the czar—destroying those branded with this symbolic mark. Freud does not mention the civil "castration" of the Jews through the pogroms in Russia during the 1880s and 1890s, when the Wolf Man would have been born. He prefers to associate this image with the consumptive Jewish footman who cleans the Wolf Man after he has defecated into his clothes at the age of four and a half.[142] The Wolf Man describes how he actually liked some of the servants in his father's house. "He emphasized the fact that they had been either sickly or Jews (which implied circumcision)."[143] He sees these as figures over whom he has power, who fulfill his compensatory needs against the power of his parents. The Wolf Man linked for Freud the image of circumcision with the discourse on disease, specifically tuberculosis, a disease about which (as with syphilis) there was a debate concerning Jewish risk or immunity.[144] Freud saw this patient as representing the "ambivalence" that "is a legacy from the psychic life of primitive races; with the Russian people, however, it is far better preserved and has remained more accessible to consciousness than elsewhere."[145] For Freud, the specific "Russian" racial memory of his patient contained the seed of his neurosis. The various types of racial memories of the peoples of the East (both Russians and Jews) reflect their specific atavistic natures.

Circumcision is associated with powerlessness and with disease. This view was later echoed by Arnold Zweig in his comments on the association of castration with the origins of anti-Semitism. Employing Freud's theoretical matrix, he noted that the Jewish prisoners in Rome had low status because they had been vanquished and because "they bore the sign of circumcision, which was associated in the eyes of the people with castration."[146] Powerlessness and circumcision are linked because of the involuntary nature of castration in Roman society and because of its association with the status of the slave. This too is echoed in the Wolf Man's evocation of the status of the sick Jew in the context of Imperial Russia.

Freud's model postulated castration as the original act, which was then modified into the symbolic act of circumcision. Circumcision is an early symbolic substitute for the castration of male children. But how can castration be a sign of past practice? Would the line not have been destroyed by the castration of males in the past? No, for in Jewish law the matrilineal line carries identity; it is through one's mother that one is a Jew. Castrating males would force Jewish females to marry outside the group (as advocated by many scientists of the time) and would raise the specter of crossbreeding. The Jewish father, rather than castrating his sons and ending his line, circumcised them and thus proved to them his power over their sexuality. This gave rise to debates about the meaning of Jewish sexual selectivity and the purity of the "race."

Circumcision and castration are closely linked, and they remain in the medical literature signs of the barbarity of the Jews. In the case of the Jewish child called Little Hans, Freud paraphrases the child's argument: "Could it be that living beings really exist which did not possess widdlers? If so, it would no longer be so incredible that they could take his own widdler away, and, as it were, make him into a woman!"[147] Castration anxiety is anxiety about losing the penis and being made into something different and less whole. To this statement Freud appended a long footnote that relates the anxiety about castration to the nature of anti-Semitism. It is important to follow Freud's stated train of thought: if—says the child—I can be circumcised and made into a Jew, can I not also be castrated and made into a woman? But this can also be read in light of the phantasm of the congenital essence of Judaism hidden in the literature on the inheritance of circumcision. If I am revealed as a Jew because of the nature of my genitalia, I can also be revealed to be a woman. These forces within me—like the eel's gonads—are only waiting to be revealed.

Freud's note attempted to "demonstrate the typical character of the train of thought" of five-year-old Little Hans:

> The castration complex is the deepest root of anti-Semitism; for even in the nursery little boys hear that a Jew has something cut off his penis—a piece of his penis, they think—and this gives them a right to despise Jews. And there is no stronger unconscious root for the sense of superiority over women. Weininger (the young philosopher who, highly gifted but sexually deranged, committed suicide after producing his remarkable book, *Geschlecht und Charakter* [*Sex and Character*, 1903]), in a chapter that attracted much attention, treated Jews and women with equal hostility and overwhelmed them with the same insults. Being neurotic, Weininger was completely under the sway of his infantile complexes; and from that standpoint what is common to Jews and women is their relation to the castration complex.[148]

Freud's example of the problematic relationship of the Jew to his circumcised penis is Otto Weininger, a figure of substantial importance to his intellectual as well as his personal life.

Otto Weininger had been a student of philosophy and biology at the University of Vienna at the turn of the century. He published his revised dissertation, *Sex and Character*, in 1903 and killed himself shortly thereafter in the house in Vienna in which Beethoven had died.[149] Weininger was both a baptized Jew and intensely confused about his sexual identity.[150] His book became an immediate best-seller and established him as a serious contributor to the discourse about the relationship between race and gender at the beginning of the century.[151] This is a work of intensive self-hatred that, however, had an unprecedented influence on the era's scientific discourse about Jews and women. Weininger's suicide shortly after the publication of this book helped publicize his views, but they were hardly new to the thinkers of the time. His polemical restatement of Arthur Schopenhauer's views on women simply extended the category of the feminine to the Jew. This book, read by Freud in an early draft, was fundamental in shaping at least some of his attitudes toward the nature of the body. Indeed, it was seen as a serious work of science by radical thinkers of the time, such as the American feminist Charlotte Perkins Gilman.[152] Ludwig Wittgenstein accepted and incorporated aspects of Weininger's philosophy into his worldview.[153] Its influence extended to the most original and influential work by Japan's leading fin de siècle philosopher, Kitārō Nishida.[154] Jewish scientists, such as Freud's friend Leopold Löwenfeld, the Munich neurologist, saw Weininger as a scientist, a "mad" scientist, but a scientist nevertheless. In his study of sexual drives, published in 1911, Löwenfeld labeled Weininger a "doubtlessly highly gifted madman whose *Sex and Character* has achieved unearned attention."[155] But then he spent two pages countering Weininger's contrast between the erotic and the sensual. It is clear from Löwenfeld's discussion that he (and his scientific readers) were intimately acquainted with Weininger's views. As late as Felix Langer's 1934 study of *The Protocols of the Elders of Zion*, which Freud owned, Weininger's suicide was evoked as proof of his weakness and madness.[156] Langer presumed his readers would recognize Weininger's name and the meaning of his life and death.

Weininger's work, while in no way innovative, established a psychological spectrum running from the Jewish psyche at one pole to the Aryan mind at the other. This scale was parallel to that on which masculine and feminine served as antithetical points. Weininger's views echoed (or plagiarized) those held by Freud's close friend Wilhelm Fliess, and the publication of Weininger's book led to the final breach of Freud's friendship with Fliess.[157] In 1904 Fliess accused Freud of having revealed the concept of bisexuality to Otto Weininger through his patient (and Weininger's friend), Hermann Swoboda. Freud claimed a total inability to recall anything about Weininger and his work. This denial did not satisfy Fliess. Indeed, in a later letter to David Abrahamsen he noted that he had seen the Weininger book only in manuscript, as a draft of the dissertation, which totally avoided the discussion of the "Jewish Question."[158] Yet Freud, in his note to the case of Little Hans, published in 1909, showed that he knew quite well the anti-Semitic dimension of Weininger's work and felt compelled to use it as the basis for a diagnosis of the author's mental state. Weininger's argument about "Jewishness" was never mentioned in the exchange of letters between Freud and Fliess in 1904. The question of the originality and creativity of the Jew, especially the Jewish scientist, was central to their exchange, but it was unspoken of in their letters.[159] This final break with Fliess was related to another Jewish text of this period, Freud's own account of the case of Dora, which was the subject of Freud's penultimate letter to Fliess prior to the explosion of the scandal about Weininger's plagiarism. Freud's account of that case remained unpublished for three years; as he noted to Fliess, he withdrew this paper from publication in 1901 "because just a little earlier I had lost my last audience in you."[160] This audience had been colored by Freud's reading of Weininger and its personal repercussions for him. The homoerotic nature of Weininger's text was clear to Freud and his contemporaries. This evocation of sexual difference, with its clear parallel to Freud's relationship with Fliess, became subsumed in Freud's reading of Weininger's image of the Jewish body.

Weininger's views on the nature of bisexuality reflect the model seen in the work of the ethnopsychologists. Qualities of the body are (usually incompletely) transferred to the psyche. Weininger's image of the sexual as a "platonic" quality of mind was in turn important in framing Freud's response to Weininger's equation of the Jewish male and the female. For Weininger the Jewish mind is closely analogous to that of the female; the assumption is that the reason for this lies in the nature of the Jewish body.

Weininger's "laws of sexual attraction" postulate the existence of a biological (in other words, "real") explanation for sexual attraction. This is much the same ground most of the post-Darwin biologists plowed. For Weininger the basis of attraction is the existence in every individual of both male and female qualities of mind. The desired end is the Aristotelian golden mean, with the male and the female qualities of both partners exactly balanced. Thus the very feminine male could find an ideal partner in the very masculine female or (and this is unstated) in the very masculine male. Just as the Jew, for Weininger, is a quality of mind that could be expunged, so too is the feminine. Masculinity and femininity are abstractions for Weininger, and thus the possibility of bisexuality exists without advocating any image of the physical difference of the homosexual. Weininger could thus deal with his "Jewishness" and his "homosexuality" (using two clinical terms of the day) by seeing them as mind-sets that could be altered. Weininger states this literally in the form of detailed mock formulas, with "M" and "W" representing the male and female mentalities and other pseudomathematical parallels. This model of the "mixed" race as outlined by Claus is carried over into his representation of the relationship between Jew and Aryan, between male and female. It is also important to see how Freud could avoid translating scientific abstractions into concrete visual images in his reading of Weininger, for Weininger translated all his concepts into these formulas, representing human sexuality as the result of a scientific process (a view already explored by Goethe in *The Elective Affinities*).

There was a model in nineteenth-century science for the relationship between sexuality and race. It had already been presented in a rather oblique way by Mantegazza. The model of racial attraction was more directly stated by the nineteenth-century French writer Abel Hermant:

> Differences of race are irreducible and between two beings who love each other they cannot fail to produce exceptional and instructive reactions. In the first superficial ebullition of love, indeed, nothing notable may be manifested, but in a fairly short time the two lovers, innately hostile, in striving to approach each other strike against an invisible partition which separates them. Their sensibilities are divergent; everything in each shocks the other; even their anatomical conformation, even the language of their gestures; all is foreign.[161]

Or to cite Havelock Ellis's view: "It is difficult to be sexually attracted to persons who are fundamentally unlike ourselves in racial constitution."[162] Weininger's first law of sexual attraction is an answer to this view. Sexual attraction is based on wholeness and complementarity. One strives to have a complete male and complete female by combining the masculine and feminine natures of two individuals, each of which has both masculine and feminine qualities. Weininger's second law attempts to explain the strength of sexual affinity in any conceivable case. For this he adds in the "race factor" as well as "the health and absence of deformity in the two individuals."[163] Weininger accepts the premise that Jews look different and that there is a "universally acquired correspondence between mind and body. . . . The science of character can be linked with morphology, [and] will be valuable not only to these sciences but to physiognomy."[164]

The biological difference of the Jew is mirrored in the representation of the reality of the Jew's body. Freud had evoked the Jewish "scientist" Otto Weininger as an anti-Semite. Weininger is like the little (non-Jewish) boy in the nursery who hears about the Jews cutting off penises, except that he, of course, knows that it is true. His hatred of the Jews is "infantile," according to Freud, since it remains fixed at that moment in all children's development when they learn about the possibility of castration. Jewish neurotics like Weininger focus on the negative difference of their bodies from ones that are "normal," and use this difference, like their evocation of the bodies of women, to define themselves. Freud's argument, however, evokes one further reading of circumcision—that, for the uncircumcised Aryan, the Jew is analogous to the woman. The circumcised penis is as clear a sign of the vulnerability of the child as is the genitalia of the female. Alfred Adler commented in 1909 about a patient of Fritz Wittels, the first biographer of Freud, who saw Wittels as a woman in a dream. He "had the impression that Wittels, too, is in some sense castrated (circumcised)." Adler noted, "thus his representation of him as a woman (in the transference) signifies also a degradation."[165] The Jewish psychoanalyst (Wittels) is unmanned again by being seen as castrated and circumcised simultaneously by another Jewish psychoanalyst (Adler).

The counterargument was given by one of the leading non-Jewish precursors of psychoanalysis, Georg Groddeck, whose work on the "id/it" provided the model for Freud's discussion of the basic drives. In a late essay (1931) Groddeck addressed the question of bisexuality.[166] For him the Jewish race is the "most masculine of races." The Jew has been robbed of his femininity (which for Groddeck, unlike Weininger, is the most positive quality) and is cast in the role of the exemplary male. What makes the Jew into the male is his circumcision. It serves as a pathological sign of his rejection of his bisexuality. Bisexuality is an attribute of the godhead (at least in Jewish mysticism) and by marking himself off from the deity, he affirms his separation from, and thus subordination to, God: "Judaism is precisely humanism: he decides to exist in this world, from which the extra-human, which is the bisexual, is excluded." And yet Groddeck is ambivalent about this role of the male Jew as the essential male, as he (like many of his non-Jewish predecessors) feels ambivalent about the Jews being those "who gave circumcision its special meaning, through which the Jew distinguishes himself from all other humans and gives him . . . the sense of his superiority to the non-Jew." The "common mental construction" of the Jew is his (false) sense of superiority, which is achieved, according to Groddeck, through his becoming "purely masculine" (*Nur-Mann*).[167]

The intact penis despises the "operated" penis, which is seen as analogous to but not the same as the "missing" genitalia of the "castrated" woman. But in the non-Jewish child, the repression of the possibility of acts such as circumcision and castration leads to a neurosis, that of anti-Semitism. The fear is that "I" can too easily become like "them." Here is Freud's first attempt—which is much more detailed in later works such as *Totem and Taboo* (in theory) and *Moses and Monotheism* (as a case study)—to deal with anti-Semitism as a disease of the uncircumcised. Anti-Semitism becomes a disease, specifically a mental illness. Following the full political emancipation of the Jews in Austria in 1848, at least one of the most impassioned opponents of the Jews was considered by the Viennese police to be "overly excited, to suffer from a 'persecution mania,' but to be without blemish from a moral and Christian point of view."[168] Cesare Lombroso had stated this position quite clearly at the turn of the century in a review of Max Nordau's polemic against modernism entitled *Degeneration*. Anti-Semitism is a sort of "disease" that afflicts people like "madness." Richard Wagner is in many of his works "not only mad but imbecile. . . . [W]hen he wrote 'Judaism in Music' [his polemic against the Jews] he had a sort of delirium of persecution against the Jews."[169] Anti-Semites are diseased. For Lombroso the "epidemic" of anti-Semitism was caused by syphilis, for "the most fanatic anti-Semites have syphilis or they show the signs of having had the disease."[170] They demonstrate signs of the "delirium . . . incited everywhere by the same virus."[171] It is a disease, indeed, caused by the presence of the intact penis and the anxiety of castration. As early as Freud's comments to the Viennese Psychoanalytic Society in 1907, anti-Semitism, as a reaction to the body of the Jew, was labeled a neurotic symptom.[172] The image of anti-Semitism as a form of psychopathology became part of Freud's understanding of the premier anti-Semite, Adolf Hitler. The historian of medicine Charles Singer spoke with Freud in the middle of November 1938 and wrote that Freud "is confident that Hitler is insane in the technical sense. He says, however, that this type of insanity is not, unfortunately, likely to lead soon to a state of confusion. Of course if it did it would be obvious to all, even to Germans."[173] This view saw anti-Semitism as the mental aberration of an individual rather than as mass hysteria. Felix Weltsch, a Jewish lawyer and Zionist from Prague, could label anti-Semitism a "mass hysteria" while not seeing the anti-Semite as necessarily clinically insane.[174] In 1941, Rudolph Loewenstein began his study of the origins of anti-Semitism in which the history of the Jewish body is also evoked as the object of the anxiety of the uncircumcised.[175] In 1946, Otto Fenichel argued that circumcision was merely one of the precipitating causes of anti-Semitism among the "uncircumcised."[176] In 1947, Herman Nunberg saw the absence of circumcision as the cause of the German's inability to "endure the restriction of aggression as demanded by Jewish-Christian ethics." The Jews "through circumcision entered into a Covenant with God . . . they learned thereby to master their own aggression from within."[177] Theodor Adorno's work on the authoritarian personality in the 1940s evoked this sense of "anti-Semitism as 'symptom' which fulfills an 'economic' function within the subject's psychology."[178] Even in contemporary discussions of Jew-hatred, psychoanalytic models have been created to exemplify the universal underpinnings of this phenomenon.[179]

The labeling of anti-Semitism as a neurosis resulting from a fantasy of the Jew's body represented the powerlessness of the Jew as analogous to the powerlessness of the female—this in a time when both the Jew and the woman were becoming more visible in the civic culture of Western Europe. It was vital to narrate the psychological processing of conflicted emotions through the application of psychological mechanisms such as projection and repression. Freud could thus generalize the experience of both the Jew and the woman as the core of the mental illness of the Aryan. The diseased body of the Jew, the sexuality of the Jew associated with circumcision, is the origin of the disease of the Aryan. The Jew's body is like the body of the woman, but is not identical to it. (This is unlike the Aryan in Freud's narrative who sees "Jew" and "woman" as interchangeable categories when confronted by them with claims on his power, a power represented by him in the intact nature of his penis. This is Freud's revision of Weininger's argument. For Weininger, "Jewishness" is the stain that marks the diseased individual. The Jew is damaged beyond hope. Freud accepts the difference of the Jewish body, as he does the difference of the Jewish mind, but sees the response of the Aryan as a kind of pathology. His view distinguishes the male Jew and the female, while projecting the discourse about disease onto the Aryan.

In a footnote, concerning castration anxiety written in 1919 to his study of the creativity of Leonardo da Vinci (1910), Freud stated, "here we may also trace one of the roots of the anti-Semitism which appears with such elemental force and finds such irrational expression among the nations of the West. Circumcision is unconsciously equated with castration. If we venture to carry our conjectures back to the primeval days of the human race we can surmise that originally circumcision must have been a milder substitute, designed to take the place of castration."[180] But circumcision is also a sign of "primitive peoples."[181] Freud, like most other commentators of the period, cites parallel cases from Australia.[182] In 1893, one of G. Stanley Hall's pupils at Clark University, Arthur H. Daniels, introduced his discussion of the meaning of circumcision with the note that "it is by no means a distinctively Jewish rite."[183] The rite of circumcision is "primeval" and is the atavistic root of the anxiety about the castrated body in the West. Its existence in "primeval" cultures in the late nineteenth century is proof of its ancient status in the West. Discussions about circumcision in the medical literature of the late nineteenth century reflected debates about the difference of the Jewish body. In seeing the act of circumcision as "primeval," Freud placed circumcision at the root of Western civilization. He takes the general opinion (espoused by Hegel as well as many anthropologists of the time) that the Jews are themselves an atavism in European culture, and generalizes this view. The anxiety about castration is a universal anxiety, while the anxiety about symbolic castration (circumcision) is a specifically Aryan one.

While Jews suffer from castration anxiety, the apprehension about the penis is not a parochially Jewish neurosis. Jewish men have the reality of

circumcision already inscribed on their bodies from their earliest awareness. The baseline for the Jew is his circumcised penis; the Aryan, like the
female, must undergo a double displacement of his anxiety. In his discussion in *Three Essays on the Theory of Sexuality* (1905) Freud outlines
boys' assumptions that everyone has a penis. Unlike Little Hans, they
deny the reality of the "little girls' " genitalia. "Little girls do not resort to
denial of this kind when they see that boys' genitals are formed differently
than their own. They are ready to recognize them immediately and are
overcome by envy for the penis—an envy culminating in the wish, which
is so important in its consequences, to be boys themselves."[184] Now
Freud's argument about circumcision presents a third variable: the circumcised male. In Freud's presentation, he is the baseline, the norm. It is
the uncircumcised male who looks at the circumcised male and responds.
He does not deny the possibility; rather he becomes anxious, fearing that
he will become a Jew himself. This reversal of "longing" and "fear"
reflects the question of status. Freud wrote in a note to the 1920 edition
of this passage, "The conviction which is finally reached by males that
women have no penis often leads them to an enduringly low opinion of
the other sex."[185] The triad is clear: the fearful, uncircumcised Aryan; the
longing, castrated female; and the Jewish male.

Freud, in discussing the Aryan's fear of circumcision, projected the
anxiety of his own precarious sense of the stability of his world onto the
aggression of the Aryan. The scientific debate about circumcision affects
the way the male Jew understands a part of his anatomy, his penis, but it
also forms his understanding of his place in society. Thus Freud, in *Civilization and Its Discontents* (1930), could without hesitation paraphrase
Havelock Ellis's view that "the genitals themselves, the sight of which is
always exciting, are nevertheless hardly ever judged to be beautiful; the
quality of beauty seems, instead, to attach to certain secondary sexual
characteristics."[186] Havelock Ellis's statement is even more direct:

> They [the sexual organs] are not aesthetically beautiful. It is fundamentally
> necessary that the intromittent organ of the male and the receptive canal of
> the female should retain their primitive characteristics; they cannot, there-
> fore, be greatly modified by sexual or natural selection. . . . Under the
> influence of art there is a tendency for the sexual organs to be diminished in
> size, and in no civilized country has the artist ever chosen to give an erect
> organ to his representation of ideal masculine beauty. It is mainly because
> the unaesthetic character of a woman's sexual region is almost imperceptible
> in any ordinary and normal position of the nude body that the feminine form
> is a more aesthetically beautiful object of contemplation than the mascu-
> line.[187]

Albert Moll wrote that "normal coition presents nothing aesthetic in itself and I believe that were we not accustomed to it through frequent

practice we could not imagine a more repulsive act."[188] Freud's comments ring with a claim for universality, but he also noted in the case of Dora that "the pride taken by women in the appearance of their genitals is quite a special feature of their vanity; and disorders of the genitals which they think calculated to inspire feelings of repugnance or even disgust have an incredible power of humiliating them, of lowering their self-esteem, and of making them irritable, sensitive, and distrustful."[189] The male thinks his genitals are ugly (the traditional antithesis of "beautiful"). But is it every male who sees his penis as unaesthetic? Or is it that only those males who see their genitalia as "disordered" feel this sense of "repugnance or even disgust"?

Freud stressed the act of looking at the genitalia. This is a leitmotif in his discussions of the anxiety about circumcision and castration. All anxiety is rooted in the act of looking at the genitalia and seeing them as different. Here the response of the female is different from that of the male. Havelock Ellis had emphasized the racial component in the evaluation of the beautiful, for the beautiful is always the "complete embodiment of the particular racial or national type."[190] The idealized genital form of the male in fin de siècle Central Europe was that of the uncircumcised male. The male looks at his genitalia and takes narcissistic pride in them, fearing that they will be taken away from him; the woman, like the Jew, is horrified by the appearance of her genitalia. Thus Theodor Reik, an early Jewish supporter of Freud, could ask in the psychoanalytic journal *Imago* in 1919 whether the "mark of Cain" could be the scar of circumcision.[191] Reik argued that the origin of circumcision lay in the self-mutilation of Cain as his punishment for an act of incest. With the rite of circumcision the boy-child is admitted to the world of men and is able to take his role in the nonincestuous sexual world. But, as Herman Nunberg observed, "why injury to the penis should make a man more masculine is not quite clear."[192] Indeed, the common wisdom of the age presented this act in precisely the opposite terms. The mutilation of the penis was a feminizing act.

In Freud's overt discussion of circumcision, the Aryan evidences the anxiety of becoming a Jew; this disguised the anxiety Jews felt about being indelibly marked as Jews. The Jew is recognized as different even without revealing his hidden nature; everyone on the streets at the turn of the century knew the Jew on sight. Looking in the mirror, seeing his own body, revealed the hidden Jew who was seemingly visible to all. Martin Freud provided an anecdote that revealed the power of the gaze. He was sitting with his father in a beer garden when a young boy clumsily failed to bring his parents their requested drinks. The assembled crowd laughed at the boy's ineptitude. Freud commented "in a cold voice, loud enough to be heard by the parents, that he hoped none of us would give so shocking a display if sent on a similar errand." Only later did Martin Freud understand what his father had seen: "the boy who has disgraced himself so much in father's eyes was plainly Jewish in an unmistakable and not attractive way, rather like a caricature of a Jewish boy; and this was quickly seen by the Gentiles in the *Biergarten* who watched the performance with amused disdain. Perhaps father had some underlying fear that his own Jewish children would meet one day with similar treatment." Indeed, Martin Freud concluded his anecdote with a fantasy of passing, of not being seen as the boy in the beer garden: "We, father's Jewish children, were never conscious of anything approaching discrimination against us because of our race. Although we were not easily recognized as Jewish, we could not be mistaken for Bavarian or Austrian Gentiles. 'Your children, Frau Professor,' a polite German lady once remarked to mother, 'look so Italian.' "[193] Being seen as different is unescapable; only how one is seen is important. The difference of the body comes to represent the instability of the social status of the Jew. (This may be the reason Freud did not have his sons ritually circumcised.)

The debate about the diseased or disordered nature of the circumcised penis places Freud's sense of the visibility of the Jew in a specific rhetorical context. Freud's argument in *Civilization and Its Discontents* that the genitalia are ugly concludes: "Happiness, in the reduced sense in which we recognize it as possible, is a problem of the economics of the individual's libido. There is no golden rule which applies to everyone: every man must find out for himself in what particular fashion he can be saved."[194] This quotation, known to every schoolboy in Germany, had been scribbled by Frederick II on the margin of a report opposing the establishment of Roman Catholic schools in Prussia in 1740. By the end of the century this phrase had become standard in the political rhetoric of Jewish emancipation, which would have shocked Frederick the Great, who shared his idol Voltaire's attitude toward the Jews.[195] Freud had used this quotation in his 1926 defense of lay analysis, another case where there was a clear subtext concerning "Jewish quackery," a theme in Viennese medicine reaching at least as far back as the von Rosas-Mannheimer exchange in the 1840s.[196] Freud contextualized his understanding of the meaning of the genitalia in the terms attributed to his body in the scientific literature of his time. The Jew cannot be "saved," the Jew cannot escape his racial identity, which is indelibly marked on his genitalia.

We are left with an interesting problem. We have a cause for and a cure of disease—circumcision—that indelibly marks the Jew as different, even when he is not circumcised. The "primeval" act of circumcision is an ancient substitute for an even more brutal act of mutilation. It pathologically marks the Jew's psyche, but only when the Jew remains fixated at an early stage of development analogous to the early stage of history during which the threat of castration was made. This is the case of the neurotic

Otto Weininger. "Normal" Jews, like Little Hans, overcome their anxiety about their own bodies by being made to understand that the real difference is not between their circumcised penises and those of uncircumcised males, but between themselves and castrated females. This too marks them; it provides them with the unknown and unknowable essence that is the Jewish psyche. It is not a pathology, a sign of disease, but rather a sign of positive, if unalterable, difference.

The debate about the impact of circumcision on the communal psyche was also closely related to Freud's discussion of the trauma theory in the late 1890s. The model of individual experience mirroring racial experience is echoed in Freud's understanding of the origin of neurosis. Hysterics "suffer mainly from reminiscences," as Freud and Josef Breuer stated in the "preliminary communication" (1893) to *Studies on Hysteria*.[197] But then so do male Jews, because of circumcision: "Circumcision is, no doubt, a trauma, releasing a tendency in the ego to repeat it in one way or another and to form reactions to it."[198] The memory of a social trauma and the resulting functional deficits form the model of explanation Jewish scientists employed throughout the eighteenth and nineteenth centuries to mitigate (they believed) the charge of the inherited constitutional difference of the Jews. Our illnesses, which are real, they argued, are the result of social trauma, either from the ghetto or from the pressure of "modern life." Our neuroses and somatic disorders are the inheritance of this memory of the ghetto, from which we have been liberated for generations. We still bear these stigmata impressed on our minds and bodies just as we bear the mark of circumcision. And they make us unable or less able to cope with the stress of contemporary civilization.

Sigmund Freud, in his pivotal paper "Heredity and the Etiology of the Neuroses," first written and published in French in 1896, attempted to dislodge this understanding of social trauma as the origin of hysteria. This paper marked his break with Jean-Martin Charcot (who had died three years earlier) and Charcot's view that hysteria was an inherited phenomenon. Freud dismissed the primacy of the inherited disposition to hysteria (such as that attributed by Charcot to the Jews). He stressed the difference between a "similar heredity," which always produces the same diseases with the same signs and symptoms (such as Huntington's chorea), and those diseases with a "dissimilar heredity," which produce seemingly unrelated illness with myriad signs and symptoms.[199] For the latter, sources other than inheritance must be sought. In his search for the etiology of such psychopathologies, Freud further distinguished between "preconditions" (heredity) and "specific causes" of a disease. Both are necessary to create similar disease profiles, while the more general "concurrent causes" are sufficient but not necessary. Freud employed the model of the continuum used in his model of "bisexuality"—he saw "preconditions" and "specific causes" on a spectrum; as one decreases in importance, the other increases. The totality produces the illness, just as the individual may be more or less male or female, the totality making up the entire personality structure.

Freud dismissed as marginal all those "concurrent causes" that had been used to explain the existence of neurosis (in Jews as well as others): "emotional disturbance, physical exhaustion, acute illness, intoxications, traumatic accidents, intellectual overwork, etc."[200] Thus he also rejected the claim that psychopathologies such as neurasthenia are the "fruits of our modern civilization." He found the roots of these neuroses in early sexual experience: "These functional pathological modifications *have as their common source the subject's sexual life, whether they lie in a disorder of his contemporary sexual life or in important events in his past life.*"[201] Freud made these "sexual disorders" the primary cause of neuroses; heredity was a peripheral cause.

Freud proposed two sets of differential diagnoses. He distinguished between neurasthenia, the product of masturbation or "a sexual constitution analogous to what is brought about in a neurasthenic as a result of masturbation," and anxiety neurosis, the result of "abstinence, unconsummated genital excitation . . . , coition which is imperfect or interrupted . . . , sexual efforts which exceed the subject's psychical capacity, etc."[202] He also differentiated between hysteria and obsessional neurosis, the former caused by "some event of the subject's sexual life appropriate for the production of a distressing emotion," the latter caused by such "an event which has given pleasure."[203] The pleasure in the sexual act is different for the male and the female: for the male, pleasure is the result of the aggressive desire of experienced sexuality; for the female, the enjoyment generated by the sexual act.

Both hysteria and obsessional neurosis are caused by real events, remembered physical contact with the child's genitalia. Hysteria is the result of "passive sexuality, an experience submitted to with indifference or with a small degree of annoyance or fright."[204] This event is real to the sufferer, not as an event in the past, but *as though it were a contemporary event.*"[205] The living of a life in the present that has been marked in the past (either of the individual or of the group) by trauma is the basic explanatory model for the present state of the difference of the Jews. Thus, Freud concludes, what appears to be hereditary in the acute symptoms of patients, such as the occurrence of "a pair of neurotic patients" in the same family, proves to be a "pair of little lovers in their earliest childhood—the man suffering from obsessions and the woman from hysteria. If they are brother and sister, one might mistake for a result of nervous heredity what is in fact the consequence of precocious experience."[206] Here Freud has gendered the differential diagnosis—the female is passive or frightened; the male feels pleasure.

Yet Freud's dismissal of heredity as the cause of the neurosis provides a rationale for restructuring the concept of trauma, removing it from the world of daily life and centering it in the world of the sexual. Jews no longer will suffer from such signs of neurasthenia as "flatulent dyspepsia, constipation, or sexual weakness"[207] (to list only a few of the traditional "Jewish" symptoms that appear on Freud's list of neurasthenic symptoms) purely because of their heredity, but because of sexual practices, such as masturbation, that are universal rather than particularly Jewish. By moving hysteria to the realm of the incestuous, Freud eliminates the trauma of circumcision, the most evident *"precocious experience of sexual relations with actual excitement of the genitals, resulting from sexual abuse committed by another person,"* from the etiology of neurosis.[208] Circumcision is clearly understood as "frightening" in much of the medical literature opposed to it and in the complicated literature on *metsitsah* at the turn of the century. Incest, especially brother-sister incest, is yet another charge brought regularly against the Jews as the etiology for specific forms of somatic and mental illness. But it is the removal of circumcision from the category of the causative factors for mental illness by dismissing the arguments about the heredity of mental illness (or its disposition), and the stress on the specific nature of sexual trauma, as opposed to other traumatic factors, that lie at the heart of Freud's final dismissal of Charcot and Charcot's model of hysteria. Freud's was clearly a minority voice, as C. H. Hughes noted about Freud's paper on the "Etiology of Hysteria" (1896): "Hysteria, whatever its exciting causes, whether in the premature or over sexual, grief, disappointment or other psychoneural sources of depression and exhausting excitation, is usually bad neuropathic endowment, dormant at birth but ready—prepared like the lucifer match—for flame when rightly struck. Herr Sigmond [*sic*] Freud should try again."[209]

He did try again. In 1897 Freud abandoned his trauma theory of neurosis. He realized that he was seeing not the specific experiences of a select (but extensive) group of individuals whom he was treating, but rather a reflex of human development. He was observing the results of the fantasy of maltreatment rather than maltreatment itself. Freud separated these two moments while continuing to see a link between the empirical and fantasy in his own empirical studies on fantasy. Freud simultaneously elided and displaced the distinction between real events and fantasy. Freud's position was that of the racial biologist who saw the factors of Jewish identity, including the *Mauscheln* of the Jews, of the misuse and abuse of language, as a sign of the racial nature of the Jews. It is unimportant whether these qualities are understood as "inherited" (congenital) or "acquired" (but now an aspect of the genotype). Through this mechanism Freud hoped to free Jews, such as himself and his father, from the charge of being diseased, of lying, of being corrupt and corrupting.

In 1895, Freud evolved a four-part formula to describe the origin of neurosis, based on Aristotle's four-part analysis of causality. Needed was (1) a precondition, (2) a specific cause, (3) a concurrent cause, and (4) a precipitating cause.[210] The precondition was the existing disposition to disease, a disposition either acquired or innate. The specific cause, such as the seduction of the child, led to the specific symptom formation, such as the *globus hystericus.* The concurrent causes, such as overwork or exhaustion, are seen as less important but as having a contributory role in the appearance of the neurosis. The actual precipitating cause was simply the final trigger that occurred before the symptoms became evident.

This model was certainly sufficient to explain the mental illnesses of the Jews. The precondition was either the inheritance of the Jews or precipitating diseases such as syphilis; the specific cause, "two thousand years of oppression," the concurrent cause, "overwork" and the "stresses of civilization," and the precipitating cause, whatever could be found in each individual case.

But Freud needed to discount the role of degeneracy, of "pathogenic heredity," as it "left no room for the acquisition of nervous disease."[211] It also meant that all Jews, including Sigmund Freud, were at risk for specific forms of mental illness. His answer was to see the inheritance of trauma, following a Lamarckian model, as the source of disease, rather than some vague "Jewish predisposition to mental illness." What was originally sufficient (the specific cause) became necessary in Freud's revision of the etiology of neurosis. Trauma became the cause of neurosis.

Once "real" seduction is abandoned as the source of hysteria, and the source of neurosis is seen as lying in the fantasy of the Oedipal struggle, then the reality of this model is drawn into question. In order to universalize the Jewish physical predisposition to illness, Freud evolved his own theory of the relationship between constitution and neurosis. He developed the law of the etiological complemental series, the idea that constitution and trauma complement one another: the weaker the constitution, the smaller the trauma needed to create a neurosis. Seeking the meaning of trauma, Freud restructured his presentation of the etiology of neurosis. In the *Introductory Lectures on Psycho-Analysis* (1916–17), Freud stressed the etiological significance of (1) hereditary (and primal) dispositions, (2) infantile impressions, and (3) adult experiences.[212] About the clinical significance of phylogeny as a universal source of the predisposition to neurosis, Freud remained adamant. "Real" trauma lies in the universal past of all human beings, not solely in the Jewish experience in the Diaspora.[213] Here degeneracy is abandoned and the inheritance of acquired characteristics becomes a means of moving Jews into the mainstream of neurosis.

All human beings become inventors of their own past. All trauma is part of the universal experience of growth and development. The Jews'

rationale that their illness is the result of two thousand years of persecution becomes no more important than any other claim of trauma. It ends
the inheritance of the acquired trauma of Jewish experience and makes it
part of the origin of that which makes all human beings human. In the
famous letter of September 21, 1897, Freud admitted to Fliess, "I no
longer believe in my neurotica."[214] Believing in the reality of trauma
would mean "in all cases, the *father*, not excluding my own, had to be
accused of being perverse." Freud abandoned a system that demands a
mimetic, psychic representation of reality for one that sees the psyche as
the place for the play of fantasy. He abandoned the act of seeing in a
manner ascribed to the Galtonian photographs. And yet he clearly never
abandoned the status of science associated with that manner of seeing. As
much as Freud was aware of the problems of positivistic epistemology,
the status of the scientific gaze overcame his sense of its limitations. Even
though he rejected mimetic representation, Freud retained the model of
the Galtonian photographs as one of his central paradigms for his work
on dreaming, written after his rejection of the seduction theory.

However, in his rejection of the seduction theory, Freud substituted
one form of mimetic representation of disease for another. He used statistical thinking, another model for the scientific gaze, to dismiss seduction
theory as an "improbability."[215] Statistical argument is the basic under-
pinning of nineteenth-century racial science, since it was incorporated
into medical science. While there is some case-study material (primarily
from Jean-Martin Charcot's clinic), the attempt to sketch the image of the
Jews' disability as a group relied heavily on probability. It is no accident
that Freud phrases his abandonment of a "scientific" theory that had paralleled the arguments about the origin of Jewish difference and hysteria in
terms of the enigmatic punch line to a Jewish joke.[216] But Freud, at the
same time, does not dismiss the potential for the reality of child abuse.
Indeed, in a 1924 footnote to the case of Katherina in *Studies on Hysteria*,
he observed that her hysterical symptoms were the result of a real seduction.[217] Thus Freud avoided the trap of diseases associated with the Jews.
Trauma is not necessary for the appearance of hysteria, but it can be a
precipitating factor. The root of hysteria is not a specific historical fault,
either of nature or nurture; it is a universal pattern to be found in all
individuals because of their developmental biology and their placement
within the family structure. This does not vitiate the possibility that specific traumas can occur, such as the trauma of castration and its replacement through circumcision, but they are not universal. The illness attributed to the Jew's body is the disease of all human beings. But there is some
individual variation because of the special mental construct of the Jew.
The disease of the Jew is limited—and here the limits are clear. Circumcision is a sign of pathology, but not for the Jew. It is the Aryan who suffers
from the trauma of the Jew's circumcision.

The result of this trauma, in the view of late-nineteenth-century psychiatry, is mental illness. This reversal presents the next stage in the dilemma
posed by the debate about the special nature of the Jewish body and its
representation in the medical literature of the age. How can the medical
debate about the nature of the Jewish body be read by a physician who is
interested in psychopathology? Sigmund Freud, even in his earliest neurological work, focused on the relationship between the aberrant nature of
the body and psychopathology (or at least anomalous mental states). In
working in this arena of fin de siècle medicine, Freud was constantly and
intensely confronted with the assumption that this link was especially
true of the male Jew. The link was one widely seen by the neurologists
and alienists (psychiatrists) of the late nineteenth century as an intrinsic
element in their topography of the special nature of the male Jewish body.
The male Jew's psyche was as clearly distinct from that of the Aryan as
was his body.

Chapter Three

JEWISH MADNESS AND GENDER

THE PREDISPOSITION OF JEWS TO SPECIFIC FORMS OF MENTAL ILLNESS

Even as the Jews of Europe followed the guidelines set out for them by the Enlightenment, even as they began to integrate themselves into the body politic during the course of the nineteenth century, the idea of the inherent susceptibility of the Jews to specific illnesses became more and more institutionalized. And no more powerful stigma could be found than the view that the Jews were susceptible to specific forms of mental illness.[1] Theodor Gomperz, one of the leading philologists of the late nineteenth century and a teacher of Freud, wrote in 1886 to his sister that "looking around our family circle, there are not too many bright points. Nearly everywhere, at the least, irritable and excited nerves—the inheritance of a very old civilized race and of the urban life."[2] Jewish mental illness was the result of the sexual practices of the Jew, such as inbreeding, which created the predisposition for disease, and the pressures of modern life in the city, which were the direct cause. The dean of fin de siècle German psychiatrists, Emil Kraepelin, professor of psychiatry in Munich and founder of the Institute for Psychiatry there, spoke with authority about the "domestication" of the Jews, their isolation from nature and their exposure to the stresses of modern life.[3] Jewish physicians themselves accepted the premise of their own potential mental collapse because of the stress of the "modern life" into which they entered simply by becoming part of the medical establishment.

The statistics cited by nineteenth- (and indeed twentieth-) century writers on the topic of the mental instability of the Jews may not, of course, reflect any specific predisposition of the European Jewish community to mental illness. The statistics, used over and over by mental-health practitioners during this period, probably reflect the higher incidence of hospitalization of Jews for mental illness due to their concentration in urban areas, which, unlike rural ones, are not so tolerant of the presence of the mentally ill in society. Also, urban Jews had developed a better network for the identification and treatment of illness, including mental illness. The overt social pressures that were mounting against the Jews, which were often repressed by acculturated Jews anxious about their status in European society, may well have increased the amount of psychic pain these individuals had to bear. It is also quite possible that some Jews in Western European urban areas, especially those who were displaced from Eastern Europe and forced to flee westward, evidenced the traumatic results of their flight. The sense of community, coupled with the impression that the mentally ill were unable to function in urban society, may have led to more frequent hospitalization, and thus to the much higher statistical incidence of psychopathology among the Jews. Jewish communal organizations certainly subscribed to the view of the greater risk of Jews for mental illness. The "Bureau for Jewish Statistics" published a study in 1918 in which the greater frequency of hysteria and neurasthenia among German Jews was detailed.[4]

Even though such notions about the predisposition of the Jews to specific forms of mental illness were current and common in Vienna, Freud's most startling exposure to such views may well have come during his stay in Paris in 1885 and 1886 when he studied with Jean-Martin Charcot. Charcot's theories may have reflected much of the common wisdom of Viennese medicine (at least in Freud's estimation), even on this matter. In the October 27, 1888 entry in Charcot's *Tuesday Lessons*, there is the stated presumption that "nervous illnesses of all types are innumerably more frequent among Jews than among other groups."[5] Charcot attributed this to inbreeding.[6] He saw "the Jews as being the best source of material for nervous illness."[7] (Charcot had a number of male Russian Jews suffering from hysteria and neurasthenia as patients. Their case notes are among his unpublished papers in Paris.) Freud, who translated the first volume of these lectures into German in 1892 (and certainly knew both volumes intimately), was also lectured by Charcot about the predisposition of Jews to specific forms of illness, such as diabetes, where "the exploration is easy" because of the intermarriage of the Jews.[8] In his letter to Freud, Charcot used the vulgar "juif" rather than the more polite "Israélite" or the more scientific "sémite."[9] In an off-the-record remark, "a French physician," probably Charcot, commented: "In my practice in Paris, . . . I have the occasion to notice that, with the Jew, the emotions seem to be more vivid, the sensibility more intense, the nervous reactions more rapid and profound." This leads to the "vital sap ris[ing] from his limbs, or his trunk, to his head [and] . . . his overstrained nervous system is often apt, in the end, to become disordered and to collapse entirely."[10] This view was certainly present in mainstream German medicine. The anthropologist-physician Georg Buschan, whose first position had been as an asylum physician in Leubus in 1886, stressed the "extraordinary incidence" of hysteria among European Jews as a sign of their racial degeneration in an address to the Organization of German Psychiatrists in Dresden on September 21, 1894.[11]

When Freud returned to Vienna and began teaching in the Medical Faculty, he found that the idea that Jews were predisposed to specific forms of mental illness was commonplace. The standard handbooks of the time repeated this view in various contexts, including those that associated the hidden taint of the Jew's potential mental illness with the visible signs of degeneracy. Georg Burgle's 1912 handbook of forensic medicine states clearly that "the Jewish race has a special predisposition for hysteria." For him this is a result of the degenerative nature of the Jew and is also marked by "physical signs of degeneration such as asymmetry and malocclusion of the skull, malocclusion of the teeth, etc."[12] The signs and symptoms of the Jew and the degenerate pointed to their susceptibility.

This view was not limited to the Jews of fin de siècle Europe. In 1907, Georges Wulfing-Luer published a detailed study of the Jews' predisposition to nervous diseases in which he traced this predisposition back to biblical times, attempting to counter the argument of the situational causation of the nervousness of the Jews.[13] Such views were espoused by noteworthy opponents to political anti-Semitism, such as the French historian Anatole Leroy-Beaulieu. He, too, agreed that "the Jew is particularly liable to the disease of our age, neurosis." He wrote that "the Jew is the most nervous of men, perhaps, because he is the most 'cerebral,' because he has lived most by his brain." He is "the most nervous and, in so far, the most modern of men."[14] The Jewish predisposition to mental illness is a reflex of the Jew's being the most modern of men.

Jews are at risk for diseases of the central nervous system such as neurasthenia, the lack of "nerve-force." The differential diagnosis between hysteria and neurasthenia was "impossible and unnecessary, as in fact numerous transitional forms and mixed forms occur."[15] One of the salient images of the Jewish male is found in the description of neurasthenia in Richard von Krafft-Ebing's study of the illness. He is "an overachiever in the arena of commerce or politics" who "reads reports, business correspondence, stock market notations during meals, for whom 'time is money.'"[16] The association of the Jew with the "American illness," through the use of the English phrase "time is money," presents the cosmopolitan Jew as the quintessential American. This view had been promulgated in 1896 in a general literary periodical with wide circulation. Jews "use too much of their brain in a restless striving for profit," which "accounts for their higher percent of mental and nervous aliments. Therefore a certain tendency for mental illness must reside in the race."[17] In the work of Heinrich Averbeck on neurasthenia, which Freud reviewed and used widely, the connection between the stressful life of modern civilization and the "neurasthenia of the stock market" is explicitly made.[18] A professor of psychiatry in Munich, H. V. Ziemssen, espoused the view that "race and tribal qualities play a major role in the etiology of neurasthenia. The Semitic race is especially predisposed to a high degree for neurasthenia. There is a neurotic quality which runs through the whole race in spite of all abilities and perseverance in their occupations." Ziemssen thought that what triggers episodes of the disease among Jews is economic failure. Sigmund Freud owned and used this text.[19]

The response of Jewish physicians of the era was complicated. Leopold Löwenfeld, one of Freud's most assiduous supporters, confronted the question of the racial predisposition of the Jews in his textbook of 1894. In his discussion of the etiology of neurasthenia and hysteria he examined the role "race and climate" might play in the origin of these diseases:

> Concerning the claimed predisposition of the Semitic race, one can only state the fact that among the Israelites today there is an unusually large number of neurasthenics and hysterics. Whether this is the result of a specific predisposition of the race seems very questionable. Historically, there is no trace of such a predisposition to be shown. The epidemics of mass hysteria observed in earlier centuries never affected members of the Semitic race. I believe it more likely that the great predisposition of the Israelites does not rest in racial qualities, but in their present quality of life. Among these would come into consideration—in East Europe, the physical poverty as well as the extraordinary moral pressure, the practice of early marriage, and the great number of children—in the West, the great number of Israelites who undertake intellectual activities.[20]

Freud read Löwenfeld's textbook carefully. The opening pages are full of debates about the inheritability of hysteria and its relationship to trauma. Löwenfeld claims that "inheritance plays a major role in the origins of neurasthenia and hysteria through the existence of an abnormal constitution of the nervous system." Freud retorts: "From where?" in the margin. Tucked away in a footnote, Löwenfeld quotes a source who claimed to have seen a large number of cases of hysteria "without a trace of hereditary neurosis."[21] Freud chuckles: "Bravo! Certainly acquired." These comments reflect Freud's preoccupation with the universal question of whether all human beings could be divided into the healthy and the degenerate, the mentally sound and the hysteric. Löwenfeld's rejection of the predisposition to hysteria for *all* Jews meant it was possible to focus on the universal rather than the racialist question. And yet Löwenfeld's distinction between Eastern Jews with their mix of social and sexual causes for their mental states and Western Jews with their (highly prized) intellectual status shows that even there a dichotomy between the religious and the secular Jew is sought. Freud seems never to have reached this section of the book; his eye remained fixed on the universal question and did not enter into the debate about Jews and madness. But in fact, he entered this debate in a complicated manner.

Freud's essay " 'Civilized' Sexual Morality and Modern Nervous Illness" (1908) provides an unspoken comment on the association of race and insanity in contemporary science. In that paper Freud links the repressive nature of modern society with the deformation of human sexuality. He begins with a paraphrase of the work of the contemporary Prague philosopher and cofounder of Gestalt psychology, Christian von Ehrenfels, who held an essentially ethnopsychological position (for many of the same reasons as did Freud). Ehrenfels had solicited Freud's contribution to a new periodical, *Sexual Problems*, which first appeared in 1908.[22] The magazine was one of the successors of an older journal, *Mother Protection*, the official publication of a eugenics group to which Freud and Ehrenfels belonged. Upon founding the journal, Ehrenfels immediately wrote to Freud for a contribution and received the essay from him.

Ehrenfels stated, in the extract cited by Freud, that "the innate character of a people" could be compared with their "cultural attainments" in order to differentiate between "civilized" and "natural" sexual morality.[23] "Civilized" morality produces "intense and productive cultural activities," while "natural" sexual morality maintains "health and efficiency." The disease of the cities, of urban life, is thus a product of the civilizing process. It is a necessary, though unfortunate, result of the suppression of human sexuality in culture. It is a problem of modern life, not of Jews in modern society.

Christian von Ehrenfels's monograph was a most interesting point of departure for Freud.[24] Published in a series of short monographs on "marginal questions" in neurology and psychology edited by Freud's friend Leopold Löwenfeld in Munich, Ehrenfels's text is explicitly indebted to Freud for much of its psychological framework. Highly influenced (like Freud) by a Darwinian model of sexual selection, Ehrenfels could not only contrast "natural" and "civilized" morality, but just as easily write of the competition between the "higher" and the "lower" races and about the "great problem of our time": resolving the demands of race in light of the "liberal-humanistic fiction of the equality of all people."[25] For Ehrenfels, the purpose of "natural sexual morals" (which was for him a natural law) "is to conserve or improve the constitution of the tribe or people."[26] He saw the need for the "white, yellow, and black" races to remain "pure" and to avoid sexual interbreeding. Like most of the racial scientists of his time, he justified colonial expansion with the rationale that the "sexual mission" of some races is best accomplished "if they place their generative powers in the service of others."[27] As the rhetoric of this statement seems to indicate, throughout Ehrenfels's discussion of race, his prime example is the "Oriental." Indeed, Freud underlined the passage in his text where Ehrenfels warns of the risk of the "Yellow Peril" overwhelming Europe. Freud reflects this image in a comment from 1915 in which he stated that it was assumed that the war that had been expected before 1914 would be between the "civilized" ("white") and "primitive" ("darker") races.[28] It is clear in this formulation that the Jews, seen as a people of culture, were to be considered "white" and, therefore, civilized.

The monograph, however, concludes with an index, prepared by the author and intended by him to enable his monograph to be used as a handbook for those seeking direct advice on topics of sexual morality. The final entry makes reference to the discussion on racial sexuality and concludes the volume with the following observation: "These same directives are applicable to the Jewish problem, inasmuch as these are the result of differences in their constitution and not—as is actually generally the case—the result of resolvable differences in their social milieu."[29] All the discussions about race are, in fact, encoded references to the Jewish question. The claim for an innate, biologically rooted difference of the Jews is the subtext of Ehrenfels's study of sexual ethics. Jews' strengths, like the strengths of each of the races, are preserved only when they remain within their own group. Intermixing leads to corruption and the weakening of the race. Rather than mixing with Aryans, the Jews, Ehrenfels implies, through their activity in Western culture, can place "their generative powers in the service of others."

Ehrenfels's demands for the purity of the race were not merely theoretical. Ehrenfels himself was an active spokesperson for eugenics and gave a talk on "breeding reform" in December 1908 before the Vienna Psychoanalytic Society. There again he warned of the dangers of monogamy as well as the threat of the "annihilation of the white race by the yellow race."[30] And yet the racial theorist who advocated the purity of the race and the distinction between "healthy" and "civilized morality" in the "higher" and "lower" races was himself Jewish by descent even though raised as a Christian. Ehrenfels publicly acknowledged his Jewish background and saw the rise of political anti-Semitism as a social anathema.[31] The real danger, Ehrenfels again stated in a talk given in 1911, was the "Yellow Peril," the "hordes of Mongols" poised to confront the "Caucasian" race: "Among a hundred whites there stand two Jews. The German peasant has been awakened and armed with the holy weapons of his ancestors—not to struggle against eighty million Mongols but to confront two Jews! Is this not the height of folly!"[32]

By 1911 Ehrenfels came to deny any substantial physiological difference between Aryans and Jews. Indeed, he came to see the Jews as suffering from all the diseases and dangers of modern society: "They suffer more than we do from the present sexual and economic order."[33] Primary among these are mental disease. Jews are, therefore, simply exaggerated Aryans. Indeed, this seems a response to Oskar Rie's question following his paper in Vienna: "would the Mongols, in taking over our culture, not take over our potential for degeneration as well[?]"[34] A number of thinkers of the period assumed that the Jews were the worst example of the impact of civilization because of their weak nervous systems. Franz Kafka mentions a response Ehrenfels made to a presentation by Felix Theilhaber on the "decline of German Jewry" to a public audience in Prague during January 1912.[35] Theilhaber had recapitulated the thesis of his controversial book: that urbanization, the struggle for profit, mixed marriages, and baptism were causing German Jewry to vanish. (The latter argument was a social variant of the older biological argument that "mixed marriages between Jews and Aryans had a noticeably lower fecundity.")[36] Ehrenfels's response, as Kafka noted, was a "comic scene" in which the philosopher (whose Jewish antecedents were well known) "smiling spoke in favor of mixed races." Freud and Ehrenfels both felt an unresolvable tension between accepting the discourse of science about race and the demand that they take a position on this discourse. Freud repressed it; Ehrenfels eventually valorized it. But Freud never forgot Ehrenfels. He recorded his death on September 9, 1932, among the very few entries concerning the passing of his contemporaries.[37]

The image of the healthy family in " 'Civilized' Sexual Morality and Modern Nervous Illness" is the antithesis of nineteenth-century anti-Semitic images of Jewish sexuality, which assumed the constant, corrupt nature of the Jewish character. It evokes, however, the idealized image of the small-town Jewish family, which was a staple of late-nineteenth-century Jewish popular culture, for example in the paintings of Moritz Oppenheim. It is of a family, "living in simple, healthy, country conditions," which had become ill when its members "had successfully established themselves in the metropolis, and in a short space of time had brought their children to a high level of culture."[38] But Freud repressed his model of the collapse of the Jewish family into madness and corruption. For him this movement was a universal one in which healthy country dwellers enter the cities and begin to decay. It was, however, the Jews who were the prime examples for such social deformation in Freud's primary sources. Freud argued that these authorities were essentially correct but that they "leave out of account precisely the most important of the etiological factors involved. If we disregard the vaguer ways of being 'nervous' and consider the specific forms of nervous illness, we shall find that the injurious influence of civilization reduces itself in the main to the harmful suppression of the sexual life of civilized peoples (or classes) [*Kulturvölker* (*oder Schichten*)] through the 'civilized' sexual morality prevalent in them."[39] Not race (Ehrenfels's point of departure) but civilization or class determines pathology. But what do Freud's sources say? Otto Binswanger stated that "among the European races the Jews present the greatest number of cases of neurasthenia."[40] Wilhelm Erb, at a birthday celebration for the king of Baden, commented on the increased nervousness among the "Semites, who already are a neurotically predisposed race. Their untamed desire for profit and their nervousness, caused by centuries of imposed life-style [*auferlegte Lebensweise*] as well as their inbreeding [*Inzucht*] and marriage within families [*Familienheiraten*], predispose them to neuroses."[41] Richard Krafft-Ebing, in one of the standard medical handbooks of the day, simply quoted Erb's comment that "Jews are especially prone to nervousness."[42] Freud commented on none of this. He wanted to move the argument about the madness of the Jews away from the question of race and to universalize it.

The conflation of two aspects of difference underlines the political implications of seeing in the "cosmopolitanism" of the Jews, in their function in the modern city, the source, on one level, of their neurasthenia. Yet this integration of the Jews into the negative image of modern civilization is contradicted by the view of the exclusivity of the Jews in their sexual isolation from Western society. This view was seconded by Moritz Alsberg, whose study of the racial mixing of the Jews pointed out the inherent disposition of the Jew to mental illnesses, "which can be traced to the impact that mental exhaustion and excitement have on the all-too-easily stimulated Jewish temperament." The cause for this is the "frequent marriage within families."[43] This position was reinforced by the 1908 statistical study of the incidence of mental illness in the (former) kingdom of Württemberg, where Jews were shown to have a rate of mental illness twice as high as their representation in the general population. (Of hospitalized cases, 1.3 percent were Jews, who represented only .5 percent of the population.) Both Catholics and Protestants were represented in proportion to their presence in the population.[44]

Jewish physicians were forced to deal with the potential of Jewish mental illness because the problem reflected on their own mental stability. The standard Jewish rationale for the higher incidence of psychopathology among the Jews came to be that of the Jewish brain's inability to compete after "a two-thousand-year Diaspora" and "a struggle for mere existence up to emancipation." This image of the origin of the potential mental illness of the Jew, especially the Jew's predisposition to neurasthenia, is found in the discourse of Viennese medicine at the time. Martin Engländer, one of the early Viennese supporters of Herzl and the Zionist movement, wrote a widely read pamphlet, *The Most Striking Appearances of Illness in the Jewish Race* (1902).[45] There he discussed the cultural predisposition of the Jews to specific forms of mental illness as a result of the "overexertion and exhaustion of the brain . . . among Jews as opposed to the non-Jewish population."[46] "The struggle, haste and drive, the hunt for happiness" caused a "reaction in their central nervous system."[47] Engländer thus attempted to dismiss the etiology of neurasthenia as a result of inbreeding, citing the Americans as an example of a "race" in which neurasthenia predominates and in which exogamous marriages are common. The cause of the Jews' illnesses is their confinement in the city, the source of all degeneracy; the cure is "land, air, light."[48]

Engländer's views are not idiosyncratic. For him the madness of the Jews was a direct result of the Jews' political and social position in the West. Cesare Lombroso, whose name is linked with the concept of "degeneration" he helped forge, was also a Jew. After writing a number of studies on the degeneracy of the prostitute and the criminal, Lombroso was confronted with the charge that Jews too were examples of a degenerate subclass of human being, a class determined by their biology. Lombroso's answer to this charge, *Anti-Semitism and the Jews in the Light of Modern Science* (1893), attempted to counter the use of medical or pseudoscientific discourse to characterize the nature of the Jew. But Lombroso also accepted the basic view that the Jew was more highly prone to specific forms of mental illness. He quoted Charcot to this effect, but like Engländer saw the reason for this tendency not in the physical nature of the Jew but in the "residual effect of persecution."[49] Both Engländer and Lombroso accepted the view that some type of degenerative process, which caused the predominance of specific forms of mental illness, exists among all Jews. The only difference was the cause of this process. In rejecting the charge of inbreeding, Jews such as Engländer and Lombroso also rejected the implication that they indulged in primitive sexual practices, practices that violate a basic human taboo against incest. The confusion of endogamous marriage with incestuous inbreeding was a result of the desire of scientific discourse to have categories circumscribing the explicit nature of the Other. The Jews are thus mentally ill, they manifest this illness in hysteria and neurasthenia, and the cause is their sexual practice or their mystical religion or their role as carriers of Western cosmopolitanism. All their mental instability can be diagnosed by their corrupt discourse. Their illness is inscribed in their corrupt use of language.

Other Jewish commentators on the nature of the mental illness of the Jews took similar positions. Moses Julius Gutmann, who wrote extensively about the predisposition of the Jews to various illnesses, including mental illness, beginning with his 1920 dissertation, wrote an extensive study of the mental illness of the Jews in 1926.[50] He, too, saw the Jews as being especially predisposed to specific forms of illness because of the early marriages among Eastern Jews, which permit individuals to pass specific types of mental illness on to their offspring before they themselves manifest any symptoms. The assumption is that these individuals would not have reproduced had they waited until they were older to marry. The Jewish physician Max Sichel, a member of the staff of the psychiatric clinic at the University of Frankfurt, while understanding the exogenous causes of mental illness, such as the transition from the closed world of the ghetto to the competitive world of modern society, also stressed the endogenous aspects of the constitution of the Jews as a major factor in their illness.[51] Sichel's work accepted the immutability of the racial characteristics of the Jew. Like most Jewish physicians, he accepted the reality of Jewish mental illness, even if it were triggered "by the constant persecution and mental torture, by the eternal struggle for naked existence and for daily bread,"[52] and in doing so accepted its inheritability, if only over the limited span of generations. But he, like most of his contemporaries, also felt that inbreeding played a major role in transmitting and causing such illnesses.[53]

Mental illness among the urbanized Jews in Germany was thought to be ubiquitous. This claim came to have a specific political dimension in Germany after the collapse of the German Empire in 1918. In a widely read essay in the popular *South German Monthly*, Emil Kraepelin, certainly the most visible German psychiatrist of the age, evoked the model of the insane Jew in condemning the German Spartacus revolutionaries in Berlin and Munich, such as Ernst Toller, as "psychopaths."[54] Jewish physicians, such as the Social Democratic politician Julius Moses, recognized the charge immediately and condemned Kraepelin's "diagnosis" as a "powerful appearance of anti-Semitism."[55] The charge of insanity, often laid against revolutionaries, was here reified with the evocation of the "common mental construction" of the Jews. Jewish revolutionaries were typically insane Jews. But the argument about the inherent mental instability of the Jew was read by Jewish physicians in often contradictory ways.

Jewish psychiatrists were constrained to answer the politicized claims about the mental illness of the Jews; this they undertook in a variety of ways. Max Sichel, like many of the physicians who emphasized the degenerative model of mental illnesses, also stressed the absence among Jews of certain forms of mental illness (alcoholism and suicide) found in other racial groups. This question continued through the 1920s and 1930s to be a popular topic of academic concern in medicine. In 1923 Max Nussbaum defended his dissertation on the racial predisposition of the Jews to mental illness.[56] His work reflected the arguments of some racial biologists who saw the Jews as a mixed race. This race would and, according to these works, did present mixed clinical images of mental illness. This view was widely held in the medical literature of the early twentieth century. In 1927 Ludwig Frigyes, writing his dissertation under the supervision of the famed German-Jewish neurologist Kurt Goldstein in Frankfurt, also argued for a racial basis for the madness of the Jews. Frigyes emphasized the "uniqueness of the Jewish psyche" as one of potential result of the racial difference of the Jews.[57] Freud would have had access to an excellent summary of these debates in the extensive essay on mental illness and the Jews written by Felix Theilhaber in the *Jewish Lexicon*.[58] These debates continued well into the 1930s.[59]

The biological presuppositions in medicine about the relationship between madness and race had a major impact even on those outside this professional arena. Bertha Pappenheim, the Anna O. of *Studies on Hysteria*, critiqued the "absence among Galician Jews of the most primitive concepts of child care, nursing care, and the care of newly delivered women, indeed the absence of any knowledge of infection or even disinfection. . . . The spas, hospitals, and mental asylums, the institutes for the blind and the deaf-dumb, show a high percent of Galician Jews. Today many of these diseases are labeled hereditary that have their sources in the ignorance of the simplest hygienic rules and the exercise of other activities detrimental to health."[60] The attempt to dismiss all diseases, even mental illness, as the result of a biological cause (here in the environment rather than in the individual) simply places the fault for Jewish illness in the world of the Eastern Jew, shielding her from the charge of her own racial susceptibility to hysteria. The image of the Eastern Jew as "filthy" (as opposed to the cleanliness and orderliness demanded of the Jew) simply transfers the locus of anxiety for the risk of madness from Western Jews (always fearful they are not quite clean enough) toward the East. In 1930, in a handbook entitled "Hygiene and the Jews," one of the products of the regular Hygiene Exhibitions held in Germany since the turn of the century, at which there was usually a Jewish pavilion, there appeared a historical essay on "why the Jews of Poland were 'filthy.' "[61] Here the comments of Bertha Pappenheim were placed in the mouth of the eighteenth-century City Physician of Warsaw, August Ferdinand von Wolff, the son of a baptized Jew, the physician Abraham Emanuel Wolff.

From the standpoint of Western Europe in the early twentieth century the Eastern Jews were at special risk for mental illness because they were either so unlike the Western Jews (as seen from a Jewish point of view) or so essentially Jewish (seen from an Aryan, racialist point of view). Beginning in the mid-nineteenth century, statistical studies of the East began to document the higher incidence of mental illness among Eastern Jews. Josef Czermak, using admission figures for a hospital in Moravia during 1857, showed that for every ten thousand Catholics there were seven Catholic patients admitted for some form of mental illness; for every ten thousand Jews, twenty-two Jewish patients.[62] Parallel findings are seen in the Baltic provinces of Russia. In 1914, H. Budul undertook a study of the frequency of certain mental illnesses in Dorpat (Tartu) in Estonia. There he found that Jews suffered more than other groups from manic-depressive illness and hysteria.[63] Harald Siebert did a similar study in Latvia, finding that Jews were racially predetermined to suffer from hysteria. He, however, made an interesting distinction: "For the educated class one finds primarily nervous disease among women; for the lower classes, among men."[64] Certainly the major figure to deal with the mental illness of Eastern Jews was the Jewish psychiatrist Hermann Oppenheim, Karl Abraham's cousin and the widely cited author of a standard psychiatric textbook of the period.[65] His essay on the psychopathology of the Russian Jews is without a doubt the most authoritative work in the field. Published in a festschrift for Auguste Forel, it begins with the complaint that "from year to year the growing hordes of patients from Russia come to us for advice and cure."[66] The "us" is Western physicians. Oppenheim states quite directly that it is "well known that Jews have a predisposition to neurosis and psychosis." Oppenheim makes an unstated distinction between the collectivity of the Eastern Jews, whose social milieu triggers the innate predisposition to mental illness, and the individual Western Jew, like himself, who may bear the taint but has not been exposed to the circumstances that trigger the illness.

What is striking in Oppenheim's account is the role played by the voice as a sign of the sensibility of the patient or nosology of the disease. He notes that even "with the simplest test for sensitivity with needle pricks the patient cries out: 'Gewalt, Gewalt!' Certainly cowardliness, the fear of pain, may play a role, but more evidently this cry seems to me a statement of the horrid path of suffering of this people, i.e., this race."[67] In another case study he describes the visit of a Russian-Jewish singer who had imagined a change in the quality of her voice upon the death of her husband. She appeared to be a hysteric according to Oppenheim, as the only sign of her putative aphonia was a slight nasality in her voice. This, he notes, "was in intimate relationship to her mental state."[68] The image of the female seems to subsume the image of the Jew and yet, for Oppenheim, the voice of the Eastern Jew permeates even the veneer of high culture. The altered voice of the Jew is a sign of the Jew's pathological relationship to the discourse of high culture.

The relationship between mental illness and the disruption of discourse has its roots in late-nineteenth-century medicine. The neurologist who listened to his hysterical patient and diagnosed "general paralysis of the insane" from the patient's monomaniacal tirades, or the psychiatrist who was able to characterize the discourse of a patient suffering from "dementia praecox" as "word salad," centered their perception of illness on the nature of the patient's language. Alterations in the nature of discourse were understood to be basic signs of pathology. Indeed, they came in the course of the closing decades of the nineteenth century to have the weight of the primary signs of psychopathology. How a patient spoke was important, and incompetent discourse was a sign of psychopathology.

The relationship between the voice of the Jew and the Jew's body informed Max Nordau's often-cited call, published in 1900, for the Jews to become "muscle Jews."[69] Max Nordau was a Hungarian-Jewish physician who wrote his French medical dissertation with Jean-Martin Charcot and was later the vice-president of the first Zionist Congresses from 1897 to 1903. Nordau's acceptance of the scientific mind-set of physicians such as Charcot, no matter how tenuous his actual relationship to his teacher, predisposed him to consider the Jew at risk. For Nordau, the reform of the Jew's body would reform the Jew's ability to control the Jew's mind and this would result in a healthy, socially acceptable discourse. Nordau's title recalls the "Muscular Christianity" of the late nineteenth century, with its advocacy of regular exercise to improve the body and to control "lascivious thinking." His model was already present in his dissertation, written with Charcot. It was on the impact of "castration" (ovariotomy) on the mental and physical life of the woman. There he established an absolute link between the physical and the mental status of the woman.[70] "Castration" (ovariotomy) was understood to have a positive therapeutic result in the treatment of hysteria.[71] Here the connection between a physical state (that of being female) and a pathological mental state had already been made. The emphasis on the body was an attempt to link spiritual and physical well-being. The further connection of Jewish nationalism in the form of Zionism with German nationalism through the code of *mens sana in corpore sano* is evident. But, of course, this earlier call by the father of German nationalism, Friedrich "Turnvater" Jahn, had been heavily overladen with anti-Semitic rhetoric. The movement from the discourse of the woman's body to that of the body of the Jew was possible for Nordau, who saw the pathology of both woman and Jew as treatable. This movement also answered the charges leveled at Jews (and at women) of their inability to function in modern life because of their impairment.

Nordau's demand that the Jews reform their bodies was yet another attempt from within the Jewish community to adapt the underlying structure of anti-Semitic rhetoric and use its strong political message for other ends. Nordau's call for a "new muscle Jew" was based on the degeneration of the Jew "in the narrow confines of the ghetto." But it was not merely the muscles of the Jews, but also their minds, that atrophied in the ghetto. The "new Jews," like the "new women," must reform their bodies, must purge them of the diseases of the past. Implicit in Nordau's message is the equation of the "old Jews" and their attitude toward life. Zionism demanded that the new muscle Jews have healthy bodies and healthy minds. Thus Nordau condemns his critics as not only having weak bodies but weak minds! This charge must be read in the context of the inner circles of the Zionist movement, in which the opponents of Zionism were viewed merely as Jews possessing all the qualities ascribed to them (including madness) by anti-Semites.

Neurasthenia, the American disease, the disease of modern life, was also the disease of the Jews, modern humans incarnate. Degeneration was the result of sexuality and was evidenced by deviant sexuality. If the best authorities were to be believed, and at least in Germany the best authorities argued that inbreeding was the cause of the neurasthenia of the Jews, there was more than a slight implication of incest. Indeed, Engländer expressly defended the Jews against the charge of "racial inbreeding" while condemning the provisions of Mosaic law that do permit marriage between uncle and niece. He thus gives evidence for the implicit charge that runs through the literature on the insanity of the Jews—that they are the cause of their own downfall through their perverse sexuality. The lack of redemption of the Jews is made manifest by this perverse sexuality, and their degeneracy is the outward sign of their fall from grace. The sexuality of the Other is always threatening. With the implicit charge of incest, one of the ultimate cultural taboos of nineteenth-century thought is invoked. Inbreeding is incestuous and is a sign of the "primitive" nature of the Jews, who exist outside the bounds of acceptable, Western sexual practice.[72]

It was thought not only that Jewish social practices led to madness, but that the Jews' undertaking these practices was a symptom of their underlying insanity. At the time, race was a major force in shaping the form, appearance, and symptoms of both neurological and psychological illness.[73] Indeed, Richard Gaupp, in his inaugural lecture as a professor of psychiatry at Tübingen in 1907, saw as one of the most needed goals of contemporary psychiatry "the clarification of the influence of race and morals, of climate and life-style," on the appearance and frequency of mental illness.[74] Thus Adolf Hitler's views about the diseased nature of the Jewish psyche were in line with many of the mainstream opinions in the Viennese academy.

The Viennese psychiatrist Alexander Pilcz, a pupil of Heinrich Obersteiner and Julius Wagner-Jauregg, wrote one of the period's standard handbooks of racial psychiatry.[75] He received his doctorate in 1895 and was the acting chair (locum tenens) for the First Department of Psychiatry at the University of Vienna from 1902 to 1907, when he became director of the mental hospital Am Steinhof. (The Second Department of Psychiatry came to be the primary one. It was chaired by Wagner-Jauregg.) Pilcz was one of the most visible members of the psychiatric faculty of the University of Vienna during Freud's tenure there as student, fellow, and faculty member, and an early reviewer of Freud's work.[76] Freud mentioned Pilcz's ideas about the relationship between the time in the course of the night when one dreams and the antiquity of the dreams' manifest content in *The Interpretation of Dreams*.[77] Freud also owned at least two of Pilcz's major works. In one of them the question of the Jewish predisposition to manic-depressive psychosis is spelled out in detail: "In conclusion, I would like to present a personal observation, which is evident from the material presented here as well as from my private practice. It seems to me that there is a very high incidence of Jews among those patients with periodic insanity. It is noticeably high in regard to the relationship between Jews and the rest of the population."[78] Pilcz then elucidates six of the cases in his study that present Jews suffering from mental illness. Of these cases, four are men and two are women. No other "racial" category (such as Hungarian or Czech) is mentioned in any of his other case studies. He employs terms such as "possessing an extraordinary dialectic and sophistry" to describe the Jews' symptoms, terms taken from the anti-Semitic rhetoric of the day. Pilcz's study seeks out the Jews as a visible "race" marked by a high rate of mental illness. For him, clearly the biological predisposition of the Jew was evident in these cases.

One needs to understand Pilcz's views as the reflection of the mainstream opinion in Viennese medicine during the period.[79] In 1901 Pilcz, then on the staff of Wagner-Jauregg's clinic in Vienna, published an often-cited essay on the occurrence of mental illness among Jews in the widely read *Viennese Clinical Survey*. Pilcz noted the greater number of Jews who showed up in his study of periodic mental illness. It was for him a question of race. Pilcz stressed that he could not sort his sample by religion, for "even though those of the Jewish confession overlapped completely with those of the Jewish race, it is evident that not all patients who were Christian could be seen as Aryan."[80] Thus he placed "baptized Jews in the rubric of Jewish patients." Pilcz felt one could never escape one's race. The madness of the Jews was an inherent racial quality. He presented his own clinical findings, noting that in Vienna, for the period from January 1, 1898, to August 1, 1901, 1219 patients were admitted, of which 134 (10.99 percent) were Jews. According to the 1900 census, the population of Vienna at the end of that year was 1,648,335, of which 146,136 (8.86 percent) were Jews. It is clear that Pilcz defined the Jews in the clinic by race. In the 1900 census they were defined by religion: Jewish converts would be found not among the 8.86 percent but among the remaining population. The diseases for which Pilcz saw the highest occurrence of Jewish patients were drug addiction (two out of six, or 33.3 percent), neurasthenia (25 percent of the neurasthenic patients), and "periodic insanity" (manic-depressive psychosis—26.08 percent were Jews). The etiology of the Jews' madness, he notes, citing Krafft-Ebing and Theodor Kirchhof, lies in their inbreeding. This essay was popular enough to warrant translation into French in 1902.[81] Pilcz lectured widely in Vienna on this topic.[82] In 1906 Pilcz, by then the assistant chairperson of the psychiatric clinic, published a detailed monograph on "comparative racial psychiatry."[83] He introduced this monograph by noting the positive reception of his earlier work on the madness of the Jews.[84] In this more extensive study, which also includes anthropological data on non-European groups, Pilcz centers on the racial groups in the Austro-Hungarian Empire: Hungarians, Germans, "North Slavs," and Jews. According to his findings Jews suffer from progressive paralysis (the final stage of neurosyphilis), dementia praecox (schizophrenia), paranoia, and periodic psychosis (manic-depressive disorder) more frequently than from any other mental or neurological illnesses, and more frequently than all other groups. Under hysteria Pilcz simply notes that "since Charcot" the "especially strong predisposition of the Jews for hysteria has been known."[85] Likewise, Jews make up the majority of neurasthenics.[86] Jews reveal a tendency toward "hereditary-degenerative psychosis."[87] He argues, citing medical and anthropological authorities, that the incidence of mental illness in Palestine is equal to that in Europe. And he closes with the statement that "since the heightened disposition is also to be found in women, it cannot be the exhausting mental life, the *struggle for life* [in English], the damage of 'civilization,' that can explain the prevalence of the Jewish insane."[88] The cause is race and nothing more. Pilcz provides us with a theoretical model for the transmittal of such tendencies (relying on the view of Wagner-Jauregg) in which he stresses the forms of mental illness that can be carried from generation to generation.[89] He notes that the "hereditary-degenerative" mental illnesses are uninfluenced by external causes. The question of proximal cause of any disease is for him secondary, except, perhaps, for those mental illnesses that could be traced to neurosyphilis. Pilcz preached the dogma of the racial transmission of mental illness to students and faculty throughout the opening decades of the twentieth century. On February 10, 1927, he lectured on this topic to the Twenty-fourth International Course for Continuing Medical Education held by the medical faculty.[90] There he spoke of the existence of an Eastern European Jewish psychosis.

In Vienna there was an attempt by Jews to answer Pilcz directly. Ignaz Zollschan, a physician-anthropologist whose work was well known to Freud, argued that "many authors have painted the future of the Jews in the blackest colors because of the great number of the mentally ill to be found among them. . . . All the biological advantages and disadvantages of the Jews are the result of inbreeding. . . . The Jew has an especially fine and sensitively organized nervous system. He responds with sensitivity to stimulation more than the nerves of the robust peasant, and can thus hardly be considered neurasthenic."[91] This seems to dismiss the Jews' "mental illness" as an artifact of the Jews' more highly developed nervous systems, and yet the epidemiological literature of the period did not leave Zollschan unaffected. Zollschan, who persuasively argued for a single, pure Jewish race, still accepted the statistical arguments that Jews do suffer more readily from forms of mental illness. Among other sources, he cited statistics from Prussia that "proved" that Jews had twice as high a rate as did Aryans (five cases per thousand of the population as opposed to two and a half cases). His rationale here is complicated and returns us to the earlier discussion of the frequency of syphilis among the Jews and its relationship to the nature of the Jew's body. Zollschan carefully argues that the higher incidence of "mental illness" is in fact a higher rate of progressive paralysis. Citing Pilcz's study of racial psychiatry, he notes that of the cases of mental illness in Prussia from 1898 to 1900, 20.5 percent had progressive paralysis. He ties progressive paralysis to syphilis directly and sees the increased rate of mental illness as a reflex of the increased rate of syphilitic infection. But why would Jews have a high rate of syphilitic infection? Zollschan, reflecting the work of Iwan Bloch, argues that the first exposure of a group to a new disease initially creates greater damage than among groups long exposed to the disease. The Jews, having been sequestered in the ghetto and practicing early marriage, were simply shielded from the ravages of syphilis until civil emancipation. "Syphilitic infection is endemic among the Jews only as a result of their assimilation." This is a powerful metaphor for Zollschan, whose Zionist agenda advocates the preservation of the pure race of the Jews from the contamination of mixed marriages and assimilation. But even here Zollschan makes one further claim to provide a rationale for the insanity of the Jews. A thousand years of mental toil, "the extraordinarily difficult struggle for existence, the haste and hunt for daily bread" also contributes to the neurosis of the Jew. (These arguments are repeated verbatim by Felix Theilhaber in the *Jewish Lexicon*.)[92] In other words, everything associated with the Jew's life in the Diaspora leads to the diseased mental state of the Jews. The sole cure: a political state, which would "preserve the individuality of the race" and provide a cure for the Jews' madness.

For some Jewish physicians, this madness came to be represented in the discourse of psychiatry by the figure of the self-hating Jew. The image of the Jewish anti-Semite was a given in Freud's culture: "[Mr. N] heard a gentleman who was himself born a Jew make a spiteful remark about the Jewish character. 'Herr Hofrat,' he said, 'your ante-Semitism was well-known to me; your anti-Semitism is new to me.' "[93] It was still a specifically Jewish manifestation. Jakob Wassermann saw this as a character fault; it came to be understood in psychiatry as a disease. It is indeed what happens when anti-Semitism, a mental illness of the non-Jew generated by the anxiety that arises when the Aryan even thinks about the circumcised body of the Jew, is transmitted to the Jew. In the Jewish medical literature of the period, the social contagion of this neurosis (or psychosis) through the internalization of the non-Jew's anxiety is at the root of the mental illness of at least those Jews, those converts to Christianity, who are manifestly diseased and whose conversion is the primary symptom of their mental instability. In 1909 the Viennese-Jewish poet Fritz Löhner, whose witty poems on Jewish themes were widely quoted by his contemporaries, could ironically refer to "that Group of Jewish anti-Semites . . . / who bear the signs of baptismal hydrocephaly! [*Sie tragen waschechte Taufwasserköpfe!*]."[94] In 1923 Joseph Prager saw modern Jewry as "sick in its soul."[95] Theodor Lessing gave it a name in 1930: "Jewish Self-Hatred."[96] Lessing's work is a study of Jews such as Otto Weininger who attempt to convert to Christianity, and who end in madness. Lessing saw it as the rejection of Jewish racial identity, an impossibility—as one cannot leave one's race—that leads to madness. By 1931 Erich Stern placed this hatred of the self in the camp of the diseases of the Jews. It became the Jewish neurosis. It was a result of the rejection of religious identity by Jews who then had little or nothing to replace this identity.[97]

A furious debate was launched in the official publication of the German Zionist organization, the *Jewish Review*, in 1934 by the publication of an article by Dr. James Kirsch of Tel Aviv critiquing a recent publication by C. G. Jung in which Jung wrote about the specifically negative Jewish perception of aspects of the psyche. Kirsch agreed with Jung in general, contradicting him only in his claim that the Jews are a nomadic people; rather, he stated, the Jews are a "people with a collective neurosis, which resulted from the loss of connectedness [to the Holy Land]."[98] Dr. Otto Juliusburger, a Berlin psychoanalyst, saw the Jews as indeed ill, but traced this to the changes in Jewish life that had taken (and were taking) place through the process of acculturation, specifically the increased consumption of alcohol.[99] He was answered by Dr. J. Steinfeld from Mannheim, who affirmed the existence of a "Jewish neurosis," which, however, only colors the universal, early childhood experiences of all people.[100] Ludwig Lewisohn saw how "the Jewish people had become as a whole neurotic" since emancipation: "Jews began to hate themselves; Jews began to accept their enemies' estimate of them."[101]

In 1935 Joseph Wortis, in a training analysis with Freud, confronted Freud on this issue. Wortis commented that "Jews . . . are more liable to neuroses because they are looked upon as inferior." Freud's response is striking:

> I am not so sure of that. . . . Gentiles have plenty of neuroses too. Only the Jew is more sensitive, more critical of himself, more dependent on the judgment of others. He has less self-confidence than the Gentiles, and is fresher—has more "chootzpa" too—both come from the same thing. Jews are less sadistic than Gentiles, and the neuroses in general develop themselves at the cost of sadism: the more reckless a person is, the less neurotic. Besides, the Gentiles drown their neurosis in alcohol, and the Jew does not drink.[102]

Jewish mental illness is different than that of the non-Jew. It is a reflex of the body (just as Jews do not exhibit the symptoms of alcoholism) and reflects itself in the special mental state of the Jews.[103] One of the signs of this, for the non-Jew, is the Jew's heightened sensitivity to "any sign of anti-Semitism," as Ernest Jones, one of Freud's first non-Jewish (and non-Germanic) followers, noted. Freud had not "escaped the Jewish persecution heritage."[104] The notion that Jews internalize the views of those about them and that this is the source of their "mental illness" points toward an acceptance of the sick role by Jews or the assignment of that sick role to other (distanced) groups of Jews. That is the case in many of the writings about "Jewish self-hatred" in which Western Jews see Eastern Jews as at risk, Zionists see assimilationists as at risk, religious Jews see Marxist Jews as at risk, and so forth.[105]

There was a rich literature on the predisposition of the Jews to mental illness that drew on psychoanalytic theory present in German, Austrian, and Swiss medicine at the end of the century. Followers of Eugen Bleuler such as Rafael Becker in Switzerland argued for a reading of such a predisposition as a sign of an Adlerian inferiority complex.[106] It was even debated before the New York Neurological Society on April 7, 1914. The presentation was made by A. A. Brill, who had worked with Bleuler at the Burghölzli clinic when Becker was there, and Morris J. Karpas.[107] They noted that the differences among the statistics reflect the national status of the Jews and that while "the Jewish race contributes a rather high percentage to the so-called functional form of insanity . . . the Jew is not disproportionately insane."[108] Functional psychopathologies, such as hysteria, were more evident among Jews even in New York City. The groups Brill and Karpas were examining were the newly arrived Eastern European Jews who were admitted to the public hospitals from which they gathered their samples. The debate that followed their presentation was intense. George H. Kirby argued that it was important to understand the frequency of the diseases, such as dementia praecox, in order better to treat the various immigrant groups. Smith Ely Jelliffe, the president of the society, threw up his hands and stated that statisticians could make what they wanted out of the figures and could make the superficial important. The physician-anthropologist Maurice Fishberg, who was present by invitation, presented his argument for the contextual cause of the higher incidence of mental illness. Jews were urban dwellers, they were engaged in "financial and commercial pursuits" more than others, and their propensity to mental illness seemed to change based on where they lived and what the local conditions were. Here is one of the hidden readings of the Jew's mental illness. It is the male Jew, the Jew engaged in the world of fin de siècle commerce, who is at risk. As a Dr. Brosius had stated in a lecture on "the psychosis of the Jews" at the Seventieth Annual Meeting of the Psychiatric Association of the Rhineland on November 15, 1902, "the

Jews have more mental illness than do Christians and . . . the male sex are in the majority."[109] The assumption of the entire debate was, however, that male Jews did suffer from specific forms of mental illnesses in greater numbers. The problem was to discover the reason.[110]

In the American psychoanalytic debates this question surfaced in a paper delivered by I. S. Wechsler to the New York Psychoanalytical Society on November 27, 1923. Entitled "The Nervousness of the Jew: An Enquiry into Racial Psychology," the paper examined the "prevalence of neuroses among Jews." Wechsler's argument accepted the difficult social context of Jews as the immediate cause of the Jews' increased incidence of psychopathology. But it was the predisposition of the Jew because of his "common mental construction" that was stressed by Wechsler. Unlike others in Western culture, the Jew cannot simply flee into the "idealism" of a religion that escapes the realities of daily life in the promises or threats of heaven and hell. The Jew's religion, because of his negative experience in this world, "permits less of vicarious neurosis." Wechsler's model is a purely phylogenic one: "Just as the individual in his growth from the childhood state of fantasy to maturity is exposed to conflict and neurosis, so the race goes through similar stages. Racial neurosis is a step in phylogenesis, as individual neurosis is in psychic ontogenesis."[111] Racial memory was real for Wechsler and part of it was the predisposition of the Jew to madness.

In 1920 the famed eugenist Abraham Myerson at the Boston State Hospital attributed the psychopathology of the Jew to "social" rather than "biological heredity." Like Becker he saw in the Jews' isolation from appropriate forms of work one of the major sources of their psychopathology. Myerson also saw in the rejection by Jews of "sports and play" one of the sources of the illness. Again following Nordau's image of the "muscle Jew," here redefined as the "all-American athlete," Myerson provided yet another theoretical restatement of this myth: "Sports and play . . . form an incomparable avenue of discharge for nervous tension. They breed confidence in oneself. Being extenser in their character, they allow for the rise of pride and courage. Circumstances excluded the Jew from their wholesome influence, and the children of the race grew up to be very serious, very earnest, too early devoted to mature efforts, excessively cerebral in their activities, and not sufficiently strenuous physically. In *other words, the Jew, through his restrictions, was cheated out of his childhood.*"[112] Myerson, like Becker, needed to locate the baneful influence on the Jews outside the Jews themselves. He placed it in another society, not America with its reevaluation of older, foreign values.[113] (Indeed, the large number of Eastern European Jews who were manual laborers under the most primitive conditions relegates his condemnation of the image of the inactive Jewish male child to the world of myth.) Myerson, a powerful advocate of sterilization as a eugenic tool, thus managed to absolve the Jews from any congenital defect. Indeed, he did not discuss the mental illness of the Jews in his widely influential study of the inheritance of mental illness.[114] The view that the socialization of the Jewish child lies at the root of a heightened rate of mental illness among Eastern Jews was not unique to the United States. Menasze Offner, an Adlerian psychoanalyst in Vienna, sounded precisely the same call in his description of the "Jewish inferiority feeling" among Eastern European Jewish children in Vienna.[115] Jewish religious education in the East lay at the center of this mental illness that afflicted the Jews. This was the disease that infected the Jews of Vienna.

In the course of the nineteenth and early twentieth centuries a number of approaches were made to the myth of the mental illness of the Jews. European biology served, especially in Germany and France, to reify accepted attitudes toward all marginal groups, especially the Jews. The scientific "fact" that the Jew was predisposed to madness would have enabled society, acting as the legal arm of science, to deal with Jews as it dealt with the insane. However, the reality was quite different. While the fantasy of the privileged group would have banished the Jews out of sight, into the asylum, the best it could do was to institutionalize the idea of the madness of the Jews. Jews, like women, possessed a basic biological predisposition to specific forms of mental illness. Thus, like women, who were also making specific political demands on the privileged group at the same moment in history, Jews could be dismissed as unworthy of becoming part of the privileged group because of their aberration. Like the American slaves who were labeled mad because they desired to escape from slavery, Jews, by acting on the promise made to them through the granting of political emancipation in the eighteenth century, proved their madness.[116] Jewish doctors, in accepting the rhetoric of nineteenth-century medicine, needed to limit the applicability of this model to themselves. They saw in various subgroups of Jews (the merchant Jew, the Eastern Jew, the disenfranchised Jew, the immigrant Jew) those groups most at risk. They removed themselves from the category of those endangered and freed themselves from the potential curse of the Jews' madness. But this emotionally laden charge did not vanish; it became part of the definition of the female.

TRAUMA AND TRAINS: THE TESTING GROUND OF MASCULINITY

The predisposition of the male, Eastern European Jew to specific forms of mental illness, such as hysteria, became a topic of great debate at the turn of the twentieth century. The atavistic Jew appears in Sigmund Freud's discourse about the hysteric. Freud's reading of the ancient Greek myth of

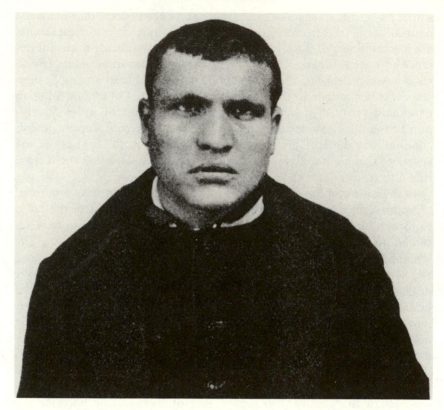

Figure 4. The physiognomy of the male hysteric as beardless degenerate. From
Wilhelm Weygandt, *Atlas und Grundriss der Psychiatrie*
(Munich: Lehmann, 1902).

the wandering womb, which when lodged in the throat created the *globus hystericus*, serves as a detailed example of the problems attendant to "seeing" the hysteric. While Oppenheim's hysterical opera singer reverted to the primeval sounds of her *Mauscheln*, in Freud's early case studies the sign of damaged discourse became a generalized and medicalized symptom. Freud's initial presentation of his work on hysteria in Vienna was a paper on male hysteria—not the Jewish male predisposition to hysteria but the universal male potential for hysteria. Freud's overt argument was evidently (the paper is lost) that men, too, suffer from hysteria, since the etiology of the disease was not in the gender of the patient but in the patient's traumatic experiences. It is well known that Freud, in the autobiographical account he wrote of the occasion some forty years after the event, recalled the "bad reception" this paper on male hysteria got when he presented it to the Viennese Society of Physicians on October 15,

1886.[117] Returning from his work with Jean-Martin Charcot in Paris and desiring to present his newly acquired insights about male hysteria to his home audience in Vienna, Freud's powerful memory was that his hearers thought that what he "said was incredible. . . . One of them, an old surgeon, actually broke out with the exclamation: 'But, my dear sir, how can you talk such nonsense? *Hysteron* [*sic*] means the uterus. So how can a man be hysterical?"[118] Freud's angry memory was aimed at the narrow-minded claim of this old man, representing the Viennese medical establishment, that it, and it alone, had command of Greek. In showing his knowledge of Greek, the Jewish psychoanalyst staked his claim to control a discourse of academic culture. Freud's memory was certainly shaped by the hostile reception psychoanalysis had gotten in the four decades following his talk. Psychoanalysis was seen as a Jewish pseudoscience and as a form of mass hysteria, a "psychic epidemic among physicians."[119] We can remember Freud's comment, rebutting Felix von Luschan's attack on the new science of psychoanalysis in 1916, that "an old Jew is tougher than a noble Prussian Teuton."[120] Freud laughed at the "old surgeon" who claimed to understand culture but whose very inability to command its language disqualified him from it. He eventually supplanted him and became—an "old Jew."

The young, French-trained Freud knew that the concept of hysteria was tied to universals (which, at that point, he thought of as trauma) and was not merely a reflex of the biological uniqueness of a subgroup. Freud wished to rescue hysteria (the hallmark of the new science) from the crabbed claws of a Viennese medical establishment that could not even get its Greek correct, for *hustera* is the correct form of the Greek noun for uterus. Thus the young Jew (and Freud had seen himself, since his exposure to the virulent "scientific" anti-Semitism of the University of Vienna, as a Jew) showed his command over not only the language of science (represented by Charcot's discourse on hysteria) but also the language of culture (Greek). Freud's sense, like that of his contemporaries, was that hysteria manifested itself as a disease not of the womb but of the imagination. It was a functional illness resulting from trauma, rather than the result of inheritance, as he had shown in his paper on heredity and inheritance. With the claim that male hysteria existed, he attempted to free the other targeted group, women, from their special risk. This did not absolve females from being the group most at risk, however, for the idea of a pathological human imagination structurally replaced the image of the floating womb as the central etiology of hysteria. Women's imagination was understood by the physicians of the time, such as P. J. Möbius, as diseased.[121] What was removed from the category of hysteria as Freud brought it back to Vienna was its insistence on another group, the Jews, as the group that essentially replaced the woman as at risk.

In the contemporary record of the discussion following Freud's paper, attributed to the young Austrian-Jewish physician and writer Arthur Schnitzler, there is a further complication.[122] Not only is there no mention of the impossibility of male hysteria, but Theodor Meynert and Moritz Rosenthal claim that, while less frequent than female hysteria, cases were well documented in the various Viennese hospitals as well as in the German medical literature. Heinrich von Bamberger, who chaired the meeting, commented further that while he certainly had seen cases of male hysteria, he was troubled by Freud's claim that his case was only the result of trauma. Indeed, he noted, the very case Freud cited "shows a hereditary predisposition" for the disease. Not trauma, which is the result of accident, but heredity, which cannot be altered, was the source of male hysteria, according to Bamberger. Thus within the concept of hysteria as Freud elaborated it, the question of the hysteric's heredity and predisposition was hotly contested.

The idea of the hysteric was as central to the imaginative world of Sigmund Freud as it was close to his self-definition. At the end of the nineteenth century the idea of seeing the hysteric was tightly bound to the idea of seeing the Jew—specifically the male Jew.[123] Indeed, if the visual representation of the hysteric in the nineteenth century was the image of the female, its subtext was that feminized males, such as Jews, were also hysterics, and they too could be "seen." The face of the Jew was as much a sign of the pathological as was the face of the hysteric. More significantly, the face of the Jew became the face of the hysteric.

Maurice Fishberg, one of the Jewish defenders of the Jews against the charge of being congenitally tainted by hysteria, stated the case boldly in *The Jews: A Study of Race and Environment* (1911): "The Jews, as is well known to every physician, are notorious sufferers of the functional disorders of the nervous system. Their nervous organization is constantly under strain, and the least injury will disturb its smooth workings."[124] The origin of this predisposition is neither consanguineous marriage ("the modern view . . . [is that they] are not at all detrimental to the health of the offspring") nor the occupations of Jews ("hysteria [is] . . . met with in the poorer classes of Jews . . . as well as in the richer classes").[125] It is the result of the urban concentration of the Jews and "the repeated persecutions and abuses to which the Jews were subjected during the two thousand years of the Diaspora."[126] According to Fishberg, these influences, found at the turn of the century primarily among Eastern Jews, show the predisposition of these specific groups of Jews to illnesses such as hysteria: "Organic as well as functional derangements of the nervous system are transmitted hereditarily from one generation to another."[127] It is not *all* Jews who are hysterics, but Eastern Jews, and primarily Eastern male Jews, in Fishberg's account: "The Jewish population of [Warsaw] alone is almost exclusively the inexhaustible source for the supply of specimens of hysterical humanity, particularly the hysteria in the male, for all the clinics of Europe."[128] Here the American Jew Fishberg misquotes the French psychiatrist Fulgence Raymond, who had stated that the Jews of Warsaw formed a major sector of the mentally ill of that city.[129] Fishberg's misquote of Raymond became the standard view in German psychiatry.[130] It appeared in Freud's circle when Isidor Sadger noted at the November 11, 1908, meeting of the Vienna Psychoanalytic Society: "In certain races (Russian and Polish Jews), almost every man is hysterical."[131] The male Jew from the East, from the provinces, was most at risk for hysteria. This view had been espoused by Charcot, who diagnosed on February 19, 1889, the case of a Hungarian Jew named Klein, "a true child of Ahasverus," as a case of male hysteria. Klein had a hysterical contracture of the hand and an extended numbness of the right arm and leg. Charcot emphasized the limping of the Jew. Klein "wandered sick and limping on foot to Paris" where he arrived on December 11, 1888. He appeared at the Salpêtrière the next day, "his feet so bloody that he could not leave his bed for many days." Klein "limped at the very beginning of his illness." Charcot reminded his listeners that the patient "is a Jew and that he has already revealed his pathological drives by his wanderings." His "travel-mania" was evident in that "as soon as he was on his feet again, he wanted to go to Brazil."[132] Wandering and limping mark the hysterical Jew as diseased, and diseased because of intermarriage. This theme was elaborated on in the work of Charcot's last major student, Henry Meige, who wrote his dissertation on these "wandering Jews," seeing them as the contemporary incarnation of the legendary Wandering Jew. In his thesis he reproduced their portraits so that one can study their physiognomy for the signs of their hysteria.[133]

The hysteria of the male Jew, especially the Eastern Jew, remained a truism of medical science through the decades. Prof. Hermann Strauss of the Jewish Hospital in Berlin, in one of the most-cited studies of the pathology of the Jews, provides a bar chart representing the risk of Jews for hysteria.[134] Here the relationship between men and women indicates that male Jews suffer twice as often from hysteria as do male non-Jews. The standard textbooks of the period reflect this view. While it is clear that women still are the predominant sufferers from the disease, it is evident from the visual representation of the cases of hysteria that there is a distinct "feminization" of the male Jew in the context of the occurrence of hysteria. This view is paralleled by the findings in the United States that "in European races, melancholic or depressive types of mental disorder are most frequent amongst the Germanic and Scandinavian peoples."[135]

The liberal Jewish neurologist Moritz Benedikt, professor of neurology at the University of Vienna at the turn of the century, also linked the

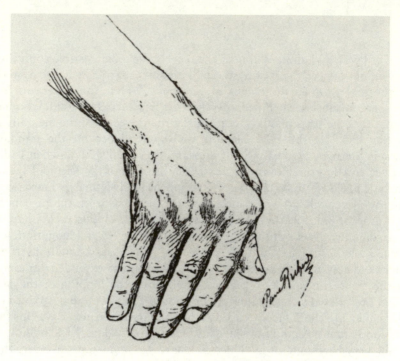

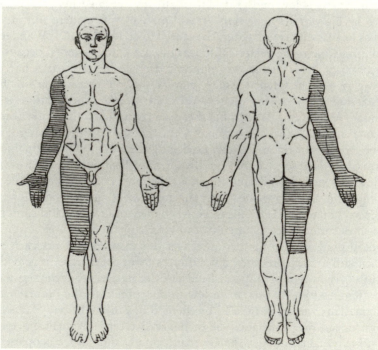

Figure 5. Images of the Hungarian Jew Klein with his limping leg from the *Poliklinische Vorträge von Prof. J. M. Charcot*, trans. Sigmund Freud and Max Kahane, 2 vols. (Leipzig: Deuticke, 1892–95). The bottom drawing represents the anesthetic areas of the hysterical Jew.

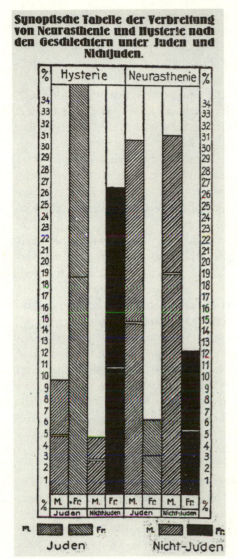

Figure 6. The Jewish hysteric as represented by a chart from Hermann Strauss, "Erkrankungen durch Alkohol und Syphilis bei den Juden," *Zeitschrift für Demographie und Statistik der Juden*, n.s. 4 (1927): 33–39; chart on p. 35. The relatively higher frequency of male hysterics among the Jews is "documented" in this image.

"American" quality of life with the appearance of hysteria, a disease accepted by him as "a uniquely feminine nervous disease"—in men.[136] (It is remarkable that only Jewish physicians in Vienna dealt with the question of male hysteria before [and including] Freud.) The struggle for life in the city causes the madness of the male Jew. According to Cecil F. Beadles: "Mental anxiety and worry are the most frequent causes of mental breakdown. They are all excitable and live excitable lives, being con-

stantly under the high pressure of business in town."[137] The reason for
this inability to cope with the stresses of modern life lies in "hereditary
influences"—in their being Jews.[138] And their "Jewishness" is a sign of
their being out of their correct space. For they are ill, "like many Orien-
tals (e.g., Mohammedans) who have a disposition to hysteria."[139]

Benedikt needed to argue against the equation of race and madness,[140]
for the "insanity of the Jew" was one of risks all Jews would have to face.
In a detailed answer to Beadles, he presented a convoluted and complex
argument about the special status of the nervousness of the Jew. He accepted the reality of Beadle's charge. It is not, however, a quality over
which "evolution has no power . . . [and] which is deeply rooted in the
organism." Benedikt argued against the uniformity of the Jews as a race
and saw the origin of the mental illness of the Jews in the external social
pressures "in times of exile, dispersion, and persecution." The Jews are
not really even a nation, for "the first condition necessary for a nation is
a common language." "Other nations could find an outlet for their passions and emotions in outward actions; the Jews found an outlet for them
usually at the expense of health, and so became more and more neurotic."
This neurosis resulted in "excessive sexual intercourse, *intra matrimo-
nium*" and caused the cases of "hysterical aphonia, in endemic form, . . .
[which] are very frequent in Jews, male and female." This caused "neurologists all over the world [to be] interested in the number, intensity, and
variety of cases seen amongst the Jews." The lost language of the Jews,
the inability to speak any tongue flawlessly, marks the Jews as ill. But
what did Benedikt see as the cause of the madness of the Jews? The "ill-
treatment and cruelty to . . . which they have been subjected." This even
explains to him why Jews, who have a lower incidence of "syphilis and
drunkenness," also have a higher rate of general paralysis, for it is clear
that syphilis cannot be the cause of the general paralysis of the insane,
luetic tabes. It is the result of social factors. With acculturation, new nervous diseases afflicted the Jews. Jewish women, "formerly pampered neurotic individuals," now became "eccentric. . . . Very many of them became, by reason of superficial learning, actually perverse." "They quickly
entered into the modern economic contest with all its fatal consequences
as regards nervous integrity." Benedikt's model, as is evident from his
examples, is the Eastern Jew, hampered by the ghetto experience.[141] And
it is Yiddish that for Benedikt was the marker of Jewish mental illness.
The so-called language, with its coarse gestures, seemed to have a magical
quality that prevented the acculturation of the Eastern Jews and pro-
longed their risk for mental illnesses. Indeed, Theodor Reik pointed out
that Eastern Jews communicated as much with "gestures and . . . facial
expressions, the rise and fall of the voice of the story-teller," as with
words.[142]

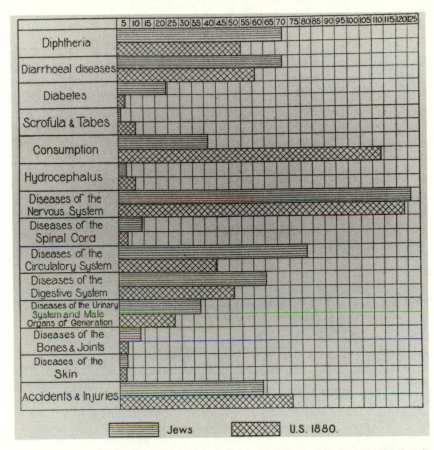

Figure 7. The comparatively higher rate of mental illness (among 60,630 Jews) in the United States in a special census of 1889. From John Shaw Billings, *Vital Statistics of the Jews in the United States*, Census Bulletin no. 19, December 30, 1890.

When Freud's earliest cases are examined it is clear that the belief about the inheritability of the madness of the Jews and its relationship to endogamous marriage was a commonplace in the Viennese clinics and asylums of the 1880s.[143] Questions concerning the status of the family were a standard part of the patient's history. Indeed, questions twelve to fourteen of the printed cover form of each medical record inquired about the presence in the nuclear and extended family of mental illnesses or "notable character traits." Of Freud's ninety-two patients for whom records have been found, eighty-six were Catholic and five were Jewish (one file did not record a religious affiliation.) Of these, fifty-eight were men and thirty-four were women. In the case of the five Jewish patients, the figures are quite the reverse. In this group there were one man and four women. All these cases were Eastern Jews from Hungary or Galicia. What is striking about these cases is that there was the assumption not only of inheritance of mental illness but of inbreeding among the Jewish patients. This can be seen in the case notes concerning Ruth B., admitted to the Lower Austrian State Asylum in Vienna in 1885 suffering from paranoia. The admitting physician (a Dr. Pleischl) noted that "a hereditary predisposition is excluded. In the entire extended family of the patient there never was a case of insanity, alcoholism, epilepsy, even though the parents and grandparents of the patient are related by blood."[144] This observation is remarkable as it shows the perception of the physician taking this history. The assumption of the physician was that there is either inherited insanity or inbreeding among these patients, or both.

On December 5, 1906, this topic came up for discussion at the Viennese Psychoanalytic Society following a paper on Wilhelm Stekel's theory of the origin of nervousness. Isidor Sadger commented "on the widespread occurrence of nervousness (especially obsessional neurosis and hysteria) among the Polish Jews."[145] The cause of this is the "Jew's addiction to rumination . . . [which] has been characteristic of the Jews for thousands of years." The inheritance of specific forms of a "common mental construction" lies at the heart of the Jew's predisposition to mental illness.[146] The view that the Eastern Jew was essentially at risk for hysteria permeated even the discussion of this circle of mainly Eastern European Jews, transplanted to Vienna. They saw at risk not themselves, but "those" Eastern Jews, an abstraction they distanced from their own personas.

Galton's model of "seeing" the Jew's gaze, of looking at the Jew looking, was part of the discourse of psychopathology during the late nineteenth century. In Charcot's clinic there was an often-stated assumption that Jews, especially Jews from the East, were at great risk for mental illness.[147] Following the collapse of the Catholic Union Generale Bank in 1882, there was a great rise in public anti-Semitism. In the spring of 1886, Edouard Drumont's best-seller *La France juive* appeared, perhaps the most important French anti-Semitic tractate. Drumont cited psychological statistics to show that Jews, especially Jews from the East, were most at risk for mental illness, and therefore presented a social danger to the French body politic. And he repeated statements made by Charcot "in his lectures in the Salpêtrière."[148]

No wonder Jewish scientists such as Jacobs, Fishberg, and Freud, in very different ways, sought to find the hysteric outside their own immutable self-images, for those images were within the biology of race. This consistency of character, with its deviant sexual nature, led to the disease that marked the Jew: hysteria. The etiology of the Jew's hysteria, like the hysteria of the woman, was to be sought in "sexual excess,"[149] specifically in the "incestuous" inbreeding of this endogamous group: "Being very neurotic, consanguineous marriages among Jews cannot but be detrimental to the progeny."[150] The converse is also true: "The excessive tendency to the neuroses [among] . . . the Jews [results] from their mode of life and consanguineous marriages through long centuries."[151] Jews (especially male Jews) are sexually different; they are hysterical and their gaze reveals it.

Race is only one category in the visualization of the hysteric that played a role in shaping the image of the hysteric during the nineteenth century. The image took many different forms, becoming a composite that revealed the "truth" about the hysteric's difference to himself or herself.

In the course of the 1890s Freud abandoned much of the work of the anti-Semitic Charcot[152]—for whom Jews, as the essential "moderns," were at special risk for hysteria—and entered a new alliance with the provincial Jew Hippolyte Bernheim.[153] Much of this is explored in Freud's French-language paper on the meaning of heredity in the etiology of hysteria (1896). Such a movement is parallel to the abandonment of the idea of trauma—still for Charcot the cause of hysteria (in women as well as in Jews)—and its replacement with the etiology of hysteria in the psyche. Freud wrote, "[The physician] will be able to convince himself of the correctness of the assertions of the school of Nancy [Bernheim] at any time on his patients, whereas he is scarcely likely to find himself in a position to confirm from his own observation the phenomena described by Charcot as 'major hypnotism,' which seem only to occur in a few sufferers from *grande hystérie*."[154] The scientific "observation," the gaze of the Jew rather than the gaze directed at the Jew, marks the distinction between Bernheim and Charcot. Freud's "conversion" to Bernheim's mode of seeing the "usual" rather than seeing the "unique" also marks the beginning of his rejection of the reduction of the origin of hysteria to a single, traumatic event.

But what does "trauma" mean? One meaning relates it to the debate about congenital circumcision and the inheritance of acquired characteristics. To trace the meaning of trauma is to see the reason the Eastern European Jew appears as a hysteric (or perhaps more accurately, the provincial Jew as a parvenu, out of his mind because he is out of his natural place). The discourse on the relationship between "trauma" and "hysteria" provides the key to Freud's—and many of his contemporaries'—ambivalence concerning models for therapy.

"Trauma" is not a neutral concept. There was a general acceptance of the historical model of the "railway spine," hysterical trauma resulting from railway accidents, as a means of understanding the traumatic nature of hysteria at the turn of the century.[155] Indeed, in much of the early work on hysteria these images haunt the literature. The hysteric suffers from traumatic neurosis similar to that caused by experiencing a train accident, as outlined by Herbert Page in his classic work *Injuries of the Spine and Spinal Cord* (1883) and accepted in toto by Charcot in his work on the neurosis of fright or shock. Men and women are therefore equally at risk for such forms of psychopathology. Hysteria is merely the direct result (brain or spinal cord lesion) or indirect result (shock) of trauma. Here the confusion between the models of hysteria evolved by Charcot and Hughlings Jackson must be noted, for the "traumatic" event causes hysteria only in those who are predisposed to being hysteric (Charcot), but the lesion caused by trauma also releases those subterranean aspects of our earlier evolution held in check by the highest order of neurological organization (Hughlings Jackson).

The image of the train as the source of modern hysteria quickly took on a symbolic function. For Max Nordau, in the 1890s, the railroad became the sign of the overloading of the nervous system through the pressures of modern life. "Even the little shocks of railway travelling, not perceived by consciousness, the perpetual noises, and the various sights in the streets of a large town . . . cost our brains wear and tear."[156] For Nordau the "constant vibrations undergone in railway travel" as well as the "effects of railway accidents" lie at the center of "modern nervousness" and the "degeneration" of the era. But for Nordau, as for Freud, the subtext, unstated in his comments, is that the nervousness attributed to modernity, with its increased speed of life, is most often and most evidently a Jewish problem. The nervousness of modern life as symbolized by the railroad is Jewish nervousness.

The Jew is predisposed to hysteria because of heredity and consanguinity as well as by the trauma of civilization, as represented by the Jews' predisposition to the somatic diseases linked to hysteria—such as syphilis. Even more directly, in one of Freud's major sources for the discussion of "railway spine," the author stressed that "national and individual vulnerability as well as nervous temperament can bring one individual to the edge of the grave while the other remains free of shock." "Psychic predisposition" determines whether one will suffer from the hysteria associated with train accidents.[157] It is not surprising that the diagnostic criteria for nervous illnesses that evolved from the preoccupation with "railway spine" became the specialty of Jewish physicians. The discussion of "spinal irritation" as the central cause of nervous illness, which had preceded (and structured) the debate about "railway spine," had been dominated by Benedict Stilling, Moritz Romberg, and August Axenfeld, all Jewish physicians.[158] The evocation of such a cause for psychopathology seemed to counter the claim that heredity and predisposition were the central factors in mental illness. Freud's rejection of simple predisposition and his search for the specific etiology of hysteria, while it indeed incorporated the "germ theory model" into psychiatry, also enabled him to displace the blanket association of all Jews because of their inherited nature with certain forms of mental illness.[159]

The image of the trauma of modern civilization was closely associated with the train at the turn of the century. As Sir Clifford Allbutt, professor of medicine at Cambridge University, stated in an essay in the *Contemporary Review* of 1895:

> To turn now . . . to nervous disability, to hysteria . . . to the frightfulness, the melancholy, the unrest due to living at a high pressure, the world of the railway, the pelting of telegrams, the strife of business . . . surely, at any rate, these maladies or the causes of these maladies are more rife than they were in the days of our fathers? To this question . . . there is, I know, but one opinion on the subject in society, in the newspapers, in the books of philosophers, even in the journals and treatises of the medical profession.[160]

Thus the railroad, railway accidents, and the "speed of modern life" all collaborate to create the hysteric. But nineteenth-century "railway" medicine faced a dilemma that later faced Sigmund Freud. Trauma—such as involvement in a railway crash—is the cause of hysteria, but why do not all individuals who are involved in railway crashes become hysteric? This question was answered in part by the neurologist C. E. Brown-Séquard, who as early as 1860 had argued that there were hereditary transmissions of acquired injuries, as in the case of "animals born of parents having been rendered epileptic by an injury to the spinal cord."[161] This view of reflex theory quickly became standard in the literature on "railway spine."[162]

But the world of the train and the meaning of trauma had a secondary context for Jews in the nineteenth century. It was one of the public spaces, defined by class and economic power, in which the Jew could purchase status. It was part of the image of the world of "modern life" that helped deform the psyche of the Jew. A ticket assured one of traveling among one's economic equals—but not as racial "equals." The association of trains and the trauma of confronting one's Jewish identity is a powerful topos at the turn of the century. Freud linked his own phobia of traveling by train to the move from the East when he was three years old and he saw the gas flames in the Breslau railroad station burning like "souls in hell."[163] But it is also clear that the anxiety associated with the train was linked by the older Freud to the sense of social displacement he felt when leaving the déclassé world of the Eastern Jew (to which he feared he always belonged). Freud's lifelong anxiety was about "missing a train" rather than about being on a train. To have missed the train west would have meant not eventually going to Vienna, and this would have made him permanently an Eastern Jew. His anxiety can be related to his early sense of change and loss associated with the world of the Eastern European Jew.[164]

Freud's sense of status anxiety permeated his relationship with Wilhelm Fliess when Freud informed his friend of Martha's anxiety about his traveling to meet him on a train: "Half an hour ago I was pulled out of my fear of the next train accident when the thought occurred to me: W. and I are also traveling, after all. This put a stop to the tomfoolery. But this must remain strictly between us."[165] The general anxiety that Martha Freud expressed about train accidents became, in Freud's daydreams, the status of Freud's relationship with Fliess. It was the relationship of two marginal Jewish, male "scientists" undertaking a two-man "scientific" congress that could be "derailed" at any moment. Is what they were doing truly Western, modern "science" or a cabal between two male Jews? Did these two men truly belong to the world of science or were they seeing the world through their own Jewish lens? The displacement of the anxiety associated with difference became associated with the "train ride," for it is on trains that frightening events occur that reveal the innate difference between the self and the Other. This anxiety appeared powerfully in Freud's admission to Fliess in the course of his self-analysis that he had seen his mother *nudam* while on a train journey from Leipzig to Vienna. In his account of that experience, Freud linked his sight of the unclothed body of the woman with the sense of displacement and guilt at the death of his younger brother. But the initial sense of displacement came in regard to his seeing the body of a woman as different, and the anxiety this evoked. If conflicts and anxiety were associated with train trips, so too was therapy. Free association was "as though, for instance, you were a traveller sitting next to the window of a railway carriage and describing to someone inside the carriage the changing views which you see outside."[166] Here the therapist was on the train and, like the analysand, was able to travel unimpeded, looking through the window of the moving vehicle. Freud's self-analysis revealed the anxiety that took place on the train, but never resolved the conflicts associated with the potential train trip. Freud retained his train neurosis. Missing the train meant remaining an Eastern Jew; making the train meant confronting his own Jewish difference. The unimpeded journey was not for Freud. As a Central European Jew, the train trip always held the anxiety of the articulation of his own difference, as striking a difference as the "castrated" body of the woman.

Confrontations with anti-Semites took place on trains. In December 1883 Freud experienced a scene in a train traveling through Saxony in which he was called a "dirty Jew" when he attempted to open a window in the car: "My first opponent also turned anti-Semitic and declared: 'We

Christians consider other people. . . .' Even a year ago I would have been speechless with agitation, but now I am different; I was not in the least frightened of that mob, asked the one to keep to himself his empty phrases which inspire no fear in me, and the other to step up and take what he deserved. I was quite ready to kill him, but he did not stand up."[167] The trauma of this incident was powerful enough that it haunted the "Count Thun" dream, recorded in August 1898. The imagery of that dream takes place on a train and reflects "a piece of anti-Semitic provocation during a railway journey in the lovely Saxon countryside."[168] Trains became part of the mental space associated with Jewishness and the trauma of that race. Freud was not a passive, feminized male Jew here, but rather an active, aggressive one. This "new" Jew, quite willing to engage in physical conflict when verbally attacked, was not like his passive father bullied by a Christian anti-Semite who knocked his "new fur cap" into the gutter and forced him to retrieve it.[169] (In reality, the cry of "hep! hep!" by an anti-Semite during his father's youth was an order to vacate the sidewalk and to step into the muck of the unpaved streets. By simply remaining on the sidewalk, Freud's father stood his ground.) The identity of the Jew as male became associated with the trip.

This masculinization of the Jew is the result of the reconstruction of the fantasy of the Jew as one who can independently cross frontiers rather than be driven across them. The crossing of frontiers (in trains) is understood as a sign of responsible masculinity. In 1898 Freud, in a most striking response to seeing Theodor Herzl's play *The New Ghetto* (1894), noted that "the Jewish problem" was a "concern about the future of one's children, to whom one cannot give a country of their own, concern about educating them in such a way that they can move freely across frontiers."[170] Freud's phrase is both metaphor and fact—one must be trained so that one knows how to respond to the trauma that can occur when crossing frontiers.

The anti-Semitic incident on the train became a set piece for the graphic sexual humor of the late nineteenth century. It was almost always the *male* Jew, in his masculinity as well as in his role as a Jew, who stood at the center of the train joke. This masculinity was disqualified by this association in jokes told about Jews by non-Jews. Thus in a collection of Slovenian blue jokes, reproduced in the seventh volume of *Anthropophyteia*, a yearbook of sexually explicit folklore to which Freud contributed, there is a tale of a Jew who falls asleep on the train and snores so loudly that his fellow travelers smear a bit of cheese under his nose. Thinking himself at home in bed, he mutters: "Sarah, cover yourself, you stink," much to the amusement of his fellow passengers.[171]

In the Jewish joke books of the turn of the century this association became one in which the aggressiveness of the male Jew was played out and the train became a space in which the marginal Jew, speaking in *Mauscheln*, had his revenge:

> A Polish Jew was traveling by train. Underway he attempted to enter into conversation with an officer traveling in his compartment. As the train passed a deforested mountain, our friend spoke: "My dear officer, kin ye tell me why no grass grows on dat mountain?" "Because a lousy Jew shat on it!" the officer nastily replied. The Jew was embarrassed and was quiet. As the journey continued the officer took his cap from his head and the Jew noticed that he was bald. He quickly took the occasion to revenge the insult and turned to his traveling companion with the following words: "Tell me, my dear officer, did a lousy Jew also shit on your head?"[172]

Freud's own study of Jewish jokes is peppered with unpleasant incidents that happen to Jews on trains.[173] The jokes he tells are, however, incidents in which a Jew (an Eastern Jew) is the butt of the joke of another Jew. These internecine jokes are self-deprecating and revealed, to Freud, a "common mental construction" analogous to the actions of his father stepping into the gutter. Freud's scientific narrative frames the telling of these jokes in precise scientific discourse, separating his own scholarly, masculine voice from the marginalized voice of the Jews in the jokes.[174] But, as we can see from his anxiety about Fliess, stories about Jews in trains were anxiety-provoking for him, as the train was the locus where he could be (and was) directly confronted by the meaning of his own Jewish identity. Unlike the squabbling, feminized Jews of the jokes he tells, his actions were those of a real man—but a "real" man whose close emotional attachment was to another man whom he met on trains. These jokes about Jews on trains haunted his dreams.

In his dreams about his conflicted desire to visit Rome he recounted two "facetious Jewish anecdotes which contain so much profound and often bitter worldly wisdom and which we so greatly enjoy quoting in our talk and our letters." The first is that of "an impecunious Jew [who] had stowed himself away without a ticket in the fast train to *Karlsbad*. He was caught, and each time tickets were inspected he was taken out of the train and treated more and more severely. At one of the stations on his *via dolorosa* he met an acquaintance, who asked him where he was travelling to. 'To Karlsbad,' was his reply, 'if my constitution can stand it.' "[175] The Jewish constitution is tried by the excesses of persecution—here, however, made the fault of the Jew acting stereotypically.

But this Jew is also the crypto-convert. Carl Schorske saw the figure as Freud himself "longing for an assimilation to the gentile world that his strong waking conscience—and even his dream censor—would deny him."[176] He seemed to be suffering on a road of pain, the Catholic term for the final journey of Christ through the streets of Jerusalem. But there is a further reading, one that acknowledges the power of the contrast between the narrative structure of the joke and its punch line. Here we have the difference between the distanced, male voice of the scientist that is represented as "neutral" precisely because he can evoke the world of high Christian discourse. (Any Jewish scientist would quickly have realized that the vocabulary of medical science, such as Charcot's "stigmata" [of the hysteric/witch], drew directly or indirectly on the world of Christian icons as much as on any other source.) The punch line is delivered in *Mauscheln*, at least in terms of its sentence structure and implied intonation. Here the introduction of the language of the Jew mirrors the hidden flaw present within the Jew.

Freud provided a clue to the meaning of "Karlsbad," the spa to which the Jew was heading. Karlsbad was where "we are in the habit of prescribing treatment . . . for anyone suffering from the constitutional complaint of diabetes."[177] Diabetes was, for the physician of the time, the Jewish disease about which one could speak, unlike the general silence that surrounded hysteria (even though, for men, impotence is a common symptom of diabetes).[178] But even this disease, because of its evident association with Jews, was seen as a sign of degeneration. William Osler, visiting Berlin in 1884, reported on the work of the internist Friedrich Theodor Frerichs on diabetes: "With reference to race, it is remarkable that 102 of the [400] patients were Jews, which he attributes to hereditary excitability of the nervous system, the keen pursuit of business, and, above all, intermarriage."[179] As late as the 1920s this view remained quite alive in German-language medicine. Diabetes was the "sole result" of "the impact of the nervous excitement on the nervous system transmitted from the time of the ghetto."[180] For the Jewish male, diabetes provided an association of Jewishness and masculinity that stressed not only the diseased nature of the Jew but also his physical and social impotence. The mind and the body of the Jew were impaired because of the very nature of the Jew, the "perverse" sexuality of his "race," and his striving for material success.

Freud associated this story about the Jewish constitution with a joke: about "a Jew who could not speak French and had been recommended when he was in Paris to ask the way to the rue Richelieu."[181] Here the displacement of the Jewish male in a strange city (like that of Eastern Jews living in Western cities) is mirrored in the language of the Jew. The Jew stops a stranger and asks him in broken French how to find this street. The individual he stops is a French Jew who answers him in Yiddish that he doesn't have to try to hide his identity, that he knows him for a Jew by his *Mauscheln*.[182] The crossing of boundaries, as in the movement from the Eastern fringes to the centers of culture, such as Paris, evokes the train. It is not circumcision that reveals the true nature of the Jew in public but the use of language, precisely that quality that marks the Jew as a Jew even when he is well-dressed, well-to-do, and riding in a first-class compartment in the train. Language is a marker of difference, but the difference is a quality of gender as well as race, for it is the *male* Jew who is disqualified from being a fully fledged member of society in all these stories.

The physician Freud linked these two jokes, one about the constitution and disease of the Jew and the other about the impact of these on the Jew's psyche and language. They are "jokes" only so long as they happen to Eastern, marginalized Jews who remain the object of study for the scholarly eye of the neutral scientist. And the Jews are Eastern Jews because of their misuse of language. The neutral scientists, Freud and Fliess, used scientific jargon (which they were in the process of creating) to provide a forum for the analysis of this aberrant discourse. Freud did not find incidents such as the one that occurred to him in reality in any way humorous. In trains the trauma of race became most evident, and Jew and Aryan confront one another. But trains were also places where male Jews could prove themselves—either in confrontations with anti-Semites or in collaboration with other male scientists.

The image of the hysteric being at risk because of inheritance limited the field from which the hysteric could be drawn. Thus the male physician could—under most circumstances—see himself as belonging to a separate category, as distanced from the hysteric as the child of alcoholics or criminals. But not the male Jewish physician. The Jewish physician was at risk no matter which theory of hysteria he accepted.[183] Some views using the model of biological determinism held that the Jew was at risk simply from inheritance; some views sought a sociological explanation. But both views, no matter what the etiology, saw a resultant inability of the Jew to deal with the complexities of the modern world, as represented by the Rousseauean city. The trauma of "modern life" was closely linked to the image of the city. For nineteenth-century medicine (whether psychiatry or public health), cities were places of disease and the Jews were the quintessential city dwellers, the Americans of Europe. Richard von Krafft-Ebing believed that civilization regularly brings forth degenerate forms of sexuality because of the "more stringent demands which circumstances make upon the nervous system" and which manifest themselves in the "psychopathological or neuropathological conditions of the nation involved."[184] For him (and most clinical psychiatrists of the time) the Jewish male was the ultimate "city person" whose sensibilities were dulled, whose sexuality was pathological, whose materialistic, money-grubbing goals were "American," whose life was without a center. The city also triggered the weakness hidden within the corrupted individual. Its turbulence, its excitement, what Auguste Forel in *The Sexual Question* (1905) called its "Americanism," led to "illnesses" such as hysteria: "Americanism.— By this term I designate an unhealthy feature of sexual life, common among the educated classes of the United States, and apparently originating in the greed for dollars, which is more prevalent in North America than anywhere else. I refer to the unnatural life which Americans lead, and more especially to its sexual aspect."[185] This was an image seen by physicians of the period as "Jewish" in all its dimensions. Jews manifest an "abnormally intensified sensuality and sexual excitement that lead to sexual errors that are of etiological significance."[186] Jewish scientists, when they addressed this question directly, looked for a developmental rather than a hereditary reason for this evidently higher rate of hysteria. They sought out the "two-thousand-year Diaspora" as the origin of trauma.[187]

But this did not free them. Given the views of Brown-Séquard there was really little escape no matter what the cause. As Ernst Lissauer observed in 1912:

> The Jews are in an intermediary stage. The emancipation of the Jews is but a hundred years hence, it began only a hundred years ago and is not yet completed. These hundred years are but a very short span of time. Our poorly educated sense of history often allows Jews and non-Jews to forget that the Jews were in the Diaspora for 1,700 years, under extraordinary pressure and need, and that the effects of such an extended time cannot be eradicated in a century. When we tabulate these figures, the "Jewish Question" acquires quite a different image. One can thus see that the Jews still possess many of the characteristics that come from the ghetto and that awake the hate of the non-Jew, but also that on the other hand many of these characteristics have been lost, as assimilation has been relatively successful.[188]

Even when a model of environmental adaptation was present, as it was in the work of most Jewish scientists at the turn of the century, the assumption was that it was gradual change, at best, that would free the Jews from their diseased, ghetto nature. The Jewish male became the hysteric and hysteria was measured by the sexual abnormality of the Jew. Thus Freud's search for the psychopathological origin of hysteria in the sexual life of the individual had already been undertaken in the medical literature of the day—but only when that individual was a Jew. The conventional reading of madness thus became a search for the etiology of the illness, and race was considered a substantial factor. What would happen when a Jewish male psychotherapist was confronted with a case study of a severely mentally ill patient that revealed that central to the male patient's delusional system was the anxiety of becoming a Jew, being marked by a sign of an immutable insanity?

READING INSANITY: MALE HOMOSEXUALITY AND THE RHETORIC OF RACE

There is a tradition in European medicine that makes the study of the autobiographical accounts of the mentally ill a part of the undertaking of science. Sigmund Freud found this in a number of the earlier studies he cited on the nature of madness. The Belgian reformer Joseph Guislain explored the meaning attached to the discourse of the mentally ill. Indeed, he provided a three-page transcript of his exchange with an individual suffering from paranoia.[189] A. Krauss in Tübingen published a long three-part essay on the "meaning in madness" in which the dreams of his patients were closely described and analyzed in order to provide some insight into the structure of their insanity.[190] Even the arch-materialist Wilhelm Griesinger stated in the middle of the nineteenth century that what seemed to be the ravings of the mentally ill appeared to have covert meanings, much like the meanings hidden in dreams.[191]

Beginning with the Enlightenment, there had been a subterranean tradition of collecting, publishing, and analyzing the reports of the mentally ill about their illnesses. Karl Phillip Moritz, an educator and psychologist, recorded them in his late-eighteenth-century journal of "experiential psychology."[192] Book-length accounts also existed. The autobiographical record of an individual suffering from idiopathic epilepsy documented the psychological (and, one might add, cultural) contexts of his illness in the 1790s.[193] One of J.E.D. Esquirol's patients, Alexis Berbiguier, published what may well be the most extensive autobiographical account of a psychosis ever made available to the reading public.[194] The firsthand account of a toxic confusional state was the basis for scholarly investigation early in the nineteenth century.[195] At midcentury the deservedly famous autobiographical account by John Perceval in Great Britain recorded the complexities of the paranoid systems of an individual claiming he had been unjustly incarcerated in asylums.[196] All these texts were available to both lay and medical readers and provided evidence that the mentally ill could represent their mental illnesses in published form.[197] The experience of mental illness could thus be shared vicariously by the reading public. These accounts also permitted professionals who dealt with mental illness to illustrate their ability to confront the essence of the disease in a direct manner. Unlike the case study, which was the physician's representation of the patient, the patient's own words would ostensibly provide an unambiguous key to the meaning of mental illness.

The publication of texts by the mentally ill became an adjunct to the evolving specialty of psychiatry. In the mid-nineteenth century Friedrich Engelken and Dietrich Georg Kieser, a professor of medicine at Jena, each recorded and analyzed autobiographical accounts by the mentally ill.[198] By the end of the nineteenth century such accounts began to appear with great frequency. In 1880 the Russian physician Victor Kandinsky printed a firsthand account of a hallucinatory episode.[199] From the psychiatric clinic in Warsaw, Karl Rychlinski presented a case of hallucinatory psychosis.[200] One of the most widely read and discussed of such documents was the autobiography of a case of mania of the distinguished retired professor of psychiatry in Zurich, Auguste Forel, in 1901.[201] By 1906 such texts could even be found in the German literary periodicals of the day.[202] These texts revealed the use of contemporary problems, settings, conflicts, political rhetoric, or religious sensitivities within the otherwise seemingly closed world of writing by the mentally ill. And all of them provided interpretations that translated this experience into a clinical setting.

The explication of texts by the mentally ill provided a set of linguistic signs of "madness" for the neurologist or alienist that were equivalent to the symptoms of somatic diseases. The fragmented sentence, the inchoate narrative, the complex neologism, all came to hold meaning as signs of psychic disruption. But the meaning the psychiatrist found in these signs was usually limited to the overt disruption of "normal" communicative language. Thus Emil Kraepelin, in his diagnostic category "word salad," saw the disruption of language as a clinical sign.[203] This was a pure phenomenological sign. What does one do when confronted with "narrative texts" that are so disrupted, so "crazy," that they represent "madness" in and of themselves? No reading, no interpretation is necessary; the very bizarreness of the text is as sure a sign of madness as were the pathognomonic signs of endemic goiter during the first half of the nineteenth century.[204] Griesinger's midcentury comment on the meaning implicit in texts by the mentally ill was understood as a purely phenomenological sign. Sigmund Freud, too, in *Studies on Hysteria*, saw the inability of the hysteric to narrate her past life as a significant sign of pathology. The inability to narrate one's life came to signify the presence of a disease process, hysteria.

If a physician as an interpreter of signs is to move beyond the phenomenological, then the complex implications of why those specific signs are selected, and what they mean within the general culture as well as within the personal vocabulary of the patient, must be taken into consideration. The thicker and more complex the text, the more evolved the interpreter must be in sorting out these implications. One of the central questions prior to any attempt to read texts by those who are severely mentally ill concerns what the contemporary associations are between the power of the organizing metaphor of a paranoid system and the contemporary culture in which both the patient and the physician live. Fin de siècle physicians such as Max Nordau recognized clearly the association between paranoid systems and the patient's contemporary context:

> It is a phenomenon observed in every kind of mania, that it receives its special coloring from the degree of culture of the invalid, and from the views prevailing at the times in which he lived. The Catholic who is prey to megalomania fancies he is the Pope; the Jew, that he is the Messiah; the German, that he is the Emperor or a field-marshal; the Frenchman, that he is the President of the Republic. In the persecution-mania, the invalid of former days complained of the wickedness and knavery of magicians and witches; today he grumbles because his imaginary enemies send electric streams through his nerves, and torment him with magnetism."[205]

Thus in the first detailed account of an "influencing machine," published in John Haslam's 1810 *Illustrations of Madness*, the "bomb-bursting, lobster-cracking, and lengthening the brain" machine portrayed by the physician reflected the general association between "machinery" in late-eighteenth-century Britain and the place where power can be located outside oneself.[206] The organizing metaphors for paranoia are seen to shift from culture to culture and age to age. The physician of the late nineteenth century understood that these metaphors were not merely window dressing for the paranoid. They focused the delusional structure, altering its form and intensity across time and in different cultural contexts. The articulation of paranoia was thought to shape the paranoid just as surely as the paranoid shaped the language of paranoia. Understanding the roots of the patient's metaphoric system was part of analyzing the system itself. If this was not done, only a partial view of the "invalid" could be given.

In examining these texts and their interpreters, it is vital to gauge the response of the physician to the power of these central, organizing metaphors. One of the keys to an understanding—not of texts by the mentally ill, but of the response of the scientific reader—is to probe the underlying resistance to the power of such images. Psychoanalysts began at the turn of the century to examine texts by severely disturbed patients as a test of their ability to read the languages of the patients for clues to the universal implications of these organizing metaphors. Freud's reading of his patients' dreams as complex, confusing texts was undertaken to throw light on the underlying processes, such as the Oedipus complex, that revealed themselves through his interpretation. The hermeneutic claim was the motivation for the title *The Interpretation of Dreams*. This movement, the attempt to analyze the bizarre form and content of a language produced to confuse and baffle, was also the project of other Jewish thinkers of the time, notably Karl Kraus in Vienna and Fritz Mauthner in Berlin.[207] In psychoanalysis it was the analysis of the products of those patients suffering from "dementia praecox" or, following Eugen Bleuler's coinage of the term in 1911, "schizophrenia," that were the basis of an attempt to make sense of the senseless.[208] Even more than the text of the hysteric, which seemed to have some superficial organization, the paranoid text would prove the existence of universal patterns of development and perception.

The notion was that the text of the paranoid came from a deeper, more atavistic level, and thus revealed its origin even more clearly. Indeed, Viktor Tausk, following Freud's reading of the meaning of paranoia (but evoking the views of his contemporary Otto Pötzl), saw the "regression in schizophrenia . . . [as] traceable to those 'engrams' of the oldest era of the race, and the theory would demand that these phylogenetic traces of function retain their capacity for being reactivated."[209] (The newly devised concept of schizophrenia, under the influence of Eugen Bleuler, came to unify aspects of the diagnosis of paranoia and general psychosis at the beginning of the twentieth century.) The schizophrenic's language and psyche reflect "the history of the species." By early 1908, Freud saw paranoia as providing the key to an "understanding of all neurosis."[210] He wrote Ferenczi in the spring of 1909, "we . . . must collect and learn" from the paranoid.[211] Paranoia became a key to understanding mental illness in general, but even more important, it became a key to understanding universal mental processes.

The root metaphors of paranoid systems in fin de siècle Germany and Austria were even less a neutral object of study for the Jewish physicians of the time. As with all such systems, they focused intensely on the perceived source of power and danger. These systems were often cast in the language of German anti-Semitism and centered on a perceived danger from an international Jewish conspiracy.[212] Paranoia and anti-Semitism were closely linked at the turn of the century. Given the sexualized and feminized definition of the male Jew in the science and popular culture of the day, it is not surprising that these images of the dangerousness of the Jew are projected by Freud onto another image of the dangerous, diseased, sexualized male—the homosexual.[213]

Homosexuality was, for Freud, a fixation at an earlier stage of sexual development. The developmental pattern Freud established presented fixed and successive stages of development. The newborn passes through a series of stages, the center of pleasure moving from the mouth to the anus, and finally to the genitals.[214] Each stage of development is also paralleled by a difference in the love object. Initially it is the self, then the mother, then the father, and finally someone of the opposite sex. Homosexuality is therefore a universal experience through which all individuals pass in order fully to mature. All human beings maintain a residue of homosexual desire. Homosexuals are those, however, who remain fixated at an earlier stage of development. Homosexuality was in no way to be seen as an illness, as it was understood by many of Freud's contemporaries, but its presence can be (although it does not have to be) the precipitating factor in an illness.[215]

Freud's views concerning the meaning of homosexuality altered over time. He came to understand that the homosexual could be completely "healthy" in his or her sexual orientation. He wrote in 1920 about "a case of homosexuality in a woman" that "the girl was not in any way ill . . . she did not suffer from anything in herself, nor did she complain of her condition." Indeed, it is clearly the parents in this case who were fixated on their daughter's sexual orientation. From the case of Dora to this case, there was a major shift in attitude. Attitudes toward male homosexuality likewise changed. From the beginning of the century, when the origins of psychopathology and homosexuality were linked, Freud came (in a letter written in English in 1935) to see homosexuality as having "no advantage, but it is nothing to be ashamed of, no vice, no degradation, it cannot be classified as an illness; we consider it a variation of sexual function."[216] The push to understand the homosexual as different but not ill may well stem from the analogy between homosexuality and Jewish identity in the medical model of Freud's time.

In Freud's view, at least at the beginning of the century, paranoia was the result of an unresolved homosexual conflict. It was this unresolvable fixation on the same-sex individual that provided the basis for the paranoid break. The fixation could not be acted on because of the self-censuring nature of the psyche, which would not let socially unacceptable thoughts be articulated in the conscious mind. Freud's position was an answer to Richard von Krafft-Ebing's view that male homosexuality was a congenital predisposition that had to be triggered by some trauma to produce the "true" homosexual.[217] Krafft-Ebing's view of Jewishness is analogous to this. The psychological collapse attendant to Jews being exposed to the trauma of "modern life" reveals their innate Jewishness, their innate flaw.

The general assumption of sexologists such as Krafft-Ebing was that the Jews, too, were fixated at an earlier stage of sexual development. This ancient topos harks back to Tacitus's description of the Jews as the "projectissima ad libidinem gens"—the most sensual of peoples. By the close of the nineteenth century it had become part of the new medical literature in Germany, which described the nature of the Jew thus in one of the standard forensic studies of the time, one Freud read and used: "Further it must be noted that the sexuality of the Semitic race is in general powerful, yes, often greatly exaggerated."[218] Or, as John S. Billings, the leading American student of Jewish illness and the head of the Surgeon General's Library in Washington, noted, when Jewish males are integrated into Western culture they "are probably more addicted to . . . sexual excesses than their ancestors were."[219] The Viennese-Jewish literary scholar Otto Rank, soon after discovering psychoanalysis in 1905, wrote of the "stress on primitive sexuality" as the "essence of Judaism."[220] These are signs of reversion to earlier stages of the history of sexual development. "Civilization" had moved from the most primitively organized system of sexual activity through the stage of Judaism to its height—modern Christianity.[221] This was Krafft-Ebing's summary of the sexual history of the human race. Freud extrapolated from this phylogeny of human sexuality the ontogeny of individual human sexual development. Homosexuals were not degenerate in Freud's view, but they were atavistic. And this developmental atavism was shown to be hidden in the paranoid's text.[222]

On December 9, 1908, the Viennese Psychoanalytic Society discussed a series of case presentations, beginning with Fritz Wittels's account of a Jewish patient who suffered from the paranoid delusion that he was being persecuted by anti-Semites because of the shape of his nose.[223] As a parallel example, Freud introduced into the discussion a case presentation by the New York–based psychoanalyst A. A. Brill. Brill, who was interested in the question of the racial predisposition of certain Jews to specific forms of mental illness, came to this question through his examination of the "disease" of anti-Semitism. Brill presented the case of a homosexual patient, I.S., whom he treated for paranoia. Brill's case material had come from his time at the psychiatric hospital of the University of Zurich, the Burghölzli, working with the Freudian psychiatrist Eugen Bleuler. Freud praised the essay (which appeared in a journal edited by his supporter Morton Prince) and he summarized it in great detail.[224]

For Freud the central feature of the case was the Oedipus complex, which was articulated by the presence of an anti-Semitic father and the "conversion" of the psychotic son from a philo-Semite to an anti-Semite. Through this act he acknowledged the power of his father over him. I.S.'s father became God for him, and through his delusional system, he returned to God the father. He converted to anti-Semitism, the belief of his father, rather than to Christianity. The gods of the anti-Semite's delusional system were taken from ancient Egypt, the land that enslaved the Jews. Freud stressed the roles the Egyptian gods Isis and Osiris played in structuring the patient's "mystic fantasies." But he also showed that they had further, complex associations. The name Osiris was identical with that of a rich Zurich banker who had recently died, and the patient had the fantasy of inheriting his millions. Linked with the name of Osiris, the father is also Isis, the mother. Freud stressed the hidden aspect of the feminine both in the paranoid system and in the patient's sense of self.

The patient's sexual confusion is reflected in his fixation on a sentence from a letter sent by his beloved in Pittsburgh, Pennsylvania. It was this beloved whom his father forbade him to marry and who emigrated to the United States where she married someone else. Freud stressed the patient's unspoken question: "Is she true to me?" and saw the patient's homoerotic fantasies as a reversal of this desire ("Is she true to me?" "Can I be true to her?"). What the patient experienced was a reversal not only of the question but also of the sex of the love object.

It is evident that Freud's reading of Brill's case marginalized the question of the patient's anti-Semitism, quickly seeing in it only a manifestation of the Oedipus complex. Freud's presentation of this case to the Viennese Psychoanalytic Society came during his treatment of the Rat Man, which, according to the case notes, had anti-Semitic overtones.[225] The Rat Man would have given Freud a clearly defined project in which to work out his reading of the meaning of anti-Semitism in the establishment of complex behavior systems. Freud's published presentation of the case in October and November 1907 did not mention this aspect at all.[226] When we turn to Brill's actual presentation, it is clear that Freud's selective reading of the case, his desire to foreground all the cultural aspects of I.S.'s paranoid system except his anti-Semitism, presents a problem in Freud's mode of interpretation.

Brill's paper, which relies on a Zurich-based reading of Freud that used word-association tests and their response times as the basis for analysis, is a remarkable document for the care given to recording the utterances of a psychotic and interpreting them. But it also explores in detail the function of the rhetoric of anti-Semitism in articulating the paranoid delusions of a patient. Brill noted that "until recently we were quite satisfied to note that the patient is delusional and demented, utters senseless phrases, and goes through a number of peculiar actions, etc. Thanks to Freud we know that all our actions and speech, both normal and abnormal, are psychically determined."[227] Brill gave meaning to the meaningless but he also tried to interpret the meaningful, specifically the role anti-Semitism played in structuring the paranoid delusion. Following Freud's lead in his earlier, published work, Brill saw this rhetoric as a veneer that revealed the homosexual cathexis in the case.

Homosexuality and anti-Semitism both became aspects of the disease process. According to Brill, I.S., a thirty-nine-year-old single bank official, had been transferred to the Burghölzli on November 16, 1907, from an asylum in Bohemia, where he had been hospitalized for four months. He was confused and hallucinatory but improved enough to give "a fluent account of his *vita anteacta*, and only now and then was it necessary to question him." The patient, I.S., recounted the tale of his father who objected to his marrying a widow, "in whose house I lived more than seven years. He strongly objected, and threatened to disown me should I disobey him. He also upbraided me for my mode of living. He is very religious and anti-Semitic, while I was an agnostic and worked among Jews for eighteen years."[228] Beginning in February 1907 he became "very nervous":

> I was alone in my room, when I began to feel a strange power influencing me. I felt ecstatic, but I knew there was something peculiar in me. It was like an electric magnetic power or ether. It suddenly forced me down on the floor on my left knee, my hands were pressed together in an attitude of prayer, and with great force I cried out: "Lord, have mercy on suffering humanity." I spoke with a stentorian voice like a preacher. I repeated "Our Father" hundreds of times. I felt an influence of the Egyptian gods Isis and Osiris. I was also forced to repeat numerous times, "Am I Parsifal, the guileless fool?" ("Parsifal reinster Thor"). This state continued for seventy-two hours, during which I had not slept at all. I also imagined that I was very wealthy. The whole thing was like a colossal suggestive influence, and the Jews played some part in it.[229]

Brill continued to recount the delusional structure of I.S. in his own words. I.S. wrote "a letter to my firm with whom I had been for eighteen years, telling them that my present views did not permit me to work for a Jewish firm."[230] He found new employment in Munich but "when I arrived there I found that the head of the firm was a Jew, so I refused it." In a series of word-association tests I.S. associated "Jews" with the *Deutsches Volksblatt* (a conservative, anti-Semitic paper) and with the word "rich." He further associated "Isis" and "Osiris" with the dead banker Osiris. Brill provided a detailed reading of the sexual implications of the delusional structure, stressing the potential homoerotic attraction of I.S. to the son of his landlady, and its roots in the repression of his feelings for his first love, who emigrated to Pennsylvania.

Brill emphasized the patient's rejection of the values of his father, in that I.S. became "an atheist and worked among Jews for eighteen years. He no longer attended church, but studied Nietzsche, Stirner, and others." By 1900 Friedrich Nietzsche had become the representative of the cultural avant-garde. Nietzsche had read (and used) much of the work of the iconoclastic thinker "Max Stirner" (Johann Kaspar Schmidt), whose anti-Semitic study *The Individual and His Possessions* (1845) had been rediscovered at the turn of the century by Nietzsche and the highly influential philosopher Eduard von Hartmann. Nietzsche's own ambiguous image of the Jews meant that he could be (and was) used by anti-Semites and as philo-Semites during the same period.[231] For Brill the reading of Nietzsche and Stirner was a simple rejection of the father who had prohibited the earlier marriage. In fact, it could well have been read as an attempt to maintain the continuity of anti-Semitic rhetoric even after the patient's initial break with his father. As Brill also noted, that I.S. "did not entirely rid himself of his early religious training, but only repressed it, is shown by the fact that he kept on subscribing for an anti-Semitic journal, and during the Dreyfus affair he was the only anti-Dreyfusard in his office. He could not be convinced that Dreyfus was not guilty (symbolic actions)."[232] But Brill was stymied by his inability to understand the role the Jews played in this delusional system: " 'The Jews played some part in it' is all we can get from the patient. He insists that he never had any differences with Jews. What part they played in his attack cannot be explained, but it may simply be a forcible reassertion of his father's doctrines."[233]

Brill's reading of the Jewish aspect of this case and Freud's reading of Brill provide a context for the complex reading of paranoia as a disease in which homosexuality and the Jews are linked. Brill was a Jew from the eastern reaches of the Austro-Hungarian Empire who was born in 1874 and emigrated to the United States at the age of fifteen.[234] Educated at New York University and the College of Physicians and Surgeons at Columbia University, Brill undertook postgraduate studies in psychiatry, first in 1907 with Pierre Janet at the Bicêtre in Paris and then with Eugen Bleuler and C. G. Jung at the Burghölzli in Zurich. He then returned to New York where he had a central position in presenting Freud's views to the American scientific and popular communities through his lectures and translations. Brill was very aware of the issue of Jewish identity and its implications in the society of his day.[235] He was also clearly marked as a Jew, both in Vienna and in the United States, by his Yiddish accent (*Mauscheln*). In 1939, the Kansas psychiatrist Karl A. Menninger recounted his own Mid-western, Christian discomfort at hearing the editor of the *New York Times*, Arthur Sulzberger, tell "a story involving the imitation of the Jewish accent of Dr. Brill which I thought was in very bad taste. As a matter of fact, it was the second time he had told it in my presence, and he admitted that he had told it in his office when he made a speech to the employees a few days ago. He is such a cultivated, dignified fellow that it is amazing to hear him come out with this ridicule of the accent of other Jews."[236] Brill's discomfort in confronting the meaning of the anti-Semitic discourse of I.S. shows his own inability to see in the rhetoric references not only to the Jews as an abstraction, but to himself as an individual marked for I.S. by his accent as a Jew.

Brill's *Mauscheln* was a sign that had been made the stigma of pathology. Brill, in his work on the predisposition of the Jews to certain forms of mental illness, could have understood that he, too, would be seen as at risk. Jewishness for Brill, too, was not a religious but a racial matter, as he wrote of Freud in 1940: "I feel that Freud's Jewish descent—constitution—and his later experiences—environment—played a great part in the molding of his character, and in directing his future interests."[237] The notion of the "common mental construction" of the Jew shaped Brill's world.[238] This sense of Jewish racial identity played a major role in Brill's inability to read fully the meaning of his patient's system. The mere presence of a visibly Jewish physician would have shaped the paranoid delusions of the institutionalized patient. Brill was not a neutral observer, giving word-association tests to his patient. He was a Jewish psychiatrist with all the attendant associations of danger and risk.[239]

Sigmund Freud universalized the image of I.S.'s father into any father's power to control his son's sexuality. The image of the Jews in I.S.'s paranoid system were removed to the periphery. In I.S.'s delusional system charges were lodged against the Jews that they were at the center of a conspiracy sexually to exploit the world about them for their own power and gain. The perceived control over the sexuality of the son was projected onto the age-old myth of Jewish world domination. Freud did not see this as central to a reading of the case. His reading of Brill's case foreshadowed a much more complex and difficult reading of a published text representing the paranoid system of a contemporary, the "most important document in psychiatry bar none," according to the Nobel Prize–winning author and memoirist of the fin de siècle Viennese scene, Elias Canetti.[240]

In the spring of 1910, C. G. Jung suggested that Freud read the autobiography of Daniel Paul Schreber, which had appeared in a limited edition in 1903. Jung had earlier used this material in *The Psychology of Dementia Praecox* (1907).[241] Daniel Paul Schreber was born in 1842, the son of Daniel Gottlob Moritz Schreber, an orthopedist and health reformer. His brother Gustav, three years his senior, committed suicide at the age of thirty-eight in 1877. Schreber married in 1878. He and his wife had no children. He was a successful civil servant in Saxony, eventually rising to the rank of chief judge of a provincial court in Chemnitz. In October 1884, he was defeated for election to the Reichstag by a Social Democrat, Bruno Geiser. Geiser was one of twelve Social Democrats elected even though the "anti-Socialist law" was still in effect. Schreber ran as the coalition candidate of the Conservative and the National Liberal parties espousing Bismarck's platform. Following his electoral defeat, he had the first of a series of psychotic episodes. In November 1884, he consulted with Paul Emil Flechsig, the chair of the Department of Psychiatry at Leipzig. From December 8, 1884, to May 31, 1885, he was in the Leipzig clinic, where he made two suicide attempts. He was released as cured in June 1885 and was immediately reappointed to the bench. From June 1885 to November 1893 he served as a judge in two regional courts and was eventually promoted to presiding judge of the court of appeals at Dresden. On November 9, 1893, at his mother's home in Leipzig, he again attempted suicide. From November 21, 1893, to December 20, 1902, he was in the university clinic in Leipzig, the Lindenhof sanatorium, and then Sonnenstein sanatorium, where he wrote his *Memoirs of a Neuropath* between February and September 1900. They were published in edited form in 1903. He died in the hospital at the age of sixty-eight on April 14, 1911, having spent fourteen years in mental institutions.

Schreber's *Memoirs of a Neuropath* was the most recent of the extensive series of primary texts by the mentally ill that had appeared in German during the late nineteenth and early twentieth centuries.[242] Freud read Schreber's account in the midst of his confrontation with Alfred Adler, which evoked his own homoerotic identification with Fliess. He wrote to Jung at the end of December 1910 that the reason the difficulty with Adler "upsets me so much is that it has opened up the wounds of the Fliess affair."[243] Freud wrote to Jung, informing him that "my Schreber is finished" and that he was unable to "judge its objective worth as was possible with earlier papers, because in working on it I have had to fight off complexes within myself (Fliess)."[244] Freud's work on Schreber, with its theme of repressed homoeroticism, evoked the image of his old friend Fliess, but it was also immediately linked in Freud's response to his conflict with Adler. Both Adler and Fliess were Jews and Freud, as noted above, was afraid that psychoanalysis was being seen as primarily a Jewish undertaking. Freud actively sought Jung as Adler's replacement as his primary disciple. The text by which Jung was fascinated, and which he suggested that Freud read, was one structured by the central metaphor of the dangerousness of the Jews. It reflected a wide range of the anti-Semitic images of the Jewish body that haunted the scientific and popular culture of Freud's day. The association of Jung and the anti-Semitic text provided a context in which Freud could consciously move away from the Jewishness and homoeroticism associated with Fliess and Adler.

Freud took the volume with him on his trip to Sicily that September and wrote his interpretation of the Schreber case during the fall and winter of 1910. He had just finished writing his analysis of Leonardo on creativity and homosexuality, in which he had explored the relationship between repressed homosexual desire and creativity. The Schreber text seemed to fit safely under this rubric. But unlike the sources for his reading of Leonardo, Schreber's text reflected the ugly rhetoric of his own day.[245] Daniel Paul Schreber was afraid he was turning into an effeminate Jew, a true composite of Weininger's images of the Jew and the woman. Schreber's basic system employed the rhetoric of the diseased Jew. Freud did not, could not, read this aspect of the text. His interpretation of Schreber was Freud's own attempt, as in his reading of Wilhelm Jensen's *Grad-*

iva, to present his own "creative" response to a text. And yet it was clear that Freud's identification with Schreber drew this clear separation between the psychoanalyst and the psychotic as writer into question. For example, in a letter written to Karl Abraham in the fall of 1910, he indicated that he wanted to get in touch with the other major non-Jewish advocate of psychoanalysis in Swiss psychiatry, Jung's professor, Eugen Bleuler. Freud noted that he wanted to get in "touch with him ('to make nerve contact with him')." It was to Schreber that he turned for the correct phrase.[246]

Freud's stated role was as a reader, and a creative one at that. Yet this reading was carefully placed within the older medical tradition of the psychiatrist dissecting the writing of the patient, looking for the etiology of the patient's disease. He was aware of the pitfalls of this role. The psychoanalyst, he noted, needs "tact and restraint whenever in the course of his work he goes beyond the standard lines of interpretation."[247] It is here that the risk is greatest. He must "guard against the risk that an increased display of acumen on his part may be accompanied by a diminution in the certainty and trustworthiness of his results."[248] That is, like the Jew, the smarter he seems to be, the more "creative" he is, the less validity and value his work will have. Freud's reading would, therefore, be very scientific, very conservative. It would be selective with a purpose.

The interpretation of the case of Schreber is presented with even greater complexity because of the nature of the text itself. The autobiography had been censored by physicians who removed material as "unsuitable and offensive": "Surely the last qualities we have a right to demand from a case history which sets out to give a picture of deranged humanity and of its struggles to rehabilitate itself are 'discretion' and 'aesthetic' charm."[249] But these are precisely the criteria that have not been applied to the autobiographical texts by the mentally ill of the period. On the contrary, as one can see in Brill's case study (which was not based on a written text) and numerous other analyses of texts by the mentally ill, it is the highly complex question of the meaning of the inner world of mental illness and the means of expressing this inner reality that these texts are supposed to reveal. When we examine Freud's reading of the Schreber autobiography, we do find a second level of "censorship," one that aims at "discretion." Brill's paper, even though it stopped before asking the final question about what the Jew in I.S.'s system truly meant, could be the stuff of discussion before the "Jewish" audience of the Viennese Psychoanalytic Society. When Freud turned to the greater public in his role as a scientist, even Brill's degree of confrontation of the rhetoric of anti-Semitism was lacking. The publication of Freud's "scientific" reading of the Schreber case avoided any reference to the anti-Semitic rhetoric, such as the leitmotif of the Wandering Jew, which seems, at least on a first reading, to be a powerful subtext in the autobiography of Daniel Paul Schreber.

Freud's reading of Schreber was based on Griesinger's dictum that a psychotic's delusions are "readable" as are dreams, a view espoused as early as *The Interpretation of Dreams*.[250] Freud's undertaking as the critic was to translate Schreber's system of psychotic representations in order to make it comprehensible to the reader, who would then understand the "meaning" of Schreber's disease. As in the case of Brill's patient, in which Brill was unable to "understand" the full meaning of I.S.'s anti-Semitism, Freud ignored the choice of the contemporary coloration of the psychotic's system. Rather, Freud concentrated on the persecution complex in which Schreber's physician, Paul Flechsig, was understood as God.[251] Freud thus revealed the universal, Oedipal tensions on which Schreber's system seemed to rest. It was the "appearance in Schreber of a feminine (that is, passive homosexual) wish-fantasy, which took as its object the figure of his doctor."[252] Schreber's own rhetoric here evoked the image of the "eternal Jew" who had to be "unmanned (transformed into a woman) to be able to bear children."[253] The conflation of castration with circumcision was a standard topos of the anti-Semitic literature of the period. Freud read over this, seeing only the affective component in the transference of Schreber's love and fear from one who was important to him (his father or his brother) to one who was indifferent or neutral, his physician, Flechsig.

Thus the Schreber case, a case of paranoia for Freud, became "the conflict [that arises because of] a homosexual wish-fantasy of *loving a man*."[254] This very thought is unacceptable to the individual because of the social stigma attached to it. The paranoid, in order to make this desire acceptable to himself, reverses it. It is not that I love a man, but that he loves me, that lies at the center of the delusional system. Indeed, this form of projection leads to a further reversal: as I do not reciprocate his love, he hates me and persecutes me. The generation of a delusional system is predicated on a context that would trigger the repressed desire. Homosexuals are not inherently ill, according to this view, but they "have not freed themselves completely from the stage of narcissism"; they have a "disposition to illness [that] must be located in that region."[255] The older language about disposition lurked within the definition of homosexuality for Freud. The illness Schreber evidenced was, for Freud, a regression to an earlier stage of development, to the stage of infants' fascination with their own bodies. Homosexuals have become fixated at this point in human development and seek out those individuals whose genitalia mirror their own. This desire for the self can be very specific or can be generalized into a love for "man"kind.

According to Freud, Schreber's illness was manifested in his fear of or desire for castration and degradation:

> For we learn that the idea of being transformed into a woman (that is, of being emasculated) was the primary delusion, that he began by regarding that act as constituting a serious injury and persecution, and that it only became related to his playing the part of the Redeemer in a secondary way. There can be no doubt, moreover, that originally he believed that the transformation was to be effected for the purpose of sexual abuse and not so as to serve higher designs. The position may be formulated by saying that a sexual delusion of persecution was later on converted in the patient's mind into a religious delusion of grandeur. The part of the persecutor was at first assigned to Professor Flechsig, the physician in whose charge he was; later, his place was taken by God Himself.[256]

For Freud, the religious coloration of Schreber's system was a subsequent rather than a primary aspect of its construction. Schreber's own anxiety in being simultaneously transformed into a woman and a Jew was ignored. The God of Wrath replaced Flechsig and thus became an acceptable focal point for the delusional system. Here one can see the parallel to Brill's reading of the case of I.S., where the "conversion" of the son turns a philo-Semite into an anti-Semite because of the power of the "Father." The castrated male becomes the Redeemer, the source of "a new race of men, born from the spirit of Schreber."[257]

The evocation of castration and its association in Freud's works with circumcision provides a context for Freud's inability to read aspects of Schreber's text. Much has been made in the critical work on Schreber (especially by William Niederland, Morton Schatzman, and Jeffrey Masson) of the discovery that Flechsig (among others) had proposed and used castration to treat hysteria, and of Freud's potential knowledge of this.[258] Whether or not Schreber knew of this procedure—that is, whether or not this was a fearful reality that translated itself into an aspect of Schreber's paranoid system or whether castration was an inherent aspect of this system because of its association with the Oedipus complex (as Freud suspected)—is not central to my argument here. What is clear is that castration was understood at the time as an alteration of the body that made it different, and more feminine in that it also made it more "Jewish." Freud, in his study of puberty (1905), responded to this view and stressed the intact nature of the personality even when castration (in men or women) occurred. Anatomy is not character (any more than is ethnic identity), "for the sex-glands do not constitute sexuality, and the observations on castrated males merely confirm what had been shown long before by removal of the ovaries—namely that it is impossible to obliterate the sexual characteristics by removing the sex-glands."[259] But Freud's source, Conrad Rieger's monograph on the social rather than the biological results of castration, labels Freud's own views on the role of sexuality in the etiology of neurosis as merely "the gossip of old women" (*Altweiber-Geschwätz*).[260] Freud, the circumcised/castrated Jew, becomes a woman in this reading of the social meaning of castration. The exclusion of the parallel between the female and the Jew from Freud's reading of the Schreber case provides an insight into Freud's defense mechanisms.

The paranoid system structures the world so that this central act of love and hate is placed in a controllable structure. For Schreber what was dangerous, what was fearful, but also what was attractive, what was seductive, became linked to the Jews. This belief was prevalent in late-nineteenth-century European thought, not only in the asylums, but on the floors of the legislatures in Vienna and Berlin, on the front pages of newspapers and magazines, throughout the political and intellectual culture of Central Europe. But for Freud, this action reflected the world of the "primitive," not of Central Europe. Schreber was "the savage . . . primitive man, as he stands revealed to us in the light of researches of archeology and of ethnology."[261] This is the last line in Freud's postscript of 1912. In this rereading of his own interpretation, Schreber is the parallel to the history of the Jews in *Totem and Taboo* and in *Moses and Monotheism* and their primitive acts and barbaric customs, such as circumcision, as the object of Western study.[262] For Freud the connection between obsessional neurosis and religious practices was clear. Schreber's text provided the matrix for understanding "a psychoanalytic explanation of the origins of religion."[263] The delusional system of the paranoid is equivalent to the organized system of theology.[264] For Freud this association evoked the past or the distant in specific ways; it did not evoke the present and the near.

Schreber's memoirs reflect many of the preoccupations of his own day. They are filled with the overt fear of emasculation and devirilization, expressed through the fear of becoming a Jew. In Schreber's system, as in the system of I.S., the Jew plays a special and specific role. The Jew is the agent of evil. Given the rhetoric of the period this would seem a natural source for a powerful image that would contain and limit fear, would place it in a specific and focused place on the social horizon. To become a Jew would be to be transformed physically into something quite different from oneself. It would be to have one's body altered and reshaped, as in the German physician-author Oskar Panizza's 1893 tale, "The Operated Jew," and its discourse about the remaking of the body of the Jew. It depicts the careful cosmetic reconstruction of the Jew Itzig Faitel Stern (one of the classic anti-Semitic literary characters of the mid-nineteenth century) into an "Aryan."[265] But this attempt to reconstruct the Jew fails (as it must) and at the close of the tale the Jew is no different than he was at the beginning in spite of the interventions of surgeons and orthopedists.

Let us turn for a moment to Daniel Paul Schreber's own account of what he intended to do in writing his *Memoirs of a Neuropath*: "My aim is solely to further knowledge of truth in a vital field, that of religion."[266] Freud's reading is quite correct, but it is not the religion of the primitive, but of the Aryan, that he is about to unravel. Schreber's goal is to inform his "wife [of] my personal experiences and religious ideas. This explains also why I have frequently thought it right to give circuitous explanations for facts already known, to translate foreign words, etc., which would really have been unnecessary for the scientifically trained reader."[267] Science is masculine. It possesses a specialized, secret language not available to all. Schreber as the scientist must explain science for the female within and outside himself. This is a text, at least for Schreber, on Aryan "religion," which lays claim to the status of the racial "science" of the turn of the century.

Schreber's paranoid system uses the vocabulary of fin de siècle scientific anti-Semitism as a rhetorical structure to represent his anxiety about his own body. Schreber senses himself being transmuted from a "beautiful," masculine Aryan to an "ugly," feminized Jew. For Schreber, the soul (*Seele*) is a physiological force—it is a reflex of biology, "the human soul is contained in the nerves of the body."[268] This view was basic to the materialist psychiatrists of Schreber's day, especially his own psychiatrist, Paul Flechsig, whose widely republished inaugural lecture at the University of Leipzig was entitled "Brain and Soul."[269] But within Schreber's system the biological reality of the soul reflected the idea of Schreber's fantasy of the living God. The central metaphors in this "religious" system related the body and the divine. He saw his views as neutral statements of the truths of racial science.

The meaning of "science" in Schreber's "religious" system lies in Schreber's claim that the transcendent power of medical science proves the validity of his new religious vision. Schreber buttressed his views of the religious value of the visions he was having with a citation from the psychiatric authority Emil Kraepelin. He attempted to understand and therefore control his illness by gaining "scientific" knowledge about his ailment. To this end, he acquired the standard psychiatric handbook of his day, Kraepelin's textbook, and read it. In his account he quotes from Kraepelin, concerning his aural hallucinations, that the "phenomenon of being in some supernatural communication with voices had frequently been observed before in human beings whose nerves were in a state of morbid excitation."[270] Actually Kraepelin simply reported the association between visual and aural hallucinations. His text (unquoted by Schreber) continued: "God or Christ gives the patient a task, a promise, or explains to him secrets of his own personality. The entire procedure usually has a somewhat dreamlike, extrasensory feeling, while the torturing and persecuting voices possess the qualities of true sensory experiences." Central to the account is Kraepelin's phenomenological orientation. What Schreber sees in Kraepelin's text is a world in which the words of the patient have value as scientific proof that the language of paranoia has status and meaning.

Kraepelin also presents a detailed account of the predisposition of the Jews to specific forms of mental illness. He notes that the "Jews [in Europe] and the blacks of North America . . . are pure races" that can be control cases for the predisposition of various races to mental illness. The Jews are predisposed to "paralysis and dementia praecox" as well as "manic depression and nervousness," which diseases result from "their preference for consanguineous marriages." They are "diseases we associate with inherited degeneration."[271] Freud knew this text, which drew on the work of Max Sichel and his Viennese colleague Alexander Pilcz. As Schreber saw his madness as the result of his "Jewification," so too Freud could have seen Kraepelin's text as the proof-text for the medical rhetoric behind Schreber's association of Jews with madness and syphilis. Was it Schreber or Kraepelin against whom Freud reacted? When Schreber attacked Kraepelin and traditional asylum psychiatry, Freud commented in the margin, "Bravo!"

But if Schreber's delusional system is a biological reading of theology, at its center stands the frightening figure of God. And Schreber's God, who indeed seems interchangeable with his physicians, especially Flechsig, is very much a Teutonic God. He has been transformed from the original Old Testament God of Wrath. This God speaks to souls who are in the process of metamorphosis from one form to another, in the process of feminization, in the "so-called 'basic language,' a somewhat antiquated but nevertheless powerful German, characterized particularly by a wealth of euphemisms (for instance, reward in the reverse sense for punishment, poison for food, juice for venom, unholy for holy, etc. God Himself was called 'concerning Him Who is and shall be'—meaning eternity—and was addressed as 'Your Majesty's obedient servant')."[272] The language of God is a complex, topsy-turvy biblical German. It is a language, like the language of science, that Schreber understands and can explain to his reader (and his wife). This language of the Teutonic God is one that Schreber commands. It is not the language of the Jew's Bible. One of the basic tenets of German anti-Semitism saw the Jews of the Bible, especially of the New Testament, as belonging to a very different category from contemporary Jewry. As early as the German Enlightenment, there had been complicated attempts to separate the discourse of the New Testament from the language of the Jews heard in the streets of Frankfurt and Berlin. Jesus could not really have been a Jew, for he spoke a different language.[273] Schreber went on to argue:

> The above statement that God used the German language in the form of the so-called "basic language," is not to be understood as though the state of Blessedness was reserved only for Germans. Nevertheless the Germans were in modern times (possibly since the Reformation, perhaps ever since the migration of nations) *God's chosen people* whose language God preferred to use. In this sense God's chosen peoples in history—as the most moral at a given time—were in order the old Jews, the old Persians, . . . the "Greco-Romans" . . . and lastly the Germans. God readily *understood* the languages of all nations by contact with their nerves.[274]

At this point Freud's scribbled "Chauvin" in the margin of the text. It was the nationalism of Schreber (without its anti-Semitic overtones) to which he was responding. The true "chosen people" are the Germans; Schreber presents to his reader a chronology that places the Jews and their holy tongue in the distant past.

The language of Schreber's transformation is a "nerve-language" of which "a healthy human being is not aware."[275] As the "nerve-language" becomes less clear to Schreber the voices become an "empty babel of ever recurring monotonous phrases; grammatically incomplete by the omission of words and even syllables."[276] These voices disintegrate into *Mauscheln*. This sounds to Schreber like "abusive and insulting phrases" that contain "Jewish" nonsense: "David and Solomon, salad and radishes."[277] While Schreber describes these voices as "neutral," it is clear that their manifest content reflects a "Jewish" discourse in its use of the Old Testament and at least one food ("radishes") strongly associated with Jews.

Schreber's God is organized into two spheres, the posterior and the anterior. The former is dominated by two gods: The lower god, Ahriman, who "seems to have felt attracted to nations of originally brunette race (the Semites) and the upper God [Ormuzd] to nations of originally blond race (the Aryan peoples)."[278] Ahriman is the evil principle in Zoroastrian theology. It represents all that is evil in the world. Schreber's "unmanning" comes from a conspiracy "between such a person and the elements of the anterior realms of God to the detriment of the Schreber race, perhaps in the direction of denying them offspring or possibly only of denying them choice of those professions which would lead to closer relations with God such as that of a nerve specialist."[279] It is the Jews who conspire with the physicians (the "person engaged in the practice of nervous diseases—having perhaps another profession besides"[280]) who attempt to control and transform Schreber.[281]

The names, at least, of Schreber's gods are taken from Zoroastrianism much as the paranoid system of Brill's patient, I.S., incorporated names from Egyptian mythology. Like those of Brill's patient, the names had specific, contemporary associations. Schreber would have associated the names with the turn-of-the-century Nietzsche cult widely disseminated in newspapers and journals. Schreber's religious rhetoric, especially his pseudo-Zoroastrianism, was highly influenced by a fin de siècle reading of Nietzsche's texts, especially his *Thus Spake Zarathustra*, but also Nietzsche's understanding of texts of the true Aryan religion, the Book of Manu. For Nietzsche the strength of the Old Testament became the smothering "love" of the New Testament. This is clear when, in *The Antichrist[ian]*, he contrasts the primitive law of Manu with the New Testament:

> Ultimately, it is a matter of the end to which one lies. That "holy" ends are lacking in Christianity is my objection to its means. Only bad ends: poisoning, slander, negation of life, contempt for the body, the degradation and self-violation of man through the concept of sin—consequently its means too are bad. It is with an opposite feeling that I read the law of Manu, an incomparably spiritual and superior work: even to mention it in the same breath with the Bible would be a sin against the spirit. One guesses immediately: there is a real philosophy behind it, in it, not merely an ill-smelling Judaine of rabbinism and superstition; it offers even the most spoiled psychologist something to chew on. Not to forget the main point, the basic difference from every kind of bible: here the noble classes, the philosophers and the warriors, stand above the mass; noble values everywhere, a feeling of perfection, an affirmation of life, a triumphant delight in oneself and in life—the sun shines on the whole book. All the things on which Christianity vents its unfathomable meanness—procreation, for example, woman, marriage—are here treated seriously, with respect, with love and trust.[282]

The laws of Manu are positive, strengthening the nature of the human being in the world; the New Testament (the world of the Jews in Nietzsche's reading) is destructive of life. For Nietzsche the New Testament enacts the ultimate success of the weakness of the modern Jews (the Christians) over the powerful world of Old Testament Jewry. But all these images are mediated by the idea of the female and the image of the sexual. The incest taboo, violated by the Jews, becomes the hidden context for the glorification of the East, the truth of the "real" Orient, the fantasy East to be found in the world of words of Arthur Schopenhauer, a world of "India," without the "crudity" of Judaism.[283] Thus the world of the Christian represents the false world of the East. Sexuality and corruption, the idea of the woman, form the centerpiece for Nietzsche's understanding of the Jew in his (yes, his) manifestation as the Christian.[284]

Nietzsche's understanding of the nature of the New Testament is important, for he sees it as an "ill-smelling Judaine of rabbinism and superstition" ("Judaine" is Nietzsche's neologism for the evil essence of Jewishness). The entire phrase points not to an image of the Jews of the New Testament, but to the rhetoric of late-nineteenth-century anti-Semitism with its stress on the false logic, the rabbinical sophistries, and the superstitions of the Jews linked to their appearance and smell. The synesthesia of smelling the illogic, of dirty sophistry, reappears in *The Antichrist[ian]* in a much more specific context: "What follows from this? That one does well to put on gloves when reading the New Testament. The proximity of so much uncleanliness almost forces one to do this. We would no more choose the 'first Christians' to associate with than Polish Jews—not that one even required any objection to them: they both do not smell good."[285] The first Christians were really just Eastern Jews. They contaminated through their very presence. Their presence, however, is felt through the smell of the word, through the stink of their language, through the stench of their rhetoric. And these external signs and symptoms reflect their inherent sexual corruption.

Nietzsche is attacking the mode of discourse of the New Testament as much as its content. The common ground of the New Testament and contemporary rabbinic tradition lies in their shared lying and corrupting rhetoric. But Christianity is the rhetoric of power with which, whether he wishes it or not, he is condemned to be linked. His attempt at exorcising the Christian demons that lurk within his self-perception, his violent parodies of the style of the New Testament in *Thus Spoke Zarathustra*, only heighten his awareness of his existence as a representative of the most dominant of all groups, of the most powerful, of the most frightening: the German Christians. For they are the "healthy," the norm that defines the diseased, and he possesses within himself the hidden Jew, the stigma of disease and madness that marks the Jew.

Nietzsche draws the New Testament and its image of the sexualized body into question:

> Really, how can one put a book in the hands of children and women that contains that vile dictum: "to avoid fornication, let every man have his own wife, and let every woman have her own husband. . . . It is better to marry than to burn"? And how can one be a Christian as long as the notion of the immaculata conceptio christianizes, that is, dirties, the origin of man?
>
> I know no other book in which so many tender and gracious things are said to woman as in the law of Manu; those old graybeards and saints have a way of being courteous to women that has perhaps never been surpassed. "The mouth of a woman"—it is written in one place—"the bosom of a girl, the prayer of a child, the smoke of the sacrifice, are always pure." Another

passage: "There is nothing purer than the light of the sun, the shadow of a cow, the air, water, fire, and the breath of a girl." A final passage—perhaps also a holy lie: "All apertures of the body above the navel are pure, all below are impure. Only in the girl is the whole body pure."[286]

Again it is the image of the female's body that represents the Christian as Jew. The male Jew's body is marked by the act of circumcision. Circumcision marked on the skin—at least for the laws of Manu, the Aryan laws that served Nietzsche as his anti-Bible—the "counterconcept, the unbred man, the mishmash man, the chandala."[287] They were marked by "circumcision for male children and the removal of the internal labia for female children." The chandala were also the source of "ghastly venereal diseases." In addition, the manner of marking difference was "to make him sick" by forcing him to eat "impure vegetables" such as "garlic and onions." This law of exclusion mirrors for Nietzsche the position of the Jew in German culture, a culture striving for precisely the same law of "pure blood" as did the ancient Aryans. And this difference is marked by the physical form (which is here the mark of male and female) and by the smell of difference.

Schreber notes this in the "foul taste and smell which such impure souls cause in the body of the person through whose mouth they have entered."[288] The smell of the Jew and the smell of the female are both incorporated to provide the sexualized stench of the Jews' rhetoric. Olfactory qualities had long been used to label the Other as different in German racial "science." The mephitic odor of difference had been one of the central markers of the Jew in the biology of race in late-nineteenth-century Germany. At the close of the nineteenth century at least one distinguished German biologist, Gustav Jaeger, suggested that the Jewish soul was marked by a specific smell, a version of the stench, the *foetor judaicus*, associated with the Jew as early as the time of the Roman poet Martial, but of central importance in defining the image of the Jew in the Middle Ages.[289] Others, such as the anthropologist Richard Andree, associated the smell of the Jew with the Jew's consumption of garlic, evoking Nietzsche's image of stench.[290] But even this he sees as a reflex of the Jew's "southern" nature, acquired from long exposure to his original Mediterranean homeland, for only "southern" peoples indulge in this disgusting habit. (This confusion of the "acquired" smell of the Jew and the Jew's inherent "stench" is paralleled by Johann Jakob Schudt, who describes the "stench" of the Frankfurt Jews as inherent, as even their infants smell, but also as a result of their dietary habits.)[291]

But the smell of the Jew acquired importance as a marker of the sexual difference of the Jew in the racial biology of the period. Jaeger's evocation of the different smell of the Jew's soul and Andree's labeling of this smell as a reflex of the Jew's culture do not negate one another. Acquired characteristics become part of the essence of the Jew; thus the Jew's smell is a sign of the measurable, observable difference attributed to the Jew. Given the centrality of olfactory impressions in the debates about the nature of human sexual attraction (from Darwin on), it is not surprising that the question of the Jew's smell came to have clinical significance. One striking document, a letter from 1912 from a young man to a professor of medicine in Bohemia, reflects the assumptions among non-Jews about the smell of the Jew's body:

> My brother, a Christian, wishes to marry a Jewess. I would like to draw your attention to one thing that could make this difficult, to wit, that the Jews have a specific racial smell, which in our terms can be outspokenly unpleasant. I would like to ask whether or not through this a certain aversion might arise that in the course of time could have a negative impact on their psychological harmony. One cannot, of course, give this a trial run; our doctors seem to have no knowledge or experience of this, as mixed marriages rarely occur here.[292]

This statement is taken quite seriously by the physician who cites it. He refers to the biology of sexual attraction, ignoring the discourse of racial difference inherent in this view.

Schreber smells himself and sees himself as a Jew. In his unmanning he has become a Jew, but not any Jew; he has become the "Wandering Jew":

> In such an event, in order to maintain the species, one single human being was spared—perhaps the relatively most moral—called by the voices that talk to me the "Eternal Jew." This appellation has therefore a somewhat different sense from that underlying the legend of the same name of the Jew Ahasverus. . . . The Eternal Jew . . . had to be unmanned (transformed into a woman) to be able to bear children. This process of unmanning consisted in the (external) male genitals (scrotum and penis) being retracted into the body and the internal sexual organs being at the same time transformed into the corresponding female sexual organs, a process which might have been completed in a sleep lasting hundreds of years, because the skeleton (pelvis, etc.) had also to be changed. . . . The rays of the lower God (Ahriman) have the power of producing the miracle of unmanning; the rays of the upper God (Ormuzd) have the power of restoring manliness when necessary.[293]

This world conspiracy of the Jews, the "Order of the World," "unmans" Schreber and makes him a Jew.[294] Schreber becomes the "Eternal Jew," the one remaining individual after the destruction of the world. This identification may itself be a literary one. It is the positive protagonist of Eugène Sue's novel The Wandering Jew (1844–45) who revealed the depth of the Roman Catholic conspiracy to rule Europe (which reappears in the discussions of the "wandering Jew" in the psychiatric literature of the day). Schreber's vocabulary is not only anti-Semitic; it is also anti-Catholic, much in line with Bismarck's attack on transmontanism, the *Kulturkampf*. But for Schreber, the Jews are behind the Church of Rome; they merely use Christianity for their own "Jewish" ends: "amongst these was a Viennese nerve specialist whose name by coincidence was identical with that of the above-named Benedictine Father [Starkiewcz], a baptized Jew and Slavophile, who wanted to make Germany Slavic through me and at the same time wanted to institute there the rule of Judaism; like Professor Flechsig for Germany, England and America (that is mainly Germanic States), he appeared to be in his capacity as nerve specialist a kind of administrator of God's interests in another of God's provinces."[295] While the names of the persecutors are Catholic, they reveal themselves really to be only Eastern European Jews. Their baptisms are false, for Jews cannot change their essence even through baptism. It is they who attempted to convert him to Catholicism, which is, of course, merely crypto-Judaism, by altering the form and the function of his body.

Freud did not comment on this aspect of Schreber's text. He made no mention of the persistent incorporation of the rhetoric of anti-Semitism. Yet up to this exact point in his reading of the text, Freud underlined each reference to castration in Schreber's account (such as that on page 4 of the German text, which Freud annotated with the comment: "Fantasy of feminization"). Indeed, at one passage (page 45 of the German edition) in which Schreber evoked the "feminization" he felt his body to have undergone, Freud commented that this was the "center of the problem" ("Kern der Sache").

It was clearly important to Freud to find documentation concerning castration anxiety in Schreber's text. The concept of castration anxiety had evolved from the evocation of Otto Weininger in the case of Little Hans. Even in its initial formulation it had reflected Freud's sense of the origins of anti-Semitism and Jewish self-hatred. But when he was confronted with Schreber's own use of this motif, in a text suggested by a non-Jew, Jung, and documenting a non-Jew's view of the hidden nature of the Jewish body and the need to "preserve the race," Freud did not remark on it. The "Jewish" response to Little Hans and Otto Weininger is one thing; a direct confrontation with the origins of their anxiety is another. Such a confrontation would draw the "neutral" nature of the scientist's own body into question, and this could not be risked.

Schreber eventually came to believe that he had become a woman in all her form and structure. This transformation, from the removal of his mustache to the "change of my whole stature," "emanated from the lower God (Ahriman)," the god of the Jews.[296] While he is given the genitalia of a woman, which "unmans" him, marking him as a Jew, he is also given the stomach of a Jew: "Concerning the stomach: already during my stay in Flechsig's Asylum the Viennese nerve specialist named in Chapter V miraculously produced in place of my healthy natural stomach a very inferior so-called 'Jew's stomach.' Later for a time the miracles were in preference directed against my stomach, partly because the souls begrudged me the sensual pleasure connected with the taking of food, partly because they considered themselves superior to human beings who require earthly nourishments."[297] Judaism, according to Ludwig Feuerbach, is merely a gastronomic cult, as it stresses the worldly aspects of religion rather than its metaphysical ones.[298] In the medical literature the "Jew's stomach" becomes "chronic dyspepsia, which is the result of too rapid eating among the Slavic lands reputedly because of the greater consumption of tea among Jews."[299] In reading Schreber's autobiography, Freud carefully underlined the words "Jew's stomach" in his copy of the text. This was the only one of the symptoms of Schreber's transformations noted by him. For Freud, the image of the diseased body of the Jew sprang from the page only in the image of the stomach. Schreber's anxiety about being castrated, about acquiring the Jew's circumcised penis, the sign of the feminization of the Jew, was not read by Freud as the internalization of Jewish difference.

Even the act of defecation was associated with an anti-Semitic image of the Jew. In contemporary culture, the Jew stank of the *foetor judaicus*. The smell, like the smell of the sewers of the nineteenth century, which epitomized the source of decay for nineteenth-century public health, was the smell of shit.[300] Within the scatological culture of Germany, Jews had a special role in the German fantasy about defecation.[301] Beginning with Luther, there had been a powerful association between the act of defecation and being Jewish. As Luther wrote in one of his late tracts against the Jews: "When we read that Judas hanged himself, that his belly burst in pieces, and that his bowels fell out, we may take this as an example of how it will go with all Christ's enemies. The Jews ought to have made a mirror of Judas, and have seen therein how they in like manner would be destroyed. An allegory or mystery lies hid, for the belly signifies the whole Kingdom of the Jews, which shall also fall away and be destroyed, so that nothing thereof shall remain. When we read that the bowels fell out, this shows the posterity of the Jews, their whole generation, shall be spoiled and go to the ground."[302] At the turn of the century, Oskar Panizza represented this as a quality of the essential Jewish body. He wrote about his Jewish protagonist:

Now in order to present a full picture I am compelled to touch on something distasteful: Faitel had a fear of the toilet. He believed in the old Hebrew spirits of the latrine and squalor who bothered people during their most urgent calls and took possession of them and could only be repulsed through certain prayers. Since he no longer knew these prayers nor could say any of them with conviction, his fear grew even greater. And only the circumstance that the spirits did not dare attack anyone in the presence of a third party enabled Faitel to dispose of such urgent business in peace—naturally only after he always provided for the proper conditions.[303]

Panizza's work evokes a theme well known to Freud from a Talmudic reference in the German translation of John Gregory Bourke's *Scatalogic Rites of All Nations*, for which he wrote the introduction in 1913.[304] Likewise, Iwan Bloch commented in his fin de siècle study of human sexuality that the early Jews used excrement in their worship of Baal-Peor, and this use of excrement tied the "act of defecation to sexual excesses of various sorts."[305]

Schreber's fearful (yet simultaneously voluptuous) attitude toward the act of defecation is parallel to the anxiety expressed by the Jews:

Whenever the need to defecate is produced by miracle, some other person in my environment is sent to the lavatory—by exciting the nerves of the person concerned—in order to prevent me from emptying myself; this I have observed so frequently (thousands of times) and so regularly that one can exclude any thought of it being coincidence. "Why do you then not sh. . .?" is followed by the capital answer "because I am somehow stupid?" . . . When I do empty myself—usually in a bucket because I almost always find the lavatory occupied—this act is always combined with a very strong development of soul-voluptuousness. Liberation from the pressure of the feces present in the guts creates an intense feeling of well-being, particularly for the nerves of voluptuousness.[306]

This act is understood as a Jewish preoccupation with constipation, one of the classic "Jewish symptoms" related to hemorrhoids.

There is a long association between Jews and hemorrhoids. A late fourteenth-century Hebrew translation of Bernard de Gordon's *Lilium Medicinae* (1305) contains the following passage:

the Jews suffer greatly from hemorrhoids for three reasons: firstly, because they are generally sedentary and therefore the excessive melancholy humors collect; secondly, because they are usually in fear and anxiety and therefore the melancholy blood becomes increased, besides (according to Hippocrates) fear and faint-heartedness, should they last a long time, produce the melancholy humor; and thirdly, it is the divine vengeance against them (as written in Psalms 78:66): and "he smote his enemies in the hinder parts, he put them to a perpetual reproach."[307]

The Hebrew translator adds to the final point: "what is written is a lie and they who believe it, lie." Hemorrhoids, like male menstruation (and, indeed, all illnesses of the Jews), are a punishment for the Jews' denial of Christ. In 1777 Elcan Isaac Wolf had already commented on the relationship between the Jews' sedentary life-style and the seemingly universal appearance of hemorrhoids.[308] This was a leitmotif in Jewish culture in Europe. Indeed, one of the puzzles of the epidemiological literature on cancer is that Jews had such a low rate of rectal cancer given the high occurrence of hemorrhoids among them.[309] But the image of hemorrhoids is associated in the medical literature with Eastern European Jews, as Maurice Fishberg noted: "among the Hasidm in Galicia and Poland a Jew without hemorrhoids is considered a curiosity. Physicians who have had experience among the Jews testify that it is rare to find a Jew who has passed the middle age without having his hemorrhoidal veins more or less enlarged. The Jews of eastern Europe attribute this condition to the habit of sitting during the greater part of the day on the hard benches of the *bet La-midrash* [school] while studying the Talmud."[310] Freud would have had this view of an Eastern Jewish predisposition reinforced by his reading of Ignaz Bernstein's collection of Jewish proverbs, to which he referred in a 1914 footnote to *The Interpretation of Dreams.*[311] Among Eastern Jews, the inheritance of this affliction became the stuff of folk wisdom: "A yiddishe yerishe is a gildene uder" [A Jew's inheritance is a golden vein, i.e., hemorrhoids] and "Vus yirushenen Yidn? Zurus un meriden!" [What do Jews inherit? Trouble and hemorrhoids!][312] For the medical practitioner at the turn of the century, "hemorrhoids are an inherent part of the image of the Hassids of Galicia and Poland."[313]

But being Jewish means, as noted above, suffering from a disease, and Schreber suffered from a disease of the body that was at the same time a disease of the mind. It was, to quote his physician Flechsig, "the body which is in the first case what makes the mind ill, and the sick brain has its own laws."[314] According to Schreber, he has the "brown plague," the disease of Ahriman, the lower God of the "brunette" Jews; it is "a disease of the nerves and hence a 'holy disease.' "[315] This "holy disease" is leprosy, "*Lepra orientalis, . . . Lepra hebraica,*"[316] the Oriental disease par excellence, the disease of the Jews. He chants in the asylum: "I am the first leper corpse and I lead a leper corpse."[317] The disease of the Jews alters the Jew's skin, the shape of the Jew's nose. It is overtly leprosy but it is also a plague unnamed in the text. It is that disease which changes "my sex organ."[318] It is syphilis, the plague associated by Schreber with the Jews and leprosy.

Syphilis—and its assumed relationship with madness—is one of the commonplaces found in the articulation of the nineteenth-century masculine anxiety about control. This age of syphilophobia understood, long before Hideyo Noguchi demonstrated this relationship in the laboratory, the association between a life of sexual debauchery and the eventual punishment for such a life through the madness and death resulting from syphilis. This was, as one can see in the case of Schreber, understood as the problem of the male; it was the male who was infected by women, it was the male who was thus unable to function in civil society, who was unable to procreate or to serve in the armed services. Such a view of the "collapse of the race" (the phrase comes from a French antivenereal poster of the day) was the direct result of men being at greater risk. This view flew in the face of all rational understanding. The model of women infecting men who would thus be unmanned, unable to fulfill their masculine function in society, ignored that women too were infected and were also exposed to eventual mental collapse and death. The fixation of the medical profession on "general paralysis of the insane," as tertiary syphilis was labeled, extended well beyond the fields of neurology, psychiatry, and syphilology (a branch of dermatology). It was the defining psychosis for the late nineteenth century, both in popular and in medical terms.[319] Ibsen's *Ghosts* (1881), with its image of hereditary syphilis and the resulting madness of the son, is a model for this disease's perceived masculinization, having been passed from the father to the son.

This is paralleled by Schreber's self-image, in his case notes, as a syphilitic. Schreber associated his wife's frequent miscarriages with his having infected her with syphilis. And Schreber's self-diagnoses, such as "softening of the brain," are precisely those associated in the medical literature and popular culture of his time with syphilitic infection. This pattern of self-determined associations was convincing enough to his physicians that they actually prescribed a specific for syphilis—potassium iodide—for his condition.[320] Syphilis was, as noted, closely linked to the Jews and to their practice of circumcision, a practice that alters the "normal" body and transforms it into that of a Jew. Here the links in the medical literature of the time are fascinating. The association of neurological and psychological illnesses with physical pathologies was commonplace. Syphilitic infection was one of the patterns for this association as it provided an altered mental state associated with specific physical signs and symptoms (such as a diminished Babinski reflex and frozen, unequal pupils). One of the cures for such an illness could be circumcision, and this was seen in the medical literature as "making a Jew out of [the patient]," as C. H. Ohr commented in 1887.[321]

The blackness of the Jew was initially associated with the diseased nature of the Jewish body as well as with the syphilitic body. Jews are black because they are different, because their sexuality is different, because their sexual pathology is written on their skin. Johann Pezzl described the typical Viennese Jew in the 1780s as "the color of a black." For him this was a sign of diseased skin, "the *plica polonica*."[322] As noted in chapter 1, the *plica polonica*, the fabled skin disease associated with the Jews and others from the East, marked the Jew as visibly different.[323] There is no question that the Jew suffers from Jewishness. Pezzl's contemporary, Josef Rohrer, stresses the "disgusting skin diseases" of the Jew as a sign of the group's general infirmity.[324] The essential Jew for Pezzl, even worse than the Polish Jew, is the Galician Jew, the Jew from the eastern reaches of the Hapsburg Empire.[325] This theme reappears in Arthur Schopenhauer's mid-nineteenth-century evocation of the Jews as "a sneaking dirty race afflicted with filthy diseases (scabies) that threaten to prove infectious."[326] The skin disease of the Jews is syphilis, the disease of Jewish sexuality.

But the disease from which Schreber believed himself to suffer was neither syphilis nor leprosy; it was the relatively newly medicalized "disease" of homosexuality. The Jewish God, the lower God, the brown God, raped Schreber: "Fancy a person who was a *Senatspräsident* allowing himself to be f. . .ked."[327] This is the language of the "posterior" gods; it is the crude language of Jewish sexuality: "The choice of the word 'f. . .king' is not due to my liking for vulgar terms, but having had to listen to the words 'f. . .k' and 'f. . .king' thousands of times, I have used the term for short in this little note to indicate the behavior of rays which was contrary to the Order of the World."[328] Sexuality, especially a sexuality that was labeled diseased by the medical culture of Schreber's world, was associated with the world of the Jews.

Schreber's vocabulary as he adapted it from the contemporary discourse about race is relatively incomplete. One aspect of this vocabulary is not so evident. Schreber cites the idea of seeing the world as a series of internalized visual representations: "Perhaps nobody but myself, not even science, knows that man retains all recollections in his memory, by virtue of lasting impressions on his nerves, as pictures in his head."[329] Schreber could evoke these pictures from his prior experience ("persons, animals and plants, of all sorts of objects in nature and objects of daily use") through the use of "ray-communication." He thus used the idea of imaging (as in the dream state) in order to see himself as female: "When I am lying in bed at night I can give myself and the rays the impression that my body has female breasts and a female sexual organ. . . . The picturing of the female buttocks on my body—*honi soit qui mal y pense*—has become such a habit that I do it almost automatically whenever I bend down."[330] These transformations, following the racial composite images of Francis Galton, are representations of the essence of the individual. Schreber could create and personify the image of the Jew or the woman by imagining its essence. By becoming a woman Schreber undertook what was expected of a Jew—that the Jew become someone else, with a different body, in order to become new.

Ever since the work of William Niederland in the 1950s great attention has been paid to the pedagogical writings of Schreber's father, Moritz Schreber, and the various orthopedic devices he employed for the correction of children's posture or to prevent their masturbation. The son's sexuality and its control by the machines of the father seem to be reflected in the son's paranoid world. It is not separate from the construction of this world, but rather a reorganized, meaningful reinterpretation of the meaning of these representations. The machines have another level of meaning. They are machines for the restructuring of the body, they are machines that feminize Schreber's body by unmanning him with magical rays. These machines also make the body into a Jew. The fascination with the world of difference and of danger is incorporated in Schreber's image of himself. Only the most coercive medicine would even attempt to make the Jew into an Aryan. In Oskar Panizza's image of the refashioning of the Jew, the body of the Jew is rebuilt in the workshop of the physician. The machinery and implements of Professor Klotz, the anatomist, begin to reshape the Jew's body. It is corrective orthopedic work as well as surgery. Jews were beginning to use cosmetic surgery to "cure" their Jewish features; like the craze to rebuild the Jewish nose began to take more and more of the time of such reconstructive surgeons as the German-Jewish innovator of aesthetic rhinoplasty ("nose jobs"), Jacques Joseph (known as "Nosef"), at the beginning of the twentieth century.[331] Panizza's image of the reconstruction of the Jewish body used implements of torture, such as those attributed in the critical literature to Schreber's father, which are part of the fantasy of altering the body, such as a barbed wire belt to correct posture: "a barbed wire belt similar to a collar was placed around his hips on his bare skin (as they do with dogs) so that he was immediately spiked when he tended to move up and down or from side to side."[332] Such a device is parallel to the devices actually developed by Schreber's father for the correction of the spines of his pupils, which may reappear in his son's narrative as the "compression of the chest miracle," which "consisted in the whole chest wall being compressed, so that the state of oppression caused by the lack of breath was transmitted to my whole body."[333] This machine kept the Jew (and Schreber as well) in his newly acquired form. Faitel removed the barbed-wire belt, the belt that had kept him erect, for his wedding night. "What I do know is that Faitel had discarded the barbed belt, the preservative of his correct posture, for the first time the night before this celebration. Nobody can reprimand him for this since the discarding was symbolical. Faitel had entered Christian society for good on this day."[334] But it is alcohol that is the Jew's undoing as he returns to his original form "making disgusting, lascivious, and bestial canine movements with his rear end" (as does Schreber) at the end of the text.[335] The rays that transform him act like the alcohol that transforms Faitel. Schreber is made to act like a Jew by the external forces that transform his body.

Freud's reading of this most complicated text ignores all of Schreber's anti-Semitic rhetoric and focuses on the meaning of Schreber's "homosexuality," his delusion of castration and of being transformed into a woman. Freud's comments on the relationship between fantasies of castration and images of the Jew should have provided, as they did to a limited extent for Brill, a context in which Schreber's anxiety about his own body could have been explored. Schreber's charge of soul-murder, his "unmanning for purposes consistent to the Order of the World, that is for the sexual satisfaction of a human being," is understood by Freud as a response to his Oedipal struggle with his father. That Schreber encodes this struggle, as does I.S., with a rich vocabulary taken from the discourse about the Jews is seemingly invisible to the reader in Freud's published analysis of the case, although it was quite evident to Freud as he read Schreber's text and annotated these passages, among others, with marginal notes. His stress was on the homoerotic meaning associated with the images Schreber evokes. The details of these images also recall the rhetoric of anti-Semitic racial science. If it follows that much of the impetus of Schreber's paranoid system came from absorbing and reacting to the system of evaluation used by his physician, Paul Flechsig, then Schreber would have been diagnosed by Flechsig as a "degenerate." For Flechsig, the line between the "healthy" and the "diseased" was drawn by the potential for disease. The degenerate, whose character deficiencies are a sign of his illness, is formed in the depths of the womb, while his disease often appears only in puberty. It is in the body of the degenerate that the origin of his perversion lies.[336] Schreber, who was clearly conversant with the psychiatric literature of his day, saw himself in the nosology of Flechsig as a degenerate, as little more than a Jew. The process of transforming the homosexual into the Jew is one with the psychiatric system in which Schreber found himself. Schreber both welcomed and feared his transformation, a conflict that reflected his incorporation of these themes into his paranoid system. Such systems generate the illusion of structure, of solidity. They are, in fact, an ever-shifting set of images and topoi, which provide a necessary illusion of permanence.

The "degenerate," the greater category into which the nosologies of the nineteenth century placed the "pervert," was—according to Max Nordau, one of the first supporters of Theodor Herzl's Zionism, quoting B. A. Morel—the "morbid deviation from an original type."[337] The difference between the original type, the middle-class, heterosexual, Protestant, white male, and the outsider was a morbid one—the outsider was diseased. Thus there is a general parallel drawn between the feminization of the Jew and the homosexual in the writings of assimilated Jews, Jews who did not seek to validate their difference from the majority during the late nineteenth century but did see themselves as potentially at risk by being perceived as such deviations from the norm. Nowhere is this illustrated with greater force than in an essay written in 1897 by the future foreign minister of the Weimar Republic, Walter Rathenau. Rathenau, who begins his essay by "confessing" to his identity as a Jew, condemns the Jews as a foreign body in the cultural as well as the political world of Germany: "Whoever wishes to hear its language can go any Sunday through the Thiergartenstrasse midday at twelve or evenings glance into the foyer of a Berlin theater. Unique Vision! In the midst of a German life, a separate, strange race. . . . On the sands of the Mark Brandenburg, an Asiatic horde." As part of this category of difference, Rathenau sees the physical deformities of the Jewish male—his "soft weakness of form," his femininity (associated with his "orientalism")—as the biological result of his oppression. This was a restructuring of the charge that Jews were inherently feminine, rather than so as a social reaction to their stigmatization.[338] David Friedrich Strauss, a great critic of Christianity, was able to speak of the "especially female" nature of the Jews.[339] (Freud read this text as a young man and it made a considerable impression on him.)[340] The evils of Christianity lie in their Jewish origin—a point Nietzsche, like many of the "Christian" critics of Christianity during the late nineteenth century, raised. The physician Moses Julius Gutmann translated this discussion of the "common mental construction" of the Jews into a reading of the anthropometric statistics of the woman as parallel to those of the male Jew. Thus the Jew has an arm span less than equivalent to his height, as does the woman.[341] It is not surprising, therefore, that the Jew is seen as overwhelmingly at risk for being (or becoming) a homosexual. Moses Julius Gutmann observed that "all the comments about the supposed stronger sexual drive among Jews have no basis in fact; most frequently they are sexual neurasthenics. Above all, the number of Jewish homosexuals is extraordinarily high."[342] This view was echoed by Alexander Pilcz, Freud's colleague in the Department of Psychiatry at the University of Vienna, who noted that "there is a relatively high incidence of homosexuality among the Jews."[343] The biological (or "ontological") difference of the Jew is the source of his feminized nature. Among Jews, according to a lecture given in 1920 by Robert Stigler, a professor of anthropology at the University of Vienna, "the physical signs of the sexual characteristics are noticeably vague. Among them, the women are often found to have a relatively narrow pelvis and relatively broad shoulders and the men to have broad hips and narrow shoulders. . . . It is important to note the attempt on the part of the Jews to eliminate the role secondary sexual characteristics instinctively play among normal people through their advocacy of the social and professional equality of man and woman."[344] Only Havelock Ellis denied this association, noting that among his homosexual patients only "two are more or less Jewish." He was surprised by the "frequent presence of the German element" among his patients.[345] This notion of the general tendency of all Jews (male and female) to homosexuality, as represented by their social and political acts as well as their biological reality, had to be modified by Jews such as Rathenau to provide a space where they were able to escape the stigma of feminization.

"Feminization" is here to be understood both in its general, cultural sense and in its specifically medical sense. "Feminization," or the existence of the "feminized man," is a form of "external pseudo-hermaphrodism."[346] It is not true hermaphrodism, but rather the sharing of external, secondary sexual characteristics, such as the shape of the body or the tone of the voice. The concept began in the middle of the nineteenth century with the introduction of the term "infemminsce," to feminize, to describe the supposed results of the castration of the male.[347] By the 1870s, the term was used to describe the "feminisme" of the male through the effects of other diseases, such as tuberculosis.[348] Henry Meige, at the Salpêtrière, saw this feminization as a form of atavism, in which the male returned to the level of the "sexless" child.[349] "Feminization" was the direct result of actual castration or its physiological equivalent, such as an intensely debilitating illness. And it reshaped the body. Freud, citing Taruffi, rejected any simple association of the form of the body of the hermaphrodite with the sexual preference of the homosexual.[350] He separated out the "common mental construction" of the homosexual from his or her physical form. His preferred reading of the meaning of castration was that of Rieger, for that reading, even though it implicated Freud as an "old woman," saw the results of castration as a social rather than a physiological reality.

At the turn of the century, male Jews were feminized and signaled their feminization through their discourse, which reflected the nature of their bodies. Their feminization recalled the association between castration and circumcision, but it formed a fantasy about the entire body, including the voice. Here again Oskar Panizza's tale, "The Operated Jew," provides a ghastly parallel. The Jew's buccal physiognomy was related to his language. "His lips were fleshy and overly creased; his teeth sparkled like pure crystal. A fatty violet tongue often thrust itself between them at the wrong time."[351] His speech consisted of a "mixture of Palatinate Semitic babble, French nasal noises and some high German vocal sounds which he had fortuitously overheard and articulated with an open position of the mouth."[352] His language is the language of the black; it "lacked a declinatory character as is the case with some Negro languages."[353] Indeed, he is seen as an exotic object, like the black: "I was attracted to him in the same way I might be to a Negro whose goggle eyes, yellow connective optical membranes, crushed nose, mollusk lips and ivory teeth and smell one perceives altogether in wonderment and whose feelings and most secret anthropological actions one wants to get to know as well!"[354] Similarly, Schreber's language and his body were well matched. They reflected his Aryan nature. The voice of the Jew, like the language of the Jew, revealed the essence of the Jewish "soul." And it is there that the key to the degeneracy of the homosexual and the Jew is to be found.

The feminizing "break of the voice," the inability to speak in a masculine manner, is one of the standard stigmata of degeneration borne by the homosexual in late-nineteenth-century medicine and popular culture. Homosexuality, by the close of the nineteenth century, was generally understood in the work of Richard von Krafft-Ebing, Benjamin Tarnowski, Albert Moll, and others as being an innate, biological error that not only manifested itself in "perverted" acts but was written on the body of the homosexual through the appearance of specific, visible signs.[355] One of the most evident degenerative stigmata, cited in almost all case reports, is the quality of the voice. At the turn of the century Dr. Theodor S. Flatau, an otolaryngologist in Berlin, undertook a study of the vocal mechanisms of homosexuals, as the voice was considered a secondary sexual characteristic. He reported that homosexual men showed markedly "female" laryngeal structures, while "mannish" women showed markedly "male" laryngeal structures.[356] Moll reported a case in which the choice of dressing like a woman began to affect all aspects of the patient's outer and inner reality: "His walk, his voice, everything in him, took on a feminine character; he finally gave himself a girl's name."[357] With the increased knowledge of the endocrinological system during the second half of the nineteenth century, the biochemical link between the breaking of the voice and sexual change during puberty became known. The change of voice signaled the masculinization of the male; its absence signaled the breaking of the voice, the male's inability to assume anything but a "perverted" sexual identity: "It is a fact that in the normal state the female voice possesses a quality and a range different from those of the male voice; when the male imitates the female voice, the result is known as a falsetto. Now, this type of voice is sometimes quite pronounced in Uranists. . . . They do so with ease; and even when in a gathering of normal individuals they find it difficult to speak in a normal tone, so easily and naturally does the falsetto voice come to them."[358] Homosexuals speak this way because it is a reflex of their essence. The voice of the homosexual mirrors his "perversion." This is the mirror of the "perverted speech" of the "insane inverts, . . . affected, for example, with *Pseudologia fantastica* (pathological swindlers), and who are also homosexual. [It] shows the intimate relationship which exists between sexual inversion (also called 'uranism') and the psychoses."[359] They are "the most consummate liars and [they] by their repulsive manners in the street and in public places often excite the disgust of honest people."[360] It is also the disease of the boastful Eastern Jew. In a letter written to Wilhelm Fliess in April 1898, Freud refers to his brother-in-law Moriz Freud (a distant cousin who married his sister Marie) as a "half-Asian" who suffered from "pseudologica fantastica."[361] He is "half-Asian" because he is from Bucharest, and the disease he is said to suffer from is the psychiatric diagnosis for those mythomanic patients who lie in order to gain status. "Pseudologia fantastica" is a syndrome in which "an extraordinary vanity forms the motor, the need for the extraordinary, the need to appear more than one is, to have experienced more than one has, more than one can experience in the course of daily life. . . . The pleasure that accompanies such vacillation is so great that it cannot be controlled, even when the substance of the lie is immediately evident; it is simply impossible for such characters to stay with the truth."[362] The homosexual's "illness" mirrors that of the Jew: "Many of these perverts are neurasthenic or hysteric, they are easily excited, suffer from headaches, suffer from all sorts of sensations in their limbs, are often unwilling to work. . . ."[363] The question is not whether there are homosexual Jews. Indeed, there is a debate whether there is the same proportion of homosexuals among the Jews as "among the other races."[364] The image of the Jew and the image of the homosexual were parallel in the fin de siècle medical culture. But within the gay culture in Germany, Jews were seen essentially as Jews even when they were also identified as gay. They were given Jewish nicknames (such as Sarah or Rebecca) even when their given names were in no way identifiably Jewish.[365]

It was, however, also accepted in the fin de siècle nosological system that those who become homosexuals, usually through the act of seduction (or trauma), have some inborn predisposition to homosexuality that may well announce itself through the stigmata of degeneration. The tension between "nature" and "nurture," between these two models of homosexuality, had its parallel in attitudes toward race during the same period, with much the same confused response on the part of those stigmatized. It is assumed that the stigmata are "real" signs of perversion, whether present or future, whether endogenous or exogenous. This assumption is internalized, often in the most complex manner, by those stereotyped. One would imagine that the endogenous explanation for difference would have been rejected by those individuals so stigmatized. Not so.

Karl Heinrich Ulrichs, the first major advocate of homosexual emancipation during the 1860s, saw homosexuals as the "third sex," a biological category of equal validity to the male and the female; likewise, some Jews, such as the early Zionists, by the 1890s began to accept the idea of racial difference as a means of establishing their own autonomy and separation.[366] Such a complex reading of categories of difference is reflected in the responses of highly acculturated German and Austrian Jews, such as Sigmund Freud, who were caught between an understanding of their own difference and a need to conceptualize it in such a way as to make it bearable.

Freud's reading of Schreber's text eliminated any discussion of the meaning of Flechsig's understanding of homosexuality as degeneration and its integration into Schreber's system in his anxiety about becoming a Jew. Is the rhetoric of anti-Semitism a natural outgrowth of the presuppositions of Flechsig's view of the degeneration of the homosexual? If, as was argued in the medical literature of the period, anti-Semitism is a neurotic symptom, how is this symptom to be read? Is it a sign of the inherent, atavistic nature of the Aryan as anti-Semite, just as the hysteria and neurasthenia of the Jew are signs of the inherent nature of the Jew?

Freud, who was quite aware of Flechsig's clinical work, managed to ignore in his narrative the clear associations in Schreber's own text and the problems they present.[367] Rather, the text became a proof of Jung's "assertion that the mythopoetic forces of mankind are not extinct, but that to this very day they give rise in the neurosis to the same psychical products as in the remotest past ages."[368] Jung's views on the "common mental construction" of the Jews are repressed, and the vision Freud gives the reader of this text is a purely "scientific" one, which bears no sign that this discourse on the nature of the degenerate and the Jew would have any special meaning for the now "neutral" scientific observer. Unlike Brill, who pursued the hidden meaning of his patient's anti-Semitism, Freud repressed this quality in Schreber's text. Freud's reading of Schreber is proof that he was truly a scientist, unencumbered by the "common mental construction" Jung ascribed to the Jew.

The images that haunted Freud's representation of Schreber—his language, the sexual acts of his imagination, their source, the relationship between pathology and infection—were all "racially" marked (at least notionally) in turn-of-the-century medical culture. For Freud, abandoning the act of seeing, an act made canonical in the work of his anti-Semitic mentor Charcot, was an abandonment of the associations of sight within this discourse of sexual difference. The case of Schreber is an example of the power over language, of Freud's control over the language of his text that revealed him not to be an Eastern Jew. As evidenced in his critique of the "bad" Greek of his critics when he held his first talk on male hysteria in Vienna, Freud was a master of the discourse of science and culture. Freud was a scientist who used language as a scientist. This is a theme well documented in his discussion of his study of Dora, a hysteric.[369] In introducing the question of the nature of Dora's attraction to Frau K., he remarks: "I must now turn to consider a further complication, to which I should certainly give no space if I were a man of letters engaged upon the creation of a mental state like this for a short story, instead of being a medical man engaged upon its dissection."[370] What the phantasm of dissection meant for Freud, here writing in the guise of the neutral physician, is clear. It was the demand of distance from the body to be studied and analyzed. The act of writing the story was the sign of his special control of a "neutral" language, one that was hardly neutral when it comes to placing Freud, the Eastern, male Jew, at its center of risk.

Hysteria, unlike paranoia, suddenly became a quality of all human beings: "After all, Möbius could say with justice that we are all to some extent hysterics."[371] Freud evoked P. J. Möbius to universalize the meaning of hysteria. Möbius, like most of his contemporaries, assumed the predisposition of the Jews to hysteria.[372] In the "Preliminary Communication" to *Studies on Hysteria*, hysterical patients had been described as momentarily insane during hypnoid states "as we all are in dreams."[373] Hysterical symptoms involve "symbolic associations" "such as healthy people form in dreams."[374] We are all dreamers, all tell jokes, all make slips—the search for the universal already is promised (as least parenthetically) in the awareness of the danger the male Jew faces. Seeing Freud as taking part in a system in which "the doctor play[s] the role of colonizer and the patients [play] the colonized people," Octave Mannoni stresses the slipperiness of Freud's sense of himself both as a physician and as a hysteric: "Freud had arrived at La Salpêtrière as a neurologist; he left it a 'hysteric'—having found that he was just hysterical enough to identify with Charcot's patients. This identification is at the origin of the discovery of psychoanalysis, since it made possible Freud's 'self-analysis' with Fliess."[375] The identification with the Jewish disease of psychoanalysis, to be cured among Jews by Jews, became a form of Freud's resistance to this model of medical colonization. But in order to accomplish this, the Jew within had to be repressed in the now neutralized discourse of science. This was achieved through a creative repression of the overt link between mental illness and Schreber's internalization of his anxiety about becoming a Jew. As with Freud's reading of the life histories of his hysterics, Schreber came to represent his own anxieties about his identity as a physician and male Jew in the culture of fin de siècle Vienna.

Neutrality in medical science, specifically in the study and treatment of mental illness, was a desirable, even necessary goal for Freud. Yet the displacement of the image of the male Jew as the essential patient into other gendered categories of psychoanalysis illustrates that Freud's struggle continued throughout his life. The final chapter of this study will illustrate how complex this dynamic form of displacement remained in Freud's psychic life. His formulation of psychosis within the framework of his definition of homosexuality, as is presented in his reading of an autobiography by a patient diagnosed as psychotic, shows a further transformation. But all these readings reflect the body of their author— Freud as the sufferer from a specific form of cancer and as the self-aware object of the increased and omnipresent anti-Semitism of Austro-fascism and Nazism during the 1930s. Freud's own male, Jewish, and diseased body and its meaning frames the image of the suffering Jew as it is reflected in the dreamwork of science.

SYSTEMIC DISEASES: CANCER AND ANTI-SEMITISM

WHOSE CANCER IS IT, ANYWAY? FREUD'S MALE BODY AS THE LOCUS OF DISEASE

Fantasies about the potential illness of the male Jew's body and psyche shaped the discourse of psychoanalysis concerning gender and identity. As long as the "reality" of the Jewish physician's distance from such cultural fantasies was maintained, these charges could be externalized. But what happened when the cultural assumptions about the diseased nature of the Jew were realized? What happened when the Jewish physician, who had been confronted with the dilemma of being physician and patient simultaneously, suddenly found himself ill? What happened when Freud discovered in 1923 that he had cancer of the jaw, and became a patient? It is relatively easy to show that there is a residue of cultural attitudes in the structuring of systems of paranoia, as one can see in Schreber's autobiography. Much more difficult is the question of the internalization and repression of those meanings associated with organic illnesses. For is not a fever, a fever; is not a tumor, a tumor? But if paranoia and homosexuality are illnesses that affect anti-Semites, just as hysteria and neurasthenia are diseases that affect Jews, is it possible that the meaning of organic diseases can also be ideologically structured? To examine this question, let us turn to what cancer, or at least cancerous tumors, were understood to be in the second half of the nineteenth century.[1]

In 1838, Johannes Müller discovered that the cell structure of a tumor is inherently different from normal cell structure. In Berlin, Hermann Lebert was able to describe in detail the morphology of the cancerous cell. By the 1860s Rudolf Virchow's view that only cells could give rise to other cells (*omnis cellula a cellula*), and, therefore, that cancer was not a foreign intrusion into the body, was accepted. Cancer was an inherent, degenerative cellular disease that, by 1886, was believed to be limited by the specific origin of the cell from which the tumor sprang (*omnis cellula e cellula eiusdem naturae*).

But what caused cancer? The theories were as diverse as the cultures of science that gave rise to them. With the success of Pasteur's view of the bacteriological origin of certain diseases, such as rabies, one focus was on bacteria. The fascination with local inflammation, and the realization that it seemed to produce tumors, gave rise to the alternative view that cancer was a disease resulting from scarring. With the central importance of the science of race in medicine, it is not surprising that at the beginning of the twentieth century, the focus turned to the question of race and its role in the origin of cancer.

In 1914, Theodor Boveri, a professor of zoology at the University of Würzburg, published a study of the origin of malignant tumors in which he argued that carcinomas had their ultimate origin in an error of the chromosomes that could be caused through either mechanical or chemical means.[2] This view augmented earlier work by David von Hansemann, who saw the growth of malignant tumors as parallel to that of normal cells; that is, he understood cancer as a type of development response to external stimulus.[3] Cancer was seen as a somatic mutation that could, therefore, be inherited, rather than as the result of some unknown infectious disease.[4] This view had been widely discussed in the course of the late nineteenth century, but the rise of greater knowledge about modes of inheritance, following the rediscovery of Mendelian genetics at the beginning of the twentieth century, led to the reestablishment of this view as one of the central theories of the origin of cancer. By the 1930s this view of cancer as a disease of the chromosomes had become part of eugenics' cadre of inherited diseases that could be eliminated by careful breeding.[5]

The debate about who suffered from cancer, and the related debate about what causes cancer, are ancient. During the course of the nineteenth century the question of race became one means of distinguishing those at risk from those who were seen to be immune from the disease. In the 1860s, Cesare Lombroso had begun to study the question of the comparative mortality of the Jews of Verona in the context of the death rate of the non-Jewish population. There he observed that Veronese Jews suffered from twice as many cases of cancer as did Veronese Christians.[6] Lombroso's statistics supported the contention that Jews were a separate and unique race, whose medical anomalies rested in this separateness. They were, to quote a study from the early twentieth century, "a race of considerable purity of stock, [which] . . . by their ubiquitous presence . . . supply the interesting phenomenon of a racial unit subjected to widely-differing geographical influences."[7] In Berlin during 1905, 8.6 percent of all deaths among Jews were attributed to cancer, while the remaining population evidenced a 6 percent death rate from cancer.[8]

The simple reversal of Lombroso's claim about a Jewish predisposition to cancer had also been made by British physicians such as James Braithwaite at the turn of the century.[9] This view, that "cancer occurs rarely among Jews," was then refuted by further statistical evidence to the contrary.[10] But if Jews were neither immune to nor predisposed to cancer, they certainly were seen as a group that presented a specific manifestation of the disease.[11]

By the beginning of the twentieth century the question was no longer whether Jews suffered from cancer, but whether Jews were predisposed to or immune to certain, specific types of tumors. There was a growing statistical literature that discussed the Jewish predisposition to certain forms of cancer. Jews, it seemed, had an immunity to some forms. In 1890, W. S. Bainbridge could cite the case of a sarcoma in a Jewish woman as a pathological curiosity.[12] In Munich Adolf Theilhaber saw the social role rather than the race of his patients playing a major factor in the frequency with which any group develops specific tumors, such as uterine tumors.[13] The religious practices of the Jews—circumcision, for example—were felt to play a role in the lower incidence of uterine cancer.[14] Theilhaber's findings were reinterpreted by the Jewish neurologist Leopold Löwenfeld in a different way. He saw the lower incidence of uterine cancer among female Jews as a reflection of types, rather than of race. The earlier menarche of Jewish women reflected the predominance of a specific type (the plethoric) among the Jew. This resulted in a lower incidence of uterine cancer because of the increased amount of blood in the organ.[15] The replacement of racial arguments with typological arguments was common at the time. Theilhaber also stressed the greater risk Jewish men have for cancer of the stomach and of the intestine.[16]

Adolf Theilhaber's son, Felix, whose work on the decline of the Jewish birthrate began with his interest in cancer while at his father's proprietary hospital for female diseases in Munich, documented the complex literature on the relationship of cancer to "race," stressing the much lower rate of cancer of the uterus and cervix for Jewish women and the much higher rate cancer of the stomach for Jewish men.[17] He clearly saw that this was in no way tied to the question of class, as the Jews he examined came from many social classes. He discounted the usual views about the lower rate of uterine and cervical cancer: Jewish women tend to have more children (his figures were from Budapest) so a lower birthrate did not account for the lower rate; they were admitted to hospitals more frequently (which would tend to provide a higher rather than a lower reporting of incidents); and they were exposed to the same surgical procedures. He noted that the "Jews are a purer race than those people among whom they live" and they suffered from many fewer cases of cervical cancer.[18] Theilhaber left open the cause of the lower rate, but his assumption was that it had to do with the etiology of the tumors.

The Theilhabers make little distinction between "racial" (endogenous) and "social" (exogenous) causes for cancer and its localization. But certain overall views can be extrapolated from their findings. For the Theilhabers, the localization of specific cancers made it possible to speak of a gender-based difference in the types of cancer among Jews. The stated rationale for the lower incidence of uterine and cervical cancer among Jewish women was the sexual practices of the Jews, specifically the "strict observance of the Mosaic Law regarding marital relations."[19] The laws governing abstinence among Jewish women during and following their menstrual cycles decrease the amount of "continued irritation," which was seen as "a potent causative factor" in the etiology of cancer. But hidden in this argument is the assumption that one further cause is the ritual circumcision of male Jews as well as their lower incidence of sexually transmitted disease.[20] There was a strong assumption in the course of the late nineteenth and early twentieth centuries (which is still held) that cervical or uterine cancer had a parasitical origin that could be sexually transmitted.[21] The etiology for the higher incidence of stomach cancer among Jewish men was the pace of life; the lower rate of cervical cancer among women was the sexual practices of the Jews. Freud would have had access to a summary of this debate in Felix Theilhaber's essay on cancer and the Jews in the *Jewish Lexicon*.[22]

Certainly the debate about the localization of cancer in both male and female Jews centered on the primary biological marker of the Jew, the circumcised penis, and its implications.[23] This sign of Jewishness was read metaphorically as a sign of the Jews' intense striving after wealth, the cause of stomach cancer in males. But there is in addition a detailed literature on the relationship between penile cancer and circumcision. Penile cancer accounted for between two and three percent of all cancerous tumors in men during the nineteenth century and was one of the most physically and psychologically devastating diseases. As early as 1882 the British surgeon Jonathan Hutchinson related the occurrence of cancer of the penis to the appearance of phimosis, the constriction of the prepuce, in infants. He also encouraged the practice of circumcision as it "must necessarily tend to cleanliness."[24] This relatively rare anomaly became one of the standard rationales for the advocacy of universal male circumcision by the end of the century.[25] In 1907, J. Dellinger Barney of the Harvard Medical School published a study of one hundred cases of cancer of the penis in which he noted "that not a single circumcised Jew was found in the hundred cases. This seems to my mind a most convincing argument in favor of circumcision."[26] Benjamin S. Barringer and Archie Dean added thirty-six cases to the literature on cancer of the penis in 1923, and noted early in their paper that "no Jews appear in this series."[27] Abraham Wolbarst of New York asked the most evident question: "Is circumcision a prophylactic against penis cancer?" His studies, which covered an additional 675 males, almost all of whom were Jews, found "not a single case of cancer of the penis."[28] The reason Wolbarst gave was the "cleanliness" circumcision affords.[29] As for the Austrian situation, V. Föderl, of von Hochenegg's surgical clinic at the University of Vienna, argued precisely the same point: he reported on forty cases from his clinic over a period of twenty-four years, of which none was a Jew. In addition he accounted for

276 cases of cancer over eleven years among men from the Viennese Jewish Hospital in which again, not a single case of penile cancer was recorded.[30] Further studies in Vienna done from 1921 to 1927 record 2,252 cases of cancer in males, in which not a single case of cancer of the penis was found.[31] These statistics implied that there was not only an immunity to penile cancer afforded by circumcision, but, taken together with Theilhaber's work on cervical cancer, that cancer of the genitalia was substantially less frequent among Jews than in the general population. Circumcision was a prophylactic against cancer and was a sign of sexual hygiene. Here, the implications of the debate about Jews and the transmission of syphilis lurked in the background.

There are complex interrelationships among many of these views concerning Jewish immunity or propensity to specific forms of disease. Given the debate about the lower (or higher) incidence of syphilis among Jews, it is not surprising that this view is linked to statistics concerning specific forms of cancer. Cancer of the mouth was assumed to be the result of scarring left by syphilis. In the standard nineteenth-century handbook on syphilis, there is an extensive discussion of this issue; "in the case of the tongue, the association of the two [cancer and syphilis] is so common, that it is difficult to avoid an impression, that syphilis must exercise some degree of predisposing influence. . . . In attempting to lay down rules for the differential diagnosis between cancer and syphilis I am most anxious to insist, as already done, on its extreme difficulty. . . . Cancerous processes may be simulated by syphilis in the closest possible manner."[32] In one study, 30 percent of all the cases of cancer of the mouth were claimed to have a syphilitic origin.[33] Maurice Sorsby used this as an illustration to rebut the assumption that the Jewish immunity to certain forms of cancer was hereditary: "A low incidence of [cancer of the tongue] among Jews would lend no support to the suggestion of racial immunity to it among Jews, for it is well known that cancer of the tongue is frequently excited by syphilis, and syphilis is by no means so common among Jews as it is among non-Jews; indeed, in the past it was almost completely absent."[34] Indeed, it was assumed that there was a low incidence of cancer of the buccal cavity (the soft tissues of the mouth and tongue) among Jews.[35]

For the period from 1924 to 1929, Sigismund Peller documented a greater incidence of death from cancer of the buccal cavity among Jewish men than among Jewish women. (In Peller's sample, 28 Jewish men died, as compared to 9 Jewish women. For every 100 cases of cancer reported, 2.5 Jewish men and .7 Jewish women suffered from buccal cancer, as opposed to 3.5 non-Jewish men and .4 non-Jewish women. In the overall statistics 37 Jews and 319 non-Jews died of buccal cancer, a ratio of 1 to 8.5.) Peller noted that Jewish men were much less likely to have cancer of the oral cavity and Jewish women much less likely to have cancer of the

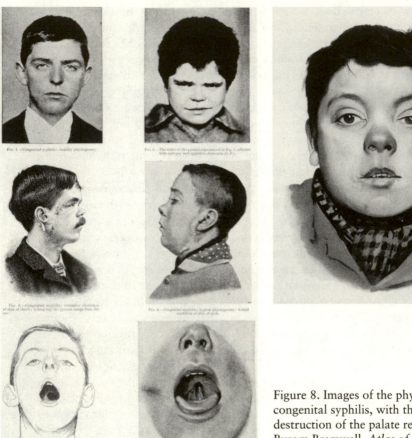

Figure 8. Images of the physiognomy of congenital syphilis, with the hidden destruction of the palate revealed. From Byrom Bramwell, *Atlas of Clinical Medicine* (Edinburgh: Constable, 1892–96).

genitalia.[36] Later work contrasted cancer of the mouth and cancer of the breast in men and women: cancer of the mouth was five times more frequent among men and cancer of the breast was seventeen times more frequent among women.[37] What the breast represented in the female, the mouth represented in the male. Except for Jews—Jewish males had a substantially lower rate of buccal tumors than the general population, but a higher rate than Jewish women. Disease was "gendered" as much as it was categorized by race.[38]

In April 1923 Freud showed his internist, Felix Deutsch (who later became a noted psychoanalyst specializing in working with organically ill patients), a lesion in his jaw and palate.[39] This lesion was initially diagnosed as a benign leukoplakia, a tumor caused by smoking. After an initial, poorly executed operation by Marcus Hajek, a professor of laryngology at the University of Vienna, that same month, when Freud almost bled to death, he was put in the hands of the best-known Austrian specialist on tumors of the jaw, the dental surgeon Hans Pichler, professor and director of the Dental Institute at the University of Vienna, under whose care he remained for the next sixteen years. By the end of the summer of 1923, after returning from a trip to Italy during which he had been in intense pain and had had a profuse hemorrhage, Freud was informed of what he had already guessed: the tumor was cancerous. In October 1923 Freud underwent two major operations to remove the cancer, which was then definitely diagnosed as squamous cell cancer, often found in cancers of the mouth. From 1923 to 1938 Freud underwent thirty-seven procedures at the hands of Pichler, many intended to adjust the prostheses that Pichler had made for him. Both Freud's speech and his hearing were affected to a limited extent. He avoided public appearances where he had to speak and was often represented at these by his daughter Anna. (The recording of Freud's voice made for the BBC upon his arrival in England in 1938 shows that while his speech was slightly impaired, it was completely comprehensible. From his perspective, however, this may well not have been the case.)

During the 1930s it seemed that he was in constant discomfort, if not outright pain, from his prostheses as well as from the effects of the surgery. By the fall of 1938, in Freud's new home in Hampstead, Max Schur, his internist, noticed a further lesion, which proved to be cancerous. Treated with radium, this final recurrence brought the aged Freud to the point where he requested Schur to administer morphine to him, and he quietly died on the night of September 23, 1939.

The question of what cancer, the "unwelcome intruder," as Freud called it, meant to Freud can be explored through an examination of the meaning of cancer as a disease of the Jews and Freud's representation of this disease in his writing of his final work, *Moses and Monotheism*. Freud insisted that the "dear old cancer with which [he had] been sharing [his] existence for 16 years" was the result of smoking.[40] Given the debate about the carcinogenic nature of tobacco that took place in the medical literature of the period, his view was well founded.[41] The view that tobacco consumption could be correlated with the occurrence of cancer had appeared as early as 1739. But by the time Rudolf Virchow wrote his study of cancerous tumors (1863–67), this view had become a standard part of that medical literature which sought specific irritants as the cause of cancer.[42] According to Virchow, the originative factors for cancerous tumors should be sought externally rather than internally, in the environment and not in heredity. Many of the standard medical handbooks of the period accepted this view, especially the association of cancer of the oral cavity and the smoking of pipes and cigars.[43] By accepting this notion Freud freed himself of a "Jewish" disease, one associated with the male Jew's sexuality in many complex ways.

One might also add that tobacco was considered a source of hysteria and, by Theodor Billroth, the great Viennese surgeon, of the "nervousness" of modern society.[44] This nervousness was the result of the competition for survival and the idea that "tired nerves need the stimulation of tea and alcohol and strong cigars" to function.[45] Indeed, there was the view that one of the primary forms of undiagnosed mental illness at the turn of the century was "Nicotinismus mentalis."[46] If excessive smoking caused nervousness, Freud's Jewish medical ally Leopold Löwenfeld saw moderate smoking, three cigars a day, as a potential therapy to "reduce nervousness."[47] That Jewish physicians tended to stress the positive aspect of tobacco addiction is not at all surprising. As early as the Christian anti-Semitic literature of the early nineteenth-century German Romantic poets, such as Clemens Brentano, it was the Jews who "in the year 1696 . . . planted the first tobacco in the Mark Brandenburg and thus suppressed the activity of the countrymen and caused the many sinful and confused thoughts . . . generated by the stench of this . . . plant."[48] The Jews were so addicted to this narcotic, stated Brentano, that they even subverted their own laws about smoking on the Sabbath by blowing smoke into a barrel on Friday that they emptied on Saturday! Such views were associated by Brentano with the "remarkable inherited diseases" of the Jews. Tobacco consumption came to be a means of describing yet another sign of the innate physical and psychological difference of the Jews. The Jewish response, linked to class identity, was to reverse this accusation and make tobacco consumption a sign of middle-class identity.

In one of the handbooks to which Freud contributed (and which he owned in both editions) there is a long and detailed study of the erotic (or rather, the antierotic) function of smoking. The author, Alexander Elster, argued that even though tobacco served as a physiological and psychological depressant or anaphrodisiac, it also had cultural significance: "The lord and master smokes 'big' cigars; the gentleman, the lover, and the young man smoke cigarillos; the lady and the prostitute smoke cigarettes." In addition, the act of smoking is given a gendered interpretation: for the man it is the reversion to the oral state; for the woman it is "playing with the idea of fellatio."[49] The association of the sexual with the world of smoking is clearly a reflex of the symbolic interpretation present in sexological discourse as a result of Freud's influence, but with social implications—that the cigar signifies the social rank of the powerful and the powerless (the master and the infant) but that it is not a sign of feminization.

At the beginning of his disease, before it was diagnosed as malignant, Freud had written to Ernest Jones that "smoking is accused as the etiology of this tissue rebellion."[50] During his treatment with Hans Pichler in 1924 he was also quite clear that, in his mind, there was a close connection between the cancer and his smoking of cigars.[51] Three decades earlier he had also linked his state of ill health with smoking. He had complained to Fliess at the time of the Emma Eckstein incident that he was "smoking heavily, owing to all the trouble which there was a great deal of recently," and that his "severe cardiac misery" was "accompanied by a mild depression."[52] Indeed, even later, in 1926, Freud's heart condition, his "myocarditis," was attributed to his consumption of cigars and Freud actually tried some nicotine-free cigars, which gave him much the same effect as untreated ones.[53] In a turn-of-the-century English anthology of tobacco-related verse that Freud owned and read, the following verse appears:

> In spite of my physician, who is, *entre nous*, a fogy
> And for every little pleasure has some pathologic bogy,
> Who will bear with no small vices, and grows dismally prophetic
> If I wander from the weary way of virtue dietetic;
>
> In spite of dire forewarnings that my brains will all be scattered,
> My memory extinguished, and my nervous system shattered,
> That my hand all take to trembling, and my heart begin to flutter,
> My digestion turn a rebel to my very bread and butter;
>
> As I puff this mild Havana, and its ashes slowly lengthen,
> I feel my courage gather and my resolution strengthen . . .
> I will smoke, and, I will praise you, my cigar, and I will light you
> With tobacco-phobic pamphlets by the learnéd prigs who fight you![54]

Freud never gave up his Havana, his "sweet habit of smoking."[55] In his daily chronicle, where only those things central to his life from 1929 to his death were recorded, he noted receiving cigars from the Frankfurt psychoanalyst Karl Landauer with the same intensity as he received great and costly works of art. Indeed, on November 2, 1930, he recorded only "first small cigar," the first since a major operation on his mouth by Pichler.[56] He (and here he was not alone)[57] believed that tobacco might actually have some salutary effect on such cancerous lesions.

For Freud a cigar was much more than a cigar. He even attributed his ability to work to tobacco.[58] Being without a cigar "was an act of self-mutilation as the fox performs in a snare when it bites off its own leg. I am not very happy, but rather feeling noticeably depersonalized," he wrote to Ferenczi in 1930 after another cardiac infarction.[59] The cigar was a central attribute of his sense of self; without it he ceased being completely human. The role the act of smoking played in his sense of self can be judged from his seeing his father as his model: "I believe I owe to the cigar a great intensification of my capacity to work and a facilitation of my self control. My model in this was my father, who was a heavy smoker and remained one for his entire life."[60] In Vienna, the Eastern Jews of Kallamon Jacob Freud's generation were seen as abusers of tobacco.[61] Tobacco was considered one of the precipitating causes of the nervous and circulatory diseases, such as intermittent claudication, from which Jews suffered.[62] But by Freud's own generation cancers of the hard palate had come to be called "rich man's cancer" because of the cost of purchasing the fifteen to twenty cigars a day deemed necessary to cause the cancer.[63] Cancer of the buccal cavity became a sign of success, much as did cardiac infarctions during the 1980s in the United States. This cancer was no longer seen as a sign of inferiority, but of acculturation. What had been a quality ascribed to foreign Jews became a quality associated with a specific economic class, as Jews became more integrated into the economic life of Vienna. Indeed, from 1900 to 1930, about the time Freud's cancer was discovered, Jewish scientists such as Maurice Sorsby recorded that the incidence of cancer among Jews, except for genital cancer, seemed to be approaching the frequency of cancer in the non-Jewish population.[64] By becoming ill they were becoming like everyone else.

Freud's description of his father's addictive behavior was in no way a conscious evocation of a Jewish predisposition to the consumption of tobacco, but rather a claim that his disease, his cancer, was—according to the best science of his day—not a Jewish disease. Rather it was a disease of a specific social class. To see it as a Jewish disease would be to evoke his own predisposition to a disease, the scientific discourse about which was linked to the perceived corrosive sexuality of the Jew. Yet lurking in Freud's statement is the sense that he was indeed his father's son in his compulsive smoking, as perhaps in other ways. Freud's relationship to his father was a complex one, as is the relationship of every son to his own father. Of the many things Freud's father represented to Freud, according to his own account, none was more central to his recollection than his image as a Jew.[65] Freud's account of his father's tale of being bullied by a Christian anti-Semite who knocked his cap into the gutter and forced him to retrieve it had provided Freud with a need for a "big, strong" Jewish father who was not an "unheroic" man.[66] Given all the negative associations Freud had with the internalized representation of his father, and with him as the representative of adult, Jewish masculinity, it is striking how Freud's association of a "capacity to work and a facilitation of self control" came to be associated with his father's image as a smoker. Here was the idealized image of the parent who nurtures (and nurtures orally) presented in the fantasy of the father as smoker. Needless to say, the qualities of hard work and self-control that Freud ascribed to his father were those of the positive stereotype of the successful, acculturated Jew in Viennese society. The internalized representation of the father as Jew and smoker was, however, poisoned. For even here the medical discourse pathologized the success of Kallamon Jacob and Sigmund Freud and their integration into Austrian society. Success, like Jewishness, made you sick. The disease of the Jews had become transformed into the disease of success. Yet both were clearly gendered—the cancer-ridden, male Jew was transformed into the cancer-ridden, successful male. Masculinity entailed specific dangers, and Jewish masculinity even more so. It is no wonder that Freud turned to Thornton Wilder during his visit on June 21, 1938, in London and observed that "it might some day be shown that cancer is allied to the 'presence of hate in the subconscious.' "[67]

The Circumcised Body as the Precipitating Factor for a Social Disease: Males and Anti-Semitism

Freud's cancer occurred during the period when there was an intense debate about why Jews do or do not develop certain forms of cancer. He and his Jewish colleagues, such as Felix Deutsch and Max Schur, saw his cancer not as a disease of the Jews but as a disease of the jaw. The supposed immunity of Jews to cancer of the mouth and jaw seemed to be vanishing, and Jews were evidencing the same signs of diseases of "civilization" as everyone else of a certain class in Vienna. Freud's own sense that his disease was caused by (and perhaps could be cured by) his smoking may well have been a means of dismissing the question of the Jewish predisposition to specific forms of disease.

The question of the Jews' immunity to diseases such as cancer had been hotly debated in the nineteenth century. The view that "the 'chosen people' are of all people most exempt from cancer" reflected a more general belief in the special status of the Jewish body.[68] There was one moment in the medical literature of the period in which this question evoked a set of specific responses that may help set the medical context for Freud's final published work, his study *The Man Moses and the Monotheistic Religion* (which Freud began to write in 1933 and published in its entirety in 1939). (I shall refer to it by its better-known English title, *Moses and Monotheism*.) In an exchange of letters in 1874, in the prestigious Philadelphia *Medical and Surgical Reporter*, Madison Marsh, a physician from Port Hudson, Louisiana, put forth this more general view in considering the question of the Jewish immunity to tuberculosis. Marsh argued that the Jews "enjoy a wonderful national immunity from, not only phthisis [tuberculosis] but all disease of the thoracic viscera."[69] The Jew does not suffer from tuberculosis because "his constitution has become so hardened and fortified against disease by centuries of national calamities,

by the dietetics, regimen and sanitas of his religion, continuing for consec-
utive years of so many ages."[70] This view was generally held during the
second half of the nineteenth century. Lucian Wolf, in a debate before the
Anthropological Society of Great Britain and Ireland in 1885, stated cate-
gorically that "figures could also be given to prove the immunity of Jews
from phthisis," and Dr. Asher, in that same debate, observed that "Jews
had an extraordinary power of resistance to phthisis."[71] Jews lived
longer, had a lower child mortality, and were generally healthier than
Christians.

The Jew's "high average physique . . . is not less remarkable than the
high average of his intelligence."[72] Jews were the "purest, finest, and
most perfect type of the Caucasian race."[73] This view was one widely
espoused by Jews, in Europe and the United States, in the late nineteenth
century. Rabbi Joseph Krauskopf informed his Reform congregation in
Philadelphia:

> Eminent physicians and statisticians have amply confirmed the truth: that
> the marvelous preservation of Israel, despite all the efforts to blot them out
> from the face of the earth, their comparative freedom from a number of
> diseases, which cause frightful ravages among the Non-Jewish people, was
> largely due to their close adherence to their excellent Sanitary Laws. Health
> was their coat of mail, it was their magic shield that caught, and warded off,
> every thrust aimed at their heart. Vitality was their birthright. . . . Their im-
> munity, which the enemy charged to magic-Arts, to alliances with the spirits
> of evil, was traceable solely to their faithful compliance with the sanitary
> requirements of their religion.[74]

Marsh added one new twist to this equation. Jews were healthier, lived
longer, were more immune to disease, and were more intelligent because
of their healthful practices, such as diet, and because they belonged to the
"white" race—or at least they did from the standpoint of a rural
Louisiana physician during Reconstruction.

A month after this report was published, it was answered in detail by
Ephraim M. Epstein, a Jewish physician practicing in Cincinnati, Ohio,
who had earlier practiced medicine in Vienna and in Russia. He rebutted
Marsh's argument point by point: Jews had no immunity to tuberculosis,
or any other disease, including those long associated with Jewish religious
practices: "I am sure I have observed no Jewish immunity from any diseases, venereal disease not excepted."[75] Jews did not have "superior longevity"; they had no advantage either because of their diet or because of
their practice of circumcision. But Jews did possess a quality lacking in
their Christian neighbors. What made Jews less at risk was the network
of support, the "close fraternity, one Jew never forsaking the material
welfare of his brother Jew, and he knows it instinctively."[76] It was indeed

the "common mental construction" of the Jew that preserved his health—that and "the constitutional stamina which that nation inherited from its progenitor, Abraham of old, and because it kept that inheritance undeteriorated by not intermarrying with other races."[77] Group dynamics and racial purity were the source of Jewish health, such as it was.

Here the battle was joined. The Southern, Christian physician saw in the Jews' social practices and their race a key to universal health. He, of course, defined race in terms of his own ideological understanding of the primary difference between the "Negro" and the "Caucasian" races. The Jews, according to the standard textbooks of the period, such as that of Carl Claus, were indeed "Caucasians."[78] But in the United States, following the Civil War, this concept was given a special, intensely political association. Whites had the potential, with good diet and the fortitude to bear oppression (such as Reconstruction), to be healthier, more intelligent, more immune from disease than—and here Marsh's readers would understand—than . . . blacks. The Eastern European Jewish physician saw any limited advantage accruing to the Jews lying in their inherited nature and sexual practices, to which non-Jews could have absolutely no access—indeed, which by definition excluded them.

Marsh's intense, vituperative response came in August 1874.[79] Initially, he called on the statistical evidence from Prussian, French, and British sources to buttress his argument about Jewish longevity. He then dismissed Epstein's argument about Jewish risk for disease completely and turned to the question of the role of what Epstein described as "the moral cause that had prevented intermarriage of the Jews with other nations, and thus preserved intact their health and tenacity of life."[80] It was circumcision as a sign of the separateness and selectivity of the Jews that Epstein evoked as the proof for his case about Jewish difference. Circumcision for Marsh was a "sanitary measure and religious rite . . . in practice by the ancient Egyptians. . . . It never became a Hebrew institution until friendly relations had been established between Abraham and the Egyptians. Then it was initiated by the circumcision of Abraham and Isaac by the express command of God."[81] Circumcision was an Egyptian ritual and "Moses, the great champion, leader and lawgiver of the Hebrew race, was himself an Egyptian priest, educated in all the deep research and arts of the Chaldean Mage and mystic philosophic development of Egyptian and Oriental science, and all that was then known of the science of medicine, in its general principles and in its application of details for the preservation of health and prevention of disease."[82] This theory with its "slight tinge of Egyptian and Indian, or Asiatic philosophy, and shadow of its teachings pervade[s] all the books of Moses."[83] (While it is clear that the term "Jew" in this exchange includes both men and women, the specific images evoked for the scientist, whether the "lying" Jewish physician

Epstein or the true, non-Jewish scientist, Moses, the "Egyptian priest," are male.) The ritual practices of the Jews are merely an amalgam of the combined knowledge of the peoples of the West. They are in no way the special product of this inbred and haughty people.

What did Epstein know about real medicine? Marsh simply dismissed Epstein as a Jew, whose authority was drawn solely from this fact: "What evidence or authority does he bring to support his pretensions to superior knowledge? His being himself a Jew, per se."[84] He affirmed his view that the Jews possessed the secret to greater health, which they were unwilling to share with the rest of the world. The subtext to Marsh's argument is that Jews had a special immunity that was the result of accident and that gave them immunity to disease. But the true secret is that this gift was not theirs at all; it was taken from the peoples among whom they lived. Jewish "physicians," like Epstein, were charlatans who tried to disguise their lying natures. The evident anger Marsh felt at Epstein's claim about the lack of a special status for the Jewish body was the source of his hatred of the Jews, as Sigmund Freud pointed out in his discussion of the origins of anti-Semitism. The Jewish body, and specifically the male body, lies at the heart of anti-Semitism. In *Moses and Monotheism*, Freud affirmed Paolo Mantegazza's charge that it was the special nature of the Jewish body that evoked the anger of the non-Jew toward the Jew's selectivity. Marsh reversed this, as he, too, wished to share in the special status of the "healthy" Jewish body. Stated in his critique is the central epistemological charge lodged against the Jewish (male) scientist, the inability of the scientist to have a truly neutral position because he was a Jewish male. Thus the Jewish scientist studying the nature of the Jewish body cannot tell the truth. His own perspective is as much inscribed by his Jewish identity as is his circumcised body.

Here Marsh's construction of the "healthy" Jewish body was supported by the reading of circumcision that came to dominate American medicine by the close of the nineteenth century. Circumcision had become a major issue in the medical practice of the United States. Indeed, the American physician Peter Charles Remondino, writing in the 1870s, could note that "circumcision is like a substantial and well-secured life annuity; . . . it ensures them better health, greater capacity for labour, longer life, less nervousness, sickness, loss of time."[85] Indeed, by the 1890s, an American association had begun to be made between "uncircumcised" and "uncivilized."[86] In this context it is not surprising that circumcision, an intervention that could be made by the physician, came to have a function in the definition of "hygiene." But it is in no way to be understood as a Jewish practice, in the terms Epstein had outlined. The medicalization of circumcision meant that the association of circumcision with the nature of the Jewish male body and his character had to be exorcised. Marsh had removed the figure of the Jewish male "physician" from this equation in his debate with Epstein, and converted him into a non-Jew who created the practices that now could benefit all, not merely Jewish males.

This debate, held during Reconstruction, with its evident racial overtones, can present a basis for a reading of Freud's final work, *Moses and Monotheism*, as a study of the problematic position of the Jew as the cause of the malady of anti-Semitism.[87] The image of the Jew as the source of disease is a simple extension of the image of the diseased Jew. Freud refused to discuss this theme in his reading of Schreber's autobiography in 1911; Freud repressed the presence of this association in his understanding of the cause of his cancer in 1923; but in his final work, written under the sign of the anti-Semitism of Austro-fascism and of the Nazis, he acknowledged this punishing association. *Moses and Monotheism*, Freud's study of the disease of anti-Semitism, was written by a diseased male Jew, the often-operated-upon Sigmund Freud, at the height of public anti-Semitic feeling in the early twentieth century. This European anti-Semitism would soon move to extirpate the "diseased Jew" from the European body politic through the Shoah. *Moses and Monotheism* was Freud's complex answer to the image of anti-Semitism as madness, the etiology of that insanity, and the paranoid system of the anti-Semite. The book was, as he wrote to Hanns Sachs on March 12, 1939, "quite a worthy exit."[88]

Freud's image of Moses as an Egyptian male who led the Jews into the desert and was killed by them certainly evoked, as a contemporary review noted, "the impressions he believes persist in the mind of the race."[89] When attacked for having written a book that could undermine Jewish resistance at this period of great anti-Semitism, Freud commented to Arnold Zweig that "my arid treatise would [not] destroy the belief of a single person brought up by heredity and training in the faith."[90] The "common mental construction" of the Jew, given the Jew's inheritance and intelligence, could not succumb to the mere words of a "scientific" study of the origin of that mind-set. Here Freud stated the dilemma with which this study has grappled: if to be Jewish is not to belong to a religious community (indeed, it seems to be here another reflex of the "common mental construction" of the Jew), what relationship does it have to the mind of the Jew, and specifically the mind of the Jewish male scientist? Is the male Jew as scientist to be understood in the context of the "common mental construction" of the Jew or the neutral ("arid") mental construction of the scientist? The images of the Jews retained by the ailing Freud can be explored in reading *Moses and Monotheism*.

In the work of Josef Popper-Lynkeus, the self-taught, Austrian-Jewish engineer, social theorist, and author, Freud believed himself to have first found mention of his central thesis of Moses as an Egyptian. Popper-Lynkeus was born in Kolin in Bohemia in 1838 and, unlike Freud, remained in the Eastern provinces until he was fifteen, attending the local religious school. He eventually attended the gymnasium and then the polytechnic in Prague, but was denied an academic position for which he was proposed because he was a Jew. A self-taught engineer, he developed a series of patents that, over decades, generated enough income to enable him to devote his time to study and writing. In the 1920s he became one of the leading opponents of scientific racialism, attacking writers such as the philosopher Eduard von Hartmann. In 1938 Freud (as well as Albert Einstein) wrote a short introduction to a study of Popper-Lynkeus by Yisrael Doryon.[91] In a letter to Doryon, Freud noted that his borrowing of the theme of Moses as an Egyptian from Popper-Lynkeus's *Fantasies of a Realist* (1899) may well have been a case of "cryptomnesia," an unconscious borrowing. This admission to an act of cryptomnesia was paralleled by Freud's uncomfortable later realization that not only Popper-Lynkeus but also the anti-Semitic theorist Houston Stewart Chamberlain, relying on Ernst Renan's comments, espoused this view.[92] Thus both the Jewish rationalist, Popper-Lynkeus, and the anti-Semite, Chamberlain, could have provided the source for Freud's image of the Egyptian Moses.

If Chamberlain was Freud's antithesis, as Wagner's son-in-law and a member of the anti-Semitic German cultural elite at the turn of the century, then Popper-Lynkeus, as an Eastern-European Jewish scientist, creative writer, and philosopher, was Freud's literary Other. It was not exclusively his image of Moses that Freud acknowledged to have found in his work, but also a clear parallel to his theory of dreams.[93] But only in his 1932 essay on Popper-Lynkeus did the writer come to be identified with the "unique mental construction" of the Jew: "A special feeling of sympathy drew me to him, since he too had painful experience of the bitterness of the life of a Jew and of the hollowness of the ideals of present-day civilization."[94] If we are to take Freud's claim seriously that he repressed his first reading of Popper-Lynkeus's story on dreaming (in 1899), then his simultaneous repression of his memory of Popper-Lynkeus's tale about "the son of the King of Egypt" can provide some further context for Freud's interpretation. This tale, which turns on the dream the pharaoh has of being strangled by the fruit of his own loins, is merely a subliminal indicator of the motivation the pharaoh has for killing all of the newborn male children of the Jews. The image of the child killing the father is initially present in a story about the Egyptian Moses and his threat to his Egyptian father. Freud made the real threat that of the Egyptianized Jews to their Egyptian leader. It is striking that the entire discourse of identification that Freud evoked here has to do with the choice of definitions of the "good" male as opposed to the "bad" male. Jewish masculinity, and specifically the masculinity of the Jewish scientist, stands at the center of Freud's identification.

As with many of his works, *Moses and Monotheism* provided a general theoretical introduction to Freud's approach. Building on the work he had written on the origins of group dynamics in *Totem and Taboo* (1912–13) and *Group Psychology* (1921), Freud sketched how he (and Otto Rank) had reconstructed "an 'average' legend that brings into prominence the essential features" of the myth of the birth of the hero. What is noteworthy is that Freud here, for the first time in decades, evoked Galton's photographic technique as the model for the procedure of reconstruction.[95] The composite photograph is the model for the manner of seeing difference in *Moses and Monotheism*. The overlapping stories provided a uniform model, which is the tale of Oedipus, and—not surprisingly—the tale of Moses. We are meant to "see" the essential qualities of the hero in Freud's representation of Moses. But this image of seeing was polluted, not only by Galton, but by the flood of illustrated racial studies during the 1920s and 1930s, which claimed to present the essence of the visual representation of Jewish difference. That the acculturated, Western Jew was virtually invisible, that the Jew often could "pass" as an Aryan, made it imperative for science to be able to represent the essence of Jewish difference.

Science makes images, but Jews do not. The religion that the Egyptian male Moses was to help establish is itself antithetical to the creation of images. It is a sign of the intensification of earlier forms through the Jews: "Jewish monotheism behaved in some respects even more harshly than did the Egyptian: for instance in forbidding pictorial representations of any kind."[96] This led to the establishment of the written language of the Jews, for "if they were subject to the prohibition against pictures, iconoclasm, they would even have had a motive for abandoning the hieroglyphic picture-writing while adapting its written characters to expressing a new language."[97] The evocation of the image as a means of speaking about a world in which images are forbidden points to the contradiction between the "insight" associated with science and that associated with religion. But it is also the Jewish response to the pressures and temptations of a world outside Judaism.

J. G. Frazer had struck a similar note in his rebuttal of Ernst Renan's theory about the origin of the prohibition of graven images. Renan had tied it to the nomadic nature of the Jews and the simple difficulty of transporting idols. Frazer saw it, as did Freud, as a response to the "black arts of their powerful neighbors." These "black arts" would have been "doubtless familiar to the Hebrews, and may have found many imitators among them. But to deeply religious minds, imbued with a profound sense of the divine majesty and goodness, these attempts to take heaven by storm must have appeared the rankest blasphemy and impiety; we need not wonder therefore that a severe prohibition of all such nefarious practices should have found a prominent place in the earliest Hebrew code."[98] The "common mental construction" of the Jew was even reflected in the written form of his language.

The letters of the alphabet represent the abstraction of the male Jewish mind. *Mauscheln*, the hidden language of the Jews, did not vanish; rather it became embedded in the form of the letters of the Jews' language. This is the theme of Freud's sense of the abandonment of his own language, German, through his flight from Austria in 1938. He wrote to the French psychoanalyst Raymond de Saussure on June 11, 1938, of "the loss of the language in which one lived and thought and which one will never be able to replace with another, for all of one's efforts at empathy. With painful comprehension I observe how otherwise familiar terms of expression fail me in English and how [Id] ["Es"] even tries to resist giving up the familiar Gothic script."[99] The Id, "Es" in German, remained fixed visually for Freud in German type. Here the letters of German replaced the Hebrew letters. Freud had noted to George Sylvester Viereck more than a decade earlier that his "language . . . is German. I considered myself German intellectually, until I noticed the growth of anti-Semitic prejudices in Germany and German Austria. Since that time, I prefer to call myself a Jew."[100] Freud was a Jew who visualized the world in terms of his embeddedness in German culture. It was part of him, yet remained distant. (It is no accident that the word Freud "sees" in Gothic script is the Id—the most elemental of all aspects of the psyche.) The final decade of entries in his daily chronicle of activities beginning in 1929 was recorded in Latin script, which gradually replaced the Gothic script in which the diary began. Indeed, when he recorded, on November 10, 1938, the great pogroms that swept Germany during the Kristallnacht, his entry read in English: "Pogroms in Germany." As Michael Molnar notes, it is as if he were a foreign reporter distanced even from the native language of those unspeakable events."[101] This language of the "foreign reporter" is the language of the male scientist whose gaze is unimpaired by his identification with his subject.

Moses was, for Freud, an Egyptian male. This view, while not unique to Freud, was thought by him to be revolutionary. Moses was an Egyptian who transformed his own religion, that of Aten, through his life and death, into biblical Judaism. It was the Egyptian Moses who provided the Jews with the form of their new religion and with its primary sign, "the custom of circumcision."[102] Freud understood circumcision as an Egyptian custom. It was in this context that Freud evoked Heinrich Heine and the image of Judaism as "the plague dragged from the Nile valley, the unhealthy beliefs of Ancient Egypt."[103] Judaism was a form of leprosy (or syphilis) that infected the Jews. Freud cited the Egyptian historian Manetho's account of the going out from Egypt in which Manetho characterized the Jews as "lepers and other polluted persons" who were exiled by Amenophis.[104] Here too, Moses was a "priest, . . . a native of Hêliopolis, named Osarsêph after the god Osiris; . . . but when he joined this people, he changed his name and was called Moses."[105]

According to Freud, circumcision was not the Jews' indigenous disease—rather, it was an Egyptian disease that they acquired only by their exposure to it during their slavery in Egypt. But, of course, circumcision is not a disease, no matter how telling Heine's metaphor seemed to Freud. Circumcision is a social practice—not an inherent sign of immutable membership in a group. If it was a sign of Egyptian ritual practices, then it was also a sign of the conversion of certain Jews during the period of Egyptian slavery to the religion of Aten. Circumcision became a sign, not of separation, but of assimilation. It was the sign of the demand for assimilation placed on the Jew. The model Freud saw was that of "two groups of people who come together to form a nation" in which one of the two groups "had an experience which must be regarded as traumatic."[106] This is a mirror of the post-Enlightenment experience of Central European Jewry. The analogy that Freud makes in this work to the development of the psyche is striking. The formation of the ego is seen as "comparable to scars."[107] And scarring, such as that caused by syphilis or constant smoking, led to cancer. Hidden behind all this rhetoric is a constant set of referents to the relationship between the Jewish male body, circumcised, and the scarred and diseased Jewish psyche.

Freud's position on the meaning of the origin of circumcision in the late 1930s paralleled the movement of other Jewish male thinkers. Earlier views tended to relate the "ancient" origin of the Hebrew ritual to the circumcision practices of other "primitive" peoples. (The subtext is that Jewish males were like the males of every other race at one time.) In 1915 Theodor Reik commented that "it might be pointed out that in the sagas of the ancient Semitic peoples the same displacement [of the rebellious feelings of young men] onto gods who demand circumcision takes place, just as in primitive peoples."[108] This equation provided a sense of the universalization of a Jewish practice affecting males that was viewed by the fin de siècle medical profession as problematic.

By 1959, in his own version of the history of Moses written after the Shoah, Reik undertook exactly the opposite rhetorical strategy: the Jewish practice of circumcision was inherently different from that of the "primitive." He wrote that "we encounter here a remarkable difference between the Hebrew ritual of the circumcision and that of the primitive tribes, a difference worthy of our attention. . . . While among the Jews circumcision is the token of the covenant between Yahweh and His people, anthropologists agree that 'distinctly religious ceremonies in combination with the rite are extremely rare' among savage tribes of Africa and Australia."[109] The Jewish males were now not "savage." Their ritual reflected a higher level of political organization and was therefore basically different from that of the "primitive." This movement from a pre-Shoah to a post-Shoah reading of the meaning of circumcision closely followed Freud's rereading of the meaning of the act of circumcision, a reading that was itself formed by the discourse about disease implicit in the medical writing about circumcision.

The image of the "Egyptian disease" is central for Freud's argument about Moses' Egyptian identity, for it explained why Moses demanded circumcision as a basic rite of his new religion. Had Moses been a Jew, Freud reasoned (and he himself saw the thinness of his logic), he would have abolished all such identifying signs of the male Jews' subjugation in Egypt. Rather, he made this a sign of Jewish assimilation to the dominant religion of Egypt. The model here was the retention of acquired characteristics, echoing the debate about the inheritability of the sign of circumcision. Jewish religious practice retained the sign of circumcision as it signified a traumatic stage through which it was necessary to have passed in order to have developed into a Jew. This sign of moving from one stage to another, from the world of the Judaism of Joseph to that of Moses, paralleled for Freud the development of the individual, following the model of the recapitulation of the species.

But all of this was cast, for Freud, in the language of competition between males. The strong male was pitted against the weak male. In the individual, the mother's threat that the father would castrate the son for his masturbatory activities, a cause of pleasure and disease, created a fear of the father.[110] This fear evoked an essential element of the "common mental construction" of all human beings, the original threat of the primal father to castrate his competing sons. Jewish masculinity was thus a relic of some earlier, deeper confrontation between men. This atavistic moment in history was marked on the Egyptian consciousness and on the Egyptian body in the practice of circumcision. Circumcision marked the essence of the borrowing from Egypt, and circumcision was but the "symbolic substitution for the castration which the primal father once inflicted upon his sons in the plenitude of his absolute power."[111] It is thus not the Jewish males who were atavistic, but rather the Egyptians; by extension, Freud saw this as a quality of the other "nation" that circumcises, the Moslems. Circumcision marks the distinction between cleanliness and the unclean in Islam: "Even to this day a Turk will abuse a Christian as an 'uncircumcised dog.' "[112] Freud's reduction of Islam, as a religious practice, to a national identity, "a Turk," reflects the distancing of religious identity throughout his work. But it also illustrates his fantasy of a nationalism defined in masculine terms. His circumcised, male "Turk" represents both the national state and the masculine simultaneously. As Philip Rieff noted: "The primitive and the child survive [for Freud] in memory, the representation of the past among the faculties. Against the overconfidence of reason, representing the future, the Lamarckian Freud asserted the ancient claim of memory to a greater power than reason had allowed."[113] But the Jewish male was not the originator of this evocation of the distant past; it was Egyptian, the Moslem.

In *Moses and Monotheism*, Freud defined who was diseased. The Egyptianized Jews first killed their leader and then repressed the memory of this act. This repression made them ill. The meaning of the "Jewish" religion, of monotheism, itself reflected a further debate about the originality and creativity of the Jews. Freud's study of the man Moses and the origin of monotheism had its seed in the debates about the nature of Judaism that surfaced in the anthropological literature of the early twentieth century, specifically in the work of the ethnologist Father Wilhelm Schmidt, whom Freud saw as his bête noire in Austria.[114] Schmidt, the author of a twelve-volume study, *The Origin of the Idea of God*, was a noted anti-Semite whose views on race mirrored the most egregious ones of his time. He tried to rebut what contemporary science called the central defining contribution of the Jews to Western culture—the creation of monotheism. For him, monotheism was in no way a discovery of a small group of male Jews. Rather, it was a universal first principle that usually degenerated into polytheistic religions.

Schmidt's views about the Jews were lodged in a conviction of the immutability of the Jewish soul rather than in genetic theory. For Schmidt it was the "psychic structure" of the Jews that defined their difference; it was that they "lost contact with their roots . . . once they rejected Christ," and this loss was mirrored in "the deepest region of their souls."[115] Even baptism, while it "removes the strongest reason separating him from us and surmounts the true and deepest cause of his otherness," was not sufficient to wipe out "the racial effects of this cause, which have made themselves apparent in the course of these two millennia."[116] The origin of monotheism, according to Schmidt, lay in the direct revelation to all "primitive" peoples of the oneness of God. It was only in the rebellion of the individual chosen as the means of this revelation that this original monotheism degenerated into polytheism. Thus Schmidt came up against Freud's view that totemism was the basis of all religion. Primitive man, for Schmidt, was neither barbaric nor neurotic: "To bring such men into connection with modern sex-ridden neurotics, as [Freud] would have us do, and from this connection to deduce the alleged fact that all thought and feeling, especially the subliminal, is founded on and saturated with sex, must remain lost labor."[117] This view was made overt in Schmidt's attacks on psychoanalysis as a corrosive (read: Jewish) force in modern society.[118] It was against Schmidt's evocation of the idea of the Jew, and Freud as the exemplary Jew, that Freud wrote *Moses and Monotheism*.

Freud's Moses is set off from the accepted biblical image of the Jewish Moses in many ways. The *Mauscheln* that marks the Jew's language, even in the form of the letters of the Hebrew alphabet, was given gender in the slowness of speech attributed to the biblical Moses. But Freud's Moses did not suffer from an "inhibition or disorder of speech" like the speech-impaired Freud suffering with his prosthesis. His Moses "spoke another language and could not communicate with his Semitic neo-Egyptians without an interpreter."[119] Moses' difficulty of speech seems to have been social rather than physiological. However, the assumption in the ethnology of the period was that the Jew's accent was a direct result of his physical constitution, rather than simply a question of his command of multiple languages.

Moses spoke well; his only problem was a noticeable accent when shifting from his native language to his new language. This was, of course, the origin and social meaning of *Mauscheln* in Freud's Vienna. But again it was not the Jew who bore the stigma of his acculturation on his tongue, but the representation of the dominant (or to use the term from the period, the "host") culture. It was the Egyptian male who had to learn the language of the Jews, not the Yiddish-speaking Jew who had to learn German. This general association of the age may well have been evoked in the context of Freud's argument about the Egyptian origin of Moses in his reading of Popper-Lynkeus's *Fantasies of a Realist*. In that volume, so intensely mined by Freud, there is a story entitled "A Table Talk with Martin Luther" that presents a *Mauschelnd* Eastern Jew who comes to visit and debate Luther. (Freud checked this tale in the table of contents of his copy.) Popper-Lynkeus presents the story, based on a true incident, of the "Polish Jew" whose exchanges with Luther are held in "his queer Polish-Jewish jargon, while turning up his arms and gesticulating with his hands, as the Jews do in talking."[120] What he says horrifies Luther and his cronies—for Rabbi Hirsch turns out to be the ultimate freethinker, an individual who believes in no laws, no rules, and who is quite willing to undermine all those held by Luther. Popper-Lynkeus's text represents the Eastern Jew speaking in *Mauscheln* as the unceasing questioner of all things. Here, too, Freud would have found a link between the male Jew as an outsider who wished to undermine all systems of belief and the popular image of the Jew as unable completely to control the language of the dominant culture. It is in the language of this male Jew that his difference from the world of German men, such as Luther, could be judged. Masculine power here is in the hands of the "real" German-speakers, who threaten Rabbi Hirsch's life; but the Jew as outsider, in spite of his lack of power, remains in intellectual control. Language remains the central quality for defining both humanness and the act of belonging to a group (*Volk*). But it is a positive quality associated with the "damaged" language of the Jew in Popper-Lynkeus's tale; in Freud's representation of Moses, it is associated with the origin of the "damaged" body of the Jew.

The primitive world mirrored by Egyptian culture in *Moses and Monotheism* is represented by the ritual of circumcision. It was a society that consisted of "small hordes, each under the domination of a powerful male. . . . It is probable that these creatures had not advanced far in the development of speech."[121] The inarticulate primitive male became the model for the Egyptian male in this book written by a speech-impaired Jewish male. This negative image of the Egyptian has a parallel in an essay certainly well known to Freud. In 1928 H. C. Jelgersma published an extensive essay on the repression of cannibalism in ancient Egypt in *Imago*.[122] Ritual cannibalism, a charge lodged over and over against Jewish males in Central Europe at the turn of the century, became a quality associated specifically with ancient Egyptian ritual practices. Jelgersma came to see this sign of masculine identity among the Egyptians as a repression of their earlier cannibalism. The Egyptians became the locus, in the discourse of psychoanalysis, for precisely those practices that had been used to define Jewish male difference.

If the Jew was infected with primitive practices and attitudes in Egyptian slavery, then the anti-Semitic response to the nature of the Jews was not at all a response to the Jews themselves, but to the world of the anti-Semite. It was thus the process of acculturation that provided the Jews with those qualities deemed objectionable by those same individuals who saw reflected in the Jews their own traditions. The Jews provided a type of narcissistic mirror held up to those cultures among which they lived and from whom they borrowed rituals such as circumcision. Central to the argument of *Moses and Monotheism* is this structure of borrowing, and specifically the borrowing of practices within the Middle East. The association of "Egypt" and "Islam" was a powerful one during the 1920s, and the violent, often brutal response of Islamic authorities to the rise of political Zionism was noted in Freud's correspondence, especially with Arnold Zweig, during the 1930s. But the real villains in Freud's piece, those primitive people who infected the Jews in exile among them with their primitive practices and attitudes, are the Germans and the Austrians. The Christian fantasy of Jewish selectivity, about which Marsh loudly complained, was a problem of Western culture, not of the Jews. The cry was that Jews brought all this hatred on themselves by their sense of superiority, which was manifested in their sexual selectivity. The question of Jewish sexual practices echoes the debate about the meaning of circumcision in the text.

Freud thus evoked in *Moses and Monotheism* the meaning of incest. He evoked the universal renunciation of instinct and the repression of polymorphous sexuality, and again rejected Edvard Westermarck's biological thesis. The Finnish sociologist Westermarck saw in the physical beauty of the female (as opposed to the strength of the male) the marker of positive sexual selection.[123] Sexual selectivity does not lead to danger, in terms of either biology or social results. Freud again rejects the tradition "which seeks to explain the horror of incest biologically and to trace it to an obscure knowledge of the danger done by inbreeding. It is not even certain, however, that there *is* any danger of damage from inbreeding—let alone that primitive peoples can have recognized it and reacted against it."[124] This is a simple recapitulation of Darwin's view. "The command in favor of exogamy" is made the desire of the father; it is not the condemnation of endogamy but the desire to keep the females of the family for the father that underlies it. This reversal of the standard interpretation of Jewish selectivity makes exogamy, rather than the refusal to permit endogamy, the constraining rule. At its center is the Jewish male and the definition of Jewish male heterosexuality, for the icon of sexual selection in Freud's text is male-centered. Freud's own view was that the Jews had at least attempted to overcome the power of the libido through their "rejection of a sexual or aggressive instinctual demand."[125] This link underlined that it was the "common mental construction" of the Jew and provided Freud with the model of the "renunciation of instinct." While this was cast within his discussion of the religious structures of Judaism (but not the practice of circumcision), it is clear that the rhetoric Freud evoked was that of the image of the sexual aggressiveness of the male Jew in Western culture.

The debate about incest was no longer a debate about racial biology. If inbreeding was benign, the only fault lay in the Jewish claim that endogamous marriage was necessary to preserve Jews' identity through their covenant with God. But the Jews, according to Freud, had "long abandoned" the view of themselves as the "chosen people." (This rejection of the special status of the Jews was a commonplace among fin de siècle acculturated Jewish thinkers.) It "still survives among that people's enemies in a belief in a conspiracy by the 'Elders of Zion.' "[126] This is analogous to the "forgotten truth [that] lies hidden in delusional ideas" of psychotics.[127] Here is the return to Schreber and to the understanding that the activity of the male anti-Semite is an activity of mental illness. It is not a neurosis, however, but rather a psychosis. It is not a single set of symptoms, but an all-consuming system of representation. The psychotic's system centers on the conspiracy of those male Jews who are the only figures in the forged *Protocols of the Elders of Zion*, as their Otherness defines the central problem, the psychotic's anxiety about his own masculinity.

It is not the claim that anti-Semitism is the inheritance of Christianity that lies at the heart of Freud's theory of anti-Semitism but the shared memory of the original sin of the Jews, their ancient killing of Moses after fleeing Egypt under his direction. This act of patricide, the recapitulation of the primitive killing of the father by his sons, shaped the Jewish experience. The struggle of the male with the male defines Jewish history in terms of the Jew's masculinity. Not the murderer, but the victim is at fault, to paraphrase the title of Oskar Kokoschka's expressionist drama. For Freud the core of anti-Semitism lay with the Jews' "continued . . . disavow[al] [of] the father's murder." The "common mental construction" of the Jews was at fault, for the Jews were "habitual[ly] stubborn."[128] The Christians, at least, admit to their own killing of "the primal picture of God, the primal father, and his later reincarnations" and thus were freed from the taint of hatred.[129] These are qualities of mind inherited across time, as are the notions that the Jews "defy all oppression" and succeed in both the economic and cultural lives of the people among whom they dwell.[130] But all these "common mental constructions" are linked to the experience of the Jews in Egypt. They are the result of the failed attempt of the Jews to assimilate and become Egyptians. The sign of this attempted assimilation is the practice of infant circumcision.

Freud's image of the Jews in *Moses and Monotheism* was a reflection of Franz Wittels's insane "baptized Jews." But Freud, who would have been represented in the text through his own discussion of the origin of Jewish identity, held himself out of the discussion by creating Moses, who belongs to and yet does not belong to the world of the Jews. It is this character with whom Freud clearly identifies in this text (and elsewhere in his work).[131] Yet Freud managed to maintain his distance from even this figure by insisting that his position was that of the "arid" scholarly observer. He was not the male Jewish fabulist, not the Popper-Lynkeus of the stories, but the neutral observer, the Popper-Lynkeus as scientist. Thus Freud did not publish the preface to his text, which argued that the text was an amalgam of the "creative" and the "scholarly," casting this in a metaphor that evoked the biological arguments about the cause of Jewish inferiority.[132]

Anti-Semitism is the inheritance of "common mental constructions" about the Jew and by the Jew. Freud thus dismissed the charge that anti-Semitism was the result of the Jews being out of their correct space. He argued that the Jews have long dwelled in cities in Germany, such as Cologne (the putative point of origin of his family), much longer than the

Germans. He refused to acknowledge that they are "different from the 'host' nations" (which is a recapitulation of his argument about the narcissism of minor differences). He saw the supposed "differences" from the "Nordic peoples" as trivial but acknowledged that they are understood as "fundamental."[133] These "differences," as he discusses them in this text, center on the definition of the male Jewish body and the sexual practices of the Jew. These minor differences come to define Jewish identity and Jewish dissimilarity in European (read: Christian) culture.

While Freud freed Christianity from the charge of being the sole origin of hatred toward the Jews, he did see that the patricide of the Jews had a formative role in Christianity. Freud's view was that the "original sin and redemption by sacrifice of a victim," the charge lodged against the Jews, became one of the "foundation stones" of Pauline Christianity.[134] Here we have the Nietzschean split between the "old" Jews and the "new" Jews—and we have the recapitulation of Freud's views of the relationship between the Jews and the Egyptians. Freud's view of the nature of Christianity, like that of Nietzsche, is that it is merely Jewish: "Christianity, having arisen out of a father-religion, became a son-religion. It has not escaped the fate of having to get rid of the father. Only a portion of the Jewish people accepted the new doctrine. Those who refused to are still called Jews today. Owing to this cleavage, they have become even more sharply divided from other peoples than before."[135] Just as the Jews adopted an Egyptian religion at Sinai, so the Jews adopted a Pauline religion after Golgotha. The "Jews," the followers of Aten, still belong to a "father-religion," having killed Moses. The followers of Paul are the "paranoids" who still believe in the "conspiracy" of the Jews for "world-domination." What Freud exposed here is the question of what happens when individuals or groups convert. Conversion is closely linked to madness, and the form of madness it takes here is anti-Semitism, the hatred of the Jews. It is the anti-Semites who are diseased. But the original Jews were or are tempted by the promises of conversion. Freud is neither. He is the scholarly observer.

The reading of *Moses and Monotheism* to this point has been in terms of the way in which Freud used certain lines of argument and certain parallel texts to reshape a narrative about the "diseased" and "primitive" nature of the Jew into a study of the origins of anti-Semitism. In writing this book, Freud understood his search for the wellsprings of the disease of anti-Semitism to be a parallel undertaking to that of Arnold Zweig in *Balance of German-Jewry 1933* (published in English as *Insulted and Exiled*). Zweig was one of the most important German-Jewish writers of the 1920s to incorporate a psychoanalytic model into his fictional and nonfictional writing. Freud wrote to Arnold Zweig on September 30,

1934, that "the starting point of my work is familiar to you—it is the same as that of your *Balance*. Faced with the new persecutions, one asks oneself again how the Jews have come to be what they are and why they should have attracted this undying hatred."[136] The *Balance* is Zweig's answer to the disease model of anti-Semitism promulgated by psychoanalysis. As with other writers deeply affected by the psychoanalytic model, Zweig's views concerning the meaning of anti-Semitism as the "Jewish disease" changed from the Weimar Republic to the period of Nazi domination.

In 1927 Zweig had published a long, detailed psychosocial study of the meaning and implication of anti-Semitism under the title *Caliban, or Politics and Passion* (1927). Dedicated to Freud and using his work in *Group Psychology* (1921), it is the major popular attempt to understand and outline the problem of the "Jewish disease" during the 1920s. Zweig's argument here is very different from his argument in 1934. Anti-Semitism is a result of mass consciousness and is, therefore, a natural, if dangerous, product. Mass psychology is merely an exaggerated form of the psychology of the individual. If it is a disease, stemming as it does from the disfigurement of natural forces through the pressures of society, it is analogous to a coping neurosis. But the question of the health of the Jews is at the center of the Jewish response to the "kernel of truth" (as Zweig sees it) of the anti-Semites' attack. It is not the anti-Semitic myth of the Jewish capitalist, but the myth of the diseased Jew, that is the most telling one for the German Jew. It is not the calumny about Jews and money but that about "the mental and physical health of their children" that is "the place where anti-Semitism truly gets at the Jew."[137] The fear for the child at risk marked the "common mental construction" of the Jew.

The pattern is set in early childhood. The Jewish family coddles the child in the home through "an exaggerated protectiveness" while the child is exposed to the torment of a hostile world outside the home: "Jewishness, which had a positive value in the home or was not mentioned there (which is very bad); or which was evoked through the use of a jargonesque special vocabulary [*Mauscheln*] (which is even worse): outside, at times when the difference in emotional valence . . . had a corrosive effect on the inner life of the child."[138] The result is a "sense of inferiority" that is in no way compensated by the older religious tradition of the sense of being one of the "chosen people." The result, according to Zweig, was that, from the "beginning of the nineteenth century neurosis was the fated disease of the Jews, with all of the illnesses, all of the functional diseases, the somatic illnesses that develop on the basis of the effect of the psyche on the endocrine system."[139] The risk of the Jews for physical illness is psychosomatic, a response to the conflicted nature of the world about them. But it is also clear that Zweig did not see this "disease" in terms of gender—the child is ungendered and the family is seen to contain both males and females.

By 1934 Zweig's view had shifted: racism was a form of mental illness and anti-Semitism was a specific form of this disease. He dismissed the argument about race at the beginning of the volume, reducing the image of race to the difference between languages and arguing the relatedness of at least all the Western languages, including the "Aryan" and the "Semitic" ones.[140] Anti-Semitism was the product of the "witches' cauldron of the affects," the sense of defeat experienced by the Germans during World War I.[141] This created in the German people a psychotic break with reality, one in which the German persecution mania isolated them from other healthy peoples.[142] As anti-Semitism is associated with war and nationalism, it is also closely associated with masculinity.

But why are the Jews at the center of the Germans' paranoid system? Zweig asked (as did Freud). Zweig answered in a most telling manner. He made a differential diagnosis between the madness in Germany and the history of European anti-Semitism, whether in the officer corps in Germany or in the state-sponsored anti-Semitism of Austria and Russia during the late nineteenth century. What he needed to know was how the current psychotic manner of seeing the Jews evolved, and he took as his model Sigmund Freud's reading of the Schreber case.[143] The model for the anti-Semite is the homosexual male. As Schreber sees his tormentor, Flechsig, divided into three segments, so too do the "Nazi agitators" divide their enemy into the Freemasons, the Catholics, and the Socialists, all in turn controlled by "the International Jew." "The Nazi neurotic needed an adversary with the following qualities. This adversary must be black, that the blond hero could stand out in radiant contrast."[144] This is undertaken by "the cult of the livery of war" whose "political leaders were photographed in uniform but this did not give them a more manly appearance."[145] The Nazis needed to dress up in fancy uniforms to feel that they were truly masculine, and in doing so they persuaded themselves as well as the onlooker. They were living out their own paranoid fantasy of masculinity, which revealed them (at least to the Jewish observer, Arnold Zweig) to be as homoerotically repressed as was Schreber. "The Nazi impulse to wear uniforms has its counterpart in the lore of mental disease."[146] For Zweig, the anti-Semitic German was the psychotic homosexual.

The worldview of the anti-Semite was that of the male psychotic, and the psychotic was similar in structure to the male homosexual. And Schreber, in whose system the rhetoric of anti-Semitism would have provided one of the keys to an understanding of his world of madness, became the prototype for the anti-Semite. Indeed, Zweig saw in the "sinister garrulousness" and "affect-drenched style" of Hitler's autobiographical *My Struggle* clear parallels to Schreber's autobiography. True masculinity, which is associated with the claims of the male scientist about his neutrality, is parodied in these psychotic texts. Both make claims to the discourse of science but are merely a "farrago of topsy-turvy science from the elementary school conjoined with topsy-turvy history from the tavern."[147] Zweig did not see the irony in this reversal. For Zweig, Germany became Schreber. Zweig saw Germany as being so psychotic that it had cut itself off from the rest of the world. The Germans were crazy and this made the Jews in Germany sick. The Jews may have internalized the charge of their own predisposition to disease, while it was the Germans who were truly ill.

In Zweig's 1934 study, Freud found Schreber evoked as the model for the etiology of German paranoia. But the model Zweig derived from Freud's study of Schreber is one of the generation of paranoia through the repression of homosexuality. It is the fantasy of the narcissist, loving himself in the form of one whose body is formed identically to his. This model works only if it is the male Aryan who is attracted to the male Jew. This is impossible for the German because of the social stigma associated with loving the body of the Jew. The "narcissism of minor differences" focuses on the circumcised penis and makes it the central marker of deviation and disease. The German male must turn the love he feels for the male Jew into hate, and the hate for the Jew into the sense that the Jewish male, the Elder of Zion, is persecuting him.

This is, of course, Zweig's own fantasy of the origin of anti-Semitism. The "narcissism of minor differences," the difference of the body of the Aryan from that of the Jew, makes the simple love of the Aryan for the Jew a Jewish fantasy. Here the image first evoked in my discussion of Freud's understanding of the masculine body in chapter 2 must return. Zweig created an idealized Jewish body in the present which was the same as that of the idealized body of the Aryan. It was clearly not so understood by the Aryan. The paranoia of the German was not the paranoia of Schreber, even though both evoked a similar rhetoric. Indeed, Schreber fearfully but intensely identified with the body of the Jew; the German anti-Semites did not. They did not fear becoming the Jew; they wished to extirpate him. Zweig attempted to translate the origin of anti-Semitism into a product of his times; Freud avoided focusing on contemporary rhetoric and sought a deeper, historical rationale. He found it in the model of racial science and his adoption of the concept of ethnopsychology.

In the mid-1940s Ernst Simmel, the Jewish cofounder of the Berlin Psychoanalytic Institute, continued Zweig's argument and saw the etiology of anti-Semitism in latent homosexuality. Using the older model of anti-Semitism as a disease, Simmel did not see the illness as evoking in its sufferers the need for a cure. The

> anti-Semite will never seek psychoanalytic help because he wants to get rid of his anti-Semitism. Above all, he has no insight into his illness and therefore does not consider himself sick. . . . We are able to draw some conclusions about anti-Semitism from the psychoanalytic treatment of those individuals who seek our help for severe neurotic ailments, and who also have anti-Semitic tendencies. From these individual treatments we have come to know that in certain cases the basic complex at the bottom of the individual obsessional idea of anti-Semitism is the latent homosexual complex, that complex which produces hate as a defense against the dangers of homosexual love.[148]

Again, anti-Semitism turns out to be a secondary effect, here, of the underlying disease process, the repression of sexual identity. As with Zweig and Freud, it is gendered as a male psychopathology. Even though Simmel seems to be evoking the concept of "homosexuality" in its broadest terms, he sees the anti-Semite as male throughout his text. It is the male anti-Semitic German who is mad, not the male Jewish scientist.

In his understanding of the history of the Jew, Freud needed the murder of the father, the murder of Moses, to be a "real" event. It had to be as real as the anti-Semitic actions taking place outside his apartment house in the Berggasse. Here it is a traumatic act, as real as the abuse felt on the streets, in the parks, at the university. Most of our contemporary critics want to see the murder as an "interpretive construction of a text, not as actual deed; as Freud too forgets that there is no literal reality to the primal seductive father."[149] The reason Freud needed the death of Moses, of the primal father, to be real is that he needed a traumatic moment in the history of the Jews to explain the uniqueness of the Jewish mind-set, the "common mental construction of the Jews." This moment must be defined by the masculine and define the masculine. This is equally true of the reality of Freud's view of the primal horde. And this "common mental construction" is a positive one. Like the model of ontogeny recapitulating phylogeny, such a traumatic moment must lie at the origin of Jewish identity.

"Racial character is the precipitate of racial history," according to Freud.[150] This is the underlying principle of the Lamarckian mnemonic inheritance evoked in Freud's claim that he has "no hesitation in declaring that men have always known (in this special way) that they once possessed a primal father and killed him."[151] This is the pattern of all his responses to the biology of race: translate biology into psychology. This transformation maintains the ideological structure of the inheritance of an acquired perceptual structure. The difference of the male Jew lies in the Jewish mind, which parallels his inheritance of the Jewish body. But

Freud made this psychological aspect at its root one that is universal. The Jewish experience, the killing of Moses, simply recapitulated the killing of the primal father on a higher level of development. Being Jewish is being male and being male is being Jewish. Here the externalization of all the charges about the nature of the male Jew—his difference, his disease, his corruption—is projected back into the history of the non-Jew or the pre-Jew, whether the Egyptian Moses or the primal father.

Freud's explanation for the "psychosis" of anti-Semitism lies in the adaptive nature of the Jews. And the Jewish male is the exemplary Jew for Freud. The question of Jewish sexual selectivity, which lies at the root of the condemnation of Jewish difference in the racial science of the day, returned to haunt the sick and dying Freud. Forced from the Vienna that, like his Jewish identity, represented many conflicted, contradictory emotions, he turned in London to the completion of this work, which he could not finish in fascist Austria. His direct response to European anti-Semitism was to complete *Moses and Monotheism*, a text that explained for him the origin of the tenacity of the "common mental construction" of the Jew. His weapon against anti-Semitism was the discourse of science.

The construction of the powerful, neutral image of the male scientist, whose gaze transcends parochial limitations, reappears here in Freud's final, published text. Freud consciously and literally rejected all the admonitions of his Jewish (and non-Jewish) contemporaries to abandon his book on Moses as it was a text that would give comfort to the enemies of the Jews and no succor to the Jews themselves in the time of their extraordinary need for heroes. But Freud used this apparent neutral voice of the male scientist to become the "tough Jew," the "big, strong," heroic Jew, unlike his image of his own father.[152] In order to do so, he had to remove himself from any charge that he was indeed "merely" a Jew, "merely" acting out of self-interest. The neutral voice of the male scientist that Freud so carefully constructed in his attempt to divide humankind into only two classes—male and female—came to his rescue in his final confrontation with the forces of darkness. But this was not the first time Freud had charged the anti-Semitic mob. In this final text we see him, as we saw him so long ago, defending his own children from anti-Semitic bullies, "swinging his stick, [as he] charged the hostile [anti-Semitic] crowd, which gave way before him and promptly dispersed, allowing him a free passage."[153] It was Freud the *man*, the author of *The MAN Moses and the Monotheistic Religion*, not Freud the *Jew*, who wrote this text in final, full awareness of the complexity of his own Jewishness and his own masculinity.

NOTES

ALL quotations from Freud's works in the notes, unless otherwise designated, are from Sigmund Freud, *Standard Edition of the Complete Psychological Works of Sigmund Freud*, ed. and trans. J. Strachey, A. Freud, A. Strachey, and A. Tyson, 24 vols. (London: Hogarth Press, 1955–74) (referred to in the notes as SE). I have compared each quotation with the original as it appears in Sigmund Freud, *Gesammelte Werke: Chronologisch Geordnet*, 19 vols. (Frankfurt a. M.: Fischer, 1952–87) (referred to in the notes as GW).

INTRODUCTION
FREUD'S JEWISH IDENTITY AND ITS INTERPRETATION

1. An extensive sample of the literature on this topic follows: Ulla Haselstein, "Poets and Prophets: The Hebrew and the Hellene in Freud's Cultural Theory," *German Life and Letters* 45 (1992): 50–65; José Brunner, "The (Ir)Relevance of Freud's Jewish Identity to the Origins of Psychoanalysis," *Psychoanalysis and Contemporary Thought* 14 (1991): 655–84; Jacquy Chemouni, *Freud, la psychanalyse, et le judaïsme: Un messianisme séculairisé* (Paris: Editions universitaires, 1991); Leon Botstein, *Judentum und Modernität: Essays zur Rolle der Juden in deutschen und österreichischen Kultur 1848 bis 1938* (Cologne: Böhlau, 1991), pp. 171–93; Harold Bloom, "Freud: Frontier Concepts, Jewishness, and Interpretation," *American Imago* 48 (1991): 135–52; Yosef Hayim Yerushalmi, *Freud's Moses: Judaism Terminable and Interminable* (New Haven: Yale University Press, 1991); Jerry V. Diller, *Freud's Jewish Identity: A Case Study in the Impact of Ethnicity* (Rutherford, N.J.: Fairleigh Dickinson University Press, 1991); Mortimer Ostow, "Sigmund and Jakob Freud and the Philippson Bible (With an Analysis of the Birthday Inscription)," *International Review of Psychoanalysis* 16 (1989): 483–92; Erich Simenauer, "Freud und die jüdische Tradition," *Jahrbuch der Psychoanalyse* 24 (1989): 29–60; Jacques Le Rider, *Modernité viennoise et crises de l'identité* (Paris: Presses universitaires de France, 1990), pp. 197–222; Gerard Haddad, *L'enfant illégitime: Sources talmudiques de la psychanalyse* (Paris: Point hors ligne, 1990); Ken Frieden, *Freud's Dream of Interpretation* (Albany: State University of New York Press, 1990); Emanuel Rice, *Freud and Moses: The Long Journey Home* (Albany: The State University of New York Press, 1990); Jakob Hessing, "Jüdische Kritiken an Sigmund Freud," *Neue deutsche Hefte* 36 (1989): 285–88; Yosef Hayim Yerushalmi, "Freud on the 'Historical Novel': From the Manuscript Draft (1934) of *Moses and Monotheism*," *International Journal of Psychoanalysis* 70 (1989): 375–95; Renate Böschenstein, "Mythos als Wasserscheide: Die jüdische Komponente der Psychoanalyse: Beobachtungen zu ihrem Zusammenhang mit der Literatur des Jahrhundertbeginns," in *Conditio Judaica: Judentum, Antisemitismus, und deutschsprachige Literatur vom 18. Jahrhundert bis zum ersten Weltkrieg*, ed. Hans Otto Horch and Horst

Denkler (Tübingen: Niemeyer, 1988), pp. 287–310; Edward Shorter, "Women and Jews in a Private Nervous Clinic in Late Nineteenth-Century Vienna," *Medical History* 33 (1989): 149–83; Robert S. Wistrich, *The Jews of Vienna in the Age of Franz Joseph* (Oxford: Oxford University Press, Littman Library of Jewish Civilization, 1989), pp. 537–82; Jakob Hessing, *Der Fluch des Propheten: Drei Abhandlung zu Sigmund Freud* (Rheda-Wiedenbrück: Daedalus, 1989); Jacquy Chemouni, "Au-delà de la psychanalyse: L'identité juive," *Frénésie* 7 (1989): 99–124; Jerzy Strojonwski, "Polish-Jewish Background of Psychoanalysis," *XXX Congrès international d'histoire de la médecine, 1986* (Düsseldorf: n.p., 1988), pp. 1224–30; Francine Beddock, *L'héritage de l'oubli—de Freud à Claude Lanzmann*, Collection TRAMES (Nice: Z'editions, 1988); Jacquy Chemouni, *Freud et le sionisme* (Paris: Solin, 1988); Paul C. Vitz, *Sigmund Freud's Christian Unconscious* (New York: Guilford Press, 1988); David S. Blatt, "The Development of the Hero: Sigmund Freud and the Reformation of the Jewish Tradition," *Psychoanalysis and Contemporary Thought* 11 (1988): 639–703; Susann Heenen-Wolff, *"Wenn ich Oberhuber hieße . . .": Die Freudsche Psychoanalyse zwischen Assimilation und Antisemitismus* (Frankfurt a. M.: Nexus, 1987); Peter Gay, *A Godless Jew: Freud, Atheism, and the Making of Psychoanalysis* (New Haven: Yale University Press, 1987); Mordechai Rotenberg, *Re-biographing and Deviance: Psychotherapeutic Narrativism and the Midrash* (New York: Praeger, 1987); Jacquy Chemouni, "Freud interprète de l'antisemitisme," *Frénésie* 4 (1987): 117–36; Jacquy Chemouni, "Freud et les associations juives: Contribution à l'étude de sa judéité," *Revue française de psychanalyse* 4 (1987): 1207–43; Harold Bloom, "Grenzbegriffe, Interpretation, und jüdisches Erbe bei Freud," *Psyche* 40 (1986): 600–616; L. J. Rather, "Disraeli, Freud, and Jewish Conspiracy Theories," *Journal of the History of Ideas* 47 (1986): 111–31; J. Kirsch, "Jung's Transference on Freud: Its Jewish Element," *American Imago* 41 (1984): 63–84; Elliott Oring, *The Jokes of Sigmund Freud: A Study in Humor and Jewish Identity* (Philadelphia: University of Pennsylvania Press, 1984); Stanley Rosenman, "A Psychohistorical Source of Psychoanalysis—Malformed Jewish Psyches in an Immolating Setting," *Israel Journal of Psychiatry and Related Sciences* 21 (1984): 103–16; H. Baruk, "Moïse, Freud, et le veau d'or," *Revue historique de la médecine hébraïque* 37 (1984): 19–23; Élaine Amado Lévy-Valensi, *Le Moïse de Freud ou la référence occulte* (Monaco: Editions Rocher, 1984); Stanley Rosenman, "The Late Conceptualization of the Self in Psychoanalysis: The German Language and Jewish Identity," *Journal of Psychohistory* 11 (1983): 9–42; Harold Bloom, "Jewish Culture and Jewish Memory," *Dialectical Anthropology* 8 (1983): 7–19; Mortimer Ostow, *Judaism and Psychoanalysis* (New York: Ktav, 1982); Avner Falk, "Freud und Herzl: Geschichte einer Beziehung in der Phantasie," *Zeitgeschichte* 9 (1982): 305–37; Susan A. Handelman, *The Slayers of Moses: The Emergence of Rabbinic Interpretation in Modern Literary Theory* (Albany: State University of New York Press, 1982), pp. 129–52; Theo Pfrimmer, *Freud: Lecteur de la Bible* (Paris: Presses universitaires de France, 1982); Max Kohn, *Freud et le Yiddish: Le préanalytique* (Paris: Bourgois, 1982); Sigmund Diamond, "Sigmund Freud, His Jewishness, and Scientific Method: The Seen and the Unseen as Evidence," *Journal of the History of Ideas* 43 (1982): 613–34; Peter Gay, "Six Names in Search of an Interpretation: A Contribution to the Debate over Sigmund Freud's Jewishness," *Hebrew Union College Annual* 53 (1982): 295–308; Marie Balmary, *Psychoanalyzing Psychoanalysis: Freud and the Hidden Fault of the Father*, trans. Ned Lukacher (Baltimore: Johns Hopkins University Press, 1982); Dennis B. Klein, *Jewish Origins of the Psychoanalytic Movement* (New York: Praeger, 1981); Justin Miller, "Interpretations of Freud's Jewishness, 1924–1974," *Journal of the History of the Behavioral Sciences* 17 (1981): 357–74; David Aberbach, "Freud's Jewish Problem," *Commentary* 69 (1980): 35–39; Carl Schorske, "Freud: The Psycho-archeology of Civilizations," *Proceedings of the Massachusetts Historical Society* 92 (1980): 52–67; C. Musatti, "Freud e l'ebraismo," *Belfagor* 35 (1980): 687–96; Carl E. Schorske, *Fin-de-siècle Vienna: Politics and Culture* (New York: Knopf, 1980), pp. 181–207; Moshe Halevi Spero, *Judaism and Psychology: Halakhic Perspectives* (New York: Ktav, 1980); Marianne Krüll, *Freud und sein Vater: Die Entstehung der Psychoanalyse und Freuds ungelöste Vaterbindung* (Munich: Beck, 1979), in English as *Freud and His Father*, trans. Arnold Pomerans (New York: Norton, 1986); Hugo Knoepfmacher, "Sigmund Freud and the B'nai B'rith," *Journal of the American Psychoanalytic Association* 27 (1979): 441–49; Fred Grubel, "Zeitgenosse Sigmund Freud," *Jahrbuch der Psychoanalyse* 11 (1979): 73–75; Avner Falk, "Freud and Herzl," *Contemporary Psychoanalysis* 14 (1978): 357–87; Avner Falk, "Freud and Herzl," *Haummah* 56 (1978): 57–75 (in Hebrew); Jeffrey Masson, "Buried Memories on the Acropolis: Freud's Response to Mysticism and Anti-Semitism," *International Journal of Psychoanalysis* 59 (1978): 199–208; Peter Gay, *Freud, Jews, and Other Germans* (New York: Oxford University Press, 1978), pp. 29–92; N. K. Dor-Shav, "To Be or Not to Be a Jew? A Dilemma of Sigmund Freud?" *Acta Psychiatrica et Neurologica Scandinavica* 56 (1977): 407–20; O. Herz, "Sigmund Freud und B'nai B'rith," in *B'nai B'rith Wien, 1895–1975* (Vienna: B'nai B'rith, 1977), pp. 50–56; Avner Falk, "Freud and Herzl," *Midstream* 23 (1977): 3–24; Martin S. Bergmann, "Moses and the Evolution of Freud's Jewish Identity," *Israel Annals of Psychiatry and Related Disciplines* 14 (1976): 3–26; Paul Roazen, *Freud and His Followers* (New York: Knopf, 1975), pp. 22–27; Reuben M. Rainey, *Freud as a Student of Religion* (Missoula, Mont.: American Academy of Religion, 1975); Léon Vogel, "Freud and Judaism: An Analysis in the Light of His Correspondence," trans. Murray Sachs, *Judaism* 24 (1975): 181–93; Robert Gordis, "The Two Faces of Freud," *Judaism* 24 (1975): 194–200; Stanley Rothman and Phillip Isenberg, "Men and Ideas: Freud and Jewish Marginality," *Encounter* 43 (1974): 46–54; Marthe Robert, *D'Œdipe à Moïse: Freud et la conscience juive* (Paris: Calmann-Lévy, 1974), in English as *From Oedipus to Moses: Freud's Jewish Identity*, trans. Ralph Manheim (Garden City, N.Y.: Anchor Books, 1976); John Murray Cuddihy, *The Ordeal of Civility: Freud, Marx, Lévi-Strauss, and the Jewish Struggle with Modernity* (New York: Basic Books, 1974); A. L. Merani, *Freud y el Talmud: Seguido de crítica de los fundamentos de la psicopatología* (Mexico City: Grijalbo, 1974); Max Schur, *Freud: Living and Dying* (New York: International Universities Press, 1972), pp. 22–27; David Singer, "Ludwig Lewisohn and Freud: The Zionist Therapeutic," *Psychoanalytic Review* 58 (1971): 169–82; A. W. Szafran, "Aspects socio-culturels judäiques de la pensée de Freud," *Evolution psychiatrique* 36 (1971): 89–107; Peter Loewenberg, " 'Sigmund Freud as a

Jew': A Study in Ambivalence and Courage," *Journal of the History of the Behavioral Sciences* 7 (1971): 363–69; Peter Loewenberg, "A Hidden Zionist Theme in Freud's 'My Son, the Myops . . .' Dream," *Journal of the History of Ideas* 31 (1970): 129–32; Donald Capps, "Hartmann's Relationship to Freud: A Reappraisal," *Journal of the History of the Behavioral Sciences* 6 (1970): 162–75; Robert Couzin, "Leibniz, Freud, and Kabbala," *Journal of the History of the Behavioral Sciences* 6 (1970): 335–48; Ignaz Maybaum, *Creation and Guilt: A Theological Assessment of Freud's Father-Son Conflict* (London: Vallentine, Mitchell, 1969); M. S. Maravon, "Contribution à l'étude critique de la psychopathologie du juif: Psychanalyse du juif" (Thesis, Paris, 1969), pp. 25–51; Lary Berkower, "The Enduring Effect of the Jewish Tradition upon Freud," *American Journal of Psychiatry* 125 (1969): 103–9; Richard L. Rubenstein, "Freud and Judaism: A Review Article," *Journal of Religion* 47 (1967): 39–44; Earl A. Grollman, *Judaism in Sigmund Freud's World* (New York: Bloch, 1965); David Bakan, *Sigmund Freud and the Jewish Mystical Tradition* (New York: Van Nostrand, 1958); Theodore Lewis, "Freud, the Jews, and Judaism," *Jewish Spectator* (March 1958): 11–14; Ernst Simon, "Sigmund Freud: The Jew," *Leo Baeck Institute Yearbook* 2 (1957): 270–305; Karl Menninger, "The Genius of the Jew in Psychiatry," *Medical Leaves* 1 (1937): 127–32, reprinted in *A Psychiatrist's World: The Selected Papers of Karl Menninger*, ed. Bernard H. Hall (New York: Viking Press, 1959); W. Aron, "Notes on Sigmund Freud's Ancestry and Jewish Contacts," YIVO *Annual of Jewish Social Sciences* 2 (1956): 286–95; Samuel Felix Mendelsohn, *Mental Healing in Judaism: Its Relationship to Christian Science and Psychoanalysis* (Chicago: Jewish Gift Shop, 1936); A. A. Roback, *Jewish Influence in Modern Thought* (Cambridge, Mass.: Sci-Art, 1929), pp. 152–97; Charles E. Maylan, *Freuds tragischer Komplex* (Munich: Reinhardt, 1929) (in the Freud Library, London); Enrico Morselli, *La psicanalisi: Studii ed appunti critici*, 2 vols. (Turin: Bocca, 1926) (in the Freud Library, London); A. A. Roback, "Freud, Chassid or Humanist," *B'nai B'rith Magazine* 40 (1926): 118; A. A. Roback, "Is Psychoanalysis a Jewish Movement?" *B'nai B'rith Magazine* 40 (1926): 118–19, 129–30, 198–201, 238–39; Ludwig Braun, "Die Persönlichkeit Freuds und seine Bedeutung als Bruder," in *Festsitzung der "Wien" anlässlich des 70. Geburtstages Br. Univ. Prof. Doktor Sigmund Freud, Wien, 1926, B'nai B'rith Mitteilung für Österreich* 26 (1926): 118–31; Arnold Kutzinki, "Sigmund Freud, ein jüdischer Forscher," *Der Jude* 8 (1924): 216–21.

2. Harold Bloom, *The Strong Light of the Canonical: Kafka, Freud, and Scholem as Revisionists of Jewish Culture and Thought*, City College Papers, no. 20 (New York: City College, 1987), p. 43.

3. I use the term "Jewish physician" to refer to those physicians who either label themselves Jews or are so labeled in the standard reference works of the time. Given that it was only in the 1890s that women were admitted to German and Austrian medical faculties, Jewish physicians primarily were male. See, for example, the listing in Solomon R. Kagan, *Jewish Medicine* (Boston: Medico-Historical Press, 1952). On the present state of the assumptions about the "diseases" attributed to Jews, see Usiel O. Schmelz and F. Keidanski, comp., *Jewish Health Statistics* (Jerusalem: Academon, 1966); Ailon Shiloh and Ida Cohen Selavan, eds., *Ethnic Groups of America: Their Morbidity, Mortality,*

and Behavior Disorders, 2 vols. (Springfield, Ill.: Thomas, 1973–74), vol. 1, *The Jews;* Richard M. Goodman, *Genetic Disorders among the Jewish People* (Baltimore: Johns Hopkins University Press, 1979); Richard M. Goodman and Arno G. Motulsky, eds., *Genetic Diseases among Ashkenazi Jews* (New York: Raven Press, 1979); Henry Rothschild, "Diseases of the Jews," in his *Biocultural Aspects of Disease* (New York: Academic Press, 1981), pp. 531–56; E. Stern, J. Blau, Y. Rusecki, M. Rafaelovsky, and M. P. Cohen, "Prevalence of Diabetes in Israel: Epidemiologic Survey," *Diabetes* 37 (1988): 297–302. On the history of this tradition, see Michael Tschoetschel, "Die Diskussion über die Häufigkeit von Krankheiten bei den Juden bis 1920" (Ph.D. diss., Mainz, 1990), and Marianne Turmann, "Jüdische Krankheiten (Historisch-kritische Betrachtungen zu einem medizinischen Problem)" (Ph.D. diss., Kiel, 1968).

4. See, for example, Emmanuel Velikovsky, "The Dreams Freud Dreamed," *Psychoanalytic Review* 30 (1941): 487–511, as well as Masson, "Buried Memories on the Acropolis," and Loewenberg, "Sigmund Freud as a Jew" and "Hidden Zionist Theme."

5. Peter Homans, *The Ability to Mourn: Disillusionment and the Social Origins of Psychoanalysis* (Chicago: University of Chicago Press, 1989), p. 71.

6. Paul Weindling, *Health, Race, and German Politics between National Unification and Nazism, 1870–1945* (Cambridge: Cambridge University Press, 1989), does discuss the question of Jewish physicians and their participation in the eugenics movement (pp. 482–84), but does not put this together with the discourse on Jewish disease. Michael H. Kater, *Doctors under Hitler* (Chapel Hill: University of North Carolina Press, 1989), has his primary focus after 1933. Sheila Faith Weiss, "The Race Hygiene Movement in Germany, 1904–1945," in *The Wellborn Science: Eugenics in Germany, France, Brazil, and Russia,* ed. Mark B. Adams (New York: Oxford University Press, 1990), pp. 8–68; Gerrit Hohendorf and Achim Magull-Seltenreich, eds., *Von der Heilkunde zur Massentötung: Medizin im Nationalsozialismus* (Heidelberg: Wunderhorn, 1990); Robert Proctor, *Racial Hygiene: Medicine under the Nazis* (Cambridge, Mass.: Harvard University Press, 1988); Peter Weingart, Jürgen Kroll, and Kurt Bayertz, *Rasse, Blut, und Gene: Geschichte der Eugenik und Rassenhygiene in Deutschland* (Frankfurt a. M.: Suhrkamp, 1988); Doris Byer, *Rassenhygiene und Wohlfahrtspflege: Zur Entstehung eines sozial-demokratischen Machtdispositivs in Österreich bis 1934* (Frankfurt a. M.: Campus, 1988); and Hans-Walter Schmuhl, *Rassenhygiene, Nationalsozialismus, Euthanasie: Von der Verhütung zur Vernichtung lebensunwerten Lebens, 1890–1945* (Göttingen: Vandenhoeck & Ruprecht, 1987), all give little attention to this topic. Of interest given the importance of French science for the German medical tradition is the study of eugenics in France during this period by William H. Schneider, *Quality and Quantity: The Quest for Biological Regeneration in Twentieth-Century France* (New York: Cambridge University Press, 1990).

7. Frank J. Sulloway, *Freud, Biologist of the Mind: Beyond the Psychoanalytic Legend* (New York: Basic Books, 1979).

8. This separation is also found in the best essay written on the question of Freud's use of and reaction to the science of race: Larry Stewart, "Freud before

Oedipus: Race and Heredity in the Origins of Psychoanalysis," *Journal of the History of Biology* 9 (1976): 215–28.

9. Gay, *A Godless Jew*, and Peter Gay, *Freud: A Life for Our Time* (New York: Norton, 1988).

10. I have expressed this view in many of my earlier studies of Freud's works in various historical contexts. See the following: Sander L. Gilman, *Jewish Self-Hatred: Anti-Semitism and the Hidden Language of the Jews* (Baltimore: Johns Hopkins University Press, 1986; reprint, 1990); *Difference and Pathology: Stereotypes of Sexuality, Race, and Madness* (Ithaca, N.Y.: Cornell University Press, 1985; 3d ed., 1989); *Disease and Representation: Images of Illness from Madness to AIDS* (Ithaca, N.Y.: Cornell University Press, 1988; 2d ed., 1990); *Sexuality: An Illustrated History* (New York: Wiley, 1989); and *The Jew's Body* (New York: Routledge, 1991).

11. I aim to show in this study how the masculine and the feminine as well as the homosexual (gay/lesbian) categories of identity are structured by the rhetoric of race. Of great value to me in this study have been the following works on the construction of gender: Ulli Olvedi, *Frauen um Freud* (Freiburg: Herder, 1992); Judith Kegan Gardiner, "Psychoanalysis and Feminism: An American Humanist's View," *Signs* 17 (1992): 435–54; Michèle Barrett, "Psychoanalysis and Feminism: A British Sociologist's View," *Signs* 17 (1992): 455–66; George J. Makari, "German Philosophy, Freud, and the Riddle of the Woman," *Journal of the American Psychoanalytic Association* 39 (1991): 183–213; Elizabeth Abel, "Race, Class, and Psychoanalysis? Opening Questions," in *Conflicts in Feminism*, ed. Marianne Hirsch and Evelyn Fox Keller, (New York: Routledge, 1990), pp. 184–204; Elisabeth Young-Bruehl, ed., *Freud on Women: A Reader* (New York: Norton, 1990); Judith Butler, *Gender Trouble: Feminism and the Subversion of Identity* (New York: Routledge, 1990), pp. 57–65; Madelon Sprengnether, *The Spectral Mother: Freud, Feminism, and Psychoanalysis* (Ithaca, N.Y.: Cornell University Press, 1990); Nancy J. Chodorow, *Feminism and Psychoanalytic Theory* (New Haven: Yale University Press, 1989), esp. pp. 165–77; Seyla Benhabib, "On Contemporary Feminist Theory," *Dissent* 36 (1989): 366–70; Kaja Silverman, *The Acoustic Mirror: The Female Voice in Psychoanalysis and Cinema* (Bloomington: Indiana University Press, 1988); Jane Gallop, *Thinking Through the Body* (New York: Columbia University Press, 1988); Eli Sagan, *Freud, Women, and Morality: The Psychology of Good and Evil* (New York: Basic Books, 1988); Edith Seifert, *Was will das Weib? Zu Begehren und Lust bei Freud und Lacan* (Weinheim: Quadriga, 1987); Jacqueline Rose, *Sexuality and the Field of Vision* (London: Verso, 1986); Sarah Kofmann, *The Enigma of Woman: Woman in Freud's Writings*, trans. Catherine Porter (Ithaca, N.Y.: Cornell University Press, 1985); Jane Gallop, *Feminism and Psychoanalysis: The Daughter's Seduction* (London: Macmillan, 1982); Renate Schlesier, *Konstruktionen der Weiblichkeit bei Sigmund Freud: Zum Problem von Entmythologisierung und Remythologisierung in der psychoanalytischen Theorie* (Frankfurt a. M.: Europäische Verlagsanstalt, 1981); Lucy Freeman and Herbert S. Stream, *Freud and Women* (New York: Ungar, 1981); Moustafa Safouan, *La sexualité féminine dans la doctrine freudienne* (Paris: Éditions du Seuil, 1976); and Juliet Mitchell, *Psychoanalysis and Feminism* (New York: Pantheon, 1974).

12. See, however, Wayne Koestenbaum, *Double Talk: The Erotics of Male Literary Collaboration* (New York: Routledge, 1989), pp. 17–42; Reuben Fine, "The Forgotten Man: Understanding the Male Psyche," *Current Issues in Psychoanalytic Practice* 3 (1986): 1–368; Joe L. Dubbert, "Progressivism and the Masculinity Crisis," *Psychoanalytic Review* 61 (1974): 443–55; on the historical background, see J. A. Mangan and James Walvin, eds., *Manliness and Morality: Middle-Class Masculinity in Britain and America, 1800–1900* (New York: St. Martin's Press, 1987), and George L. Mosse, *Nationalism and Sexuality: Respectability and Abnormal Sexuality in Modern Europe* (New York: Fertig, 1985); on Freud's construction of masculinity, see Bernd Widdig, *Männerbünde und Massen: Zur Krise männlicher Identität in der Literatur der Moderne* (Opladen: Westdeutscher, 1991), pp. 101–23.

13. Judith Van Herik, *Freud on Femininity and Faith* (Berkeley and Los Angeles: University of California Press, 1982).

14. Estelle Roith, *The Riddle of Freud: Jewish Influences on His Theory of Female Sexuality* (New York: Tavistock Press, 1987).

15. Lesley A. Hall, *Hidden Anxieties: Male Sexuality, 1900–1950* (London: Polity Press, 1991), pp. 1–14.

16. I believe that the reading given to the representation of the feminine in Wittels and Freud presented by Hannah S. Decker in *Freud, Dora, and Vienna, 1900* (New York: Free Press, 1990), pp. 201–2, is incomplete.

17. Rosenman, "A Psychohistorical Source of Psychoanalysis," p. 107.

18. On a model of modern science that is useful in writing this type of history of psychoanalysis, see Lewis S. Feuer, *The Scientific Intellectual: The Psychological and Sociological Origins of Modern Science* (New Brunswick, N.J.: Transaction Books, 1992) (with a new introduction on the critical reception of this book).

CHAPTER ONE
SIGMUND FREUD AND THE EPISTEMOLOGY OF RACE

1. On Freud's recognition of the violent disruption of lectures by Jewish professors, such as the anatomist Joseph Tandler in 1929, see *The Diary of Sigmund Freud, 1929–1939: A Record of the Final Decade*, ed. and trans. Michael Molnar (New York: Scribner's, 1992), p. 45.

2. Peter Winch, *The Idea of a Social Science and Its Relation to Philosophy* (London: Routledge, 1958), p. 15.

3. SE 5:442. See Emmanuel Velikovsky, "The Dreams Freud Dreamed," *Psychoanalytic Review* 30 (1941): 487–511; Peter Loewenberg, " 'Sigmund Freud as a Jew': A Study in Ambivalence and Courage," *Journal of the History of the Behavioral Sciences* 7 (1971): 363–69; Peter Loewenberg, "A Hidden Zionist Theme in Freud's 'My Son, the Myops . . .' Dream," *Journal of the History of Ideas* 31 (1970): 129–32; and Jeffrey Masson, "Buried Memories on the Acropolis: Freud's Response to Mysticism and Anti-Semitism," *International Journal of Psychoanalysis* 59 (1978): 199–208.

4. Sigmund Freud, "Some Early Unpublished Letters," trans. Ilse Scheier, *International Journal of Psychoanalysis* 50 (1969): 419–27; here, 420.

5. Berhard Blechmann, *Ein Beitrag zur Anthropologie der Juden* (Dorpat: Just, 1882), p. 11.

6. M. J. Schleiden, "Die Bedeutung der Juden für Erhaltung und Wiederbelebung der Wissenschaften im Mittelalter," *Westermann's Jahrbuch der Illustrirten Deutschen Monatshefte* 41 (1877): 52–60, 156–69; here, 156.

7. Cited from the standard work on the anthropology of the Jews in the 1920s and 1930s, Hans F. K. Günther, *Rassenkunde des jüdischen Volkes* (1922; Munich: Lehmann, 1931), p. 12.

8. SE 20:7–8.

9. Jerzy Strojonwski, "Polish-Jewish Background of Psychoanalysis," *XXX Congrès international d'histoire de la médecine, 1986* (Düsseldorf: n.p., 1988), pp. 1224–30.

10. Josef Sajner, "Sigmund Freuds Beziehung zu seiner Heimat," *Atti de XXI Congresso internazionale di storia della medicina,* 2 vols. (Rome: n.p., [1969]), 2:1350–53.

11. Didier Anzieu, *Freud's Self-Analysis,* trans. Peter Graham (London: Hogarth Press, 1986), pp. 1–2. See also Billa Zanuso, *The Young Freud: The Origins of Psychoanalysis in Late Nineteenth-Century Viennese Culture* (Oxford: Blackwell, 1986).

12. Peter Pulzer, *The Rise of Political Anti-Semitism in Germany and Austria,* rev. ed. (London: Halban, 1988).

13. Susanne Cassirer Bernfeld, "Freud and Archeology," *American Imago* 8 (1951): 107–28; here, 118.

14. Ruth Beckermann, *Die Mazzesinsel: Juden in der Wiener Leopoldstadt, 1918–1938* (Vienna: Löcker, 1984).

15. "Autobiography of Josef Breuer," trans. C. P. Oberndorf, *International Journal of Psychoanalysis* 34 (1953): 64.

16. Stanley Rosenman, "The Late Conceptualization of the Self in Psychoanalysis: The German Language and Jewish Identity," *Journal of Psychohistory* 11 (1983): 9–42, and Ilse Grubich-Simitis, "Reflections on Sigmund Freud's Relationship to the German Language and to Some German-speaking Authors of the Enlightenment," *International Journal of Psychoanalysis* 67 (1986): 287–94.

17. From a letter to A. A. Roback, March 24, 1930, reprinted in A. A. Roback, *Freudiana* (Cambridge, Mass.: Sci-Art, 1957), p. 34.

18. Sigmund Freud, *Jugendbriefe an Eduard Silberstein 1871–1881,* ed. Walter Boehlich (Frankfurt a. M.: Fischer, 1989), p. 137; translation from *The Letters of Sigmund Freud to Eduard Silberstein, 1871–1881,* trans. Arnold J. Pomerans (Cambridge, Mass.: Harvard University Press, Belknap Press, 1990), p. 121.

19. Ibid., p. 193.

20. Smiley Blanton, *Diary of My Analysis with Sigmund Freud* (New York: Hawthorn Books, 1971), p. 92.

21. SE 4:196.

22. George Sylvester Viereck, *Glimpses of the Great* (New York: Macaulay, 1930), p. 30. Compare M. Johnson, "Pro-Freud and Pro-Nazi: The Paradox of George S. Viereck," *Psychoanalytic Review* 58 (1971–72): 553–62.

23. SE 20:9.

24. The best reading of this letter with its complicated sexual and religious implications can be found in Klaus Theweleit, *Objektwahl (All You Need Is Love . . .): Über Paarbildungsstrategien und Bruchstrück einer Freudbiographie* (Frankfurt a. M.: Stroemfeld/Roter Stern, 1990), pp. 64–67.

25. Sigmund Freud, *Brautbriefe: Briefe an Martha Bernays aus den Jahren 1882 bis 1886*, ed. Ernst L. Freud (Frankfurt a. M.: Fischer, 1960), pp. 20–25; translation from *Letters of Sigmund Freud, 1873–1939*, ed. Ernst L. Freud, trans. Tania and James Stern (London: Hogarth Press, 1961), p. 39.

26. Freud, *Brautbriefe*, pp. 142–43. Letter to Martha of February 10, 1886; translation from Freud, *Letters of Sigmund Freud, 1873–1939*, pp. 222–23.

27. SE 1:95.

28. Ibid. 18:101.

29. Anton Edler von Rosas, "Über die Quellen des heutigen ärtzlichen Missbehagens, und die Mittel um demselben wirksam zu steuern," *Medizinische Jahrbücher des kaiserlichen königlichen österreichischen Staates* 40 (1842): 16–19.

30. Ibid., pp. 18–19.

31. See the detailed accusations in Georg Pictorius, *Von zernichten Artzten: Clarer Bericht ob die Christen von den jüdischen Artzten, vertrewlich Artzney gebrauchen mögen* (Strassburg: Knoblauch, 1557) (especially on the false cures for venereal diseases); Ludwig von Hornigk, *Medicaster apella; oder, Juden Artzt* (Strassburg: Mary von der Heiden, 1631); and Christian Trewmundt, *Dess Christiani Trewmundts Gewissen-loser Juden-Doctor in welchem erstlich das wahre Conterfeit eines christlichen Medici, und dessen nothwendige Wissenschafften, wie auch gewissenhaffte Praxis, zweytens die hingegen abscheuliche Gestalt . . .* (Freiburg: n.p., 1698). The latter two authors call on the work of the convert Antonius Margaritha, *Der gantz Jüdisch glaub* (Augsburg: Steyner, 1530), and his comments on the "Jewish quack." On the self-defense of Jewish physicians against these charges, see Harry Friedenwald, *The Jews and Medicine: Essays*, 2 vols. (Baltimore: Johns Hopkins University Press, 1944), 1:31–68. Freud's own 1926 defense of Theodor Reik against the accusation of quackery (SE 20:179–258, as well as GW Nachtragsband: 715–17) should be read in this context; see Sander L. Gilman, *Disease and Representation: Images of Illness from Madness to AIDS* (Ithaca, N.Y.: Cornell University Press, 1988), pp. 182–201. On Reik, see Jean-Marc Alby, *Theodor Reik: Le trajet d'un psychanalyste de Vienne "fin de siècle" aux États-Unis* (Paris: Clancier-Guenaud, 1985).

32. Von Rosas, "Über die Quellen," p. 19.

33. It was Mannheimer who officiated at the marriage of Sigmund Freud's parents, Kallamon Jacob Freud and Amalia Nathanson, on July 29, 1855.

34. Isaac Noah Mannheimer, "Einige Worte über Juden und Judenthum . . . ," *Oesterreichische Medicinische Wochenschrift*, Ausserordentliche Beilage zur Wochenschrift 34 (1842): 1–10. A further fifteen-page rebuttal by a self-described Jewish physician, Dr. J. Hayne, appeared as a supplement to volume 38 of the same journal.

35. Anton Edler von Rosas, "Erwiederung auf Herrn Mannheimer's Einrede, bezüglich auf den Andrang der Israeliten zur Medicin," *Oesterreichische Medicinische Wochenschrift*, Ausserordentliche Beilage zur Wochenschrift 34

(1842): 11–16. Von Rosas admits to being overly inclusive in his condemnation of Jewish doctors as quacks. In a classic act of self-defense, he calls on his own Jewish students as witnesses for his lack of prejudice; he closes his piece with a bit of late-Enlightenment rhetoric evoking Lessing's *Nathan der Weise*, the epitome of toleration. All in all, an object lesson that overt public anti-Semitism was not quite acceptable in the Viennese medical establishment of the 1840s.

36. Theodor Billroth, *Über das Lehren und Lernen der medicinischen Wissen-schaften an den Universitäten der deutschen Nation nebst allgemeinen Bemer-kungen über Universitäten: Eine culturhistorische Studie* (Vienna: Carl Gerold's Sohn, 1876), pp. 146–54. Billroth's image of the Eastern Jewish medical student remained a "classic" characterization, according to *Ostdeutsche Rundschau* in 1911, well after its author had radically altered his own view. See Christoph Stölzl, *Kafkas böses Böhmen: Zur Sozialgeschichte eines Prager Juden* (Munich: Text und Kritik, 1975), p. 44. On the response to Billroth on the part of the German-Jewish writer Bertold Auerbach, see Paul Lawrence Rose, *Revolutionary Antisemitism in Germany from Kant to Wagner* (Princeton: Princeton University Press, 1990), pp. 238–39.

37. William J. McGrath, *Freud's Discovery of Psychoanalysis: The Politics of Hysteria* (Ithaca, N.Y.: Cornell University Press, 1986), p. 184.

38. Theodor Reik, *From Thirty Years with Freud*, trans. Richard Winston (New York: Farrar and Rinehart, 1940), p. 110; cited in *Freud anekdotisch*, ed. Jörg Drews (Munich: Kindler, 1970), p. 91.

39. Joseph Roth, "Das Spinnennetz," in his *Werke*, ed. Hermann Kesten, 4 vols. (Cologne: Kiepenheuer & Witsch, 1975), 1:57.

40. Franz Kafka, *Letters to Milena*, trans. Philip Boehm (New York: Schocken, 1990), p. 136.

41. Milena Jesenská, *Alles ist Leben*, ed. Dorothea Rein (Frankfurt a. M.: Neue Kritik, 1984), pp. 132–35.

42. David Berger, ed. and trans., *The Jewish-Christian Debate in the High Middle Ages: A Critical Edition of the Nizzahon Vetus* (Philadelphia: Jewish Pub-lication Society of America, 1979), p. 224.

43. Ibid., p. 340.

44. Johann Pezzl, *Skizze von Wien: Ein Kultur- und Sittenbild as der josephin-ischen Zeit*, ed. Gustav Gugitz and Anton Schlossar (Graz: Leykam, 1923), pp. 107–8.

45. On the meaning of this disease in the medical literature of the period, see the following: Michael Scheiba, *Dissertatio inauguralis medica, sistens quaedam plicae pathologica: Germ. Juden-Zopff, Polon. Koltun: quam . . . in Academia Albertina pro gradu doctoris . . . subjiciet defensurus Michael Scheiba . . .* (Regiomonti: Litteris Reusnerianis, [1739]), and Hieronymus Ludolf, *Dissertatio inauguralis medica de plica, vom Juden-Zopff . . .* (Erfordiae: Typis Groschianis, [1724]).

46. Elcan Isaac Wolf, *Von den Krankheiten der Juden* (Mannheim: Schwan, 1777), p. 12.

47. Houston Stewart Chamberlain, *Foundations of the Nineteenth Century*, trans. John Lees, 2 vols. (London: John Lane/The Bodley Head, 1913), 1:389. This topic was extremely important to those Jewish anthropologists who at-

tempted to argue for a positive reading of the concept of the Jewish race. Fritz Kahn, *Die Juden als Rasse und Kulturvolk* (Berlin: Welt, 1921), pp. 32–33, spends two full pages bringing parallel comments about the Russians, French, Poles, and so forth, to show that Chamberlain's rhetoric is not scientific but political.

48. Robert Knox, *The Races of Men: A Fragment* (Philadelphia: Lea & Blanchard, 1850), p. 134.

49. SE 14:191; GW 10:289–90.

50. See the discussion of Heinrich Heine's conversion in Peter Heinegg, "Heine's Conversion and the Critics," *German Life and Letters* 30 (1976): 45–51, for a model case.

51. Hugo von Hofmannsthal, Unpublished Diaries and Notebooks, 147.11.3, Houghton Library, Harvard University, Cambridge, Mass.

52. SE 11:199; 18:101; 21:114.

53. Chamberlain, *Foundations of the Nineteenth Century*, 1:332.

54. W. W. Kopp, "Beobachtung an Halbjuden in Berliner Schulen," *Volk und Rasse* 10 (1935): 392.

55. M. Lerche, "Beobachtung deutsch-jüdischer Rassenkreuzeung an Berliner Schulen," *Die medizinische Welt* (September 17, 1927): 1222. On the question of the definition and meaning of the *Mischling*, see Paul Weindling, *Health, Race, and German Politics between National Unification and Nazism, 1870–1945* (Cambridge: Cambridge University Press, 1989), pp. 531–32.

56. Joseph Jacobs, *Studies in Jewish Statistics* (London: Nutt, 1891), p. xxiii.

57. Weindling, *Health, Race, and German Politics*, p. 250.

58. SE 11:199; 18:101; 21:114.

59. Ibid. 21:120.

60. *Sigmund Freud–Oskar Pfister: Briefe, 1909–1939*, ed. Ernst L. Freud and Heinrich Meng (Frankfurt a. M.: Fischer, 1963), p. 64.

61. SE 21:168.

62. GW Nachtragsband: 775.

63. Ernest Jones, *The Life and Work of Sigmund Freud*, 3 vols. (New York: Basic Books, 1953–57), 1:22.

64. Gustave Le Bon, "Applications de la psychologie à la classification des races," *Revue philosophique* 22 (1886): 593–619; Gustave Le Bon, *Rôle des juifs dans la civilisation* (Paris: Amis de Gustave Le Bon, 1985). See the discussion of Le Bon's attitude toward the Jews in Robert Nye, *The Origins of Crowd Psychology: Gustave Le Bon and the Crisis of Mass Democracy in the Third Republic* (London and Beverly Hills, Calif.: Sage, 1975), p. 56, and Elisabeth Roudinesco, *La bataille de cent ans*, 2 vols. (Paris: Ramsay, 1982), especially her chapters "L'inconscient à la française (de Gustave Le Bon à l'affaire Dreyfus)," 1:181–221, and "Judéité, israélisme, antisémitisme," 1:395–411.

65. Roback, *Freudiana*, p. 35.

66. See David Lawrence Preston, "Science, Society, and the German Jews, 1870–1933" (Ph.D. diss., University of Illinois, 1971); Monika Richarz, *Der Eintritt der Juden in die akademischen Berufe* (Tübingen: Mohr, 1974); and T. Schlich, "Der Eintritt von Juden in das Bildungsburgertum des 18. und 19. Jahrhunderts: Die jüdisch-christliche Arztfamilie Speyer," *Medizinhistorisches*

Jahrbuch 25 (1990): 129–42. On the historical context of the Jews of Vienna, see Dirk Van Arkel, "Antisemitism in Austria" (Ph.D. diss., Leiden, 1966); Alfred Schick, "The Vienna of Sigmund Freud," *Psychoanalytic Review* 55 (1968–69): 529–51; John Reginald Peter Theobold, "The Response of the Jewish Intelligentsia in Vienna to the Rise of Anti-Semitism, with Special Reference to Karl Kraus" (Ph.D. diss., University of Southampton, 1975); Peter Schmidtbauer, "Households and Household Forms of Viennese Jews in 1857," *Journal of Family History* 5 (1980): 375–89; Eric Fischer, "Seven Viennese Jewish Families: From the Ghetto to the Holocaust and Beyond," *Jewish Social Studies* 42 (1980): 345–60; John W. Boyer, *Political Radicalism in Late Imperial Vienna: Origins of the Christian Social Movement, 1848–1897* (Chicago: University of Chicago Press, 1981); George Clare, *Last Waltz in Vienna: The Rise and Destruction of a Family, 1842–1942* (New York: Holt, Rinehart, and Winston, 1982); Marsha L. Rozenblit, *The Jews of Vienna, 1867–1914: Assimilation and Identity* (Albany: State University of New York Press, 1983); Ezra Mendelsohn, *The Jews of East Central Europe between the World Wars* (Bloomington: Indiana University Press, 1983); Léon Poliakov, *The History of Anti-Semitism*, 4 vols. (Oxford: Oxford University Press, 1985), vol. 4, *Suicidal Europe, 1870–1933*, trans. George Klim; Norbert Leser, ed., *Theodor Herzl und das Wien des Fin de siècle* (Vienna: Böhlau, 1987); Ivar Oxaal, Michael Pollak, and Gerhard Botz, eds., *Jews, Antisemitism, and Culture in Vienna* (London and New York: Routledge, 1987); Michael Mitterauer, ed., *Gelobt sei, der dem Schwachen Kraft verlieht: Zehn Generationen einer jüdischen Familie im alten und neuen Österreich* (Vienna: Böhlau, 1987); George E. Berkley, *Vienna and Its Jews: The Tragedy of Success, 1880–1980s* (Cambridge, Mass.: Abt/Madison, 1988); William O. McCagg, Jr., *A History of Habsburg Jews, 1670–1918* (Bloomington: Indiana University Press, 1989); Robert S. Wistrich, *The Jews of Vienna in the Age of Franz Joseph* (Oxford: Oxford University Press, Littman Library of Jewish Civilization, 1989); Steven Beller, *Vienna and the Jews, 1867–1938: A Cultural History* (Cambridge: Cambridge University Press, 1989); Harriet Pass Freidenreich, *Jewish Politics in Vienna, 1918–1938* (Bloomington: Indiana University Press, 1991).

67. SE 18:74.

68. Gustave Le Bon, *The Crowd: A Study of the Popular Mind* (New York: Viking Press, 1960), p. 83.

69. Richard Andree, *Zur Volkskunde der Juden* (Leipzig: Velhagen & Klasing, 1881), pp. 24–25; translation from Maurice Fishberg, "Materials for the Physical Anthropology of the Eastern European Jew," *Memoirs of the American Anthropological Association* 1 (1905–7): 6–7.

70. Theodor Reik, " 'Jessica, My Child,' " *American Imago* 8 (1951): 3–27; here, 5.

71. SE 20:274; GW 17:49–53.

72. Theodor Reik, *Jewish Wit* (New York: Gamut Press, 1962), p. 12.

73. William James, *The Principles of Psychology*, 2 vols. (New York: Henry Holt, 1890), 2:678.

74. SE 17:247–48.

75. Heinrich Schnitzler, ed., "Briefe Sigmund Freud an Arthur Schnitzler," *Neue Rundschau* 66 (1955): 95–106; here, 100. The "confession" that Schnitzler

was his "double" was made on May 15, 1922 (p. 96). On the background of these two Jewish physicians in the medical establishment of their time, see Bernd Urban, "Schnitzler and Freud as Doubles: Poetic Intuition and Early Research on Hysteria," *Psychoanalytic Review* 65, (1978): 131–65. and Mark Luprecht, *"What People Call Pessimism": Sigmund Freud, Arthur Schnitzler, and Nineteenth-Century Controversy at the University of Vienna Medical School* (Riverside, Calif.: Ariadne Press, 1990).

76. Philip Rieff, *Freud: The Mind of the Moralist* (New York: Viking Press, 1959), p. 261.

77. SE 18:83–85, 96–97.

78. William McDougall, *The Group Mind* (Cambridge: Cambridge University Press, 1920), pp. 159–60.

79. *B'nai B'rith: Zwi Perez Chajes Loge, 1895–1975* (Vienna: B'nai B'rith, 1976), and Hugo Knoepfmacher, "Sigmund Freud and the B'nai B'rith," *Journal of the American Psychoanalytic Association* 27 (1979): 441–49. In Freud's London library there is a copy of the *B'nai B'rith Mitteilung für Österreich* 26 (1926): 101–38, which is the *Festsitzung der "Wien" anlässlich des 70. Geburtstages Br. Univ. Prof. Doktor Sigmund Freud, Wien, 1926.* This special issue was devoted to Freud's role in the Jewish world of Vienna.

80. Theodor Reik, "Die Pubertätsriten der Wilden: Über einige Übereinstimmungen im Seelenleben der Wilden und der Neurotiker," *Imago* 6 (1915–16): 125–44, 189–222; English translation from Theodor Reik, *Ritual: Psycho-Analytic Studies*, trans. Douglas Bryan (London: Hogarth Press, 1931), pp. 91–166; here, pp. 156–57.

81. See the discussion of this concept, without any reference to the psychological or medical literature, in Beller, *Vienna and the Jews*, pp. 73–83.

82. Ludwig Wittgenstein, *Culture and Value*, ed. G. H. von Wright and Heikki Nyman (Oxford: Blackwell, 1980), pp. 18–19.

83. Freud, "Some Early Unpublished Letters," p. 426.

84. Werner Sombart, *The Jews and Modern Capitalism*, trans. M. Epstein (Glencoe, Ill.: Free Press, 1951), p. 320. On the meaning of the "genius" of the Jew, see the detailed exposition by the French historian Anatole Leroy-Beaulieu, *Israel among the Nations: A Study of the Jews and Antisemitism*, trans. Frances Hellman (New York: Putnam's, 1895), pp. 225–62. In refuting the claims about Jewish creativity, he manages to catalogue most of them.

85. Beller, *Vienna and the Jews*, pp. 78–83.

86. Chamberlain, *Foundations of the Nineteenth Century* 1:418. On Freud's reading of Chamberlain, see GW Nachtragsband: 787.

87. Wittgenstein, *Culture and Value*, p. 19.

88. Adolf Hitler, *Mein Kampf*, trans. Ralph Manheim (Boston: Houghton Mifflin, 1943), pp. 302–3.

89. SE 16:396.

90. Ibid.

91. Moritz Lazarus and Heymann Steinthal, "Einleitende Gedanken über Völkerpsychologie," *Zeitschrift für Völkerpsychologie und Sprachwissenschaft* 1 (1860): 1–73. See, in this context, their letters: *Moritz Lazarus und Heymann Steinthal: Die Begründer der Völkerpsychologie in ihren Briefen*, ed. Ingrid Belke,

2 vols. (Tübingen: Mohr, 1971–86). On their relationship to the medicine of the late nineteenth century, see Heinz-Peter Schmiedebach, "Die Völkerpsychologie von Moritz Lazarus (1824–1903) und ihre Beziehung zur naturwissenschaftlichen Psychiatrie," *XXX Congrès international d'histoire de la médecine, 1986* (Düsseldorf: n.p., 1988), pp. 311–21.

92. Wilhelm Wundt, *Elements of Folk Psychology: Outlines of a Psychological History of the Development of Mankind,* trans. Edward Leroy Schaub (London: Allen & Unwin, 1916), p. 2. See also Christina Maria Schneider, *Wilhelm Wundts Völkerpsychologie: Entstehung und Entwicklung eines in Vergessenheit geratenen, wissenschafts-historisch relevanten Fachgebietes* (Bonn: Bouvier, 1990).

93. On Freud and Wundt, see Christfried Tögel, "Freud und Wundt: Von der Hypnose bis zur Völkerpsychologie," in *Freud und die akademische Psychologie: Beiträge zu einer historischen Kontroverse,* ed. Bernd Nitzschke (Munich: Psychologie Verlags Union, 1989), pp. 97–106. For their reciprocal influences, see Tilman J. Elliger, *S. Freud und die akademische Psychologie: Ein Beitrag zur Rezeptionsgeschichte der Psychoanalyse in der deutschen Psychologie (1895–1945)* (Weinheim: Deutscher Studien, 1986), and Carl Eduard Scheidt, *Die Rezeption der Psychoanalyse in der deutschsprachigen Philosophie vor 1940* (Frankfurt a. M.: Suhrkamp, 1986).

94. James Mark Baldwin, *Mental Development in the Child and the Race* (New York: Macmillan, 1898), pp. 14–15. See SE 7:173.

95. SE 22:158–59.

96. Jacques Le Rider, "Freud zwischen Aufklärung und Gegenaufklärung," in *Aufklärung und Gegenaufklärung in der europäischen Literatur, Philosophie, und Politik von der Antike bis zur Gegenwart,* ed. Jochen Schmidt (Darmstadt: Wissenschaftliche Buchgesellschaft, 1989), pp. 475–96.

97. Cited in Reik, *From Thirty Years with Freud,* p. 30.

98. Lazarus and Steinthal, "Einleitende Gedanken," p. 5.

99. Moritz Lazarus, "Über das Verhältnis des Einzelnen zur Gesammtheit," *Zeitschrift für Völkerpsychologie und Sprachwissenschaft* 2 (1862): 437.

100. Lazarus and Steinthal, "Einleitende Gedanken," p. 35.

101. Ibid., pp. 35–36.

102. Ibid., p. 37.

103. Ibid.

104. Ibid., p. 38.

105. Ibid., p. 39.

106. SE 21:30–31.

107. Ibid. 21:89.

108. In this context, see Dagmar Barnouw, "Modernism in Vienna: Freud and a Normative Poetics of the Self," *Modern Austrian Literature* 22 (1989): 327–44, on the question of Freud's construction of fictions of the self.

109. Blanton, *Diary,* p. 43. No better indicator of Freud's sense of his double audience exists than the recently rediscovered text of an early draft of *Thoughts for the Times on War and Death* (1915), which he delivered to the Vienna lodge of the B'nai B'rith. It is clear that this talk was geared to the interests of his Jewish audience. When the published version appeared, all the "Jewish" references had

been removed. See Bernd Nitzschke, "Freuds Vortrag vor dem israelitischen Humanitätsverein 'Wien' des Ordens B'nai B'rith: Wir und den Tod (1915). Ein wiedergefundenes Dokument," *Psyche* 45 (1991): 97–131.

110. SE 21:249.

111. *Sigmund Freud–C. G. Jung: Briefwechsel*, ed. William McGuire and Wolfgang Sauerländer (Frankfurt a. M.: Fischer, 1974), p. 71, in English as *The Freud/Jung Letters: The Correspondence between Sigmund Freud and C. G. Jung*, ed. William McGuire, trans. Ralph Manheim and R.F.C. Hull (Princeton: Princeton University Press, 1974), p. 145.

112. Jones, *Life and Work of Sigmund Freud* 2:42–43. See also the description of this meeting in his autobiography: Ernest Jones, *Free Associations: Memories of a Psycho-Analyst* (London: Hogarth Press, 1959), p. 166.

113. See the discussion in Phyllis Grosskurth, *The Secret Ring: Freud's Inner Circle and the Politics of Psychoanalysis* (Reading, Mass.: Addison-Wesley, 1991), pp. 132–33.

114. Hanns Sachs, *Freud: Master and Friend* (Cambridge, Mass.: Harvard University Press, 1946), p. 48.

115. Cited by Molnar in Freud, p. 100, from the letter of August 3, 1931, from Freud to Eitingon.

116. Jones, *Life and Work of Sigmund Freud* 2:168.

117. Leroy-Beaulieu, *Israel among the Nations*, p. 51.

118. Fritz Wittels, *Sigmund Freud: His Personality, His Teaching, and His School*, trans. Eden Paul and Ceder Paul (London: Allen & Unwin, 1924), p. 140. This translation corrected many errors (listed by Freud) in the original German.

119. Carl G. Jung, *Collected Works*, ed. Herbert Read et al., trans. R.F.C. Hull, 20 vols. (London: Routledge, 1957–79), 10:13.

120. Ibid. 7:149 n. 8. The question of Jewish creativity is closely linked to the traditional medical image of woman as "full of fantasy, but without the creative power and intelligence of man." This formulation is found in the standard scientific introduction to modern physiology written by Johannes Müller, *Handbuch der Physiologie des Menschen für Vorlesungen*, 2 vols. (Koblenz: Hölscher, 1890), 2:623 (in the Freud Library, London, with Freud's name and the date 5.8.1880).

121. Ibid. 10:534.

122. Ibid. 10:165–66. For the earlier relationship, see also Duane Schultz, *Intimate Friends, Dangerous Rivals: The Turbulent Relationship between Freud and Jung* (Los Angeles: Tarcher; New York: distributed by St. Martin's Press, 1990). See Aryeh Maidenbaum and Stephen Martin, eds., *Lingering Shadows: Jungians, Freudians, and Anti-Semitism* (Boston: Shambhala, 1991), and Victor Brome, *Freud and His Disciples: The Struggle for Supremacy* (London: Caliban Books, 1984), pp. 142–53, for a discussion of this material. See also Aniela Jaffé, *From the Life and Work of C. G. Jung*, trans. R.F.C. Hull (London: Hodder and Stoughten, 1972), pp. 78–98, for a Jewish defense of Jung's relationship to anti-Semitism, as well as the issue entitled "Jung face au nazisme" of the *Cahiers de psychologie jungienne* 12 (1977) for the facts of Jung's anti-Semitism and a possible reading of them. Recently, a more critical stance has been taken within the field of analytic psychology; see Andrew Samuels, "National Psychology, Na-

tional Socialism, and Analytic Psychology: Reflections on Jung and Anti-Semitism," *Journal of Analytic Psychology* 37 (1992): 3–28, 127–47.

123. Quoted by Mortimer Ostow, "Letter to the Editor," *International Review of Psychoanalysis* 4 (1977): 377.

124. Jung, *Collected Works* 10:165.

125. Ibid. 10:166.

126. Ibid. 10:508.

127. Aldo Carotenuto, *A Secret Symmetry: Sabina Spielrein between Jung and Freud*, trans. Arno Pomerans, John Shepley, and Krishna Winston (New York: Pantheon, 1982), pp. 120–21.

128. *Hippocrates*, trans. W.H.S. Jones, 6 vols. (Cambridge, Mass.: Harvard University Press, 1959), 2:311.

129. George A. Aitken, ed., *The Tatler*, 4 vols. (London: Duckworth, 1899), 4:162 (for September 19, 1710).

130. Blanton, *Diary*, p. 43.

131. Abraham Kardiner, *My Analysis with Freud: Reminiscences* (New York: Norton, 1977), p. 70.

132. Sigmund Freud, *Briefe, 1873–1939*, ed. Ernst and Lucie Freud (Frankfurt a. M.: Fischer, 1960), p. 443.

133. GW Nachtragsband: 735.

134. *Sigmund Freud–Karl Abraham, Briefe, 1907–1926*, ed. Hilda C. Abraham and Ernst L. Freud (Frankfurt a. M.: Fischer, 1980), p. 47; translation from *A Psycho-Analytic Dialogue: The Letters of Sigmund Freud and Karl Abraham, 1907–1926*, ed. Hilda C. Abraham and Ernst L. Freud, trans. Bernard Marsh and Hilda C. Abraham (London: Hogarth Press, 1965), p. 34.

135. On the context of this exchange, see Peter Homans, *The Ability to Mourn: Disillusionment and the Social Origins of Psychoanalysis* (Chicago: University of Chicago Press, 1989), pp. 35–41.

136. Abraham to Freud, May 11, 1908, in *Sigmund Freud–Karl Abraham, Briefe*, pp. 48–49; translation from *A Psycho-Analytic Dialogue*, p. 36.

137. *Sigmund Freud–Karl Abraham, Briefe*, p. 57; translation from *A Psycho-Analytic Dialogue*, p. 46.

138. Freud to Ferenczi, July 28, 1912, Freud Collection, Library of Congress; cited in Peter Gay, *Freud: A Life for Our Time* (New York: Norton, 1988), p. 231.

139. Freud to Rank, August 18, 1912, Rank Collection, Columbia University Library; cited in Gay, *Freud*, p. 231.

140. Carotenuto, *Secret Symmetry*, pp. 120–21.

141. Reik, *Jewish Wit*, p. 33.

142. SE 19:222.

143. Enrico Morselli was the author of *La psicanalisi: Studii ed appunti critici*, 2 vols. (Turin: Bocca, 1926) (in the Freud Library, London), which argued that psychoanalysis was a Jewish discovery because of the predisposition of Jews to theoretical solutions for material problems. See also his essay "La psicologia etnica e la scienza eugenistica," *International Eugenics Congress—1912*, 2 vols. (London: Eugenics Education Society, 1912), 1:58–62. On Morselli, see Patrizia Guanieri, *Individualità difformi: La psichiatria antropologica di Enrico Morselli*

(Milan: Angeli, 1986). Freud detested Morselli's *Psicanalisi: Studii ed appunti critici*, noting in a letter to Edoardo Weiss that its "only value is its undoubted proof that he is a donkey. It contains numerous large and small mistakes. . . . Furthermore, it is covered by a layer of false courtesy, as used to be characteristic for the *Katzelmacher* [pejorative term for Italian] in old Austria." Freud's letter, phrased in equally obsequious terms, should be read in this context. Weiss, at Freud's behest, savaged the book both in German and in Italian reviews. It is important to note the extraordinary ambivalence in Freud's response to Morselli and in his damning note on Morselli to Weiss. See Edoardo Weiss, *Sigmund Freud as a Consultant: Reflections of a Pioneer in Psychoanalysis* (New York: International Medical Book, 1970), pp. 51–55.

144. Freud, *Briefe*, p. 380.

145. Cited in the introduction by Molnar to Freud, *Diary*, p. xxiv.

146. SE 19:291; GW 14:556.

147. Josef Philip Hes, "A Note on an As Yet Unpublished Letter by Sigmund Freud," *Jewish Social Studies* 48 (1986): 322.

148. SE 13:xv; GW 14:569. On this trope, see Shulamit Volkov, "Die Erfindung einer Tradition: Zur Entstehung des modernen Judentums in Deutschland," *Historische Zeitschrift* 253 (1991): 603–28; here, 609.

149. SE 19:142.

150. Paul Näcke, "Über Kontrast-Träume und speziell sexuelle Kontrast-Träume," *Archiv für Kriminal-Anthropologie und Kriminalistik* 28 (1907): 1–19; here, 13. See SE 5:396. On Freud and Näcke, see Helmut Gröger, "Sigmund Freud an Paul Näcke, Erstveröffentlichung zweier Freud-Briefe," *Luzifer Amor* 3 (1990): 144–62.

151. SE 7:151; GW 5:50.

152. This aspect of my work has been greatly influenced by the work of George L. Mosse, especially his ground-breaking study *Nationalism and Sexuality: Respectability and Abnormal Sexuality in Modern Europe* (New York: Fertig, 1985); see his chapter "Race and Sexuality: The Outsider," pp. 133–52. I quote here from his introduction (p. 17). An excellent collection of essays has followed up on Mosse's suggestions: Andrew Parker, Mary Russo, Doris Sommer, and Patricia Yaeger, eds., *Nationalisms and Sexualities* (New York: Routledge, 1992).

153. Sigmund Diamond, "Sigmund Freud, His Jewishness, and Scientific Method: the Seen and the Unseen as Evidence," *Journal of the History of Ideas* 43 (1982): 613–34. I also note here the work of Jean-François Lyotard on Heidegger and the Jews, in which Lyotard regards Heidegger's refusal to speak of the Shoah as a form of the refusal to remember, which is closely tied to the role the Jews play in the cultural world of Christianity as the ultimate object of projection. The Jew, caught up in such a system of representation, has little choice: the essential Jew, who internalizes the horrors projected onto the Jew, and which are embodied in the Jew's physical being, represses what the Jew is. See Jean-François Lyotard, *Heidegger et "les juifs"* (Paris: Galilée, 1988).

154. SE 9:211.

155. See the detailed overview of the psychoanalytic debates concerning "penis envy" in Shahla Chehrazi, "Female Psychology: A Review," *Journal of the American Psychoanalytic Association* 34 (1986): 141–62.

156. SE 20:212.

157. Sander L. Gilman, *Difference and Pathology: Stereotypes of Sexuality, Race, and Madness* (Ithaca, N.Y.: Cornell University Press, 1985), pp. 76–108.

158. SE 15:155.

159. See, for example, F.D.F. Souchay, *De l'homologie sexuelle chez l'homme* (Paris: Rignoux, 1855). This topic is central to the argument in Thomas Laqueur, *Making Sex: Body and Gender from the Greeks to Freud* (Cambridge, Mass.: Harvard University Press, 1990).

160. Karl Reiskel, "Idioticon viennense eroticum," *Anthropophyteia* 2 (1905): 1–13; here, 9. Freud makes reference to this volume in SE 10:215 n. 1. On Freud's relation to the editor of the journal, see Johannes Reichmeyr, "Friedrich Salomon Krauss und Sigmund Freud—Begegnung unorthodoxer Gelehrter," *Luzifer Amor* 1 (1988): 133–55, and Mirjam Morad, "Friedrich Salomo Krauss: Vom Blick in die Seele zum Seelenzergliederer," in *Wunderblock: Eine Geschichte der modernen Seele,* ed. Jean Clair, Catharin Pichler, and Wolfgang Pirchner, (Vienna: Löcker, 1989), pp. 501–6.

161. E. J. Schoen, "Ode to the Circumcised Male," *American Journal of Diseases of Childhood* 141 (1987): 128.

162. SE 7:195.

163. SE 7:187.

164. *Eros oder Wörterbuch über die Physiologie und über die Natur- und Cultur-Geschichte des Menschen in Hinsicht auf seine Sexualität,* 2 vols. (Berlin: Rücker, 1823), 1:76–77 (in the Freud Library, London).

165. Freud owned a reference work that includes accurate images of male and female sexual anatomy. See J. Henke, *Handbuch der Eingeweidelehre des Menschen* (Braunschweig: Vieweg, 1873), pp. 446–47 (in the Freud Library, London, with Freud's signature and the date 22.XII.81 on the flyleaf). A detailed discussion of the contemporary understanding of the structure and function of the clitoris is found in the survey by W. Liepmann, "Klitoris," in *Handwörterbuch der Sexualwissenschaft,* ed. Max Marcuse (Bonn: Marcus & E. Webers, 1926), pp. 372–73 (in the Freud Library, London).

166. SE 21:232–33.

167. Elaine Showalter, *The Female Malady: Women, Madness, and English Culture, 1830–1980* (New York: Pantheon, 1985).

168. John M. Eyler, *Victorian Social Medicine: The Ideas and Methods of William Farr* (Baltimore: Johns Hopkins University Press, 1979), p. 100.

169. On the image of the woman in fin de siècle medicine, see Lilian Berna-Simons, *Weibliche Identität und Sexualität: Das Bild der Weiblichkeit im 19. Jahrhundert und in Sigmund Freud* (Frankfurt a. M.: Materialis, 1984); on Möbius, see Francis Schiller, *A Möbius Strip: Fin-de-siècle Neuropsychiatry and Paul Möbius* (Berkeley and Los Angeles: University of California Press, 1982). Freud distances himself from Möbius's biological work on femininity; he sees instead the limitations present within the feminine as a reflex of the suppression of female sexuality in Western culture. (See SE 9:198–99 for Freud's rebuttal of Möbius.)

170. SE 20:38.

171. Cited in Jones, *Life and Work of Sigmund Freud* 2:468. See William G. Niederland, "The Source of Freud's Question about What Women Want," *American Journal of Psychiatry* 146 (1989): 409–10.

172. See Jacques Le Rider, *Modernité viennoise et crises de l'identité* (Paris: Presses universitaires de France, 1990), pp. 197–222.

173. Heinrich Singer, *Allgemeine und spezielle Krankheitslehre der Juden* (Leipzig: Konegen, 1904), p. 9.

174. Hans Gross, *Kriminal-Psychologie* (Leipzig: Vogel, 1905), p. 121.

175. Leroy-Beaulieu, *Israel among the Nations*, p. 163.

176. Adolf Jellinek, *Der jüdische Stamm: Ethnographische Studien* (Vienna: Herzfeld und Bauer, 1869), pp. 89–90.

177. Jones, *Life and Work of Sigmund Freud* 2:119; see also 2:398–99.

178. Felix von Luschan, "Altweiber-Psychologie," *Deutsche medizinische Wochenschrift* 42 (January 6, 1916): 20.

179. SE 22:113.

180. Ludwig Hirschfeld, *Was nicht im Baedeker steht: Wien und Budapest* (Munich: Piper, 1927), p. 56.

181. Kardiner, *My Analysis with Freud*, p. 92.

182. *Protokolle der Wiener Psychoanalytischen Vereinigung*, ed. Herman Nunberg and Ernst Federn, 4 vols. (Frankfurt a. M.: Fischer, 1976–81), 1:132; translation from *Minutes of the Vienna Psychoanalytic Society*, trans. M. Nunberg, 4 vols. (New York: International Universities Press, 1962–75), 1:140. Freud's comment on this case stressed the conflict between the desire to be baptized and the unchangeable Jewishness of the penis.

183. Martin Freud, *Glory Reflected: Sigmund Freud—Man and Father* (London: Angus and Robertson, 1957), p. 16.

184. See "The Jewish Reader: Freud Reads Heine Reads Freud," in Sander L. Gilman, *The Jew's Body* (New York: Routledge, 1991), pp. 150–68.

185. SE 14:69–102; here, 88–89.

186. Leroy-Beaulieu, *Israel among the Nations*, p. 113.

187. SE 14:89.

188. Leroy-Beaulieu, *Israel among the Nations*, pp. 191–93.

189. Hugo Bettauer, *Die Stadt ohne Juden: Ein Roman von Übermorgen* (1922; Salzburg: Hannibal, 1980).

CHAPTER TWO
THE CONSTRUCTION OF THE MALE JEW

1. Jacob R. Marcus, *The Colonial American Jew, 1492–1776*, 3 vols. (Detroit: Wayne State University Press, 1970), 2:984. On the American tradition, see Jay Brodbar-Nemzer, Peter Conrad, and Shelly Tenenbaum, "American Circumcision Practices and Social Reality," *Sociology and Social Research* 71 (1987): 275–79.

2. Richard Andree, *Zur Volkskunde der Juden* (Leipzig: Velhagen & Klasing, 1881), p. 157.

3. Humphrey Carpenter, *A Serious Character: The Life of Ezra Pound* (Boston: Houghton Mifflin, 1988), p. 362.

4. Richard Burton, *Love, War, and Fancy: The Customs and Manners of the East from the Writings on "The Arabian Nights,"* ed. Kenneth Walker (London: Kimber, 1964), p. 106.

5. See the exemplary use of the discussion of the Jews as a race in Richard Weinberg, "Zur Theorie einer anatomischen Rassensystematik," *Archiv für Rassen- und Gesellschafts-Biologie* 2 (1905): 198–214, especially pp. 205–6. Weinberg notes ten different physical characteristics that determine the definition of racial difference.

6. A summary of the German-Jewish views on the meaning of this practice in the 1920s can be found in the essay on "Berit mila" in *Jüdisches Lexikon,* ed. Georg Herlitz and Bruno Kirschner, 4 vols. in 5 (Berlin: Jüdischer Verlag, 1927–30), 1:861–66 (in the Freud Library, London). This essay stresses seven different readings of infant circumcision: as a hygienic practice, as the remains of older practices of castration, as the mark of stigmatization, as a sign of tribal membership, as a test of the child, as a sanctification of the penis, and as a prophylactic against incest. For the last, psychoanalytic theory is evoked. A comparable survey, which Freud would also have known, is "Beschneidung" by O. F. Scheuer in *Handwörterbuch der Sexualwissenschaft,* ed. Max Marcuse (Bonn: Marcus & E. Webers, 1926), pp. 50–52 (in the Freud Library, London). For the basic study from the 1930s, see Felix Bryk, *Die Beschneidung bei Mann und Weib: Ihre Geschichte, Psychologie, und Ethnologie* (Neubrandenburg: Feller, 1931), and, for a recent history of the visualization of the procedure, see Elliot A. Grossman, *Circumcision: A Pictorial Atlas of Its History, Instrument Development, and Operative Techniques* (Great Neck, N.Y.: Todd and Honeywell, 1982). On the Jewish views of the meaning and function of this practice see J. David Bleich, *Judaism and Healing: Halakhic Perspectives* (New York: Ktav, 1981), pp. 47–50. On the history of the Jewish tradition, see Julius Preuss, *Biblisch-talmudische Medizin: Beiträge zur Geschichte der Heilkunde und der Kultur überhaupt* (Berlin: Karger, 1927), p. 279. Compare John J. Collins, "A Symbol of Otherness: Circumcision and Salvation in the First Century," in *"To See Ourselves as Others See Us": Christians, Jews, "Others," in Late Antiquity,* ed. Jacob Neusner and Ernest S. Frerichs (Chico, Calif.: Scholars Press, 1985), pp. 163–85, and Nigel Allan, "A Polish Rabbi's Circumcision Manual," *Medical History* 33 (1989): 247–54.

7. "Die rituelle Beschneidung bei den Juden und ihre Gefahren," *Journal für Kinderkrankheiten* 59 (1872): 367–72.

8. G. S. Thompson, "Circumcision—A Barbarous and Unnecessary Mutilation," *British Medical Journal* 1 (1920): 437.

9. See, in this context, the most recent and most extensive presentation of this argument: Rosemary Romberg, ed., *Circumcision: The Painful Dilemma* (South Hadley, Mass.: Bergin & Garvey, 1985), which was published in conjunction with the INTACT Educational Foundation. The most recent debate about the medical implications in the United States of this widespread practice was begun by E. N. Preston, "Whither the Foreskin? A Consideration of Routine Neonatal Circumcision," *Journal of the American Medical Association* 216 (1970): 1853–58. In this vein, see also Edward Wallerstein, "Circumcision: The Uniquely American Medical Enigma," *Urologic Clinics of North America* 12 (1985): 123–32, which discusses the debates about infection in the context of an attack on the

practice. In this context, see Moisés Trachtenberg and Philip Slotkin, "Circumcision, Crucifixion, and Anti-Semitism: The Antithetical Character of Ideologies and Their Symbols which Contain Crossed Lines," *International Review of Psychoanalysis* 16 (1989): 459–71; E. A. Grossman and N. A. Posner, "The Circumcision Controversy: An Update," *Obstetrics and Gynecological Annual* 13 (1984): 181–95; E. A. Grossman and N. A. Posner, "Surgical Circumcision of Neonates: A History of Its Development," *Obstetrics and Gynecology* 58 (1981): 241–46; S. J. Waszak, "The Historic Significance of Circumcision," *Obstetrics and Gynecology* 51 (1978): 499–501.

The anthropological literature on this topic is often critical and superficial; see Desmond Morris, *Bodywatching* (London: Jonathan Cape, 1985), pp. 218–20. By far the best anthropological discussion of what the circumcised body means is found in the published work of James Boon: *Other Tribes, Other Scribes* (New York: Cambridge University Press, 1982), pp. 162–68; *Affinities and Extremes* (Chicago: University of Chicago Press, 1990), pp. 55–60; and his unpublished paper "Circumscribing Circumcision/Uncircumcision" (1990), in which the meaning of the act of circumcision is most intelligently and most sophisticatedly drawn into question. The reading of the Jewish practice in light of the history of nineteenth-century anthropology is extraordinarily well documented in Howard Eilberg-Schwartz, *The Savage in Judaism: An Anthropology of Israelite Religion and Ancient Judaism* (Bloomington: Indiana University Press, 1990), pp. 141–76. See also Moisés Trachtenberg, *Psicanálise da circuncisão* (Pôrto Alegre: Sagra, 1990), and Claude Lévi-Strauss, "Exode sur exode," *Homme* 28 (1988): 106–7.

10. See Sander L. Gilman, "Jewish Writers and German Letters: Anti-Semitism and the Hidden Language of the Jews," *Jewish Quarterly Review* 77 (1986–87): 119–48, and "Male Sexuality and Contemporary Jewish Literature in German: The Damaged Body as an Image of the Damaged Psyche," *Genders* (forthcoming).

11. Jakov Lind, the Viennese-Jewish novelist, long a resident of Great Britain, stated it most clearly in his autobiography:

> All he needed was a foreskin,
> otherwise he felt all right.
> He lived it up like a Duke in his castle,
> with pheasant shooting and old paintings,
> all he needed was a little foreskin,
> otherwise he was all right.
>
> He lived it up like the Roi de Soleil
> on Trianon, they fed him oysters with a spoon,
> all he needed was a bit of skin,
> otherwise he was all right.
>
> He lived it up like Zeus in the Parthenon,
> makes it only with Goddesses,
> all he needs is a bit more skin
> and everything will be fine.

Jakov Lind, *Counting My Steps: An Autobiography* (London: Macmillan, 1969), pp. 135–36.

12. Rudolf Virchow, "Gesamtbericht über die Farbe der Haut, der Haare, und der Augen der Schulkinder in Deutschland," *Archiv für Anthropologie* 16 (1886): 275–475.

13. Felix von Luschan, *Völker, Rasse, und Sprachen* (Berlin: Welt, 1922), p. 169.

14. On the colonial implications of the debate about circumcision in Great Britain and its association with Islam as well as with the Jews, see Ronald Hyam, *Empire and Sexuality: The British Experience* (Manchester: Manchester University Press, 1990), pp. 76–79.

15. Johann Jakob Schudt, *Jüdische Merckwürdigkeiten*, 4 vols. in 2 (Frankfurt a. M.: Hocker, 1714–18), 2:296. Schudt's work presents a deformed reading of controversies within rabbinic Judaism. In rabbinic Judaism, the figure of Adam is understood as having been created circumcised, as his body reflected the physical nature of the divine (see the discussion in the *Avot de Rabbi Nattan*). On the Talmudic tradition concerning congenital circumcision and its role in discussing the definition of anti-Semitism, see Sander L. Gilman and Steven T. Katz, eds., *Anti-Semitism in Times of Crisis* (New York: New York University Press, 1991), pp. 110–11.

16. Johann David Michaelis, *Mosäisches Recht*, 6 vols. (Reutlingen: Grözinger, 1785), 4:37.

17. Johann David Michaelis, *Orientalische und Exegetische Bibliothek*, 24 vols. (Frankfurt a. M.: Johann Gottlieb Garbe, 1773), 4:94.

18. Johann Friedrich Blumenbach, *Über den Bildungstrieb und das Zeugungsgeschäfte*, ed. L. V. Kàrolyi (Stuttgart: Gustav Fischer, 1971), p. 69.

19. Friedrich Schiller, *Werke*, 38 vols. (Weimar: Hermann Böhlaus Nachfolger, 1943–), 3:22. On Schiller and the Jews, see Norbert Oellers, "Goethe und Schiller in ihrem Verhältnis zum Judentum," in *Conditio Judaica: Judentum, Antisemitismus, und deutschsprachige Literatur vom 18. Jahrhundert bis zum ersten Weltkrieg*, ed. Hans Otto Horch and Horst Denkler, (Tübingen: Niemeyer, 1988), pp. 108–30. Neither Oellers nor any of the earlier writers on this play discusses this aspect of the play. See Hans Mayer, "Der weise Nathan und der Räuber Spiegelberg: Antinomien der jüdischen Emanzipation in Deutschland," *Jahrbuch der deutschen Schillergesellschaft* 17 (1973): 253–72, and Philipp F. Veit, "Moritz Spiegelberg: Eine Charakterstudie zu Schillers Räubern," *Jahrbuch der deutschen Schillergesellschaft* 17 (1973): 273–90. On Freud and *The Robbers*, see William J. McGrath, *Freud's Discovery of Psychoanalysis: The Politics of Hysteria* (Ithaca, N.Y.: Cornell University Press, 1986), pp. 21, 66–68.

20. Schiller, *Werke* 3:249.

21. Johann Heinrich Ferdinand von Autenrieth, "Über die beschnittengebohrnen Judenkinder," *Archiv für die Physiologie* 7 (1807): 296–98.

22. Melchior Fribe, "De pene in inferiore parte perforato," *Miscellanea curiosa medico-physica academiæ* 1 (1681): 135–37.

23. Salomon Reisel, "Cardialgia periodica vernalis," *Miscellanea curiosa medico-physica academiæ* 7 (1716): 12–13.

24. Gideon Brecher, *Die Beschneidung der Juden von der historischen, praktisch-operativen, und ritualen Seite* (Vienna: Verlag des Verfassers, 1845), pp. 65–66.

25. Cited by P. Ascherson, "Über angeborenen Mangel der Vorhaut bei beschnittenen Völkern," *Berliner Gesellschaft für Anthropologie, Ethnologie, und Urgeschichte* 20 (1888): 126–30, without any specific source.

26. C. Lederer, "Die Circumcision," *Wiener Medizinische Presse* 7 (1871): col. 661.

27. Charles Darwin, *The Variation of Animals and Plants under Domestication*, 2 vols. (London: Murray, 1868), 2:23. (in the Freud Library, London).

28. Ernst Mayr, *The Growth of Biological Thought: Diversity, Evolution, and Inheritance* (Cambridge, Mass.: Harvard University Press, Belknap Press, 1982), p. 698.

29. August Weismann, *Essays upon Heredity and Kindred Biological Problems*, trans. Edward B. Poulton, Selmar Schönland, and Arthur Shipley, Translations of Foreign Biological Memoirs, 4 (Oxford: Clarendon Press, 1889), p. 434. On Weismann, see SE 18:45–47, 56.

30. Dr. Levy, "Ueber Erblichkeit des Vorhautmangels bei Juden," *Virchows Archiv* 116 (1889): 539–40. Levy mentions the lecture by Weismann.

31. Eugene S. Talbot, "Inheritance of Circumcision Effects," *Medicine* 4 (1898): 473–75.

32. Ignaz Zollschan, *Das Rassenproblem unter besonderer Berücksichtigung der theoretischen Grundlagen der jüdischen Rassenfrage* (Vienna: Braumüller, 1911), p. 235 (in the Freud Library, London, with a dedication from the author).

33. Heinrich Singer, *Allgemeine und spezielle Krankheitslehre der Juden* (Leipzig: Konegen, 1904), p. 130.

34. M. J. Gutmann, *Über den heutigen Stand der Rasse- und Krankheitsfrage der Juden* (Munich: Rudolph Müller & Steinicke, 1920), p. 31.

35. Theodore James, "A Causerie on Circumcision, Congenital and Acquired," *South African Medical Journal* 45 (1971): 151–54.

36. There is no comprehensive study of the German debates on circumcision. See Julius Preuss, "Die Beschneidung nach Bibel und Talmud," *Wiener klinische Rundschau* 11 (1897): 708–9, 724–27; J. Alkvist, "Geschichte der Circumcision," *Janus* 30 (1926): 86–104, 152–71, as well as Samuel Krauss, *Geschichte der jüdischen Ärzte vom frühsten Mittelalter bis zur Gleichberechtigung* (Vienna: Bettelheim-Stiftung, 1930), pp. 157–58.

37. At least one Jewish convert to Christianity in the sixteenth century, Antonius Margaritha, while stressing the evident pain of the infant, does not condemn the ritual practice. See his *Der gantz Jüdisch glaub* (Augsburg: Steyner, 1530), pp. H1v–H2r. On Margaritha, see Sander L. Gilman, *Jewish Self-Hatred: Anti-Semitism and the Hidden Language of the Jews* (Baltimore: Johns Hopkins University Press, 1985), pp. 62–66.

38. The relevant passages in the German edition, Paolo Mantegazza, *Anthropologisch-kulturhistorische Studien über die Geschlechtsverhältnisse des Menschen* (Jena: Costenoble, 1886), are on pp. 132–37. All the quotations from Mantegazza are to the English translation: Paolo Mantegazza, *The Sexual Relations of Mankind*, trans. Samuel Putnam (New York: Eugenics, 1938).

39. See the discussion in Sander L. Gilman, *The Jew's Body* (New York: Routledge, 1991), pp. 89–92.

40. Spinoza's text, often cited and often commented on in the nineteenth century, labels circumcision the primary reason for the survival of the Jews as "they have incurred universal hatred by cutting themselves off completely from all other peoples." It also made them "effeminate" and, thus, unlikely to assume a political role in the future. Benedict de Spinoza, *The Political Works*, trans. A. G. Wernham (Oxford: Oxford University Press, 1958), p. 63. I am grateful to Jay Geller for this source.

41. Mantegazza, *Sexual Relations*, p. 99.

42. Edvard Westermarck, *The History of Marriage*, 3 vols. (London: Macmillan, 1921), 1:561. See also Israel Schur, *Wesen und Motive der Beschneidung im Licht der alttestamentlichen Quellen und der Völkerkunde. (Mit Berücksichtigung von Sabbath und Pesah.) Am 14. Dezember 1936: von R. Karsten und E. Westermarck vorgelegt* (Helsingfors: Finska vetenskaps-societeten, 1937).

43. Mantegazza, *Sexual Relations*, pp. 98–99.

44. Auguste Forel, *Die sexuelle Frage* (Munich: Reinhardt, 1906), p. 172, in English as *The Sexual Question*, trans. C. F. Marshall (New York: Medical Art Agency, 1922), p. 158 (in the Freud Library, London, in the 1905 edition). Forel cites Edvard Westermarck as his authority.

45. William Osler, "Israel and Medicine" (1914), in his *Men and Books*, ed. Earl F. Nation (Pasadena, Calif.: Castle Press, 1959), p. 56.

46. Ernest Crawley, *The Mystic Rose: A Study of Primitive Marriage* (London: Macmillan, 1902), p. 138. See SE 11:194, 195, 198–99; 13:13–14.

47. Johann Heinrich Ferdinand von Autenrieth, *Abhandlung über den Ursprung der Beschneidung bei wilden und halbwilden Völkern, mit Beziehung auf die Beschneidung der Israeliten. Mit einer Kritik von C. C. v. Flatt begleitet.* . . . (Tübingen: Laupp, 1829). On the older medical attitude toward circumcision in Germany, see Rudolph Augustin Vogel, *Zweifel wider den medicinischen Nutzen der Beschneidung* (Weiz: Beyfus Anselmus Schloss, 1774), and D. Salomon, *Kurzgefasste Abhandlung von der Phimosis, Paraphimosis und einigen andern Krankheiten der Vorhaut des männlichen Gliedes, mit Beschreibung der verschiedenen Operationsmethoden und der Beschneidung der Israeliten* (Quedlinburg: Basse, 1833). On the parallel theological view, see Paul Christian Kirchner, *Jüdisches Ceremoniel, oder, Beschreibung dererjenigen Gebräuche, welche die Jüden so wol inn—als ausser dem Tempel, bey alten und jeden Fest-Tägen, im Gebet, bey der Beschneidung, bey Hochzeiten, Auslösung der Erst-Geburt, im Sterben, bey der Begräbnüss und dergleichen, in acht zu nehmen pflegen* (Nuremberg: Monath, 1726).

48. John Lubbock, *The Origin of Civilization and the Primitive Condition of Man* (1870; Chicago: University of Chicago Press, 1978), p. 237. See SE 13:13, 111.

49. Lubbock, *Origin of Civilization*, p. 243.

50. Dr. Hacker, "Die Bescheidung der Juden, ein Ueberrest der Barbarei dieses Volkes, und ein Ersatz für seine früheren Menschenopfer," *Medicinischer Argos* 5 (1843): 375–79.

51. Wilhelm Wundt, *Elements of Folk Psychology: Outlines of a Psychological History of the Development of Mankind*, trans. Edward Leroy Schaub (London: Allen & Unwin, 1916), p. 445. See SE 13:101, 106–7, 119.

52. Wundt, *Elements of Folk Psychology*, p. 498.

53. *Philo*, trans. F. H. Colson, 12 vols. (Cambridge, Mass.: Harvard University Press, 1953–63), 7:103–5 (*De specialibus legibus*, 1:4–7). See Theodore James, "Philo on Circumcision," *South African Medical Journal* 50 (1976): 1409–12.

54. Roy S. Wolper, "Circumcision as Polemic in the Jew Bill of 1753: The Cutter Cut?" *Eighteenth-Century Life* 7 (1982): 28–36.

55. See Sander L. Gilman, *Sexuality: An Illustrated History* (New York: Wiley, 1989).

56. Samuel Holdheim, *Über die Beschneidung zunächst in religiös-dogmatischer Beziehung* (Schwerin: Kürschner, 1844). On the debates concerning circumcision in the mid-nineteenth century, see P. Wolfers, *Die Beschneidung der Juden: Eine Anweisung fur Beschneider, Ärtze und Wundärtze* (Lemförde: Helwing, 1831); Elias Collin, *Die Beschneidung der Israeliten und ihre Nachbehandlung* (Leipzig: Ludwig Schreck, 1842); Salomon Abraham Trier, *Rabbinische Gutachten über die Beschneidung* (Frankfurt a. M.: Bach, 1844); Joseph Bergson, *Die Beschneidung vom historischen, kritischen, und medicinischen Standpunkt mit Bezug auf die neuesten Debatten und Reformvorschläge* (Berlin: Scherk, 1844); M. G. Salomon, *Die Beschneidung: Historisch und medizinisch beleuchtet* (Braunschweig: Vieweg, 1844); Leopold Zunz, *Gutachten über die Beschneidung* (Frankfurt a. M.: J.F. Bach, 1844); on the specific debate about the *metsitsah*, see L. Terquem, *Die Beschneidung in pathologischer, überhaupt wissenschaftlicher Bedeutung mit der Auseinandersetzung eines neuen Verfahrens in Bezug der Ausübung der zweiten Actes der Operation* (Magdeburg: Baensch, 1844).

57. Bergson, *Die Beschneidung*.

58. Dr. Wolfers, "Ueber die Beschneidung der Judenkinder," *Zeitschrift für Staatsarzneikunde* 9 (1825): 205–9.

59. See the discussion in Salomon, *Die Beschneidung*.

60. Dr. Klein, "Die rituelle Circumcision, eine sanitätspolizeiliche Frage," *Allgemeine Medizinische Central-Zeitung* 22 (1853): 368–69.

61. S. Arnhold, *Die Beschneidung und ihre Reform* (Leipzig: n.p., 1847), pp. 50–51.

62. See Claude Quétel, *History of Syphilis*, trans. Judith Braddock and Brian Pike (Oxford: Polity Press, 1990). For the American context during this period, see Alan M. Brandt, *No Magic Bullet: A Social History of Venereal Disease in the United States since 1880* (New York: Oxford University Press, 1985).

63. See the first-rate study by Anna Foa, "Il nuovo e il vecchio: L'insorgere della sifilide (1494–1530)," *Quaderni storici* 55 (1984): 11–34, trans. Carole C. Gallucci in *Sex and Gender in Historical Perspective*, ed. Edward Muir and Guido Ruggiero (Baltimore: Johns Hopkins University Press, 1990), pp. 24–45. On Jews and syphilis, see also Klaus Theweleit, *Male Fantasies*, trans. Erica Carter and Chris Turner, 2 vols. (Minneapolis: University of Minnesota Press, 1987–89), 2:16.

64. Cited by Harry Friedenwald, *The Jews and Medicine: Essays*, 2 vols. (Baltimore: Johns Hopkins University Press, 1944), 2:531.

65. Armand-Louis-Joseph Béraud, *Étude de pathologie comparée: Essai sur la pathologie des sémites* (Bordeaux: Cassignol, 1897), p. 55.

66. Singer, *Allgemeine*, p. 49.

67. Cited by A. A. Brill and Morris J. Karpas, "Insanity among the Jews," *Medical Record* 86 (1914): 577–79; here, 577.

68. Alexander Pilcz, *Beitrag zur vergleichenden Rassen-Psychiatrie* (Leipzig: Deuticke, 1906), p. 29.

69. Joseph Adolf Hirschl, "Zur Ätiologie der progressiven Paralyse," *Jahrbücher für Psychiatrie* 14 (1896): 321–541; here, 449; Joseph Adolf Hirschl and Otto Marburg, *Syphilis des Nervensystems, einschliesslich Tabes und Paralyse* (Vienna: Hölder, 1914).

70. Bertha Pappenheim and Sara Rabinowitsch, *Zur Lage der jüdischen Bevölkerung in Galizien: Reise-Eindrücke und Vorschläge zur Besserung der Verhältnisse* (Frankfurt a. M.: Neuer Frankfurter, 1904), pp. 46–51.

71. Adolf Hitler, *Mein Kampf*, trans. Ralph Manheim (Boston: Houghton Mifflin, 1943), p. 247.

72. Compare Edward J. Bristow, *Prostitution and Prejudice: The Jewish Fight against White Slavery, 1870–1939* (Oxford: Clarendon Press, 1982), and J. L. Joseph, "The Mafkeh and the Lady: Jews, Prostitutes, and Progressives in New York City, 1900–1930" (Ph.D. diss., State University of New York, Stony Brook, 1986).

73. Cited by Friedenwald, *The Jews and Medicine* 2:529.

74. Cited by Peter Charles Remondino, *History of Circumcision from the Earliest Times to the Present. Moral and Physical Reasons for Its Performance, with a History of Eunuchism, Hermaphrodism, etc., and of the Different Operations Practiced upon the Prepuce* (Philadelphia: Davis, 1891), p. 187.

75. Benjamin Ward Richardson, *Diseases of Modern Life* (New York: Bermingham, 1882), p. 20.

76. Madison Marsh, "Jews and Christians," *Medical and Surgical Reporter* (Philadelphia) 30 (1874): 343–44; here, 343.

77. N. Balaban and A. Molotschek, "Progressive Paralyse bei den Bevölkerungen der Krim," *Allgemeine Zeitschrift für Psychiatrie* 94 (1931): 373–83. An overview of the debate on the predisposition of Jews to syphilis can be found in Jizchok Taitz, "Psychosen und Neurosen bei Juden" (Ph.D. diss., Basel, 1937), pp. 28–29.

78. Paul Julius Möbius, *Neurologische Beiträge*, 5 vols. (Leipzig: Barth, 1894–98), 3:76, 90 (in the Freud Collection, New York). See SE 3:98.

79. H. Budul, "Beitrag zur vergleichenden Rassenpsychiatrie," *Monatsschrift für Psychiatrie und Neurologie* 37 (1915): 199–204.

80. Brill and Karpas, "Insanity among the Jews," p. 578.

81. Max Sichel, "Die Paralyse der Juden in sexuologischer Beleuchtung," *Zeitschrift für Sexualwissenschaft* 7 (1919–20): 98–104; Max Sichel, "Nervöse Folgezustände von Alkohol und Syphilis bei den Juden," *Zeitschrift für Demographie und Statistik der Juden* 7 (1919): 137–41.

82. Hugo Hoppe, *Krankheiten und Sterblichkeit bei Juden und Nichtjuden* (Berlin: Calvary, 1903), pp. 42–43.

83. Ephraim M. Epstein, "Have the Jews Any Immunity from Certain Diseases?" *Medical and Surgical Reporter* (Philadelphia) 30 (1874): 440–42; here, 440.

84. Hermann Strauss, "Erkrankungen durch Alkohol und Syphilis bei den Juden," *Zeitschrift für Demographie und Statistik der Juden,* n.s. 4 (1927): 33–39.

85. James H. Jones, *Bad Blood: The Tuskegee Syphilis Experiment—A Tragedy of Race and Medicine* (New York: Free Press, 1981).

86. Moritz Mombert, *Das gesetzlich verordnete Kellerquellenbad der Israelitinnen* (Mühlhausen: Pietsch, 1828), p. 57.

87. Dr. Niemann, "Die Beschneidung der Juden, inbesondere von Seiten der Sanitäts-Polizei betrachtet," *Vierteljahrsschrift für gerichtliche und öffentliche Medizin* 7 (1855): 286.

88. S. N. Kutna, "Über den Werth der Frühbeschneidung (rituelle Circumcision)," *Medicinische Blätter* 25 (1902): 299–302. Concerning the late-nineteenth-century understanding of Jewish ritual circumcision, see Josef Grunwald, *Die rituelle Circumcision (Beschneidung) operativ und rituell bearbeitet* (Frankfurt a. M.: Kauffmann, 1892); Carl Alexander, *Die hygienische Bedeutung der Beschneidung: Vortrag gehalten im Liberalen Verein der Synagogen-Gemeinde zu Breslau am 15. April 1902* (Breslau: Schatzky, 1902); Samuel Kohn, *Die Geschichte der Beschneidung bei den Juden, von den ältesten Zeiten bis auf die Gegenwart* (Cracow: Fuchs, 1903); Simon Bamberger, *Die Beschneidung: Eine populäre Darstellung ihrer Bedeutung und Vollziehung* (Wandsbeck: Verlag von A. Goldschmidt-Hamburg, 1913).

89. Remondino, *History of Circumcision,* p. 195.

90. The first use of this term in this context seems to be Dr. Klein, "Noch ein Wort zur rituellen Circumcision," *Deutsche Klinik* 8 (1856): 59–60.

91. Herbert Spencer, *The Principles of Sociology,* 3 vols. (New York: Appleton, 1900–1901), 2:67. See SE 13:77, 93, 110.

92. A. J. Storfer, *Marias jungfräuliche Mutterschaft: Ein völkerpsychologisches Fragment über Sexualsymbolik* (Berlin: Barsdorf, 1914), p. 35 n. 2.

93. G. M. Beard, "Circumcision as a Cure of Nervous Symptoms," *Medical Bulletin of Philadelphia* 4 (1882): 248. This debate reappears in the literature on circumcision as a means of AIDS prevention. See the debate in the *Journal of the Royal Medical Society* beginning with the letter of A. J. Fink, "Newborn Circumcision: A Long-term Strategy for AIDS Prevention," *Journal of the Royal Medical Society* 82 (1989): 695, with comment in 82 (1989): 319–20 and 83 (1990): 278. See also the discussion in R. L. Poland, "The Question of Routine Neonatal Circumcision," *New England Journal of Medicine* 322 (1990): 1312–1517, and N. O'Farrell, "Transmission of HIV: Genital Ulceration, Sexual Behavior, and Circumcision," *Lancet* 8627 (1989): 1157.

94. Hermann Rohleder, *Die Masturbation: Eine Monographie für Ärzte und Pädagogen* (Berlin: Fischer's Medicinische Buchhandlung, 1899), p. 304. See SE 7:185.

95. Bergson, *Die Beschneidung,* pp. 106–24.

96. Niemann, "Die Beschneidung der Juden," pp. 291–92.

97. Dr. Beer, "Die Frage zur Beschneidung der Israeliten," *Deutsche Klinik* 26 (1874): 289–91.

98. Brecher, *Die Beschneidung der Juden*, p. 48.

99. Niemann, "Die Beschneidung der Juden," p. 298.

100. R. W. Taylor, "On the Question of the Transmission of Syphilitic Contagion in the Rite of Circumcision," *New York Medical Journal* 18 (1873): 561–82.

101. "Die rituelle Beschneidung," p. 371.

102. [Dr. Levit], *Die Circumcision der Israeliten beleuchtet vom ärztlichen und humanen Standpunkte von einem alten Artze* (Vienna: Carl Gerold's Sohn, 1874).

103. Ibid., pp. 6–7.

104. Ibid., p. 11.

105. See the discussion by Prof. Emil Kohn in *Mittheilung des Ärtzlichen Vereines in Wien* 3 (1874): 169–72.

106. Dr. Lewin, "Bedenken gegen die Circumcision," *Charité-Annalen* 1 (1874): 628–39.

107. Julius Jaffé, *Die rituelle Circumcision im Lichte der Antiseptischen Chirurgie mit Berücksichtigung der religiösen Vorschriften* (Leipzig: Fock, 1886), p. 27.

108. Jonathan Hutchinson, *Syphilis* (London: Cassell, 1887), pp. 458–60. The German translation is Jonathan Hutchinson, *Syphilis*, trans. Artur Kollmann (Leipzig: Arnold, 1888).

109. Hutchinson, *Syphilis*, pp. 115–18.

110. Jonathan Hutchinson, "On Circumcision," *Archives of Surgery* (London) 4 (1893): 379–80.

111. A. Glassberg, ed., *Die Beschneidung in ihrer geschichtlichen, ethnographischen, religiösen, und medicinischen Bedeutung* (Berlin: Boas, 1896), pp. 26–28.

112. Singer, *Allgemeine*, p. 130.

113. Max Grunwald, *Vienna*, Jewish Communities Series (Philadelphia: Jewish Publication Society of America, 1936), p. 376.

114. Phyllis Cohen Albert, *The Modernization of French Jewry* (Waltham, Mass.: Brandeis University Press, 1977), p. 232, and Remondino, *History of Circumcision*, pp. 156–57. See also P. Hidiroglou, "Langues de circoncision historique en France," *Revue de études juives* 143 (1984): 113–34.

115. Franz Kafka, *Tagebücher*, ed. Hans-Gerd Koch, Michael Müller, and Malcolm Pasley (Frankfurt a. M.: Fischer, 1990), pp. 316–17 (Russian Jews); pp. 310–12 (Prague Jews).

116. Alexander, *Die hygienische Bedeutung*, p. 18.

117. See, for example, the discussion by Dr. Bamberger, "Die Hygiene der Beschneidung," in *Die Hygiene der Juden: Im Anschluß an die internationale Hygiene-Ausstellung*, ed. Max Grunwald (Dresden: Verlag der historischen Abteilung der internationale Hygiene-Ausstellung, 1911), pp. 103–12 (on the hygienic side), and W. Hammer, "Zur Beschneidungsfrage," *Zeitschrift für Bahnärzte* 1 (1916) (on the alternate view). The first text is clearly a defense of the nature of the Jews; the second is a condemnation of their nature as well as their practices. On the general context, see Alfons Labisch, "Die soziale Konstruktion der 'Gesundheit' und des 'Homo Hygienicus,' " *Österreichische Zeitschrift für Soziologie* 3–4 (1986): 60–82.

118. *Herr Moritz Deutschösterreicher: Eine jüdische Erzählung zwischen As-similation und Exil*, ed. Jürgen Egyptien (Vienna: Droschl, 1988), p. 5.

119. SE 23: 190. See Michel de Wolf, "La castration dans l'oeuvre et l'expéri-ence freudiennes" (Ph.D. diss., Louvain, 1971), and Stephen Kern, "The Prehis-tory of Freud's Theory of Castration Anxiety," *Psychoanalytic Review* 62 (1975): 309–14. On the cross-cultural dimensions, see Orphan M. Ozturk, "Ritual Cir-cumcision and Castration Anxiety," *Psychiatry* 36 (1973): 49–60.

120. On the general background of Freud's use of the phylogenetic model, see Jean Laplanche, *Life and Death in Psychoanalysis*, trans. Jeffrey Mehlman (Balti-more: Johns Hopkins University Press, 1976).

121. On Freud and the biology of his day, see Frank J. Sulloway, *Freud, Biolo-gist of the Mind: Beyond the Psychoanalytic Legend* (New York: Basic Books, 1979); Stephen Jay Gould, *Ontogeny and Phylogeny* (Cambridge, Mass.: Har-vard University Press, Belknap Press, 1977), pp. 155–64; and Lucille B. Ritvo, *Darwin's Influence on Freud: A Tale of Two Sciences* (New Haven: Yale Univer-sity Press, 1990). See also Ritvo's earlier studies (all of which are summarized or included in her book): "The Impact of Darwin on Freud," *Psychoanalytic Quar-terly* 43 (1974): 177–92; "Freud's neo-lamarckistische Darwin-Interpretation," *Psyche* 27 (1973): 460–74; "Carl Claus, Freud, und die Darwinsche Biologie," *Psyche* 27 (1973): 475–86; "Carl Claus as Freud's Professor of the New Darwin-ian Biology," *International Journal of Psychoanalysis* 53 (1972): 277–83. See also S. Yearley, "Imputing Intentionality: Popper, Demarcation, and Darwin, Freud, and Marx," *Studies in the History and Philosophy of Science* 16 (1985): 337–50. None addresses the racial implications of this theory for Freud, even though Gould discusses these questions in detail elsewhere in his study.

122. See the "lost" metapsychological paper and the introduction to it pub-lished as Sigmund Freud, *A Phylogenetic Fantasy: Overview of the Transference Neuroses*, ed. Ilse Grubich-Simitis, trans. Axel Hoffer and Peter T. Hoffer (Cam-bridge, Mass.: Harvard University Press, Belknap Press, 1987).

123. Lorenz Oken, *Elements of Physiophilosophy* (London: Ray Society, 1847), p. 492.

124. SE 23:189–90.

125. Géza Róheim, "The Transition Rites," *Psycho-Analytic Quarterly* 11 (1942): 336–74.

126. Cited (with photographs) in Joseph Jacobs, *Studies in Jewish Statistics* (London: Nutt, 1891), p. xl. These plates were reproduced from scholarly jour-nals (in the *Photographic News* 29 [April 17 and 24, 1885], as unnumbered insets and as the frontispiece to vol. 16 [1886] of the *Journal of the Anthropological Institute*, which included the first publication of Joseph Jacobs, "On the Racial Characteristics of Modern Jews," 23–63, as well as A. Neubauer, "Notes on the Race Types of the Jews," 17–22). On the tradition of photographic evidence in the history of anthropology, see Alan Sekula, "The Body and the Archive," *Octo-ber* 39 (1986): 40–55, and Joanna Cohan Scherer, ed., "Picturing Cultures: His-torical Photographs in Anthropological Inquiry," *Visual Anthropology* (special issue) 3 (2–3) (1990). The image of race also plays a major role in the work of Lombroso. See F. Bazzi and R. Bèttica-Giovannini, "L'atlante fisiognomonico e frenologico del sig. Ysabeau tra quelli di Lavater e di Fall e quello di Lombroso,"

Annali dell Ospedale Maria Vittoria di Torino 23 (1980): 343–416, and A. T. Caffaratto, "La raccolta di fotografie segnaletiche del Museo di Antropologia Criminale di Torino: La fotografia come documento e testimonianza dell'opera di Cesare Lombroso," *Annali dell Ospedale Maria Vittoria di Torino* 23 (1980): 295–332. The tradition of fixing the racial gaze continued into the world of the scientific motion picture in the 1890s, such as the chronophotograph. See Elizabeth Cartwright, "Physiological Modernism: Cinematography as a Medical Research Technology" (Ph.D. diss., Yale University, 1991), p. 38.

127. Francis Galton, "Photographic Composites," *Photographic News* 29 (April 17, 1885): 243–46; here, 243.

128. See Hervé Huot, *Du sujet à l'image: Une histoire de l'oeil chez Freud* (Paris: Éditions universitaires, 1987).

129. Carl Heinrich Stratz, *Was sind Juden? Eine ethnographisch-anthropologische Studie* (Vienna: Tempsky, 1903), p. 7 (in the Freud Library, London). Stratz cites Joseph Deniker, *Races of Man* (London: Scott, 1900), p. 423.

130. Hans F. K. Günther, *Rassenkunde des jüdischen Volkes*, (1922; Munich: Lehmann, 1931), p. 70 (on the physiology of the Jewish eye); pp. 210–11 (Galton's photographs); p. 217 (on the Jewish gaze).

131. Robert Burton, *The Anatomy of Melancholy*, ed. Holbrook Jackson (New York: Vintage, 1977), pp. 211–12.

132. Redcliffe N. Salaman, M.D., "Heredity and the Jew," *Eugenics Review* 3 (1912): 190.

133. SE 4:139, 293. See also the mentions of this technique at 4:494 and 649, as well as 15:172 n. 1 and 23:10. See Nathan Roth, "Freud and Galton," *Comprehensive Psychiatry* 3 (1962): 77–83.

134. Houston Stewart Chamberlain, *Foundations of the Nineteenth Century*, trans. John Lees, 2 vols. (London: John Lane/The Bodley Head, 1913), 1:389. On Freud's reading of Chamberlain, see GW Nachtragsband: 787.

135. Sigmund Freud, "Beobachtungen über Gestaltung und feineren Bau der als Hoden beschriebenen Lappenorgane des Aals (Vorgelegt in Sitzung am 15. März 1877 bei Prof. Claus)," *Sitzungsberichte der mathematisch-naturwissenschaftlichen Classe der Kaiserlichen Akademie der Wissenschaften*, div. 1, vol. 75 (1877): 419–33. Peter Gay dismisses this as merely an "assignment" *(Freud: A Life for Our Time* [New York: Norton, 1988], p. 32). This was certainly true, but this does not mean that it had no significance for Freud. Note Freud's rejection of Claus while he accepted much of the Darwinian science he espoused. See the discussion in Johann Georg Reicheneder, *Zum Konstitutionsprozeß der Psychoanalyse* (Stuttgart: Frommann, 1990), pp. 12–89.

136. See the discussion by Alexander Grinstein, *Sigmund Freud's Dreams* (New York: International Universities Press, 1980), pp. 297–361, of the "non vixit" dream (SE 4:421–22).

137. Carl Claus, *Grundzüge der Zoologie zum Gebrauche an Universitäten und höheren Lehranstalten sowie zum Selbststudium*, 2 vols. (Marburg: Elwerts Universitäts-Buchhandlung, 1872), 1:46.

138. Ibid.

139. Ernest Jones, *The Life and Work of Sigmund Freud*, 3 vols. (New York: Basic Books, 1953–57), 1:38.

140. SE 17:86.

141. Ibid.

142. Ibid. 17:88.

143. Ibid.

144. The argument about immunity is made by John S. Billings, "Vital Statistics of the Jews," *North American Review* 153 (1891): 70–84, and N. Haltrecht, "Das Tuberkuloseproblem bei den Juden," *Zeitschrift für Demographie und Statistik der Juden* 2 (1925): 26–33; on the prevalence of risk, see Hermann Strauss, "Das Tuberkulose-Probleme bei den Juden," *Zeitschrift für Demographie und Statistik der Juden* 3 (1926): 42–45, and Emil Bogen, "Tuberculosis among the Jews," *Medical Leaves* 3 (1940): 123–27. On the question of the stereotypes of race and disease in German culture at the turn of the century, see Dan Latimer, "Erotic Susceptibility and Tuberculosis: Literary Images of a Pathology," *Modern Language Notes* 105 (1990): 1016–31.

145. Letter to Stefan Zweig of October 19, 1920. Sigmund Freud, *Briefe, 1873–1939*, ed. Ernst and Lucie Freud (Frankfurt a. M.: Fischer, 1960), p. 349; translation from *Letters of Sigmund Freud, 1873–1939*, ed. Ernst L. Freud, trans. Tania and James Stern (London: Hogarth Press, 1961), p. 338.

146. Arnold Zweig, "Antisemitismus," in Herlitz and Kirschner, *Jüdisches Lexikon* 1:331–34; here, 332.

147. SE 10:36.

148. Ibid. On the meaning given circumcision and its relationship to anti-Semitism within the psychoanalytic tradition, see Georges Maranz, "Les conséquences de la circoncision: Essai d'explication psychanalytique de l'antisémitisme," *Psyché-Paris* 2 (1947): 731–45; B. Grunberger, "Circoncision et l'antisémitisme: En marge d'un article de Georges Maranz," *Psyché-Paris* 2 (1947): 1221–28; Jules Glenn, "Circumcision and Anti-Semitism," *Psychoanalytic Quarterly* 29 (1960): 395–99. An extensive psychoanalytic reading of circumcision is found in Bruno Bettelheim, *Symbolic Wounds: Puberty Rites and the Envious Male* (Glencoe, Ill.: Free Press, 1954; rev. ed., New York: Collier, 1962).

149. On Weininger, see Gilman, *Jewish Self-Hatred*, pp. 244–51; Manfried Rösner, "Eine prinzipielle Unmöglichkeit: Bemerkungen zu Otto Weiningers *Geschlecht und Charakter*," in *Wunderblock: Eine Geschichte der modernen Seele*, ed. Jean Clair, Catharin Pichler, and Wolfgang Pirchner (Vienna: Löcker, 1989), pp. 497–500; Jacques Le Rider, *Der Fall Otto Weininger: Wurzeln des Antifeminismus und Antisemitismus*, trans. Dieter Hornig (Vienna: Löcker, 1985); Jacques Le Rider and Norbert, Leser, eds., *Otto Weininger: Werk und Wirkung* (Vienna: Österreichischer Bundesverlag, 1984); Peter Heller, "A Quarrel over Bisexuality," in *The Turn of the Century: German Literature and Art, 1890–1915*, ed. Gerald Chapple and Hans H. Schulte (Bonn: Bouvier, 1978), pp. 87–116; and Franco Nicolino, *Indagini su Freud e sulla psicoanalisi* (Naples: Liguori editore, n.d.), pp. 103–10.

150. I use the term "homosexual" throughout this and earlier discussions as a reflection of the medical debates about male and female gay identity within the medical literature of the period. I use the term "gay" to designate the in-group self-representation. While a number of different medical terms are used to represent male gay identity (including *homosexual* and *uranist*), it seemed clearest to

reduce these to a single label. See, in this context, Richard Green, "Homosexuality as a Mental Illness," in *Concepts of Health and Disease: Interdisciplinary Perspectives*, ed. Arthur L. Caplan et al. (London: Addison-Wesley, 1981), pp. 333–51, and G. Hekma, "Sodomites, Platonic Lovers, Contrary Lovers: The Backgrounds of the Modern Homosexual," *Journal of Homosexuality* 16 (1988): 433–55.

151. See, for example, the discussion in Carl Dallago, *Otto Weininger und sein Werk* (Innsbruck: Brenner, 1912), and Emil Lucka, *Otto Weininger: Sein Werk und seine Persönlichkeit* (Berlin: Schuster & Loeffler, 1921), esp. pp. 37–80.

152. Charlotte Perkins Gilman, "Review of Dr. Weininger's *Sex and Character*," *Critic* 12 (1906): 414.

153. Jacques Le Rider, "Wittgenstein et Weininger," *Wittgenstein et la critique du monde moderne* (Brussels: La lettre volée, 1990), pp. 43–65.

154. Kitāro Nishida, *An Inquiry into the Good*, trans. Masao Abe and Christopher Ives (New Haven: Yale University Press, 1989).

155. Leopold Löwenfeld, *Über die sexuelle Konstitution und andere Sexualprobleme* (Wiesbaden: Bergmann, 1911), p. 146 (in the Freud Library, London).

156. Felix Langer, *Die Protokolle der Weisen von Zion: Rassenhass und Rassenhetze* (Vienna: Saturn, 1934), p. 40 (in the Freud Library, London).

157. The question of the chronology and source of the ideas was hotly debated at the time. See Wilhelm Fliess, *In eigener Sache: Gegen Otto Weininger und Hermann Swoboda* (Berlin: Goldschmidt, 1906) (in the Freud Library, London), and Hermann Swoboda, *Die gemeinnützige Forschung und der eigennützige Forscher: Antwort auf die von Wilhelm Fliess gegen Otto Weininger und mich erhobenen Beschuldigungen* (Vienna: Braumüller, 1906) (in the Freud Library, London).

158. Le Rider, *Der Fall Otto Weininger*, p. 96. The original draft of Otto Weininger's dissertation has now been published and it shows that Freud's memory of the text was accurate. It does not contain the long chapter on the Jews. However, a companion manuscript, discovered at the same time as the draft of the dissertation and entitled "On the Theory of Life" (1902), does reveal the baneful influence of Schopenhauer's attitude toward the Jews. See Otto Weininger, *Eros und Psyche: Studien und Briefe, 1899–1902*, ed. Hannelore Rodlauer (Vienna: Verlag der Österreichischen Akademie der Wissenschaft, 1990).

159. Indeed, this is the one case in which Fliess's letters are actually preserved and we can read both sides of the correspondence: Jeffrey Moussaieff Masson, ed., *The Complete Letters of Sigmund Freud to Wilhelm Fliess, 1887–1904* (Cambridge, Mass.: Harvard University Press, 1985), pp. 459–68. On the question of creativity, see "The Jewish Genius: Freud and the Jewishness of the Creative," in Gilman, *The Jew's Body*, pp. 128–49.

160. Masson, *Complete Letters of Sigmund Freud to Wilhelm Fliess*, p. 456.

161. Abel Hermant, *Confession d'un enfant d'hier*, cited by Havelock Ellis, *Studies in the Psychology of Sex*, 7 vols. (Philadelphia: Davis, 1900–28), 4:176 (in the Freud Library, London).

162. Ibid.

163. Otto Weininger, *Sex and Character* (London: Heinemann, 1906), p. 38.

164. Ibid., p. 60.

165. *Protokolle der Wiener Psychoanalytischen Vereinigung*, ed. Herman Nunberg and Ernst Federn, 4 vols. (Frankfurt a. M.: Fischer, 1976–81), 2:260; translation from *Minutes of the Vienna Psychoanalytic Society*, trans. M. Nunberg, 4 vols. (New York: International Universities Press, 1962–75), 2:288.

166. Georg Groddeck, "Das Zwiegeschlecht des Menschen," in his *Psychoanalytische Schriften zur Psychosomatik* (Wiesbaden: Limes, [1966]), pp. 256–63; 259 (masculine); 262 (circumcision).

167. This discussion of Groddeck relies on the work of Roger Lewinter, "Georg Groddeck: (Anti)judaïsme et bisexualité," *Nouvelle revue de psychanalyse* 7 (1973): 199–205.

168. Erika Weinzierl, "Katholizismus in Österreich," in *Kirche und Synagoge: Handbuch zur Geschichte von Christen und Juden*, ed. Karl Heinrich Rengstorf and Siegfried von Kortzfleisch, 2 vols. (Stuttgart: Klett, 1970), 2:483–531; here, 2:495.

169. Cesare Lombroso, "Nordau's 'Degeneration': Its Value and Its Errors," *Century Magazine* 28 (October 1895): 936–40. On the tradition of labeling anti-Semitism a disease, see Hans-Peter Söder, "Disease and Health as Contexts of Fin-de-siècle Modernity: Max Nordau's Theory of Degeneration" (Ph.D. diss., Cornell University, 1991), pp. 299–300.

170. Cesare Lombroso, *Der Antisemitismus und die Juden im Lichte der modernen Wissenschaft*, trans. H. Kurella (Leipzig: Wigand, 1894), p. 17.

171. Hershel Meyer, "The Psychopathology of Nazism," *Medical Leaves* 2 (1939): 118–130; here, 119.

172. *Protokolle der Wiener Psychoanalytischen Vereinigung*, 1:134–37; translation from *Minutes of the Vienna Psychoanalytic Society*, 1:142–45.

173. Cited from a letter of November 21, 1938, from Charles Singer to Henry Sigerist by Genevieve Miller, "Charles and Dorothea Singer's Aid to Nazi Victims," *Koroth* 8 (1985): 207–17; here, 215.

174. Felix Weltsch, *Antisemitism als Völkerhysterie* (Prague: Barissia, 1931). A recent survey of five psychoanalysts' interpretations of anti-Semitism (Otto Fenichel, Ernst Simmel, Erik Erikson, Rudolph Loewenstein, and Bruno Bettelheim) points out the pronounced ambivalence of these "Jewish" figures to their own Jewish identity. See David James Fisher, "Vers une compréhension psychanalytique du fascisme et de l'antisémitisme: Perceptions des années 1940," *Revue internationale d'histoire de la psychanalyse* 5 (1992): 221–41.

175. See Rudolph M. Loewenstein, *Psychanalyse de l'antisémitisme* (Paris: Presses universitaires de France, 1952).

176. Otto Fenichel, "Elemente einer psychoanalytischen Theorie des Antisemitismus," cited in *Vom Judenhass zum Antisemitismus: Materialien einer verleugneten Geschichte*, ed. Detlev Claussen (Darmstadt-Neuwied: Luchterhand, 1987), p. 227.

177. Herman Nunberg, *Problems of Bisexuality as Reflected in Circumcision* (London: Imago, 1949), pp. 82–83.

178. Theodor Adorno, Else Frenkel-Brunswik, Daniel J. Levinson, and R. Nevitt Sanford, *The Authoritarian Personality* (New York: Harper, 1950), p. 627.

179. See, for example, the following studies from the early 1930s: Erich Kuttner, *Pathologie des Rassenantisemitismus* (Berlin: Philo, 1930); Ewald Bohm, "Antisemitismus im Lichte der Psychoanalyse," *Menorah* 8 (1930): 312–19; F. A. Feller, *Antisemitismus: Versuch einer psychoanalytischen Lösung des Problems* (Berlin: Verlag des Archivs für angewandte Psychologie, 1931). This view has not vanished; see M. Ostow, "A Contribution to the Study of Anti-Semitism," *Israel Journal of Psychiatry and Related Sciences* 20 (1983): 95–118.

180. SE 11:95–96.

181. Ibid. 22:86.

182. Ibid. 15:155.

183. Arthur H. Daniels, "The New Life: A Study of Regeneration," *American Journal of Psychology* 6 (1893): 63.

184. SE 7:195.

185. Ibid.

186. Ibid. 21:83.

187. Ellis, *Studies in the Psychology of Sex* 4:161–62.

188. Albert Moll, *Die konträre Sexualempfindung* (Berlin: Fischer, 1893), p. 308; Albert Moll, *Perversions of the Sex Instinct: A Study of Sexual Inversion*, trans. Maurice Popkin (Newark, N.J.: Julian Press, 1931), p. 212.

189. SE 7:84.

190. Ellis, *Studies in the Psychology of Sex* 4:183.

191. Theodor Reik, "Das Kainszeichen: Ein psychoanalytischer Beitrag zur Bibelerklärung," *Imago* 5 (1917): 31–42. See the rebuttal by Ludwig Levy, "Ist das Kainszeichen die Beschneidung? Ein kritischer Beitrag zur Bibelexegese," *Imago* 5 (1919): 290–93.

192. Nunberg, *Problems of Bisexuality*, p. 1.

193. Martin Freud, *Glory Reflected: Sigmund Freud—Man and Father* (London: Angus and Robertson, 1957), pp. 100–101.

194. SE 21:83.

195. See the use of the phrase in the fin de siècle text reprinted in Sander L. Gilman, "Hofprediger Stöcker and the Wandering Jew," *Journal of Jewish Studies* 19 (1969): 63–69; here, 69.

196. SE 20:236.

197. Ibid. 2:7.

198. Nunberg, *Problems of Bisexuality*, p. 2.

199. SE 3:145.

200. Ibid. 3:148.

201. Ibid. 3:149. Emphasis in the original.

202. Ibid. 3:150–51.

203. Ibid. 3:155.

204. Ibid.

205. Ibid. 3:154. Emphasis in the original.

206. Ibid. 3:156.

207. Ibid. 3:150.

208. Ibid. 3:152. Emphasis in the original.

209. Cited from Norman Kiell, ed., *Freud without Hindsight: Reviews of His Works (1893–1939)* (Madison, Conn.: International Universities Press, 1988), p. 36.

210. SE 3:135–36.

211. Ibid. 3:23.

212. Ibid. 16:362.

213. On the discussion of Jewish experience after the Shoah and the reintroduction of the question of trauma, see Shoshana Felman and Dori Laub, *Testimony: Crises of Witnessing in Literature, Psychoanalysis, and History* (New York: Routledge, 1992).

214. Masson, *Complete Letters of Sigmund Freud to Wilhelm Fliess*, pp. 264–66.

215. See Ian Hacking, *The Taming of Chance* (Cambridge: Cambridge University Press, 1990).

216. Peter Brask, "Rebecca, er det mig so taler?" *Kritik* 36 (1975): 103–26.

217. SE 2:134.

CHAPTER THREE
JEWISH MADNESS AND GENDER

1. Whether or not Jews actually had a substantially higher incidence of "nervous illness" during this period cannot be reconstructed from the materials and statistics employed in such discussions. They are simply too fragmentary and biased. (For example, they do not correct for the urban concentration of Jews in Western and Central Europe.) It would not be surprising to learn that Jews did have a higher incidence of mental illness given the greater social stresses they were under from the time of civil emancipation through the end of the century. But this cannot be substantiated from the materials employed to buttress this discussion in the nineteenth and early twentieth centuries. What is of interest are the rationales employed to provide an etiology for this supposed prevalence of mental illness. See the discussion in Sander L. Gilman, *Difference and Pathology: Stereotypes of Sexuality, Race, and Madness* (Ithaca, N.Y.: Cornell University Press, 1985), pp. 150–63.

2. Cited by Peter J. Swales, "Freud, His Teacher, and the Birth of Psychoanalysis," in *Freud: Appraisals and Reappraisals*, ed. Paul E. Stepansky, 3 vols. (Hillsdale, N.J.: Analytic Press, 1986–89), p. 28.

3. Emil Kraepelin, "Zur Entartungsfrage," *Zentralblatt für Nervenheilkunde und Psychiatrie* 19 (1908): 745–51; here, 748.

4. Dr. Maretzki, "Die Gesundheitverhältnisse der Juden," in *Statistik der Juden: Eine Sammelschrift* (Berlin: Jüdischer, 1918), pp. 123–51. On the historiography of hysteria, see Mark S. Micale, "Hysteria and Its Historiography," *History of Science* 27 (1989): 223–61, 319–51. See also the work on the early history of hysteria by Helmut-Johannes Lorentz, "Si mulier obticuerit: Ein Hysterierezept des Pseudo-Apuleius," *Sudhoffs Archiv* 38 (1954): 20–28; Ilza Veith, *Hysteria: The History of a Disease* (Chicago and London: University of Chicago Press, 1965); Umberto de Martini, "L'isterismo: Da Ippocrate a Charcot," *Pagine di*

storia della medicina 12 (1968): 42–49; Annemarie Leibbrand and Werner Leibbrand, "Die 'kopernikanische Wendung' des Hysteriebegriffes bei Paracelsus," *Paracelsus Werk und Wirkung: Festgabe für Kurt Goldammer zum 60. Geburtstag*, ed. Sepp Domandl (Vienna: Verband der Wissenschaftlichen Gesellschaften Österreichs, 1975), pp. 125–33; John R. Wright, "Hysteria and Mechanical Man," *Journal of the History of Ideas* 41 (1980): 233–47; H. Merskey, "Hysteria: The History of an Idea," *Canadian Journal of Psychiatry* 28 (1983): 428–33; H. Merskey, "The Importance of Hysteria," *British Journal of Psychiatry* 149 (1986): 23–28; John Mullan, "Hypochondria and Hysteria: Sensibility and the Physicians," *Eighteenth Century* 25 (1983): 141–73; Monique David-Ménard, *Hysteria from Freud to Lacan: Body and Language in Psychoanalysis*, trans. Catherine Porter (Ithaca, N.Y.: Cornell University Press, 1989); Phillip R. Slavney, *Perspectives on "Hysteria"* (Baltimore: Johns Hopkins University Press, 1990).

5. J. M. Charcot, *Leçons du Mardi à la Salpêtrière*, 2 vols. (Paris: Progrès médical, 1889), 2:11–12. See *Poliklinische Vorträge von Prof. J. M. Charcot*, trans. Sigmund Freud (vol. 1) and Max Kahane (vol. 2), 2 vols. (Leipzig: Deuticke, 1892–95), 2:11.

6. Charcot's influence was felt immediately. See Gustav Lagneau, "Sur la race juive et sa pathologie," *Académie de médecine* (Paris), bulletin 3, ser. 26 (1891): 287–309.

7. Charcot, *Leçons du Mardi* 1:131; see Freud's translation of the *Poliklinische Vorträge* 1: 112.

8. Toby Gelfand, " 'Mon Cher Docteur Freud': Charcot's Unpublished Correspondence to Freud, 1888–1893," *Bulletin of the History of Medicine* 62 (1988): 563–88; here, 574.

9. Toby Gelfand, "Charcot's Response to Freud's Rebellion," *Journal of the History of Ideas* 50 (1989): 293–307; here, 304.

10. Anatole Leroy-Beaulieu, *Israel among the Nations: A Study of the Jews and Antisemitism*, trans. Frances Hellman (New York: Putnam's, 1895), p. 168.

11. Cited in E. Morpurgo, *Sulle condizioni somatiche e psichiche degli Israeliti in Europa*, Bibliotece dell'idea Sionisa, 2 (Modena: Tip. Operai, 1903), pp. 66–67.

12. Georg Burgle, *Die Hysterie und die strafrechtliche Verantwortlichkeit der Hysterischen: Ein praktisches Handbuch für Ärzte und Juristen* (Stuttgart: Enke, 1912), p. 19.

13. Georges Wulfing-Luer, *La pathologie nerveuse et mentale chez les anciens hébreux et la race juive* (Paris: Steinheil, 1907).

14. Leroy-Beaulieu, *Israel among the Nations*, pp. 168–69.

15. Wilhelm A. Freund, *Über Neurasthenia hysterica und die Hysteria der Frau* (Berlin: Simion, 1904), p. 29.

16. Richard von Krafft-Ebing, *Nervosität und Neurasthenische Zustände* (Vienna: Hölder, 1895), p. 57. (This was also published as part of vol. 12 of *Specielle Pathologie und Therapie*, ed. Hermann Nothnagel, 24 vols. [Vienna: Hölder, 1894–1908]). For the context, see T. J. Jackson Lear, *No Place of Grace: Anti-Modernism and the Transformation of American Culture* (New York: Pantheon,

1981). On the question of such illnesses of the will as "male" diseases, see John H. Smith, "Abulia: Sexuality and Disease of the Will in the Late Nineteenth Century," *Genders* 6 (1989): 102–24.

17. "Einfluss der Rasse auf pathologische Erscheinungen," *Prochaska's illustrirte Monatsbände* 8 (1896): 199.

18. Heinrich Averbeck, *Die akute Neurasthenie, die plötzliche Erschöpfung der nervösen Energie: Ein ärztliches Kulturbild* (Berlin: Grosser, 1886), pp. 23–25. See SE 1:35; 7:293, 301, 313, 325, 337.

19. H. v. Ziemssen, *Die Neurasthenie und ihre Behandlung* (Leipzig: Vogel, 1889), pp. 7–8 (in the Freud Library, London).

20. Leopold Löwenfeld, *Pathologie und Therapie der Neurasthenie und Hysterie* (Wiesbaden: Bergmann, 1894), pp. 44–45 (in the Freud Library, London).

21. Ibid., p. 19 (inheritance); p. 20n (on hysteria).

22. On the background of the essay, see Wilhelm Hemcker, " 'Ihr Brief war mir so wertvoll . . .' Christian von Ehrenfels und Sigmund Freud—eine verschollene Korrespondenz," in *Wunderblock: Eine Geschichte der modernen Seele*, ed. Jean Clair, Catharin Pichler, and Wolfgang Pirchner (Vienna: Löcker, 1989), pp. 561–70. See also Peter Brückner, *Sigmund Freuds Privatlektüre* (Cologne: Verlag Rolf Horst, 1975), p. 62.

23. SE 9:181.

24. Christian von Ehrenfels, *Sexualethik* (Wiesbaden: Bergmann, 1907) (in the Freud Library, London, with extensive marginalia). This is reprinted in Christian von Ehrenfels, *Philosophische Schriften*, ed. Reinhard Fabian, 4 vols. (Munich: Philosophia, 1982–90), 3:265–356. All references are to this edition. On von Ehrenfels and racial hygiene, see Peter Emil Becker, *Zur Geschichte der Rassenhygiene: Wege ins Dritte Reich* (Stuttgart: Thieme, 1988), pp. 278–328.

25. On his debt to Freud, see von Ehrenfels, *Sexualethik*, 3:296 n. 1; on the problem of our time, 3:352; on the question of the "higher" and "lower" races, see von Ehrenfels's essay "Über den Einfluss des Darwinismus auf die moderne Soziologie," *Volkswirtschaftliche Wochenschrift* (Vienna) 42 (1904): 256–59, and *Die Wage* (Vienna) 7 (1904): 363–64, 382–85; *Philosophische Schriften* 3:251–64.

26. Von Ehrenfels, *Sexualethik* 3:275.

27. Ibid. 3:276.

28. SE 14:274.

29. Von Ehrenfels, *Sexualethik* 3:356.

30. *Protokolle der Wiener Psychoanalytischen Vereinigung*, ed. Herman Nunberg and Ernst Federn, 4 vols. (Frankfurt a. M.: Fischer, 1976–81), 2:84–91; translation from *Minutes of the Vienna Psychoanalytic Society*, trans. M. Nunberg, 4 vols. (New York: International Universities Press, 1962–75), 2:93–100; here, 93. He also discussed Fritz Wittels's monograph on sexuality, 2:74–83, 83–92.

31. On von Ehrenfels's sense of his own Jewish ancestry, see Max Brod, *Streitbares Leben* (Munich: Herbig, 1969), p. 211. See also his review of Otto Weininger's monograph "Geschlecht und Charakter," *Politisch-anthropologische Revue* 3 (1905): 481–84.

32. Christian von Ehrenfels, "Rassenproblem und Judenfrage," *Prager Tageblatt* 36 (December 1, 1911): 1–2. Reprinted in *Philosophische Schriften* 4:334–42; here, 337.

33. Von Ehrenfels, *Philosophische Schriften* 4:341.

34. *Protokolle der Wiener Psychoanalytischen Vereinigung* 2:84–91; translation from *Minutes of the Vienna Psychoanalytic Society* 2:93–100; here, 99.

35. Franz Kafka, *Tagebücher*, ed. Hans-Gerd Koch, Michael Müller, and Malcolm Pasley (Frankfurt a. M.: Fischer, 1990), pp. 370–71.

36. Heinrich Singer, *Allgemeine und spezielle Krankheitslehre der Juden* (Leipzig: Konegen, 1904), p. 25.

37. *The Diary of Sigmund Freud, 1929–1939: A Record of the Final Decade*, ed. and trans. Michael Molnar (New York: Scribner's, 1992), p. 132.

38. SE 9:182.

39. Ibid. 9:185; GW 7:148.

40. Otto Binswanger, *Die Pathologie und Therapie der Neurasthenie* (Jena: Gustav Fischer, 1896), p. 46; SE 9:184–85.

41. Wilhelm Erb, *Über die wachsende Nervosität unserer Zeit: Akademische Rede zum Geburtsfeste . . . Karl Friedrich am 22. November 1893* (Heidelberg: Universitäts-Buchdruckerei J. Höring, 1893), p. 22.

42. Krafft-Ebing, *Nervosität und Neurasthenische Zustände*, p. 54.

43. Moritz Alsberg, *Rassenmischung im Judentum* (Hamburg: Verlagsanstalt und Druckerei, 1891), p. 34.

44. "Bericht über die im Königreich Württemberg bestehenden Staats- und Privatanstalten für Geisteskranke, Schwachsinnige, und Epileptische für das Jahr 1908," *Psychiatrisch-Neurologische Wochenschrift* 12 (1910–11): 91–98; here, 93.

45. Martin Engländer, *Die auffallend häufigen Krankheitserscheinungen der jüdischen Rasse* (Vienna: Pollak, 1902), p. 54.

46. Ibid., p. 12.

47. Ibid., p. 17.

48. Ibid., p. 46.

49. Cesare Lombroso, *L'antisemitismo e la scienze moderne* (Turin: Roux, 1894), p. 83.

50. M. J. Gutmann, "Geisteskranken bei Juden," *Zeitschrift für Demographie und Statistik der Juden*, n.s. 3 (1926): 103–16.

51. Max Sichel, *Die Geistesstörungen bei den Juden: Eine klinisch-historische Studie* (Leipzig: Kaufmann, 1909); "Über die Geistesstörung bei den Juden," *Neurologisches Centralblatt* 27 (1908): 351–67; "Nervöse Folgezustände von Alkohol und Syphilis bei den Juden," *Zeitschrift für Demographie und Statistik der Juden* 7 (1919): 137–41; and "Die psychischen Erkrankungen der Juden in Kriegs- und Friedenszeiten," *Monatsschrift für Psychiatrie und Neurologie* 55 (1923): 207–28.

52. Max Sichel, "Zur Ätiologie der Geistesstörung bei den Juden," *Monatsschrift für Psychiatrie und Neurologie* 43 (1918): 246–64; here, 247.

53. Ibid., p. 249.

54. Eric J. Engstrom, "Emil Kraepelin: Psychiatry and Public Affairs in Wilhelmine Germany," *History of Psychiatry* 2 (1991): 111–32.

55. Julius Moses, "Psychopathie und Revolution," *Freiheit: Berliner Organ der USPD* (November 2, 1921): p. 1. See Susanne Hahn, "Antisemitismus in der Wissenschafts- und Gesundheitspolitik der Weimarer Republik—Zum besonderen Gedächtnis an Julius Moses (1868–1942)," *Zeitschrift für die gesamte innere Medizin* 44 (1989): 313–16.

56. Max Nussbaum, "Über die Geisteskrankheiten bei den Juden" (Ph.D. diss., Würzburg, 1923).

57. Ludwig Frigyes, "Über Geistes- und Nervenkrankheiten und Gebrechlichkeiten unter den Juden" (Ph.D. diss., Frankfurt a. M., 1927).

58. Felix A. Theilhaber, "Gesundheitsverhältnisse," in *Jüdisches Lexikon*, ed. Georg Herlitz and Bruno Kirschner, 4 vols. in 5 (Berlin: Jüdischer Verlag, 1927–30), 2:1120–41; here, 1128–32 (in the Freud Library, London).

59. Rafael Becker, "Bibliographische Übersicht der Literatur aus dem Gebiete: 'Geisteserkrankungen bei den Juden,' " *Allgemeine Zeitschrift für Psychiatrie* 98 (1932): 241–76, which catalogues 191 items, mainly in German.

60. P. Berthold [Bertha Pappenheim], *Zur Judenfrage in Galizien* (Frankfurt a. M.: Knauer, 1900), pp. 18–19.

61. Jacob Jacobson, "Warum wurden die polnischen Juden 'schmutzig'?" *Hygiene und Judentum* (Dresden: Sternlicht, 1930), pp. 73–74.

62. Josef Czermak, "Ein Beitrag zur Statistik der Psychosen," *Allgemeine Zeitschrift für Psychiatrie* 15 (1858): 265.

63. H. Budul, "Beitrag zur vergleichenden Rassenpsychiatrie," *Monatsschrift für Psychiatrie und Neurologie* 37 (1915): 199–204.

64. Harald Siebert, "Die Psychosen bei der Bevölkerung Kurlands," *Allgemeine Zeitschrift für Psychiatrie* 73 (1917): 493–535; here, 523.

65. Hermann Oppenheim, *Lehrbuch der Nervenkrankheiten fur Ärzte und Studierende*, 2 vols. (Berlin: Karger, 1894–1913).

66. Hermann Oppenheim, "Zur Psychopathologie und Nosologie der russisch-jüdischen Bevölkerung," *Journal für Psychologie und Neurologie* 13 (1908): 1–9 [Festschrift Forel].

67. Ibid., p. 4.

68. Ibid., p. 6.

69. Max Nordau, *Zionistische Schriften* (Cologne: Jüdischer, 1909), pp. 379–81. This call, articulated at the second Zionist Congress, followed his address on the state of the Jews, which keynoted the first Zionist Congress. There he spoke on the "physical, spiritual, and economic status of the Jews." In July 1902, Nordau recapitulated his views in an essay in the *Jüdische Turnzeitung* entitled "Was bedeutet das Turnen für uns Juden" (*Zionistische Schriften*, pp. 382–84). On Nordau, see P. M. Baldwin, "Liberalism, Nationalism, and Degeneration: The Case of Max Nordau," *Central European History* 13 (1980): 99–120.

70. Max Nordau, *De la castration de la femme* (Paris: Adrien Delahaye et Émile Lecrosnier, 1882).

71. Ibid., pp. 15, 28–31.

72. See Mary Douglas, *Purity and Danger: An Analysis of Concepts of Pollution and Taboo* (Harmondsworth: Penguin, n.d.), pp. 94–113, on the power of the symbols of defilement and taboo.

73. Georg Buschan, "Einfluss der Rasse auf die Häufigkeit und die Formen der Geistes- und Nervenkrankheiten," *Allgemeine medicinische Central-Zeitung* 9 (1897): 104–5.

74. Richard Gaupp, *Wege und Ziele psychiatrischer Forschung: Eine akademische Antrittsvorlesung* (Tübingen: Laupp, 1907), p. 23.

75. Alexander Pilcz, *Lehrbuch der speziellen Psychiatrie für Studierende und Ärzte* (Leipzig: Deuticke, 1904, 1909, 1912, 1926); *Die Anfangsstadien der wichtigsten Geisteskrankheiten*, Bucher der ärztlichen praxis 1 (Vienna and Berlin: Springer, 1928); *Spezielle gerichtliche Psychiatrie fur Juristen und Mediziner* (Leipzig: Deuticke, 1908); *Die periodischen Geistesstörungen: Eine klinische Studie* (Jena: Gustav Fischer, 1901) (in the Freud Collection, New York).

76. Alexander Pilcz, "Über den Traum," *Wiener klinische Rundschau* 16 (1902): 962.

77. SE 4:20.

78. Pilcz, *Die periodischen Geistesstörungen*, and *Lehrbuch*, (1904) (in the Freud Library, London). The quoted material is from the former: p. 18 (on the predisposition of the Jews); p. 32 (sophistry). The cases are to be found on pp. 32–33, 37–38, and 94.

79. This aspect of the response of Jewish physicians is underrated by Edward Shorter, "Women and Jews in a Private Nervous Clinic in Late Nineteenth-Century Vienna," *Medical History* 33 (1989): 149–83.

80. Alexander Pilcz, "Geistesstörung bei den Juden," *Wiener klinische Rundschau* 15 (1901): 888–90, 908–10.

81. Alexander Pilcz, "Sur les psychoses chez les juifs," *Annales médicopsychologiques* 15 (1902): 5–20.

82. As, for example, at the Viennese Anthropological Society on January 16, 1905. See the account in the *Monatsschrift für Kriminalpsychologie und Strafrechtsreform* 2 (1905): 754. This was evidently a topic of wide interest. See Emil Feer's lecture held on January 31, 1905, in Basel, and published under the title *Die Macht der Vererbung* (Basel: Helbing & Lichtenhan, 1905). Feer was at that time a lecturer in the medical faculty at Basel. He discusses the predisposition of the Jews for mental illness on p. 23.

83. Alexander Pilcz, *Beitrag zur vergleichenden Rassen-Psychiatrie* (Leipzig: Deuticke, 1906).

84. Ibid., p. ii.

85. Ibid., p. 18.

86. Ibid., p. 19.

87. Ibid., p. 29.

88. Ibid., p. 31. Emphasis added.

89. Alexander Pilcz, "Beitrag zur Lehre von der Heredität," *Arbeiten des Neurologisches Instituts* 15 (1907): 282–309.

90. Alexander Pilcz, "Über vergleichend-rassenpsychiatrische Studien," *Wiener Medizinische Wochenschrift* 77 (March 5, 1927): 311–14. This lecture is typical of the academic activities of such scholars. For an overview of the German academic presentations of racial theory, see Hans-Walter Schmuhl, *Rassenhygiene, Nationalsozialismus, Euthanasie: Von der Verhütung zur Vernichtung le-*

bensunwerten Lebens, 1890–1945 (Göttingen: Vandenhoeck & Ruprecht, 1987), p. 79.

91. Ignaz Zollschan, *Das Rassenproblem unter besonderer Berücksichtigung der theoretischen Grundlagen der jüdischen Rassenfrage* (Vienna: Braumüller, 1911), pp. 266–67 (on the sensitivity of the Jew); p. 268 (on syphilis); p. 269 (on the struggle of existence); p. 421 (on preserving the race) (in the Freud Library, London, with a dedication from the author).

92. Theilhaber, "Gesundheitsverhältnisse" 2:1120–41; here, 1128–32.

93. SE 8:33.

94. "Beda" [Fritz Löhner], *Israeliten und andere Antisemiten* (Vienna and Berlin: Löwit, 1919), p. 15.

95. Joseph Prager, "Verdrängung und Durchbruch in der jüdischen Seele," *Der Jude* 7 (1923): 677.

96. Theodor Lessing, *Der jüdische Selbsthass* (Berlin: Jüdischer, 1930). See the discussion of the medicalization of this category in Sander L. Gilman, *Jewish Self-Hatred: Anti-Semitism and the Hidden Language of the Jews* (Baltimore: Johns Hopkins University Press, 1986), pp. 286–308. In Freud's library there were two very late texts on this topic, evidently sent to him by their authors: C. Berneri, *Le juif anti-sémite* (Paris: Éditions Vita, 1936) (in the Freud Collection, Washington), and Hans Ehrenwald, "Über jüdischen Antisemitismus," in his *Über den sogenannten jüdischen Geist: Eine Aufsatzfolge* (Bratislava: Kreis, 1938), pp. 47–58 (in the Freud Library, London).

97. Erich Stern, "Religöse Entwurzelung und Neurose," *Der Morgen* 7 (1931): 162–77. On the general background of such debates, see Albrecht Hirschmüller, "Psychoanalyse und Antisemitismus," *Luzifer Amor* 1 (1988): 41–54.

98. James Kirsch, "Die Judenfrage in der Psychotherapie," *Jüdische Rundschau* 39 (May 5, 1934): 11.

99. Otto Juliusburger, "Die Judenfrage in der Psychotherapie," *Jüdische Rundschau* 39 (June 15, 1934): 10.

100. J. Steinfeld, "Die Judenfrage in der Psychotherapie," *Jüdische Rundschau* 39 (June 22, 1934): 14.

101. Ludwig Lewisohn, letter to Eugene Saxton, May 21, 1931. Cited in David Singer, "Ludwig Lewisohn and Freud: The Zionist Therapeutic," *Psychoanalytic Review* 58 (1971): 177.

102. Joseph Wortis, *Fragments of an Analysis with Freud* (New York: Aronson, 1984), p. 158.

103. See the discussion in Louis Lieberman, "Jewish Alcoholism and the Disease Concept," *Journal of Psychology and Judaism* 11 (1987): 165–80.

104. Wortis, *Fragments of an Analysis*, p. 161.

105. See, for example, Hershel Meyer, "Nationalism and Jewish Self-Hatred," *Medical Leaves* 3 (1940): 108–18, in which he calls this a disease of "reactionary assimilationists and intellectual Marxists" (p. 110).

106. Rafael Becker, "Die Geisteskrankungen bei den Juden in der Schweiz," *Zeitschrift für Demographie und Statistik der Juden* 4 (1919): 52–56; "Über die Verbreitung der Geistenkrankheiten bei den Juden in Polen und die Frage derer Versorgung," *OSE-Rundschau* 3 (1928): 8–11; "Ein Beitrag zur Frage der Ver-

breitung der Geisteskrankheiten bei den Juden in Polen," *Psychiatrisch-Neurologische Wochenschrift* 31 (1929): 509–12, 410–13; and "Die Geisteskrankungen bei den Juden in Polen," *Allgemeine Zeitschrift für Psychiatrie und ihre Grenzgebiete* 96 (1931): 47–66. See the discussion in Gilman, *Difference and Pathology*, pp. 150–63.

107. A. A. Brill and Morris J. Karpas, "Insanity among the Jews," *Medical Record* 86 (1914): 577–79.

108. Ibid., p. 579.

109. See the summary of Dr. Brosius's talk in *Psychiatrisch-Neurologische Wochenschrift* 4 (1902–3): 386.

110. The debate is summarized in detail in the "preliminary communication" by A. A. Brill and M. J. Karpas, "Insanity among the Jews: Is the Jew Disproportionately Insane?" *Journal of Nervous and Mental Disease* 41 (1914): 512–17.

111. A summary of Wechsler's paper was published by Adolph Stern in *International Journal of Psychoanalysis* 5 (1924): 257.

112. A. Myerson, "The 'Nervousness' of the Jew," *Mental Hygiene* 4 (1920): 65–72; here, 96. Emphasis in the original. Compare *Medical Record* (New York) (February 16, 1918): 269–75.

113. The social realities were quite different. See Jacob Jay Lindenthal, "Abi Gezunt: Health and the Eastern European Jewish Immigrant," *American Jewish History* 70 (1981): 420–41.

114. Abraham Myerson, *The Inheritance of Mental Diseases* (Baltimore: Williams & Wilkins, 1925).

115. Menasze Offner, "Die seelischen Nöte des ostjüdischen Kindes," *Internationale Zeitschrift für Individualpsychologie* 10 (1932): 136–46.

116. Gilman, *Difference and Pathology*, pp. 131–51.

117. This is the "myth" that Frank J. Sulloway, in *Freud, Biologist of the Mind: Beyond the Psychoanalytic Legend* (New York: Basic Books, 1979), p. 592, wishes to identify as "Myth One," the primal myth, in Freud's falsification of his own history. It is clear that this (and the other "myths") are fascinating insights into Freud's understanding of his own career and provide the material for interpretation, not censure.

118. SE 20:15. On the background and meaning of male hysteria, see Mark Micale, "Charcot and the Idea of Hysteria in the Male: Gender, Mental Science, and Medical Diagnosis in Late Nineteenth-Century France," *Medical History* 34 (1990): 363–411. Micale does not link the question of the gender specificity of hysteria to that of race.

119. See the comments by the neurologists Theodor Sommers and Alfred Hoche quoted in *Psychiatrisch-Neurologische Wochenschrift* 12 (1910): 128.

120. Ernest Jones, *The Life and Work of Sigmund Freud*, 3 vols. (New York: Basic Books, 1953–57), 2:119; see also 2:398–99.

121. Paul Julius Möbius, *Über den physiologischen Schwachsinn des Weibes* (Halle: Marhold, 1901). The eighth edition of this work appeared in 1908.

122. Arthur Schnitzler, *Medizinische Schriften*, ed. Horst Thomé (Vienna: Zsolnay, 1988), pp. 75–80. There are other accounts of this talk that supplement this report; see Sulloway, *Freud*, p. 38.

123. In this context, see John Marshall Townsend, "Stereotypes of Mental Illness: A Comparison with Ethnic Stereotypes," *Culture, Medicine, and Psychiatry* 3 (1979): 205–29.

124. Maurice Fishberg, *The Jews: A Study of Race and Environment* (New York: W. Scott, 1911), p. 6. Compare his statement in *The Jewish Encyclopedia*, 12 vols. (New York: Funk and Wagnalls, 1904), s.v. "Nervous Diseases," 9:225–27; here, 225: "Some physicians of large experience among Jews have even gone so far as to state that most of them are neurasthenic and hysterical."

125. Fishberg, "Nervous Diseases," p. 225.

126. Ibid.

127. Ibid.

128. Fishberg, *The Jews*, pp. 324–25.

129. "La population israélite fournit à elle seule presque tout le contingent des hystériques mâles." Fulgence Raymond, *L'étude des maladies du système nerveux en Russie* (Paris: Doin, 1889), p. 71.

130. As quoted, for example, in Hugo Hoppe, *Krankheiten und Sterblichkeit bei Juden und Nichtjuden* (Berlin: Calvary, 1903), p. 26.

131. *Protokolle der Wiener Psychoanalytischen Vereinigung* 2:40; translation from *Minutes of the Vienna Psychoanalytic Society* 2:44.

132. Charcot, *Leçons du Mardi* 2:347–53; see Max Kahane's translation of *Poliklinische Vorträge* 2:299–304.

133. Henry Meige, *Étude sur certains néuropathes voyageurs: Le juif-errant à la Salpêtrière* (Paris: Bataille, 1893). On Meige and this text, see Jan Goldstein, "The Wandering Jew and the Problem of Psychiatric Anti-Semitism in Fin-de-siècle France," *Journal of Contemporary History* 20 (1985): 521–52. See the images and the discussion in Sander L. Gilman, *The Jew's Body* (New York: Routledge, 1991), pp. 60–103.

134. Hermann Strauss, "Erkrankungen durch Alkohol und Syphilis bei den Juden," *Zeitschrift für Demographie und Statistik der Juden,* n.s. 4 (1927): 33–39; chart on p. 35.

135. H. M. Bannister and Ludwig Hektoen, "Race and Insanity," *American Journal of Insanity* 44 (1888): 456–70; here, 464.

136. Moriz Benedikt, *Die Seelenkunde des Menschen als reine Erfahrungswissenschaft* (Leipzig: Reisland, 1895), pp. 186–87, 223–26.

137. Cecil F. Beadles, "The Insane Jew," *Journal of Mental Science* 46 (1900): 736.

138. Frank G. Hyde, "Notes on the Hebrew Insane," *American Journal of Insanity* 58 (1901–2): 470. On the statistical background to the shift between the primarily German-Jewish population and the huge influx of Eastern European Jews into the United States, see John Shaw Billings, *Vital Statistics of the Jews in the United States*, Census Bulletin no. 19, December 30, 1890, p. 23. This is based on a questionnaire sent to 15,000 and responses received from 10,618 Jewish families (60,630 persons), whose names had been obtained from "rabbis and presidents of congregations." This study showed that 227 Jews (116 men, 111 women) had died of "diseases of the nervous system" (including mental diseases: 18 men; 17 women) between 1885 and 1889. The "Jews have suffered a relatively greater loss than their neighbors by deaths from . . . disease of the nervous system

... than the other peoples with whom they are compared" (p. 15). This report was condensed and published in a "popular" version as "Vital Statistics of the Jews," *North American Review* 153 (1891): 70–84.

139. Wilhelm Weygandt, *Atlas und Grundriss der Psychiatrie* (Munich: Lehmann, 1902), p. 32.

140. Moriz Benedikt, "The Insane Jew: An Open Letter to Dr. C. F. Beadles," *Journal of Mental Science* 47 (1901): 503–9; 503 (evolution); 505 (nation); 506 (sexuality and hysteria); 508 (syphilis).

141. Moriz Benedikt, "Der geisteskranke Jude," *Nord und Süd* 167 (1918): 266–70. This is also a detailed attack on Rafael Becker's Zionist explanation of the mental illness of the Jews.

142. Theodor Reik, *Jewish Wit* (New York: Gamut Press, 1962), pp. 33–34.

143. These cases are printed in Albrecht Hirschmüller, *Freuds Begegnung mit der Psychiatrie: Von der Hirnmythologie zur Neurosenlehre* (Tübingen: Discord, 1991). The Jewish cases are: Samuel V. (pp. 270–71); Johanna K. (pp. 316–21); Bertha B. (pp. 362–64); Ruth B. (pp. 385–88); and Rahel G. (pp. 478–79). See also Albrecht Hirschmüller, "Eine bisher unbekannte Krankengeschichte Sigmund Freuds und Josef Breuers aus der Entstehungszeit der *Studien über Hysterie*," *Jahrbuch der Psychoanalyse* 10 (1978): 136–68.

144. Hirschmüller, *Freuds Begegnung*, p. 386.

145. *Protokolle der Wiener Psychoanalytischen Vereinigung* 1:70; translation from *Minutes of the Vienna Psychoanalytic Society* 1:73.

146. *Protokolle der Wiener Psychoanalytischen Vereinigung* 1:93; translation from *Minutes of the Vienna Psychoanalytic Society* 1:98.

147. See Jan Goldstein, *Console and Classify: The French Psychiatric Profession in the Nineteenth Century* (New York: Cambridge University Press, 1987).

148. Eduoard Drumont, *La France juive: Essai d'histoire contemporaine*, 2 vols. (Paris: Marpon et Flammarion, 1886), 1:105–6. On the complicated issue of the structure of this argument and the Jewish response in the German-speaking lands, see Gilman, *Difference and Pathology*, pp. 150–62.

149. Beadles, "The Insane Jew," p. 732.

150. Fishberg, *The Jews*, p. 349.

151. J. Mitchell Clarke, "Hysteria and Neurasthenia," *Brain* 17 (1894): 118–78; here, 150. Freud cites this volume in SE 3:74.

152. See the discussion in Gilman, *Difference and Pathology*, pp. 150–62. See also Yves Chevalier, "Freud et l'antisémitisme—jalousie," *Amitié judéochrétienne de France* 37 (1985): 45–50.

153. Wesley G. Morgan, "Freud's Lithograph of Charcot: A Historical Note," *Bulletin of the History of Medicine* 63 (1989): 268–72.

154. SE 1:98.

155. See, for example, George Frederick Drinka, *The Birth of Neurosis: Myth, Malady, and the Victorians* (New York: Simon and Schuster, 1984), pp. 108–22. See also Esther Fischer-Homburger, *Die traumatische Neurose: Vom somatischen zum sozialen Leiden* (Bern: Huber, 1975).

156. Max Nordau, *Degeneration* (1892–93; London: Heinemann, 1913), pp. 38–39. On the general context, see Wolfgang Schivelbusch, *The Railroad Jour-*

ney: The Industrialization of Time and Space in the Nineteenth Century (Berkeley and Los Angeles: University of California Press, 1986).

157. Gustav Hubert Groeningen, *Über den Schock—eine kritische Studie auf physiologischer Grundlage* (Wiesbaden: Bergmann, 1885), pp. 99–100 (national temperaments); p. 176 (psychic predisposition). This text offers a compact summary of the major literature, including the work of Erichsen and Page, pp. 172–78 (in the Freud Library, London).

158. Edward Shorter, *From Paralysis to Fatigue: A History of Psychosomatic Illness in the Modern Era* (New York: Free Press, 1992), p. 35.

159. K. Codell Carter, "German Theory, Hysteria, and Freud's Early Work in Psychopathology," *Medical History* 24 (1980): 259–74.

160. Sir Clifford Allbutt, "Nervous Disease and Modern Life," *Contemporary Review* 67 (1895): 214–15.

161. C. E. Brown-Séquard, "On the Hereditary Transmission of Effects of Certain Injuries to the Nervous System," *Lancet* (January 2, 1875): 7–8.

162. As in John Eric Erichsen, *On Concussion of the Spine, Nervous Shock, and Other Obscure Injuries to the Nervous System in Their Clinical and Medico-Legal Aspects* (New York: Wood, 1886), p. 2, or in Hans Schmaus, "Zur Casuistik und pathologischen Anatomie der Rückenmarkserschütterung," *Archiv für klinische Chirurgie* 42 (1891): 112–22, with plates.

163. Jeffrey Moussaieff Masson, *The Complete Letters of Sigmund Freud to Wilhelm Fliess, 1887–1904* (Cambridge, Mass.: Harvard University Press, 1985), p. 285. See Laurence A. Rickels, *The Case of California* (Baltimore: Johns Hopkins University Press, 1991), pp. 195–98.

164. Jones, *Life and Work of Sigmund Freud* 2:14 (hell), 198, 335–36 (missing).

165. Masson, *Complete Letters of Sigmund Freud to Wilhelm Fliess*, p. 262.

166. SE 12:135.

167. Sigmund Freud, *Brautbriefe: Briefe an Martha Bernays aus den Jahren 1882 bis 1886*, ed. Ernst L. Freud (Frankfurt a. M.: Fischer, 1960), p. 66. Compare Bertram D. Lewin, "The Train Ride: A Study of One of Freud's Figures of Speech," *Psychoanalytic Quarterly* 39 (1970): 71–89, which does not evoke the question of the Jewish associations with the train.

168. SE 4:212. On the historical context for this dream, see Carl Schorske, *Fin-de-siècle Vienna: Politics and Culture* (New York: Knopf, 1980), pp. 185–97.

169. SE 4:197.

170. Ibid. 5:442.

171. J.K., "Erzählungen aus dem Görzischen," *Anthropophyteia* 7 (1910): 324–36; here, 327.

172. Avrom Reitzer, *Solem Alechem: Nix für Kinder, E Waggon feiner, vescher, safter Lozelach, Schmozes takef pickfeiner Schmüs für unsere Leut* (Vienna: Deubler, n.d.), p. 5.

173. SE 8:80, 115.

174. Gilman, *Difference and Pathology*, pp. 175–91.

175. SE 4:195.

176. Schorske, *Fin-de-siècle Vienna*, p. 190.

177. SE 4:195.

178. Freud would have found references to diabetes as a Jewish disease in the standard textbook of internal medicine of the period, Adolf Strümpell, ed., *Lehrbuch der speciellen Pathologie und Therapie der inneren Krankheiten für Studirende und Ärzte*, 18 vols. (Leipzig: Vogel, 1883–1912), excerpted as *A Text-Book of Medicine*, trans. Herman F. Vickery and Philip Coombs Knapp (New York: Appleton, 1893), p. 967. See SE 4:23. The "Jewish" nature of this disease is discussed widely in the medical literature of the period. In addition to Strümpell, Buschan and Charcot wrote on this question. See the literature summarized in Morpurgo, *Sulle condizioni somatiche*, pp. 61–62. On the history of diabetes without covering this topic, see Dietrich von Engelhardt, ed., *Diabetes: Its Medical and Cultural History* (Berlin: Springer, 1989).

179. W[illiam] O[sler], "Letters from Berlin," *Canada Medical and Surgical Journal* 12 (1884): 721–28; here, 723.

180. Dr. A. Kühner, *Arterienverkalkung heilbar! Neue Mittel und Wege* (Leipzig: Gloeckner, [1920]), p. 19.

181. SE 4:195.

182. Alexander Grinstein, *Sigmund Freud's Dreams* (New York: International Universities Press, 1980), pp. 72–73.

183. Compare Otto Binswanger, *Hysterie* (Vienna: Deuticke, 1904), p. 82.

184. Richard von Krafft-Ebing, *Psychopathia Sexualis: A Medico-Forensic Study*, rev. and trans. Harry E. Wedeck (New York: Putnam's, 1965), p. 24 (in the Freud Library, London, in the 1892, 1894, and 1901 editions).

185. Auguste Forel, *Die sexuelle Frage* (Munich: Reinhardt, 1906), p. 172; pp. 354–55; in English as *The Sexual Question*, trans. C. F. Marshall (New York: Medical Art Agency, 1922), pp. 331–32 (in the Freud Library, London, in the 1905 edition). See also Anson Rabinbach, *The Human Motor: Energy, Fatigue, and the Origin of Modernity* (New York: Basic Books, 1990).

186. Richard von Krafft-Ebing, *Text-Book of Insanity*, trans. Charles Gilbert Chaddock (Philadelphia: Davis, 1904), p. 143 (in the Freud Library, London, in the 1888 and 1893 editions).

187. Engländer, *Die auffallend häufigen Krankheitserscheinungen*, p. 12.

188. Ernst Lissauer, "Deutschtum und Judentum," *Kunstwart* 25 (1912): 6–12; here, 8.

189. Joseph Guislain, *Klinische Vorträge über Geistes-Krankheiten*, trans. Heinrich Laehr (Berlin: Hirschwald, 1854), pp. 16–19. Cited in SE 4:89.

190. A. Krauss, "Der Sinn in Wahnsinn: Eine psychiatrische Untersuchung," *Allgemeine Zeitschrift für Psychiatrie* 15 (1858): 617–71; 16 (1859): 10–35, 222–81. Cited in SE 4:36–37, 88–90, 92.

191. Wilhelm Griesinger, *Die Pathologie und Therapie der psychischen Krankheiten* (1867; Amsterdam: Bonset, 1964), p. 106. Freud cites this in *The Interpretation of Dreams*, SE 4:91, 135 (in the Freud Library, London, in the 1871 edition). A major phenomonological dissertation was written in Heidelberg under Karl Wilmanns at the same time that Hans Prinzhorn's study of the art of the insane was written. This is, for the 1920s, a major resource in understanding a nonpsychoanalytic approach to the writing of the mentally ill. See Wilhelm Mayer-Gross, *Selbstschilderungen der Verwirrtheit: Die onairoide Erlebnisform* (Berlin: Springer, 1924).

192. D. Dünker, "Merkwürdiger Gang der Phantasie in einem Delirium," *Magazin zur Erfahrungsseelenkunde* 2 (1784): 1–11.

193. Diateophilus [Karl Wilhelm, Freiherr von Drais], *Physisiche und psychologische Geschichte seiner siebenjährigen Epilepsie*, 2 vols. (Zurich: Orell, 1798).

194. Alexis Vincent Charles Berbiguier, *Les Farfadets, ou tous les démons ne sont pas de l'autre monde*, 3 vols. (Paris: Gueffier, 1821).

195. Paul Slade Knight, *Observations on the Causes, Symptoms, and Treatment of Derangement of the Mind, founded on an Extensive Moral and Medical Practice in the Treatment of Lunatics. Together with the Particulars of the Sensations and Ideas of a Gentleman during Mental Alienation, Written by Himself during His Convalescence* (London: Longman, Rees, Orme, Brown, and Green, 1827).

196. John Perceval, *A Narrative of the Treatment Experienced by a Gentleman during a State of Mental Derangement, Designed to Explain the Causes and the Nature of Insanity*, 2 vols. (London: Wilson, 1838–40).

197. See Roy Porter, ed., *A Social History of Madness: Stories of the Insane* (London: Weidenfeld and Nicolson, 1987).

198. Friedrich Engelken, "Selbstbericht einer genesenen Geisteskranken, nebst Krankheitsgeschichte und Bemerkungen," *Allgemeine Zeitschrift für Psychiatrie* 6 (1849): 586–653, and D. G. Kieser, "Melancholia daemonomaniaca occulta, in einem Selbstbekenntniss des Kranken geschildert," *Allgemeine Zeitschrift für Psychiatrie* 10 (1853): 423–57.

199. Victor Kandinsky, "Zur Lehr von den Hallucinationen," *Archiv für Psychiatrie* 9 (1880): 453–64.

200. Karl Rychlinski, "Ein Fall hallucinatorisch-periodischer Psychose," *Archiv für Psychiatrie* 28 (1898): 625–39.

201. Auguste Forel, "Selbst-Biographie eines Falles von Mania acuta," *Archiv für Psychiatrie und Nervenkrankheiten* 34 (1901): 960–97.

202. J. J. David, "Halluzinationen," *Die neue Rundschau* 2 (1906): 874–80.

203. Emil Kraepelin, *Psychiatrie: Ein Lehrbuch für Studierende und Ärzte*, 4 vols. (Leipzig: Barth, 1913), 3:741–45 (in the Freud Library, London). This category is found in all the earlier editions of this handbook.

204. Sander L. Gilman, *Disease and Representation: Images of Illness from Madness to AIDS* (Ithaca, N.Y.: Cornell University Press, 1988), pp. 231–44.

205. Nordau, *Degeneration*, p. 43.

206. John Haslam, *Illustrations of Madness*, ed. with an introduction by Roy Porter (London and New York: Routledge, 1988).

207. Gilman, *Jewish Self-Hatred*, pp. 209–18.

208. Gilman, *Disease and Representation*, pp. 202–30.

209. Viktor Tausk, "Über die Entstehung des 'Beeinflussungsapparates' in der Schizophrenie," *Internationale Zeitschrift für ärztliche Psychoanalyse* 5 (1919): 1–33; translation from *The Psycho-Analytic Reader*, ed. Robert Fliess (New York: International Universities Press, 1948), pp. 31–64; here, p. 58 n. 14.

210. Freud to Ferenczi, February 11, 1908, cited by Peter Gay, *Freud: A Life for Our Time* (New York: Norton, 1988), p. 277.

211. Freud to Ferenczi, March 25, 1908, cited in Gay, *Freud*, p. 278.

212. This can be seen most clearly in the materials collected by Hans Prinzhorn during the early 1920s that are now in the University Clinic in Heidelberg. See Hans Gercke and Inge Jarchov, eds., *Die Prinzhornsammlung* (Königstein: Athenäum, 1980).

213. See the complex presentation of the "medicalization of homosexuality" in David F. Greenberg, *Construction of Homosexuality* (Chicago: The University of Chicago Press, 1988), pp. 397–433, and Kenneth Lewes, *The Psychoanalytic Theory of Male Homosexuality* (New York: New American Library, 1988).

214. On the implications of this model, see John R. Morss, *The Biologising of Childhood: Developmental Psychology and the Darwinian Myth* (Hove and London: Lawrence Erlbaum Associates, 1990), pp. 43–47.

215. SE 18:150.

216. Sigmund Freud, *Briefe, 1873–1939*, ed. Ernst and Lucie Freud (Frankfurt a. M.: Fischer, 1960), p. 438.

217. Sulloway, *Freud*, pp. 281–82.

218. Erich Wulffen, *Der Sexualverbrecher* (Berlin: Langenscheidt, 1910), p. 302. This was considered one of the major innovative contributions to the criminology of the day. See the review in *Jahrbuch für sexuelle Zwischenstufen*, n.s. 3 (1911): 376–78.

219. Billings, "Vital Statistics of the Jews," 84. In this context, see David Biale, *Eros and the Jews: From Biblical Israel to Contemporary America* (New York: Basic Books, 1992).

220. All references to this hitherto unpublished essay is to the translation by Dennis B. Klein, published as appendix C to his *Jewish Origins of the Psychoanalytic Movement* (New York: Praeger, 1981); here, p. 171.

221. Krafft-Ebing, *Psychopathia Sexualis*, pp. 7–12.

222. Gilman, *Disease and Representation*, pp. 155–81.

223. *Protokolle der Wiener Psychoanalytischen Vereinigung*, 1:66–67; translation from *Minutes of the Vienna Psychoanalytic Society* 2:60–61.

224. *Protokolle der Wiener Psychoanalytischen Vereinigung* 2:71–72; translation from *Minutes of the Vienna Psychoanalytic Society* 2:78–79.

225. SE 10:276.

226. See the discussion in *Protokolle der Wiener Psychoanalytischen Vereinigung* 1:189–98, 212–23; translation from *Minutes of the Vienna Psychoanalytic Society* 1:204–11, 227–37.

227. A. A. Brill, "Psychological Factors in Dementia Praecox: An Analysis," *Journal of Abnormal Psychology* 3 (1908): 219–39; here, 233. Brill's account of this case and its relationship to Freud can be found in A. A. Brill, *Freud's Contribution to Psychiatry* (New York: Norton, 1944), pp. 93–101.

228. Brill, "Psychological Factors," p. 220.

229. Ibid., p. 220.

230. Ibid., p. 221.

231. Gilman, *Difference and Pathology*, pp. 59–76.

232. Brill, "Psychological Factors,"p. 232.

233. Ibid., p. 235.

234. A. A. Brill, "Reflections, Reminiscences of Sigmund Freud," *Medical Leaves* 3 (1940): 18–29, reprinted in *Freud as We Knew Him*, ed. Hendrick M. Ruitenbeek (Detroit: Wayne State University Press, 1973), pp. 154–69.

235. A. A. Brill, "The Adjustment of the Jew to the American Environment," *Mental Hygiene* 2 (1918): 219–31.

236. Howard J. Faulkner and Virginia D. Pruitt, eds., *The Selected Correspondence of Karl A. Menninger, 1919–1945* (New Haven: Yale University Press, 1988), p. 282. Menninger supplies his own reading of Sulzberger's reason for distinguishing between his discourse and that of someone whom Menninger sees as a "fellow Jew." Menninger comments that Sulzberger was "timid about being known to be a Jewish newspaper owner" (p. 284).

237. Brill, "Reflections, Reminiscences," p. 161.

238. A. A. Brill, "The Conception of Homosexuality," *Journal of the American Medical Association* 61 (1913): 335–40.

239. One of the strengths of psychoanalysis was to provide an outlet for Jewish physicians to address the question of race at least in terms of the critique of religion. Freud's cultural periodical *Imago* (1912–1937) is full of detailed discussions of Jewish religious practices, including circumcision, as reflections of underlying psychological archetypes. The other major journal and movement founded by a Jewish physician was Magnus Hirschfeld's *Jahrbuch der sexuelle Zwischenstufen unter besonderer Berücksichtigung der Homosexualität* (1899–1913). What is noticeable, if one examines this work volume by volume, is the total lack of mention of any Jewish topic, including the rise of anti-Semitism, while other movements, such as the women's movement, are discussed.

240. Elias Canetti, *Macht und Überleben: Drei Essays* (Berlin: Literarisches Colloquium, 1972), p. 21.

241. Carl G. Jung, *Collected Works*, ed. Herbert Read et al., trans. R.F.C. Hull, 20 vols. (London: Routledge, 1957–79), 3:73–74, 76, 153.

242. One might note that the essay following Brill's in the *Journal of Abnormal Psychology* is a similar firsthand account: B.C.A., "My Life as a Dissociated Personality," *Journal of Abnormal Psychology* 3 (1908): 240–60.

243. *Sigmund Freud—C. G. Jung: Briefwechsel*, ed. William McGuire and Wolfgang Sauerländer (Frankfurt a. M.: Fischer, 1974), p. 422; translation from *The Freud/Jung Letters: The Correspondence between Sigmund Freud and C. G. Jung*, ed. William McGuire, trans. Ralph Manheim and R.F.C. Hull (Princeton: Princeton University Press, 1974), p. 382.

244. Freud and Jung, *Briefwechsel*, p. 420; translation from McGuire, *Freud/Jung Letters*, p. 380.

245. On the sources for the Leonardo essay, see Gilman, *Disease and Representation*, pp. 50–62.

246. *Sigmund Freud–Karl Abraham, Briefe, 1907–1926*, ed. Hilda C. Abraham and Ernst L. Freud (Frankfurt a. M.: Fischer, 1980), p. 100; translation from *A Psycho-Analytic Dialogue: The Letters of Sigmund Freud and Karl Abraham, 1907–1926*, ed. Hilda C. Abraham and Ernst L. Freud, trans. Bernard Marsh and Hilda C. Abraham (London: Hogarth Press, 1965), p. 95. The power of this discourse should not be underestimated. Abraham used it in a letter to Freud on May 1, 1920 (*Sigmund Freud–Karl Abraham, Briefe*, p. 286).

247. SE 12:15.

248. Ibid.

249. Ibid. 12:37.

250. Ibid. 4:91, 135.

251. On the Schreber text, see Han Israëls, *Schreber: Father and Son* (Madison, Conn.: International Universities Press, 1989), and Gerhard Busse, *Schreber, Freud, und die Suche nach dem Vater : Über die realitätschaffende Kraft einer wissenschaftlichen Hypothese* (Frankfurt a. M.: Lang, 1991), which present a detailed history of the family as well as a critique of all the earlier, psychoanalytic readings of the case. See also M. Ruse, "Medicine as Social Science: The Case of Freud on Homosexuality," *Journal of Medicine and Philosophy* 6 (1981): 361–86; C. Barry Chabot, *Freud on Schreber: Psychoanalytic Theory and the Critical Act* (Amherst, Mass.: University of Massachusetts Press, 1982); Henry Abelove, "Freud, Male Homosexuality, and the Americans," *Dissent* (New York) 33 (1986): 59–69; James Hillman, "On Paranoia," *Eranos Yearbook* 54 (1985): 269–324; Alvaro Villar Gaviria, *Freud, la mujer y los "homosexuales"* (Bogota: Valencia, 1986) (which links the concept of the feminine and the homosexual, but excludes the Jew); David Allison, Prado de Oliveira, Mark S. Roberts, and Allen S. Weiss, eds., *Psychosis and Sexual Identity: Toward a Post-Analytic View of the Schreber Case* (New York: State University of New York Press, 1988); Peter Horn, "Halluzinierte Vögel, oder Wann ist Paranoia literarisch? Zu E.T.A. Hoffmann, Robert Musil, und Daniel Paul Schreber," *Acta Germanica*, supp. 1 (1990): 97–123; Jonathan Dollimore, *Sexual Dissidence: Augustine to Wilde, Freud to Foucault* (Oxford: Clarendon Press, 1991), pp. 169–90; and Zvi Lothane, *In Defense of Schreber: Soul Murder and Psychiatry* (Hillsdale, N.J.: Analytic Press, 1992); Jay Geller, "The Unmanning of the Wandering Jew," *American Imago* 49 (1992): 227–60.

252. SE 12:47.

253. Daniel Paul Schreber, *Denkwürdigkeiten eines Nervenkranken nebst Nachträgen und einem Anhang über die Frage: "Unter welchen Voraussetzungen darf eine für geisteskrank erachtete Person gegen ihren Willen in einer festgehalten werden?"* (Leipzig: Mutze, 1903) (in the Freud Library, London, with marginalia). All quotations are taken from the English translation, *Memoirs of My Nervous Illness*, trans. and ed. Ida Macalpine and Richard A. Hunter (London: Dawson, 1955); here, p. 73.

254. SE 12:62.

255. Ibid.

256. Ibid. 12:18.

257. Ibid. 12:58.

258. See the discussion of this debate in Janet Malcolm, *In the Freud Archives* (New York: Vintage, 1984), pp. 77–85, and in Jeffrey Moussaieff Masson, *Freud, the Assault on Truth: Freud's Suppression of the Seduction Theory* (London and Boston: Faber and Faber, 1984).

259. SE 7:214 n. 2.

260. Conrad Rieger, *Die Castration in rechtlicher, socialer, und vitaler Hinsicht* (Jena: Gustav Fischer, 1900), p. 106. See SE 7:214.

261. SE 12:82.

262. The association between religious practice and paranoia was a powerful one for Jewish psychoanalysts of the turn of the century. In Sabina Spielrein's essay on the delusional system of a schizophrenic, published in the same volume of the *Yearbook of Psychoanalysis* as the first half of Freud's study of Schreber (and cited by Freud in his postscript to the case), the presentation of the case

material begins with the religious fantasies of the female patient. (Sabina Spielrein, "Über den psychologischen Inhalt eines Falles von Schizophrenie [Dementia praecox]," *Jahrbuch für psychoanalytische und psychopathologische Forschungen* 3 [1912]: 329–400; here, 332–34.) The Protestant patient's preoccupation with her involuntary "catholicization" becomes the initial thread that Sabina Spielrein follows in order to begin to unravel the underlying tensions of the system. Just as Schreber becomes a Jew, so Spielrein's patient becomes a Catholic. In the course of her analysis, it is revealed that the patient's husband is a Catholic and their religious conflict looms large in her own symbolic representation of her illness. Spielrein too is struck by the role the physician plays in the delusional system of her patient, as the symbol of power and as the focus of the patient's fixations—but she is also aware that the physician the patient chooses for her fixation, Auguste Forel, has had no contact with the patient (p. 347). Forel, whose study of human sexuality was a popular handbook of the day, comes to have the same sort of symbolic reference in this patient's system as does the Roman Catholic Church. Religion and sexuality are linked in an overt manner, as frightening abstractions.

263. SE 12:81.

264. When in 1923 Freud published his second reading of a historic account of paranoia, that of "a seventeenth-century demonological neurosis," his views about the origin of homosexuality had begun to shift (SE 19:72–105). The image of castration, seen by Freud earlier in his reading of the case of "Little Hans" in connection with the question of circumcision, remains separate from this problem in his reading of this text. The autobiographical account by Christoph Haizmann is parallel to many of the texts on which Jean-Martin Charcot had drawn for his historical studies of possession and hysteria, some of which Freud translated in 1886 and 1893. The imagery of the Haizmann text, unlike that of Schreber, does not make any specific reference to the question of the Jews. The text is available in English as *Schizophrenia 1677: A Psychiatric Study of an Illustrated Autobiographical Record of Demonical Possession*, ed. and trans. Ida Macalpine and Richard A. Hunter (London: Dawson, 1956).

265. See Jack Zipes, "Oscar Panizza: The Operated German as Operated Jew," *New German Critique* 21 (1980): 47–61, and Michael Bauer, *Oskar Panizza: Ein literarisches Porträt* (Munich: Hanser, 1984).

266. Schreber, *Memoirs*, p. 33.

267. Ibid., p. 41.

268. Ibid., p. 45.

269. Paul Flechsig, *Gehirn und Seele: Rede, gehalten am 31. October 1894 in der Universitätskirche zu Leipzig* (Leipzig: Veit, 1896) (in the Freud Library, London); in French as *Études sur le cerveau*, trans. L. Levi (Paris: Vigot, 1898). On the relationship of this text to Schreber's autobiography, see Martin Stinglein, "Paul Emil Flechsig: Die Berechnung der menschlichen Seele," in Clair, Pichler, Pirchner, *Wunderblock*, pp. 297–307. See also Flechsig's *Meine myelogenetische Hirnlehre mit biographischer Einleitung* (Berlin: Springer, 1927).

270. Schreber, *Memoirs*, pp. 89–90. He cites Emil Kraepelin, *Psychiatrie: Ein Lehrbuch für Studirende und Ärzte*, 5th ed. (1896; reprint, New York: Arno Press, 1976), p. 110.

271. Emil Kraepelin, *Psychiatrie: Ein Lehrbuch für Studierende und Ärzte*, 3 vols. (Leipzig: Barth, 1909–15), 1:153–54 and 157 (in the Freud Library, London).

272. Schreber, *Memoirs*, p. 50.

273. Gilman, *Jewish Self-Hatred*, pp. 101–2.

274. Schreber, *Memoirs*, p. 50.

275. Ibid., p. 69.

276. Ibid., p. 139.

277. Ibid., p. 151.

278. Ibid., p. 53.

279. Ibid., p. 57.

280. Ibid., p. 57.

281. The question of the incestuous nature of the Jew, a natural parallel for the struggle with the father in Schreber's system, is evoked in the text by Schreber's reading of Lord Byron's *Manfred* (1817), mentioned twice in the text. Byron also employed the name Ariman (Schreber, *Memoirs*, 53, 55). Schreber quotes from the play, which was influenced by Goethe's *Faust*, and was one of the most popular Romantic dramas in Germany during the nineteenth century. Indeed, Schreber seems to have borrowed the central vocabulary for his pantheon directly from Byron's work. The plot of Byron's play, with its fury-driven hero, whose incestuous relationship with his sister has made him insane, haunts the image of the madman present in Schreber. The "agony" of Manfred, whose tortured death closed the drama, is incorporated in the image of "raving madness," with its solitary figure of the madman. Madness is externalized through the image of Manfred's furies, which are present in Schreber's image of madness as the spheres of Ahriman and Ormuzd, the two segments of the godhead. The projection of internalized guilt, with its sexual references, onto the external world is thus perceived in an aesthetic mode and can become the material for art. It is doubly projected—first, outside the self onto the world, and second, onto the world within the clear artifice of the work of art.

282. All references to Nietzsche's works here are to the only complete critical edition, Friedrich Nietzsche, *Sämtliche Werke: Kritische Studienausgabe*, ed. Giorgio Colli and Mazzino Montinari, 15 vols. (Berlin and Munich: dtv and de Gruyter, 1980); here, 6:240. All translations from Nietzsche's works are by the author; some of these translations have been modified from those by Walter Kaufmann. Freud had the great "Weimar" edition of Nietzsche's work in his London library, but this was a gift to him in 1926 from Otto Rank. The question of Freud's early exposure to Nietzsche is discussed by William J. McGrath, *Freud's Discovery of Psychoanalysis: The Politics of Hysteria* (Ithaca, N.Y.: Cornell University Press, 1986), pp. 138–39.

283. See Léon Poliakov, *The History of Anti-Semitism*, 4 vols. (Oxford: Oxford University Press, 1985), vol. 4, *Suicidal Europe, 1870–1933*, trans. George Klim, p. 6.

284. See Donald F. Nelson, "Nietzsche, Zarathustra, and Jesus *redivivus*," *Germanic Review* 48 (1973): 175–88.

285. Nietzsche, *Sämtliche Werke*, 6:223.

286. Ibid., 6:240.

287. Ibid., 6:100–101. Translation from *The Portable Nietzsche*, trans. and ed. Walter Kaufmann (New York: Viking Press, 1954), p. 504.

288. Schreber, *Memoirs*, p. 92.

289. Gustav Jaeger, *Die Entdeckung der Seele* (Leipzig: Günther, 1880), pp. 106–9 (in the Freud Collection, New York). For a catalogue of the smells attributed to the Jew, see Hans F. K. Günther, "Der rasseeigene Geruch der Hautausdünstung," *Zeitschrift für Rassenphysiologie* 2 (1930): 94–99; here, 97–99. Günther strongly believes in the reality of the Jew's smell and offers his own as well as historical testimony. This is repeated in summary in Hans F. K. Günther, *Rassenkunde des jüdischen Volkes* (1922; Munich: Lehmann, 1931), pp. 260–67.

290. Richard Andree, *Zur Volkskunde der Juden* (Leipzig: Velhagen & Klasing, 1881), pp. 68–69.

291. Johann Jakob Schudt, *Jüdische Merckwürdigkeiten*, 4 vols. in 2 (Frankfurt a. M.: Hocker, 1714–18), 1:349.

292. Max Marcuse, "Die christliche-jüdische Mischehe," *Sexual-Probleme* 7 (1912): 691–749; here, 714 n. 24.

293. Schreber, *Memoirs*, pp. 73–74.

294. Ibid., p. 72.

295. Ibid., p. 71.

296. Ibid., p. 132.

297. Ibid., p. 133.

298. Ludwig Feuerbach, *Essence of Christianity*, trans. George Eliot (New York: Harper, 1957), p. 114. See also C. Dimitrov and I. Gerdjikov, "Ludwig Feuerbach und Sigmund Freud: Zur Erinnerung an den 101. Todestag Ludwig Feuerbachs," *Zeitschrift für Psychosomatische Medizin und Psychoanalyse* 20 (1974): 87–98.

299. M. J. Gutmann, *Über den heutigen Stand der Rasse- und Krankheitsfrage der Juden* (Munich: Rudolph Müller & Steinicke, 1920), p. 39.

300. Gilman, *Difference and Pathology*, p. 117.

301. Alan Dundes, *Life Is Like a Chicken Coop Ladder: A Portrait of German Culture through Folklore* (New York: Columbia University Press, 1984).

302. See William Hazlitt, ed., *The Table Talk of Martin Luther* (London: Bell, 1911), p. 289.

303. Oskar Panizza, "The Operated Jew," trans. Jack Zipes, *New German Critique* 21 (1980): 63–79; here, 73.

304. John Gregory Bourke, *Der Unrat in Sitte, Brauch, Glauben, und Gewohnheitrecht der Völker*, trans. Friedrich S. Krauss and H. Ihm (Leipzig: Ethnologischer Verlag, 1913), pp. 134–35, on Jews' belief that the inability to defecate can be the result of being possessed by an evil spirit. SE 12:179, 334–37.

305. Iwan Bloch, *Beiträge zur Ätiologie der Psychopathia Sexualis*, 2 vols. (Dresden: Dohrn, 1902–3), 2:235–36. Freud's use of this is found in SE 7:51, 139; 16:307.

306. Schreber, *Memoirs*, p. 178.

307. Harry Friedenwald, *The Jews and Medicine: Essays*, 2 vols. (Baltimore: Johns Hopkins University Press, 1944), 2:527.

308. Elcan Isaac Wolf, *Von den Krankheiten der Juden* (Mannheim: Schwan, 1777), p. 84.

309. Maurice Fishberg, "Cancer," in *The Jewish Encyclopedia* 3:531, and Sigismund Peller, "Über Krebssterblichkeit der Juden," *Zeitschrift für Krebsforschung* 34 (1931): 128–47; here, 134.

310. Maurice Fishberg, "Morbidity," in *The Jewish Encyclopedia* 9:4.

311. SE 4:132 n. 1.

312. Ignaz Bernstein, *Jüdische Sprichwörter and Redensarten* (Warsaw and Frankfurt a. M.: Kauffmann, 1908). The role of Bernstein's proverb collections in providing a source for the Western understanding of the sexuality of the Eastern Jew is documented in A. A. Roback's letter of March 10, 1930, to Freud. See A. A. Roback, *Freudiana* (Cambridge, Mass.: Sci-Art, 1957), p. 31. On the centrality of the proverb for an understanding of the image of the Eastern Jew in psychoanalysis, see Theodor Reik, "The Echo of the Proverb," in *From Thirty Years with Freud*, trans. Richard Winston (New York: Farrar and Rinehart, 1940), pp. 228–41. On the negative use of these proverbs, see Wolfgang Mieder, "Proverbs in Nazi Germany: The Promulgation of Anti-Semitism and Stereotypes through Folklore," *Journal of American Folklore* 95 (1982): 435–64; p. 437 (on Bernstein).

313. Gutmann, *Rass- und Krankheitsfrage*, p. 38.

314. Paul Flechsig, *Die Grenzen geistiger Gesundheit und Krankheit* (Leipzig: Veit, 1896), p. 17.

315. Schreber, *Memoirs*, p. 98.

316. Ibid., p. 97.

317. Ibid., pp. 97–98.

318. Ibid., p. 97.

319. Gilman, *Disease and Representation*, pp. 208–9.

320. See the discussion in the case notes in Franz Baumeyer, "Der Fall Schreber," *Psyche* 9 (1955): 513–33; here, 514.

321. C. H. Ohr, "Genito-Reflex Neurosis in the Female," *American Journal of Obstetrics* 16 (1883): 50–64, 168–80; here, 64. See Shorter, *From Paralysis to Fatigue*, p. 51.

322. Johann Pezzl, *Skizze von Wien: Ein Kultur- und Sittenbild as der josephinischen Zeit*, ed. Gustav Gugitz and Anton Schlossar (Graz: Leykam, 1923), pp. 107–8.

323. See Michael Scheiba, *Dissertatio inauguralis medica, sistens quaedam plicae pathologica: Germ. Juden-Zopff, Polon. Koltun: quam . . . in Academia Albertina pro gradu doctoris . . . subjiciet defensurus Michael Scheiba . . .* (Regiomonti: Litteris Reusnerianis, [1739]), and Hieronymus Ludolf, *Dissertatio inauguralis medica de plica, vom Juden-Zopff . . .* (Erfordiae: Typis Groschianis, [1724]).

324. Joseph Rohrer, *Versuch über die jüdischen Bewohner der österreichischen Monarchie* (Vienna: n.p., 1804), p. 26. The debate about the special tendency of the Jews to suffer from skin diseases, especially *plica polonica*, went on well into the twentieth century. See Richard Weinberg, "Zur Pathologie der Juden," *Zeitschrift für Demographie und Statistik der Juden* 1 (1905): 10–11.

325. Wolfgang Häusler, *Das galizische Judentum in der Habsburgermonarchie im Lichte der zeitgenössischen Publizistik und Reiseliteratur von 1772–1848* (Vienna: Verlag für Geschichte und Politik, 1979). On the status of the debates about the pathology of the Jews in the East after 1919, see *Voprosy biologii i patologii evreev* (Leningrad: State Publishing House, 1926).

326. Arthur Schopenhauer, *Parerga and Paralipomena*, trans. E.F.J. Payne, 2 vols. (Oxford: Clarendon Press, 1973), 2:357.

327. Schreber, *Memoirs*, p. 148.

328. Ibid., p. 156.

329. Ibid., p. 180.

330. Ibid., p. 181.

331. See Sander L. Gilman, "The Jewish Nose: Are Jews White? or the History of the Nose Job," in Gilman, *The Jew's Body*, pp. 169–93.

332. Panizza, "The Operated Jew," p. 68.

333. Schreber, *Memoirs*, p. 133.

334. Panizza, "The Operated Jew," p. 77.

335. Ibid., p. 79.

336. Flechsig, *Grenzen*, pp. 32–34.

337. Cited from the English translation, Nordau, *Degeneration*, p. 16.

338. See Walter Rathenau, "Höre, Israel!" *Die Zukunft* (March 6, 1897): 454–62.

339. David Friedrich Strauss, *Der alte und der neue Glaube: Ein Bekenntnis* (Leipzig: Hirzel, 1872), p. 71.

340. Hugo Knoepfmacher, "Sigmund Freud in High School," *American Imago* 36 (1979): 287–300, as well as Robert R. Holt, "Freud's Adolescent Reading: Some Possible Effects on His Work," in Stepansky, *Freud* 3:167–92; here, 185–88.

341. Gutmann, *Rasse- und Krankheitsfrage*, p. 18.

342. Ibid., pp. 25–26.

343. Cited by Günther, *Rassenkunde des jüdischen Volkes*, p. 273.

344. Robert Stigler, "Die rassenphysiologische Bedeutung der sekundären Geschlechtscharaktere," *Sitzungsberichte der anthopologischen Gesellschaft in Wien* (1919/20), pp. 6–9; here, p. 7. Published as a special issue of *Mitteilungen der anthropologischen Gesellschaft in Wien* 50 (1920).

345. Havelock Ellis, *Studies in the Psychology of Sex*, 7 vols. (Philadelphia: Davis, 1920–28), vol. 2, *Sexual Inversion*, p. 264 (in the Freud Library, London).

346. Freud's primary source on this topic was Cesare Taruffi, *Hermaphrodismus und Zeugungsunfähigkeit: Eine systematische Darstellung des Missbildungen der menschlichen Geschlechtsorgane*, trans. R. Teuscher (Berlin: Barsdorf, 1903), pp. 96–103.

347. Ibid., p. 97.

348. Ferdinand-Valère Faneau de la Cour, *Du féminisme et de l'infantilisme chez les tuberculeux* (Paris: Parent, 1871).

349. Henri Meige, "L'infantilisme, féminisme, et les hérmaphrodites antiques," *L'anthropologie* 15 (1895): 257–64.

350. SE 7:141–42.

351. Panizza, "The Operated Jew," pp. 63–64.

352. Ibid., 65.

353. Ibid.

354. Ibid., 66.

355. See the discussion of the idea of degeneration in J. E. Chamberlin and Sander L. Gilman, eds., *Degeneration: The Dark Side of Progress* (New York: Columbia University Press, 1985), and Daniel Pick, *Faces of Degeneration: A European Disorder, c. 1848– c. 1918* (New York: Cambridge University Press, 1989).

356. This was done together with Albert Moll and reported by him in his *Untersuchungen über die Libido sexualis*, 2 vols. (Berlin: Fischer's Medicinische Buchhandlung, 1897–88), 1:339. See SE 3:102; 7:169, 180; 8:98; 18:255.

357. Albert Moll, *Die konträre Sexualempfindung* (Berlin: Fischer, 1893), p. 84; Albert Moll, *Perversions of the Sex Instinct: A Study of Sexual Inversion*, trans. Maurice Popkin (Newark, N.J.: Julian Press, 1931), p. 67.

358. Moll, *Sexualempfindung*, p. 94; *Perversions*, pp. 71–72.

359. Forel, *Die sexuelle Frage*, pp. 172, 260; *The Sexual Question*, p. 245.

360. Moll, *Perversions*, pp. 208–9.

361. Masson, *Complete Letters of Sigmund Freud to Wilhelm Fliess*, p. 311.

362. The diagnosis and description of the syndrome of "pseudologia phantastica" is taken from the third edition of Pilcz, *Lehrbuch*, pp. 272–73.

363. Albert Moll, *Sexuelle Perversionen, Geisteskrankheit, und Zurechnungsfähigkeit* (Berlin: Simion, 1905), p. 12.

364. Moll, *Sexualempfindung*, p. 78; *Perversions*, p. 63.

365. Moll, *Sexualempfindung*, p. 116. The translation (*Perversions*), p. 86, misses this sentence.

366. See Hubert Kennedy, *Ulrichs: The Life and Works of Karl Heinrich Ulrichs, Pioneer of the Modern Gay Movement* (Boston: Alyson, 1988).

367. SE 12:15.

368. Ibid. 12:82.

369. My interpretations of Freud's reading of the hysteric, including the case of Dora, have appeared in Gilman, *Difference and Pathology*, pp. 182–84, and *The Jew's Body*, pp. 81–89.

370. SE 7:77.

371. Ibid. 7:171.

372. Paul Julius Möbius, *Die Nervosität* (Leipzig: Weber, 1906), pp. 80–81.

373. SE 2:13.

374. Ibid. 2:5.

375. Octave Mannoni, "Psychoanalysis and the Decolonization of Mankind," trans. Nicholas Fry, in *Freud: The Man, His World, His Influence*, ed. Jonathan Miller (London: Weidenfeld and Nicolson, 1972), p. 93.

CONCLUSION
SYSTEMIC DISEASES: CANCER AND ANTI-SEMITISM

1. See L. J. Rather, *The Genesis of Cancer: A Study in the History of Ideas* (Baltimore: Johns Hopkins University Press, 1978). Rather's book stops at the end of the nineteenth century. See also J. A. Witkowski, "The Inherited Character of Cancer: An Historical Survey," *Cancer Cells* 2 (1990): 228–57; James S. Olson,

ed., *The History of Cancer: An Annotated Bibliography* (New York: Greenwood Press, 1989); S. E. Lederer, "A Cultural History of Cancer," *Medical Humanities Review* 2 (1988): 65–68; J. T. Patterson, *The Dread Disease: Cancer and Modern American Culture* (Cambridge, Mass.: Harvard University Press, 1987); M. J. Imbault-Huart, "Histoire du cancer," *Histoire* (1984): 74–77; B. B. Gallucci, "Selected Concepts of Cancer as a Disease: From the Greeks to 1900," *Oncology Nursing Forum* (1985): 67–71; T. J. Deeley, "A Brief History of Cancer," *Clinical Radiology* (1983): 597–608; S. Peller, *Cancer Research since 1900* (New York: Philosophical Library, 1979).

2. Theodor Boveri, *Zur Frage der Entstehung malingner Tumoren* (Jena: Gustav Fischer, 1914).

3. David von Hansemann, *Die mikroskopische Diagnose der bösartigen Geschwülste* (Berlin: Hirschwald, 1897).

4. Jean de Grouchy, "Theodor Boveri et la théorie chromosomique de la cancerogènese," *Nouvelle revue française d'hématologie/Blood Cells* 18 (1977): 1–4.

5. See B. Fischer-Wasels, *Die Vererbung der Krebskrankheit* (Berlin: Metzner, 1935) which appeared in a series, Schriften zur Erblehre und Rassenhygiene, edited by the eugenist Günther Just.

6. Cesare Lombroso, "Sulla mortalità degli Ebrei di Verona nel Decennio 1855–1864," *Rivista clinica di Bologna* 6 (1867): 3–37.

7. Maurice Sorsby, *Cancer and Race: A Study of the Incidence of Cancer among Jews* (London: John Bale, Sons & Danielsson, 1931), p. 1. (Sorsby's initial publications on this topic are under the name Sourasky.) Following Sorsby, I. Davidsohn, "Cancer among Jews," *Medical Leaves* 2 (1939): 19–27, surveys this question until the end of the decade. (This work is in the Freud Library, London.)

8. M. J. Gutmann, *Über der heutigen Stand der Rasse- und Krankheitsfrage der Juden* (Munich: Rudolph Müller & Steinicke, 1920), pp. 50–51.

9. See Maurice Fishberg's presentation of the fin de siècle material in "Cancer," in *The Jewish Encyclopedia* 12 vols. (New York's Funk and Wagnalls, 1904), 3:529–31.

10. "Cancer among Jews," *The British Medical Journal* (March 15, 1902): 681–82; here, 681.

11. This debate is outlined in more detail by the Viennese physician Sigismund Peller, "Über Krebssterblichkeit der Juden," *Zeitschrift für Krebsforschung* 34 (1931): 128–47; here, 129–31.

12. Sorsby, *Cancer and Race*, p. 77.

13. A. Theilhaber, "Zur Lehre von der Entstehung der Uterustumoren," *Münchener Medizinische Wochenschrift* 56 (1909): 1272–73.

14. See his discussion in Felix Theilhaber, *Die Beschneidung* (Berlin: Lamm, 1927).

15. Leopold Löwenfeld, *Über die sexuelle Konstitution und andere Sexualprobleme* (Wiesbaden: Bergmann, 1911), p. 128 (in the Freud Library, London).

16. A. Theilhaber and S. Greischer, "Zur Aetiologie des Carcinoms," *Zeitschrift für Krebsforschung* 9 (1910): 530–54; here, 548.

17. Felix Theilhaber, "Zur Lehre von dem Zusammenhang der sozialen Stellung und der Rasse mit der Entstehung der Uteruscarcinome" (Ph.D. diss., Munich, 1910), pp. 11–14, and "Zur Lehre von dem Zusammenhang der sozialen

Stellung und der Rasse mit der Entstehung der Uteruscarcinome," *Zeitschrift für Krebsforschung* 8 (1909): 466–88; here, 475–78.

18. F. Theilhaber, "Zusammenhang" (diss.), p. 13.

19. H. N. Vineberg, "The Relative Infrequency of Cancer of the Uterus in Women of the Hebrew Race," *Contributions to Medical and Biological Research Dedicated to Sir William Osler*, 2 vols. (New York: Hoeber, 1919), 2:1217–25; here, 1224.

20. M. H. Pejovic and M. Thuaire, "Étiologie des cancers du col de l'uterus: Le point sur 150 ans de recherché," *Journal de gynécologie, obstétrice, biologie, et reproduction* 15 (1986): 37–43.

21. Wilson I. B. Onuigbo, "Historical Notes on Cancer in Married Couples," *Netherlands Journal of Surgery* 36 (1984): 112–15.

22. Felix A. Theilhaber, "Gesundheitsverhältnisse," in *Jüdisches Lexikon*, ed. Georg Herlitz and Bruno Kirschner, 4 vols. in 5 (Berlin: Jüdischer, 1927–30), 2:1120–41; here, 1138–39 (in the Freud Library, London).

23. See the discussion of cancer in Peter Charles Remondino, *History of Circumcision from the Earliest Times to the Present. Moral and Physical Reasons for Its Performance, with a History of Eunuchism, Hermaphrodism, etc., and of the Different Operations Practiced upon the Prepuce* (Philadelphia: Davis, 1891), pp. 226–30.

24. See the case material on circumcision in Jonathan Hutchinson's periodical, *Archives of Surgery* (London) 2 (1891): 15, 267–69.

25. Jonathan Hutchinson, "The Pre-cancerous Stage of Cancer and the Importance of Early Operations," *British Medical Journal* (1882): 4–7.

26. J. Dellinger Barney, "Epithelioma of the Penis: An Analysis of One Hundred Cases," *Annals of Surgery* 46 (1907): 890–914; here, 894.

27. Benjamin S. Barringer and Archie Dean, "Epithelioma of the Penis," *Journal of Urology* 11 (1924): 497–514, here, 497.

28. Abraham L. Wolbarst, "Is Circumcision a Prophylactic against Penis Cancer?" *Cancer* 3 (1925–26): 301–9; here, 308. This view has a long history. See Abraham Ravich, *Preventing V.D. and Cancer by Circumcision* (New York: Philosophical Library, 1973).

29. Ibid., p. 302.

30. V. Föderl, "Zur Klinik und Statistik des Peniskarzinomes," *Deutsche Zeitschrift für Chirurgie* 198 (1926): 207–30; here, 208.

31. Sorsby, *Cancer and Race*, p. 65.

32. Jonathan Hutchinson, *Syphilis* (London: Cassell, 1887), p. 512. The German translation is Jonathan Hutchinson, *Syphilis*, trans. Artur Kollmann (Leipzig: Arnold, 1888).

33. A. Theilhaber and Felix Theilhaber, "Zur Lehre vom Zusammenhänge von Krebs und Narbe," *Zeitschrift für Krebsforschung* 9 (1910): 554–69; here, 561.

34. Sorsby, *Cancer and Race*, pp. 2–3.

35. Ibid., pp. 79–80.

36. Peller, "Über Krebssterblichkeit der Juden," p. 139.

37. Hans Auler, "Rasse und bösartige Gewächse," in *Rasse und Krankheit*, ed. Johannes Schottky (Munich: Lehmann, 1937), pp. 388–99; here, 395.

38. So, for example, in the summary by the Bucharest physician M. Schachter, "Cancer et race: A propos du cancer chez les Juifs," *Le progrès médical* 50 (December 5, 1931): 2213–14.

39. The most detailed account of the disease is Sharon Romm, *The Unwelcome Intruder: Freud's Struggle with Cancer* (New York: Praeger, 1983). I have also used the following studies: Jose Schavelzon, *Freud, un paciente con cancer* (Buenos Aires: Editorial Paidos, 1983) and Sharon Golub, "Coping with Cancer: Freud's Experiences," *Psychoanalytic Review* 68 (1981): 191–200. I have used also the excerpt from Romm's book included in her *Symposium on Historical Perspectives of Plastic Surgery* (Philadelphia: Saunders, 1983), pp. 709–14, and the commentary on it in that volume by Edward A. Luce, "The Ordeal of Sigmund Freud," pp. 715–16, as well as C. T. Brown, "Freud and Cancer," *Texas Medicine* 70 (1974): 62–64. In addition, I have used the following biographical studies: Max Schur, *Freud: Living and Dying* (New York: International Universities Press, 1972), and Jacob Meitlis, "The Last Days of Sigmund Freud," *Jewish Frontier* 18 (1951): 20–22. Of special interest, as it provides one of the first readings of Freud's cancer, is the parallel drawn between the oral bleeding resulting from Freud's cancer and the oral bleeding in the case of Emma Eckstein by Madelon Sprengnether, *The Spectral Mother: Freud, Feminism, and Psychoanalysis* (Ithaca, N.Y.: Cornell University Press, 1990), pp. 169–71.

40. From a letter to the surgeon Wilfried Trotter, who treated him in London in 1938 and 1939, cited by Schur, *Freud*, p. 520.

41. R. B. Walker, "Medical Aspects of Tobacco Smoking and the Anti-Tobacco Movement in Britain in the Nineteenth Century," *Medical History* 24 (1980): 391–402; here, 395.

42. See Juraj Körbler, "Der Tabak in der Krebslehre zu Anfang des 19. Jahrhunderts," *Atti des 21 internazionale di storia della medici*, 2 vols. (Rome: n.p., 1969), 2:1179–83.

43. Loebisch, "Tabak," in *Real-Encyclopädie der gesammten Heilkunde*, ed. Albert Eulenburg, 26 vols. (Berlin: Urban and Schwarzenberg, 1894–1901): 24:7–22, here, p. 19.

44. M. A. Gilbert, "Hystérie tabagique," *La lancette française* 62 (1889): 1173–74, and Count [Egon Caesar] Corti, *A History of Smoking* (London: Harrap, 1931), p. 260.

45. Leopold Löwenfeld, *Pathologie und Therapie der Neurasthenie und Hysterie* (Wiesbaden: Bergmann, 1894), p. 46 (in the Freud Library, London).

46. See the detailed account of the literature compiled by Paul Näcke, "Der Tabak in der Ätiologie der Psychosen, " *Wiener Klinische Rundschau* 23 (1909): 805–7, 821–24, 840–42.

47. Leopold Löwenfeld, *Die moderne Behandlung der Nervenschwäche (Neurasthenie) der Hysterie und verwandten Leiden* (Wiesbaden: Bergmann, 1887), p. 28 (in the Freud Library, London).

48. Clemens Brentano, "Über die Kennzeichen des Judenthums," reproduced as an appendix to Heinz Härtl, "Arnim und Goethe: Zum Goethe-Verständnis der Romantik im ersten Jahrzehnt des 19. Jahrhunderts" (Ph.D. diss., Halle, 1971), pp. 471–90; see especially p. 474 (on tobacco farming); p. 473 (on tobacco consumption); pp. 484–86 (on the disease of the Jews).

49. Alexander Elster, "Tabakrauchen," in *Handwörterbuch der Sexualwissenschaft*, ed. Max Marcuse (Bonn: Marcus & E. Webers, 1926), pp. 768–69 (in the Freud Library, London).

50. Ernest Jones, *The Life and Work of Sigmund Freud*, 3 vols. (New York: Basic Books, 1953–57), 3:89.

51. Pichler, clinical notes, May 5, 1924, cited in Romm, *Unwelcome Intruder*, p. 88.

52. Jeffrey Moussaieff Masson, ed., *The Complete Letters of Sigmund Freud to Wilhelm Fliess, 1887–1904* (Cambridge, Mass.: Harvard University Press, 1985), p. 60 (smoking heavily); p. 67 (cardiac misery); p. 68 (nicotine heart); p. 84 (depression); p. 124 (depressing business).

53. Jones, *Life and Work of Sigmund Freud* 3:120.

54. Arthur W. Grundy, "My Cigar," in *Pipe and Pouch: The Smoker's Own Book of Poetry*, ed. Joseph Knight (London: Simpkin, Marshall, Hamilton, Kent [1894?]), pp. 2–4; here, pp. 2–3 (in the Freud Library, London). A popular history of tobacco has recently appeared that does not refer in any depth to the medical significance. See V. G. Kiernan, *Tobacco: A History* (London: Hutchinson Radius, 1991).

55. Jones, *Life and Work of Sigmund Freud* 3:121.

56. *The Diary of Sigmund Freud, 1929–1939: A Record of the Final Decade*, ed. and trans. Michael Molnar (New York: Scribner's, 1992), p. 55 (Landauer); p. 85 ("first cigar").

57. Körbler, "Tabak," 2:1183.

58. Felix Deutsch, "Reflections on Freud's One Hundredth Birthday," *Psychosomatic Medicine* 18 (1956): 279.

59. Freud, *Diary*, p. 69. Molnar comments: "the fact that flight from his native land and abstinence from smoking could arouse the same imagery is one small indication—if any more were needed—of the importance of Freud's tobacco addiction" (p. 276).

60. Schur, *Freud*, p. 86.

61. Toby Cohn, "Nervenkrankheiten bei Juden," *Zeitschrift für Demographie und Statistik der Juden*, n.s. 3 (1926): 76–85; here, 85.

62. Gustave Le Bon, *La fumée du tabac: Recherches chimiques et physiologiques* (Paris: Asselin, 1880), p. 37.

63. Romm, *Unwelcome Intruder*, p. 38.

64. Sorsby, *Cancer and Race*, p. 34.

65. See, for example, Marianne Krüll, *Freud und sein Vater: Die Entstehung der Psychoanalyse und Freuds ungelöste Vaterbindung* (Munich: Beck, 1979), and Marie Balmary, *L'homme aux statues: Freud et la faute cachée du père* (Paris: Grasset, 1979).

66. SE 4:197.

67. Cited by Molnar in Freud, *Diary*, p. 297.

68. B. W. Richardson, "Cancer amongst the Jews," *Asclepiad* 8 (1891): 145–46.

69. Madison Marsh, "Jews and Christians," *Medical and Surgical Reporter* (Philadelphia) 30 (1874): 343–44; here, 343.

70. Ibid., p. 343.

71. See the debate following the presentation of Joseph Jacobs, "On the Racial Characteristics of Modern Jews," *Journal of the Anthropological Institute* 16 (1886): 23–63; here, 56 and 61.

72. Marsh, "Jews and Christians," p. 344.

73. Ibid.

74. Joseph Krauskopf, *Sanitary Science: A Sunday Lecture* (Philadelphia: Goodman, 1889), p. 7.

75. Ephraim M. Epstein, "Have the Jews Any Immunity from Certain Diseases?" *Medical and Surgical Reporter* (Philadelphia) 30 (1874): 440–41; here, 440.

76. Ibid., 441.

77. Ibid.

78. Carl Claus, *Grundzüge der Zoologie zum Gebrauche an Universitäten und höheren Lehranstalten sowie zum Selbststudium*, 2 vols. (Marburg: Elwerts Universitäts-Buchhandlung, 1872).

79. Madison Marsh, "Have the Jews Any Immunity from Certain Diseases?" *Medical and Surgical Reporter* (Philadelphia) 31 (1874): 132–34.

80. Ibid., 133.

81. Ibid.

82. Ibid.

83. Ibid.

84. Ibid., 134.

85. Remondino, *History of Circumcision*, p. 186. Remondino's book was only published in 1891, but he notes in his introduction that it had been written decades earlier.

86. Stuart Creighton Miller, *"Benevolent Assimilation": The American Conquest of the Philippines, 1899–1903* (New Haven: Yale University Press, 1982), p. 75.

87. See, in this context, Ilse Grubich-Simitis, *Freuds Moses-Studie als Tagestraum: Ein biographischer Essay* (Weinheim: Verlag internationale Psychoanalyse, 1991); Susann Heenen-Wolff, "Les travaux de Freud sur Moïse et sa relation au judaïsme et à l'antisémitisme," *Le coq-héron* 120 (1991): 9–17; David Bakan, "A Note on Freud's Idea that Moses Was an Egyptian as Scriptural and Traditional," *Journal of the History of the Behavioral Sciences* 25 (1989): 163–64; Ritchie Robertson, "Freud's Testament: *Moses and Monotheism*," in *Freud in Exile*, ed. Edward Timms and Naomi Segal (New Haven: Yale University Press, 1988), pp. 80–89; Michael P. Carroll, "*Moses and Monotheism* and the Psychoanalytic Study of Early Christian Mythology," *Journal of Psychohistory* 15 (1988): 295–310; Philip Rieff, "Intimations of Therapeutic Truth: Decoding Appendix G in *Moses and Monotheism*," *Humanities in Society* 4 (1981): 197–201; Jean Jofen, "A Freudian Interpretation of Freud's *Moses and Monotheism*," *Michigan Academician* 12 (1979–80): 231–40; Edwin R. Wallace IV, "The Psychodynamic Determinants of *Moses and Monotheism*," *Psychiatry* 40 (1977): 79–87; Martin S. Bergmann, "Moses and the Evolution of Freud's Jewish Identity," *Israel Annals of Psychiatry and Related Disciplines* 14 (1976): 3–26.

88. Cited by Molnar in Freud, *Diary*, p. 255.

89. From a review in the *New York Times* by Charles Poore, reprinted in *Freud without Hindsight: Reviews of His Work (1893–1939)*, ed. Norman Kiell (Madison, Conn.: International Universities Press, 1988), p. 640.

90. *Sigmund Freud–Arnold Zweig: Briefwechsel*, ed. Ernst L. Freud (Frankfurt a. M.: Fischer, 1968), p. 172; translation from *The Letters of Sigmund Freud and Arnold Zweig*, ed. Ernst L. Freud, trans. Elaine Robson-Scott and William Robson-Scott (New York: Harcourt, Brace & World, 1970), p. 163. Compare Johannes Cremerius, "Arnold Zweig—Sigmund Freud: Das Schicksal einer agierten Übertragungsliebe," *Psyche* 27 (1973): 658–68, and Arie Wolf, *Grösse und Tragik Arnold Zweigs: Ein jüdisch-deutsches Dichterschicksal in Jüdischer Sicht* (London: World of Books, 1991).

91. GW Nachtragsband: 784.

92. Houston Stewart Chamberlain, *Foundations of the Nineteenth Century*, trans. John Lees, 2 vols. (London: John Lane/The Bodley Head, 1913), 1:442–43; GW Nachtragsband; 787.

93. SE 4:94–95, 102–3, 308–9; 14:13–20; 18:263–65; 19:261–63.

94. Ibid. 22:224.

95. Ibid. 23:10.

96. Ibid. 23:25–26.

97. Ibid. 23:43.

98. J. G. Frazer, *Totemism and Exogamy: A Treatise on Certain Early Forms of Superstition and Society*, 4 vols. (1910; London: Dawsons of Pall Mall, 1968), 4:26.

99. Cited by Molnar in Freud, *Diary*, p. xvi.

100. George Sylvester Viereck, *Glimpses of the Great* (New York: Macaulay, 1930), p. 30.

101. Molnar, in Freud, *Diary*, p. xvii.

102. The complexities of the Freudian approach to the meaning of circumcision can be judged in Herman Nunberg, *Problems of Bisexuality as Reflected in Circumcision* (London: Imago, 1949).

103. SE 23:30–31.

104. *Manetho*, trans. W. G. Waddell (Cambridge, Mass.: Harvard University Press, 1940), p. 123; SE 22:105.

105. *Manetho*, p. 131.

106. SE 23:52.

107. Ibid. 23:77

108. Theodor Reik, "Die Pubertätsriten der Wilden: Über einige Übereinstimmungen im Seelenleben der Wilden und der Neurotiker," *Imago* 6 (1915–16): 125–44, 189–222; English translation in Theodor Reik, *Ritual: Psycho-Analytic Studies*, trans. Douglas Bryan (London: Hogarth Press, 1931), p. 111.

109. Theodor Reik, *Mystery on the Mountain: The Drama of the Sinai Revelation* (New York: Harper, 1959), p. 90.

110. SE 23:79.

111. Ibid. 23:122.

112. Ibid. 23:30.

113. Philip Rieff, "The Authority of the Past: Sickness and Society in Freud's Thought," *Social Research* 51 (1984): 527–50; here, 533.

114. Ritchie Robertson, " 'My True Enemy': Freud and the Catholic Church, 1927–39," in *Austria in the Thirties: Culture and History*, ed. Kenneth Segar and John Warren (Riverside, Calif.: Ariadne Press, 1991), pp. 328–44, and Yosef Hayim Yerushalmi, *Freud's Moses: Judaism Terminable and Interminable* (New Haven: Yale University Press, 1991), pp. 28–29.

115. Wilhelm Schmidt, "Das Rassenprinzip des Nationalsozialismus," *Schönere Zukunft* 7 (1932): 999–1000.

116. Wilhelm Schmidt, "Zur Judenfrage," *Schönere Zukunft* 9 (1934): 408–9.

117. Wilhelm Schmidt, *The Origin and Growth of Religion*, trans. H. J. Rose (London: Methuen, 1931), p. 115.

118. Wilhelm Schmidt, "Der Ödipus-Komplex der Freudschen Psychoanalyse und die Ehegestaltung des Bolschwismus," *Nationalwirtschaft* (Berlin) 2 (1929): 401–36.

119. SE 23:33.

120. Josef Popper-Lynkeus, *Phantasien eines Realisten* (Leipzig: Kiepenheuer, 1986), p. 44 (in the Freud Library, London, in the 1909 edition; Freud checked two titles in the table of contents: one, the story of Confucius, the other, the tale of the confrontation of Martin Luther with an Eastern Jew). See Jacques Le Rider, "La signification de Josef Popper-Lynkeus pour Sigmund Freud," *Austriaca* 11 (1985): 27–33; O. Renik, "Neurotic and Narcissistic Transferences in Freud's Relationship with Josef Popper," *Psychoanalytic Quarterly* 47 (1978): 389–418; and E. S. Wolf, "Freud and Popper-Lynkeus," *Journal of the American Psychoanalytic Association* 22 (1974): 123–41.

121. SE 23:81.

122. H. C. Jelgersma, "Der Kannibalismus und seine Verdrängung im alten Ägypten," *Imago* 14 (1928): 275–92.

123. See David H. Spain et al., "The Westermarck-Freud Incest Theory Debate: An Evaluation and Reformulation," *Current Anthropology* 28 (1987): 623–35, and M. L. Rodrigues de Areia and David H. Spain, "On the Westermarck-Freud Incest Theory Debate," *Current Anthropology* 29 (1988): 313–14.

124. SE 23:121.

125. Ibid. This rejection may also have a personal dimension. Freud's anxiety about methods of birth control and his fear of impotence lead to the image of an individual struggling with the realities of his own sexuality in the context of his aging and his wife's (and his) health. See the discussion in Peter Gay, *Freud: A Life for Our Time* (New York: Norton, 1988), pp. 162–64.

126. SE 23:85.

127. Ibid.

128. Ibid. 23:90.

129. Ibid.

130. Ibid. 23:90–91.

131. Harold P. Blum, "Freud and the Figure of Moses: The Moses of Freud," *Journal of the American Psychoanalytic Association* 39 (1991): 513–35.

132. Freud evoked the questions of incest, inbreeding, and crossbreeding associated with the Jews in the unpublished preface to *Moses and Monotheism*. Freud's project in writing his "historical novel" about Moses was an attempt to

create a fruitful hybrid. Freud began his preface with a theoretical statement about the nature of the relationship between fiction and history: "As the sexual union of horse and donkey produces two different hybrids, the mule and the hinny, so the mixture of historical writing and free invention gives rise to different products which, under the common designation of historical novel, sometimes want to be appreciated as history, sometimes as a novel" (Yosef Hayim Yerushalmi, "Freud on the 'Historical Novel': From the Manuscript Draft [1934] of *Moses and Monotheism*," *International Journal of Psychoanalysis* 70 [1989]: 375–95; here, 379). Following the completion of this chapter, I read Yerushalmi's longer historical analysis of Freud's text, *Freud's Moses*, which outlines the historical context of the writing of this text and stresses the importance of this text to any discussion of Freud's Jewish identity.

133. SE 23:90–91.

134. Ibid. 23:135.

135. Ibid. 23:136.

136. Freud and Zweig, *Briefwechsel*, pp. 101–4; here, p. 102; translation from *Letters of Sigmund Freud and Arnold Zweig*, p. 91.

137. Arnold Zweig, *Caliban oder Politik und Leidenschaft: Versuch über die menschlichen Gruppenleidensschaften dargetan am Antisemitismus* (Potsdam: Kiepenheuer, 1927), p. 188.

138. Ibid., p. 190.

139. Ibid., p. 193.

140. Arnold Zweig, *Bilanz der deutschen Judenheit 1933* (Amsterdam: Querido, 1934), pp. 63–66 (in the Freud Library, London). The translation is *Insulted and Exiled: The Truth about the German Jews*, trans. Eden Paul and Ceder Paul (London: Miles, 1937); here, p. 43. On the background of this text, see Jost Hermand, " 'Jetzt wohin?' Arnold Zweigs *Bilanz der deutschen Judenheit 1933*," in *Internationales Arnold Zweig-Symposium aus Anlass des 100. Geburtstage*, ed. David Midgley, Hans-Harald Müller, and Geoffrey Davis (Bern: Lang, 1989), pp. 202–18.

141. Zweig, *Bilanz*, p. 68; *Insulted and Exiled*, p. 46.

142. Zweig, *Bilanz*, pp. 68–75; *Insulted and Exiled*, pp. 46–55.

143. Zweig, *Bilanz*, pp. 93–97; *Insulted and Exiled*, pp. 67–72.

144. Zweig, *Bilanz*, p. 93; *Insulted and Exiled*, p. 67.

145. Zweig, *Bilanz*, p. 88; *Insulted and Exiled*, p. 62.

146. Zweig, *Bilanz*, p. 93; *Insulted and Exiled*, p. 67.

147. Zweig, *Bilanz*, p. 99; *Insulted and Exiled*, p. 72.

148. Ernst Simmel, "Anti-Semitism and Mass Psychology," in *Anti-Semitism: A Social Disease*, ed. Ernst Simmel (New York: International Universities Press, 1946), pp. 33–78; here, p. 35.

149. Susan A. Handelman, *The Slayers of Moses: The Emergence of Rabbinic Interpretation in Modern Literary Theory* (Albany: State University of New York Press, 1982), p. 139.

150. Quoted by Sándor Ferenczi in a paper written in 1913, "Stages in the Development of the Sense of Reality," in his *First Contributions to Psycho-Analysis*, trans. Ernest Jones (London: Hogarth Press, 1952), p. 237.

151. SE 23:101.

152. Paul Brienes, *Tough Jews: Political Fantasies and the Moral Dilemma of American Jewry* (New York: Basic Books, 1990), especially the chapter "Sigmund Freud's Tough Jewish Fantasy, Philip Roth's, and Mine," pp. 1–75. My reading is quite different from that of Brienes.

153. Martin Freud, *Glory Reflected: Sigmund Freud—Man and Father* (London: Angus and Robertson, 1957), p. 71.

INDEX

Page numbers in boldface type refer to illustrations.

Abraham, Karl, 104, 249n.246; on Jewish discourse, 34; letters to, 34, 143
Abrahamsen, David: letter to, 78
Abravanel, Isaac, 63
Adler, Alfred, 31, 44–45, 81, 142
Adorno, Theodor, 82
Alexander, Carl, 68
Allbutt, Sir Clifford, 125
Alsberg, Moritz, 100
Americans: debate among, about circumcision, 182–83, 220n.9; diseases of, 95, 106, 119, 130; psychoanalytic debates of, about Jews, 112–13, **121**; studies of mental diseases by, 243–44n.138
Andree, Richard, 23, 49, 152
Anthropophyteia, 127
anti-Semitism: as anxiety of the uncircumcised, 77, 81–82; associated with trains, 126–27; in European medicine, 12, 64–65, 93, 94, 98, 102, 115, 209–10n.35, 210n.36; and German and Austrian nationalism, 35, 105, 168, 183, 186; Jewish, 78, 109–11; Jewish body at heart of, 182; linked to paranoia and homosexuality, 135, 196–98; in Paris, 23; perceived as disease, 81–82, 137–38, 183, 191–92, 194; period of, in Europe, 13, 39, 122, 168; studies and interpretations of, 76, 195–98, 233n.174. *See also* Germans; Vienna, fin de siècle
Anzieu, Didier, 15
Aristotle, 79, 90
Aryans: and anxiety about castration, 82–83, 84, 91, 109; vs. Jews, 17, 21, 44, 49, 79, 80–81, 98, 176; male, vs. male Jews, 10, 40, 61, 92; mind of, Freud on, 23, 30, 32–33, 83, 110
Asher, Dr., 180
Autenrieth, Johann Heinrich Ferdinand von, 54; lecture by, on circumcision, 58
Averbeck, Heinrich, 95
Axenfeld, August, 124

Bainbridge, W. S., 171
Baldwin, James Mark, 27
Bamberger, Heinrich von, 116
Barney, J. Dellinger, 172
Barringer, Benjamin S., 172
Beadles, Cecil F., 119–20
Becker, Raphael, 6, 111, 112
Benedikt, Moritz, 117–18, **120**
Berbiguier, Alexis, 132
Bergson, J., 60, 66
Bernard de Gordon: *Lilium Medicinae*, 156–57
Bernays, Isaac, 17
Bernays, Minna: letter to, 17
Bernheim, Hippolyte: Freud and, 123
Bernstein, Ignaz: proverb collection of, 157, 254n.312
Bettauer, Hugo: *The City without Jews*, 48
Bettelheim, Bruno, 233n.174
Bettelheim, Josef, 16
Bible: Jews of the, 148–49; New Testament, Nietzsche and, 150, 151
Billings, John S., 136–37
Billroth, Theodor, 18
Binswanger, Otto, 99
bisexuality: Freud's views of, 47, 79, 87–88; Groddeck on, 81; Weiniger's theory of, 78–80
Bismarck, Otto von, 154
blacks, 32; Jews as, **19**, 19–22, 158, 164; Tuskegee experiments on, 64; whites vs., 18, 32, 181
Blanton, Smiley, 16, 29, 33
Bleuler, Eugen, 11, 135, 137, 140, 143
Bloch, Iwan, 109, 156
Bloom, Harold, 3
Blumenbach, Johann Friedrich, 53, 54
B'nai B'rith: Freud's membership in and address to, 24, 25, 214n.109; link of, to circumcision, 25
body, Jewish, 11, 24; Aryan fantasy concerning, 81–82; and defecation, 155–56, 253n.304; as different, 53, 83–84, 152–

body, Jewish (*cont.*)
53; Freud's evocation of, 25, 38; need for muscular development of, 104–5, 112; stomach, 155; as superior and healthy, debates about, 20, 63, 179–83. *See also* circumcision; genitalia; homosexuality; male, Jewish; odor; physiognomy, Jewish; skin (of Jews); voice (of Jews)
Bonaparte, Marie (princess of Greece), 42
Bourke, John Gregory: *Scatalogic Rites of All Nations*, 156
Boveri, Theodor, 170
Braithwaite, James, 170
Braun, Leopold, 34
Brecher, Gideon, 54, 66
Brentano, Clemens, 176
Breuer, Josef, 6, 15, 26, 62; *Studies on Hysteria* (with Freud), 87, 91, 103, 167
Brill, Abraham Aron, 63, 137; background of, 6, 111, 140; and case of I.S., 137–40, 143–46, 161, 166; on Jewishness as a racial matter, 140–41
Brosius, Dr., 111–12
Brown-Séquard, C. E., 125, 131
Brücke, Ernst Wilhelm, 71
Budul, H., 63, 103
Burgle, Georg, 95
Burton, Sir Richard, 49
Burton, Robert: *The Anatomy of Melancholy*, 74
Buschan, Georg, 94, 246n.178
Byron, George Gordon, Lord: *Manfred*, 252n.281

cancer: Jews and certain forms of, debate about, 179; Jews as susceptible to, 20, 170–74, 187; and race, role of in origin of, 170–74; studies of (mouth and jaw), 173–74, **174**, 179; studies of (penile), 172–73; understanding of, in late 19th century, 169–70
Canetti, Elias, 141
castration: Aryan anxiety about, 82–83, 84, 91, 109; and females, 77, 81, 84, 85, 87, 105. *See also* circumcision; Freud, Sigmund: Publications and writings—topics, themes, views
Chadwick, Edwin, 41
Chamberlain, Houston Stewart, 21, 184
Charcot, Jean-Martin, 91, 101, 117, 122, 129, 167, 246n.178, 251n.264; Freud's break with, 87, 89, 166; Freud's study

with, 23, 115, 123; his model of hysteria, 124; Nordau's dissertation with, 105; *Tuesday Lessons*, 94
Christians, Christianity: critiques of, 150, 151, 162; Freud on, 193, 194; vs. Jews, 9, 12, 32, 34, 157, 194; meaning of circumcision for, 57, 60, 75–76; in medical tests vs. Jews, 100, 103, 121–22
circumcision: attacks on, 57–58; and castration complex, 70, 71–72, 83, 144, 251n.264; as common and universal practice, 51, 172; congenital, debate over, 52–56, 66; and definition of Jew, 49, 57, 60; different meanings for, 220n.6, 221n.9; Freud and, 70–77, 83–89, 91, 186, 187, 188–92; link of, with syphilis, 66–69, 158; as marker of difference, 21, 44–45, 46, 51, 52, 53, 62, 81, 85–86, 152, 172, 181; medical and prophylactic considerations about, 40, 59, 60–62, 65–69, 171, 172, 182–83; move to abolish, and debate, 59–60, 67–68; religious and ritual meanings of, 25, 49–51, 50, 56–59, 77, 187–88; ritual instruments of, 50, 60, 67. See also *metsitsah*
city, the: and Jews, 62, 93, 97, 101, 102, 111, 119–20, 130, 235n.1; as place of disease, 130
Claus, Carl, 71, 79, 181, 230n.135; Freud's work with, 74, 75
Cohen, Israel: letter to, 23
Crawley, Ernest, 58
Czermak, Josef, 103

Daniels, Arthur H., 83
Darwin, Charles, 72, 230n.135; his model of inheritance, 71; his model of sexual selection, 97, 153, 192; *The Variation of Animals and Plants under Domestication*, 54
Dean, Archie, 172
Deutsch, Felix, 174, 179
Diaspora: the Jew in, 10, 62, 90, 100, 109, 116, 131
disease (and Jews), 3–4, 11; immunity of, to certain types, and debate, 179–83. *See also* Jews, racial stereotypes concerning
diseases of Jews: alcoholism, 64, 102, 110, 111, 160–61; "Americanism," 130–31; "civilization," 62, 87, 90, 95, 97–99, 111, 119–20, 124, 130; drug addiction, 107; hemorrhoids, 156–57; "Jewish-

ness," 66, 101, 110, 159; leprosy, 61, 157; of nervous system, 243–44n.138; sexually transmitted, 65, 66, 69; tuberculosis, 76. *See also* cancer; syphilis

Doryon, Yisrael: letter to, 184

Drumont, Edouard: *La France juive*, 122

Eckstein, Emma, 177, 259n.39

Eder, Montague David, 33

Egyptians: ancient, and enslavement of Jews, 137; and circumcision, 187–88; Moses as leader of, 181, 184; religion of, 185–86, 189; ritual practice of, 191

Ehrenfels, Christian von, 97–99

Einstein, Albert, 184

Eitingon, Max: letter to, 30

Ellis, Havelock, 80, 84, 85, 163

Elster, Alexander, 176

Engelken, Friedrich, 132–33

Engländer, Martin: *The Most Striking Appearances of Illness in the Jewish Race*, 100–101, 106

Enlightenment, the, 22, 93, 148

Epstein, Ephraim M., 64; and debate about Jews and health, 180–83

Erasmus, Desiderius, 57

Erb, Wilhelm, 99–100

Erikson, Erik, 233n.174

Esquirol, J.E.D., 132

Eusebius, 57

Feer, Emil, 240n.82

female: as castrated, 77, 81, 84, 85, 87, 105, 126; vs. male, 8, 40; and mental illness, 40, 113, 115; as narcissistic, 46–48; as needed and desired object, 48; as powerless, 82–83; stereotypes of, 7, 8–9; as unknowable, 36, 38, 41, 42. *See also* genitalia; male, Jewish

Fenichel, Otto, 82, 233n.174

Ferenczi, Sándor, 6; letters to, 30, 34, 43, 135, 177

Feuerbach, Ludwig, 155

Fishberg, Maurice, 111, 157; *The Jews: A Study of Race and Environment*, 116–17, 122

Flateau, Dr. Theodor S., 164

Flechsig, Paul Emil, 141, 144, 145, 147, 150, 154, 157, 161, 164

Fliess, Wilhelm, 43; his correspondence with Freud, 79, 91, 165, 177; his relationship with Freud, 126, 128, 142, 167; and Weiniger's book, 78–79

Fluss, Emile: letters to, 13, 26

Föderl, V., 172

Forel, Auguste, 58, 104, 133, 251n.262; Freud's review of, 17, 18, 29; *The Sexual Question*, 130–31

Frazer, J. B., 185

Frederick II (king of Prussia), 86

Frerichs, Friedrich Theodor, 129

Freud, Adolfine (aunt), 45

Freud, Amalia Nathanson (mother), 70

Freud, Anna (daughter), 175

Freud, Kallamon Jacob (father), 3, 70, 89, 91; as model, 127, 178–79, 199

Freud, Martha (wife), 126

Freud, Martin (son), 45, 85–86

Freud, Moriz (brother-in-law), 165

FREUD, SIGMUND. Life and career

—anti-Semitism: constructs of, avoidance, 141, 143; experiences of, 13, 16, 18, 23, 126–27, 178, 198, 199

—events and stages: birth and circumcision, 70; cancer of jaw, 165, 174–75, 177, 178, 259n.39; death, 177; flight from Austria and settling in England, 175, 186, 199; home in Vienna, 14; at University of Vienna, 18, 62, 94–95, 106

—family and friends: father as model, 127, 178–79, 199; homoerotic identification with Fliess, 142; parents, 70

—Jewish identity: as central problem, 6, 10–11, 128, 140–41; distancing from, 15, 178; dreams about, 12, 126, 127, 128; falsification of personal history, 242n.117; feeling of solidarity, 35; given name, 70; as male, 8, 116, 127; as male scientist-physician, 3, 5, 10, 12, 31, 33, 37, 126, 129, 130, 167, 184–85, 204n.3; as racial, 6, 19, 23; and religion, 7, 22–23, 188; scholarly questions about, 3–5; self-analysis, 126, 167; self-hatred, 154; status, anxiety about, 12, 125–26, 167, 186; and train neurosis, 125–28; and women scientists, 10

—language and discourse, 16; as different from Eastern European Jew, 15; German language, 13, 16, 186; and illness, with resulting difficulty of speech, 175, 190; scientific, mastery of, 115, 166–67

—library, books in, 50, 78, 96, 106–7, 176, 177, 218n.165, 252n.282, 263n.120

FREUD, SIGMUND (*cont.*)
—membership in groups and societies: B'nai B'rith, 24, 25; International Society for the Protection of Mothers and Sexual Reform, 22, 97; Reading Circle of the German Students in Vienna, 18; Vienna Psychoanalytic Society, 35
—readings, 56, 75, 94, 96, 162, 172, 177
—scientific model: and biological thinking, phylogenic model, 24, 70, 75; distance and neutrality, as essential to, 41, 44, 146, 166, 167, 186, 193, 194, 199; his focus on universal, rather than racial, 96, 100, 115, 131; and Lamarkian model, 70, 71, 189, 198; and statistical argument, 91; and status of scientific observation, 37, 44, 91, 123, 166
—smoking habit, 174, 175–76, 177, 260n.59; seen as beneficial, 177–78
—speeches and lectures: on anxiety, 26; to B'nai B'rith, 24, 25; on feminity, 45, 46–47; on male hysteria, 114–15; at Psychoanalytic Congress, 31
—studies and medical background: in biological science and eel gonads, 71, 74–75; experience in syphilogy, 61; in Paris, 23, 115, 167; in Vienna, 15, 16
FREUD, SIGMUND. Publications and writings, general
—genres: autobiography, 14; lecture on femininity, 45, 46–47; letters, 13, 16, 17, 22, 23, 26, 29, 30, 32–35, 43, 78, 91, 135, 136, 143, 165, 177, 183, 184, 186, 217n.143; "reading" of cases, 137–38, 140–41, 143–46, 196; review of Forel, 17, 18, 29; translation of Charcot, 94, 251n.264
—on Jews: as colored, 19, 32–33; common mental and racial memory of, 24–25, 33–35, 43, 89, 192, 193, 198; and construction of masculinity, 15, 37–38, 127, 188–89, 192, 198–99; as different, 16, 22, 28, 43, 44; Eastern European, 13–16, 30, 165; mind, and emotional construction of, 22, 26–28, 30–31, 33–36; as mixed race, 21, 28, 42, 44; as psychologically different from Aryans, 23, 30, 110; as unknowable, 34–35, 36
—sources, 23, 25, 27, 57, 58, 63, 95–96, 99–100, 145–46
—special cases and studies: Dora, 57, 79, 84, 167; Leonardo, 83, 142; Little Hans,

72, 77, 78, 84, 87, 154, 251n.264; madness, 132; male hysteria, 114–15; Rat Man, 138; Wolf Man, 75–76. *See also* Schreber, Daniel Paul
—topics, themes, views: anti-Semitism, 28–29, 81–83, 182, 191–94, 197, 199; bisexuality, 47, 79, 87–88; castration complex, 70, 71–72, 76–77, 83, 85, 145, 146, 154, 163; circumcision, 70, 74–75, 80–81, 83, 85; dreams, theory of, 184; female sexuality, 38–40, 218nn.165 and 169; healthy family, 99; homosexuality, 83, 135–38, 140–41, 142, 144, 163, 168; hysteria, 88–91, 113–15, 122, 124, 146; Jewish role in psychoanalysis, 29–30, 33–35, 42; narcissism, 46–47; neuroses, trauma theory of, 87–89, 123, 125; Oedipus complex, 3, 70, 90, 134, 137, 144, 145, 185; paranoia, 135, 146, 167, 251n.264; puberty, 145; race and gender, as central, 10, 37, 43, 46; sexuality, 41–42, 74, 75; trauma, 87–89, 123–26, 129–30
FREUD, SIGMUND. Works
—*Civilization and Its Discontents*, 22, 29, 84, 86
—" 'Civilized' Sexual Morality and Modern Nervous Illness," 96–97, 99
—"Etiology of Hysteria," 89
—*Future of an Illusion, The*, 29
—*Group Psychology*, 185, 195
—"Heredity and the Etiology of the Neuroses," 87–89
—*Interpretation of Dreams, The*, 106, 134, 144, 157, 246n.191
—*Introductory Lectures on Psycho-Analysis*, 90
—*Jokes and Their Relationship to the Unconscious*, 34, 128–30
—*Moses and Monotheism (The Man Moses and the Monotheistic Religion)*: on anti-Semitism, 183, 191–92; history of Jews in, 182, 193–94, 198, 199; image of Moses in, 183–84, 186, 193; importance of, 183, 264n.132; language of Moses, 190; murder of Moses, 193, 198, 199; religion of Moses, 185, 186, 188–89; sources for, 183–85; unpublished preface to, 263–64n.132
—*New Introductory Lectures on Psychoanalysis*: on role of scientist, 43–44
—*Outline of Psychoanalysis, An*, 70
—*Psychopathology of Everyday Life*, 27

—*Studies on Hysteria* (with Breuer), 87, 133, 167; case of Anna O., 103; case of Katherina, 91
—*Thoughts for the Times on War and Death*, 214n.109
—*Three Essays on the Theory of Sexuality*, 36–37, 39
—*Totem and Taboo*, 27, 81, 146, 185; preface to Hebrew edition, 35–36
Fribe, Melchior, 54
Frigyes, Ludwig, 102

Galton, Francis: his model of seeing the Jew's gaze, 122; his photographs of the "essence" of the Jew, 72–74, **73**, 91, 159, 185
Gaupp, Richard, 106
Gay, Peter: biographical work on Freud, 6–7; *A Godless Jew*, 6
Geiser, Bruno, 141
gender: and cancer, 171–72, 173; and causes of neuroses, 88; as discourse in Freud's writings, 37, 45; and hysteria, 7, 115, 242n.118
genitalia: aesthetic qualities, 84–85, 86; and castration complex, 71–72, 77; female, clitoris, 38–39, 42; male, 38–39, 40, 49; and sexual identity, 45. *See also* male, Jewish; penis
German(s): anti-Semitism of, 82, 135, 168, 183, 186, 192; as chosen people, 149; Freud and the, 27–28; language, 13, 16, 149, 186, 190; national movement, 35, 105, 168, 183, 186; and paranoia about Jews, 135, 196–97; view of women, 40
Gilman, Charlotte Perkins, 78
globus hystericus, 90, 113–14, 115
Goethe, Johann Wolfgang von: *The Elective Affinities*, 80; *Faust*, 252n.281
Goldstein, Kurt, 102
Gomperz, Theodor, 93
Griesinger, Wilhelm: study of mentally ill, 132, 133, 144
Groddeck, Georg, 81
Gross, Hans, 42
Gross, Otto, 42
Günther, Hans F. K., 74, 253n.289
Gutmann, Moses Julius, 56, 101, 162

Haeckel, Ernst, 71
Haizmann, Christoph, 251n.264
Hajek, Marcus, 174–75
Hall, G. Stanley, 83

Hall, Leslie A., 8
Hansemann, David von, 170
Hartmann, Eduard von, 139, 184
Haslam, John: *Illustrations of Madness*, 134
Heberstreit, E.B.C., 41
Hegel, G.F.W., 83
Heidegger, Martin, 217n.153
Heine, Heinrich, 45, 186, 187
Herik, Judith Van, 7
Hermant, Abel, 80
"Herr Moriz Deutschösterreicher," 69
Herzl, Theodor, 13, 14, 100, 161; *The New Ghetto*, 12, 127
Hilferding, Margarete, 10
Hintschmann, Eduard, 24
Hippocrates: *The Physician*, 33
Hirschfeld, Magnus, 43, 47
Hirschl, Joseph Adolf, 62
Hitler, Adolf, 82, 106; *My Struggle*, 62–63, 196–97
Hofmannsthal, Hugo von, 21, 22
Holdheim, Samuel, 59–60, 67
Homan, Peter, 4
homosexuality, 79, 231n.150; anti-Semitism linked to, 196–98; Freud's interpretation of, 135–38, 140–41, 142, 144, 163, 168, 251n.264; linked to the Jews, 136, 162–65; as "third sex," 43, 47, 166; the voice and, 164–65
Hoppe, Hugo, 64
Horn, Siegfried, 19
Horowitz, Lazar, 68
Hughes, C. W., 89
Hutchinson, Jonathan, 63, 67, 172
"Hygiene and the Jews," 103
hysteria: causes of, 88, 89, 114, 115, 125; Jews and, 62, 64, 94, 111, 115; linked to tobacco, 176; as universal illness, 91, 115, 167
hysteria, male: Eastern European Jews subject to, 111, 116–17, **118**, **119**, 120, 122–23; Freud's study of, 114–15, 116, 166–67; trauma as cause for, 123

Ibsen, Henrik, 158; *Ghosts*, 158
Imago, 85, 191, 249n.239
International Society for the Protection of Mothers and Sexual Reform, 22

Jackson, Hughlings, 124
Jacobs, Joseph, 122

Jaeger, Gustav, 152
Jaffé, Julius, 67
Jahn, Friedrich "Turnvater," 105
James, William, 24
Janet, Pierre, 140
Jekels, Ludwig, 6
Jelgersma, H. C., 191
Jellife, Smith Ely, 111
Jellinek, Adolf, 42–43
Jensen, Wilhelm: *Gradiva*, 142–43
Jesenská, Milena, 20
Jews, Eastern European, 26; as dirty, 103,
    151; and disease, 63, 103, 157; as essen-
    tial Jew, 159, 165; as excluded Other, 9,
    14, 15, 16, 76, 190; Freud and, 13–16,
    165; as hysteria prone, 116–17, **118, 119,**
    120, 122; language of, 13, 15, 16, 130,
    190; sexuality of, 254n.312; at special
    risk of mental illness, 94, 103, 111, 113,
    120; and trauma of moves to West, 94,
    109; in U.S., 111, 112; vs. Western Euro-
    pean Jews, 9–10, 68, 96, 104
Jews, images of: as dangerous, 26, 135, 142;
    as limping, 117, **118**; of unstable social
    status, 86; Wandering Jew, 12–13, 31,
    117, 144, 153–54. *See also* Jews, racial
    stereotypes concerning
Jews, racial stereotypes concerning: vs. Ary-
    ans, 17, 21, 44, 49, 79, 80–81, 98, 176;
    as black(s), **19,** 19–22, 158, 164; with
    common mental construction, 112, 122;
    as corrupt and degenerate, 21, 62, 82, 99,
    101, 106, 129, 161, 165; as different, 8,
    9, 12–13, 49, 51, 152–53; as diseased,
    20–21, 33, 37, 45, 51, 61–63, 65, 69,
    183, 187, 195; as healthy and immune
    from disease, 20, 63, 179–83; as hidden
    and unknowable, 36–37, 42, 182; as infe-
    rior, 18, 29, 74; as a mixed race, 21, 22,
    102; as narcissistic, 47–48; as racially
    pure, 180; as unchanging, 23–24, 53,
    102; as white, 181. *See also* body, Jewish;
    diseases of Jews; mental illness: predispo-
    sition of Jews to
Jews, Western European: as acculturated
    and successful, 13, 14, 179; and Eastern
    European Jews, 9–10, 68, 96, 103, 104;
    as indistinguishable from non-Jews, 51–
    52, 61–62
jokes, Jewish, 91, 127–29
Jones, Ernest, 30, 75, 111; letters to, 29, 34,
    177

Joseph, Jacques, 160
Judaism: attacks on, 59; called a gastro-
    nomical cult, 155; as a disease, 186–87;
    essence of, linked to circumcision, 57, 77,
    222n.15; Freud and, 22–23; and gender,
    7; and paranoia, 250n.262; and racial
    identity, 17, 107; reformed, platform for,
    59. *See also* religious practices, Jewish
Judenkratze, 20
Juliusburger, Otto, 110
Jung, Carl Gustav, 140, 141, 143; on femi-
    ninity of Jewish male, 31–32, 42, 43;
    Freud and, 32–33, 34, 142; on the Jews,
    31–32, 110, 166; *The Psychology of De-
    mentia Praecox*, 142

Kafka, Franz, 20, 68, 99
Kandinsky, Victor, 13
Kardiner, Abraham, 33, 45
Karpas, Morris J., 111
Kelsen, Hans, 6
Kieser, Dietrich Georg, 132–33
Kirby, George H., 111
Kirchhof, Theodor, 107
Kirsch, Dr. James, 110
Klein, Dr., 60
Knox, Robert, 21
Kohn, Emil, 67
Kokoschka, Oskar, 193
Kraepelin, Emil, 93, 102, 147–48; and defi-
    nition of "word salad," 104, 133; on
    Jews and mental illness, 148
Krafft-Ebing, Richard von, 95, 100, 107,
    130, 136, 137, 164
Kraus, Karl, 134
Krauskopf, Joseph, 180
Krauss, A., 132
Kutna, S. N., 65

Lamarck, Jean Baptiste Pierre Antoine de
    Monet de: Freud and, 70, 71, 189, 198;
    his model of inheritance of acquired char-
    acteristics, 24, 26, 27, 90
Landauer, Karl, 177
Langer, Felix: *The Protocols of the Elders of
    Zion*, 78
language (and Jews), 186; corrupt use of,
    101; for Freud, 15, 186; German, repre-
    senting high culture, 13, 16, 149, 190; as
    marker of difference, 30, 163–64, 190–
    91; muscular construction and, 13; per-
    ceived as secret, hidden, 34, 54; and racial

origin, 22; as sign of pathology, 16, 104, 114, 120, 133. See also *Mauscheln*

Lazarus, Moritz, 27, 28

Lebert, Hermann, 169

Le Bon, Gustave, 23, 24

Lederer, C., 54

Leroy-Beaulieu, Anatole, 30–31, 95

Lessing, Gotthold Ephraim, 210n.35

Lessing, Theodor, 110

Levit, Dr., 66–67

Levy, Dr.: response to Weismann, 55–56

Lewin, Dr., 67

Lewisohn, Ludwig, 110

Liébeault, Ambroise Auguste, 30

Lind, Jakov, 221n.11

Lissauer, Ernst, 131

Loewenstein, Rudolph, 82, 233n.174

Löhner, Fritz, 110

Lombroso, Cesare, 6, 35, 40, 170, 229n.126; *Anti-Semitism and the Jews in the Light of Modern Science*, 101; review of Nordau, 82

Löwenfeld, Leopold, 78, 96, 97, 171, 176

Lubbock, John, 58

Luschan, Felix von, 43, 51–52, 115

Luther, Martin, 57, 155, 190

Lyotard, Jean-François, 217n.152

McDougall, William: *The Group Mind*, 25

male, Jewish: circumcised, as baseline, 53, 84; as definition of Jew, 49; feminization of, and linked with feminine, 9, 25, 31–32, 36, 39, 42–43, 57, 69, 78, 79, 81, 82, 117, 161, 162, 163, 215n.120; genitalia of, as different, 8, 21, 39, 40, 44–48, 69, 85–86, 123; as masculine, 10, 15, 37–38, 127–28, 188, 192; as third sex, 43, 47

Manetho, 61, 187

Mannheimer, Isaac Noah, 18, 67–68, 70; debate with von Rosas, 17–18, 86

Mannoni, Octave, 167

Mantegazza, Paolo, 57, 80, 182; attacks on circumcision, 57–58, 61

Manu, Book of, 150, 152

Marcus, Jacob R., 49

Margaritha, Antonious, 209n.31, 223n.37

Marsh, Madison, 179–80, 181–82, 191

Martial, 152

Masson, Jeffrey, 145

masturbation, 39; circumcision linked to, 39–40, 52, 60, 61, 65, 68, 70, 71; female,

65; and neurosis, 89; seen as sin and illness, 52–53

Mauscheln, 114, 149, 186, 195; described by Freud, 13; of Eastern European Jew, 15, 16, 190; and Jewish jokes, 128, 129; as marker, 34, 89, 140, 190

Mauthner, Fritz, 134

medicine, European: anti-Semitic substance of, 12, 64–65, 93, 94, 98, 102, 115, 209–10n.35, 210n.36; and the Jew, 49, 58, 63; role of Jewish physician in, debate over, 17–18, 86; and studies of Jews, 100, 103, 107, 121–22. *See also* circumcision; disease (and Jews); diseases of Jews; mental illness; physician, Jewish; psychiatry; psychoanalysis

Meige, Henry, 117, 163

Menninger, Karl A., 140, 249n.236

mental illness: autobiographical accounts of, study of, 102, 132–33; linked to syphilis, 109, 148, 157–58; origin of, 100; women at risk, 40, 113. *See also* hysteria; neurasthenia; neurosis; paranoia; schizophrenia

mental illness, predisposition of Jews to, 40, 93, 94–102, 107–9, 111–13, 117, 121, 122, 124–25, 148, 235n.1; racial basis of, 96–97, 102–4, 108, 131; religious education and, 112, 113; sexual practices and, 93, 94, 102, 106, 120, 123, 131; urban existence as cause of, 62, 93, 97, 101, 102. *See also* hysteria; neurasthenia; neurosis; paranoia; schizophrenia

mentally ill patients, autobiographical accounts of: language of, 133; physicians' reading of, 133–34, 138–41; publication of, 133. *See also* Schreber, Daniel Paul

metsitsah, 50, 89; defined, 66; linked to disease, and hygenic implications of, 66–69, 70; practice abolished, 68

Meynert, Theodore H., 71, 116

Micale, Mark, 242n.118

Michaelis, Johann David, 52–53, 59

mind, Jewish: as atrophied, 105; and creativity, 31, 215n.120; Jews' views of, 26–30, 34–35; as overdeveloped, 95; as real marker of difference, 198–99

Mischling: image of, applied to Jews, 21, 22

Möbius, Paul Julius, 8, 37, 41, 63, 115, 167, 218n.169

Moll, Albert, 84–85, 164

Molnar, Michael, 186

Mombert, Moritz, 65
Monteux, Pierre, 19
Morel, B. A., 161
Moritz, Karl Phillip, 132
Morselli, Enrico: letter to, 35
Moses (history and representations of):
Freud's, 183–86, 190, 193; Marsh's, 181;
Popper-Lynkeus's, 184
Moses, Julius, 102
Mosse, George, 37
Mother Protection, 97
Müller, Johannes, 27, 169
Myerson, Abraham, 112–13

Näcke, Paul, 36
National Socialism, 32; and anti-Semitic labels, 35; Freud's personal experience
with, 28, 168, 186; and German paranoia, 196, 197
Nazi. See National Socialism
Nemon, Oscar, 30
neurasthenia, 88; as American disease, 95,
106; Jews as prone to, 95–96, 99–102,
106, 108
neurosis: anti-Semitism as, 81–83; and anxiety, 88, 119–20; Freud's explanations of,
88, 90–92; as Jewish disease, 195–96;
Jewish self-hatred as, 109–11. See also
trauma
New York: Eastern European Jews in, 111
Niederland, William, 145
Niemann, Dr., 65
Nietzsche, Friedrich, 139, 194; anti-Semitic
pronouncements of, 150–52; cult of, 150.
Works: The Antichrist[ian], 150, 151,
162, 194; Thus Spake Zarathustra, 150,
151
Nishida, Kitāmaro, 78
Noguchi, Hideyo, 157–58
Nordau, Max, 104–5, 112; Degeneration,
82, 124, 134, 161–62
Nunberg, Herman, 82, 85
Nussbaum, Max, 102

Obersteiner, Heinrich, 106
odor: and difference, 41; Jews and, 40, 152–
53, 155, 253nn. 289 and 304; women
and, 40–41, 152
Offner, Menasze, 113
Ohr, C. H., 158
Oken, Lorenz, 71
Olsen, Charles, 49

Oppenheim, Hermann, 104, 114
Oppenheim, Moritz, 99
Origen, 57
Osler, William, 58, 129
Other, 48; Eastern European Jews as, 9, 15,
16; "good" vs. "bad," 8–9; knowability
of, 38; sexuality of, 106; smell of, 152

Page, Herbert: Injuries of the Spine and Spinal Chord, 124
Panizza, Oskar: "The Operated Jew," 146–
47, 155–56, 160–61, 163–64
Pappenheim, Bertha (Anna O.), 62, 103
paranoia, 134; Freud and, 135, 146, 167,
251n.264; linked to homosexuality, 136;
linked to Jewish religious practice, 140,
146, 250n.262
Pasteur, Louis, 169–70
Peller, Sigismund, 173–74
penis, 38–39, 40, 219n.182; cancer of,
and circumcision, 172–73; circumcised,
45, 49–51, 65, 84, 172, 197; female
envy of, 38–39, 84; Jewish, as different,
40, 46
Perceval, John, 132
Pezzl, Johann, 20, 158–59
Pfister, Oskar, 34; letter to, 6, 22
Philo, 53, 59
physicians, Jewish, 124, 135, 169, 181,
204n.3; as male, 181–82, 204n.3; need
of, to be healthy, 33, 100; and other Jews,
113; stereotyped as quacks, 17–18, 86,
209–10n.35
physiognomy, Jewish, 72, 74; face, 16, 30,
74; nose, reshaping of, 160; visage, and
gaze, 72, 122
Pichler, Hans, 175, 177
Pilcz, Alexander, 62, 162; and Freud, 106–
7; his studies on mental illness among
Jews, 107–8, 109, 148
plica polonica, 20, 159, 254n.324
Popper-Lynkeus, Josef, 183–84, 193; Fantasies of a Realist, 190–91; Freud's borrowing from, 184, 190
Pötzl, Otto, 135
Pound, Ezra, 49
Prager, Joseph, 110
Prinzhorn, Hans, 246n.191, 248n.212
prostitution, prostitutes, 8, 41; linked with
Jews, 9, 62, 64
psychiatry: German, central views of, 117;
and image of self-hating Jew, 109–11;

Jews practicing, 141; and study of accounts of mentally ill, 102, 132–33
psychoanalysis: attack on, 43; Freud's views of, 29–30, 33–35, 42; and Jewish physicians, 249n.239; perceived as Jewish product, 30–31, 115, 142, 190, 216n.143; and role of the female, 48; and study of autobiographical accounts of mentally ill, 134–35
psychoanalysts, Jewish: association of religious practice and mental illness, 250n.262; strong Eastern European presence among, 6
public health issues: circumcision as, 41, 60, 171, 172–73; Jews and health, debate about, 179–83

race: demand for purity of, 98; idea of (shift from biological to psychological), 23, 131; and Jewish identity, 6, 16–17, 30, 43, 44–45, 50; Jews vs. Christians as issue of, 18, 31; question of, for Freud, 3–5, 12–14, 16, 18, 22, 99; and sexual attraction, 79–81. See also Freud, Sigmund: Life and career—Jewish identity; mental illness, predisposition of Jews to; science, biological
Rank, Otto, 32, 137, 185, 252n.282; letter to, 34
Rathenau, Walter, 162
Raymond, Fulgence, 117
Reik, Theodor, 6, 25, 34, 85, 120, 187, 209n.31
Reisel, Salomon, 54
religious practices, Jewish: discussions of, 249n.239; linked to disease, 60, 171, 172; linked to mental illness, 112, 113, 250n.262. See also circumcision
Remondino, Peter Charles, 182
Renan, Ernest, 31, 184, 195
Rie, Oskar, 98
Rieff, Philip, 24, 189
Rieger, Conrad, 146, 163
Roback, A. A., 23; letter to Freud, 254n.312
Róheim, Géza, 72
Rohleder, Hermann, 65
Rohrer, Josef, 159
Roith, Estelle, 7
Romberg, Moritz, 124
Rosenman, Stanley, 10
Rosenthal, Moritz, 116

Roth, Joseph, 19–20
Rychlinski, Karl, 133

Sachs, Hanns, 6, 30; letter to, 183
Sadger, Isidor, 6, 117, 122
Saussure, Raymond de: letter to, 186
Schatzman, Morton, 145
Schiller, Friedrich: The Robbers, 53–54, 75; "Song of the Bell," parody of, 19
Schmidt, Johann Kaspar [pseud. Max Stirner]: The Individual and His Possessions, 139
Schmidt, Wilhelm: The Origin of the Idea of God, 189–90
schizophrenia (dementia praecox): and Jews, 148; and language, 104, 134–35; studies of, 250–51n.262
Schnitzler, Arthur, 116; letter to, 24
Schopenhauer, Arthur, 8, 41, 78, 150, 232n.158
Schorske, Carl, 128–29
Schreber, Daniel Gottlob Moritz, 141, 160, 161
Schreber, Daniel Paul: and his father, 160–61; life of, 142
—Memoirs of a Neuropath, 141, 147; content and theme of, 142, 148, 152; and disease of homosexuality, 144, 159, 196; edited by physicians, 143; and feminization of the body, 146, 147, 154–55, 159, 161, 164; Freud's creative reading of, 142–46, 148, 154, 161, 166, 183, 196, 250n.262; rhetoric of anti-Semitism in, 152–54, 156, 157; and theme of Wandering Jew, 144, 153–54; view of God in, 144, 145, 147–50
Schreber, Gustav, 141
Schudt, Johann Jakob, 52, 53, 152–53, 222n.15
Schur, Max, 175, 179
Schwechten, Eduard: Das Lied vom Levi, illustration from, 19
science, biological (fin de siècle): definition and documentation of Jews in, 51–52; and question of transmission of acquired characteristics, 52–56; racial component in, 4, 5, 7, 17–18, 30, 37, 46, 52, 70–71, 198; and use of statistics, 93; view of Eastern European male Jew in, 26
sexuality: of Jews, 4, 64, 80, 99, 152, 254n.312; linked to smell, 153; of the Other, 106; power of, and masturbation,

sexuality: of Jews (*cont.*)
61; and race, 80; smoking and, 176; studies of, 53. *See also* bisexuality; Freud, Sigmund: Publications and writings—topics, themes, views; homosexuality; male, Jewish

sexual practices, Jewish, perceptions of: as cause for mental illness, 93, 94, 102, 106, 120, 123, 131; as excessive, 136–37; and inbreeding, 93, 94, 98, 106, 107, 123, 192; as incestuous, 106, 123, 150, 192, 252n.281; and link to cancer, 171–72; as perverse, 106; and sexual selectivity, 100, 182, 192, 194, 199

Sexual Problems, 97

Shoah, 12, 51, 183, 188

Showalter, Elaine, 40

Sichel, Max, 6, 101, 102, 148

Siebert, Harald, 103–4

Silberstein, Eduard: letter to, 16

Simmel, Ernst, 197–98, 233n.174

Singer, Charles, 82

Singer, Heinrich, 42, 56, 62, 67

skin (of Jews): color of, 19–20, 51, 158; diseases of, 20, 159, 254n.254

smoking: and tobacco addiction, 175. *See also* Freud, Sigmund: Life and career—smoking habit

Sofer, Moses, 68

Sokolov, Nahum, 16

Sorsby, Maurice, 173

Spencer, Herbert, 65

Spielrein, Sabina, 250–51n.262; background of, 6; her daughter, 32, 33; letters to, 32, 34

Spinoza, Benedict de, 57, 224n.40

Steinfeld, J., 110

Stekel, Wilhelm, 122

Stenthal, Heymann, 27, 28

Stern, Erich, 110

Stigler, Robert, 162–63

Stilling, Benedict, 124

Stirner, Max. *See* Schmidt, Johann Kaspar

Storfer, A. J., 65

Strauss, David Friedrich, 162

Strauss, Hermann, 64, 117, 119

Sue, Eugène: *The Wandering Jew*, 153–54

Sulloway, Frank J., 5–6, 242n.117

Sulzberger, Arthur, 140, 249n.236

Swoboda, Hermann, 43, 78

syphilis (and Jews), 29, 159; higher susceptibility to, 61–63, 109, 124; linked to circumcision, 66–69, 158, 173; linked to mental illness, 109, 148, 157–58; lower rate of, 63–65

Tacitus, 136

Talbot, Eugene, 56

Talmud, 52, 53, 156; as source of Jewish error, 34; tradition of, and congenital circumcision, 222n.15

Tarnowski, Benjamin, 164

Tausk, Viktor, 6, 135

Theilhaber, Adolf, 171–72, 173

Theilhaber, Felix, 99, 171–72; essay in *Jewish Lexikon*, 102–3, 109, 172

Toller, Ernst, 102

trains: Jewish jokes about, 127–29; as locus of anti-Semitic attacks, 126–27; neurosis about, Freud's, 125–28; as source of trauma, 124, 125–26, 129–30

Vienna, fin de siècle: acculturated Jew in, 178–79; anti-Semitism of, 6, 12–13, 15, 18, 23, 45, 86, 106, 115; compared to Jerusalem, 35; Eastern European Jews in, 6, 14, 15, 122; in fiction, 48; medical students in, 17. *See also* Freud, Sigmund: Life and career

Vienna Psychoanalytic Society, 10, 35, 82, 98, 117, 122; cases presented to, 137–38, 143

Viereck, George Sylvester, 16, 186

Vinci, Leonardo da: Freud's study of, 83, 142

Virchow, Rudolf, 51, 54; his study of cancerous tumors, 169, 175

voice (of Jews), 43, 104–5, 163, 164. *See also* language (and Jews)

Voltaire, 86

von Rosas, Anton Edler: debate with Mannheimer, 17–18, 86

Wagner, Richard, 82, 184

Wagner-Jauregg, Julius, 62, 106, 107, 108

Wasserman, Jakob, 109–10

Wechsler, I. S., 112

Weininger, Otto, 86–87, 110, 154

—*Sex and Character*, 77, 80, 142, 232n.158; and Fleiss, 78–79; and Freud, 77–80, 83; impact of, 78

Weismann, August, 55, 70, 71; responses
    to, 55–56
Weiss, Edoardo: letter to, 217n.143
Weltsch, Felix, 82
Westermarck, Edvard, 58, 192
Wilder, Thornton, 179
Wilmanns, Karl, 246n.191
Winch, Peter, 12
Wise, Isaac, 63
Wittels, Fritz, 10, 81, 137, 193
Wittgenstein, Ludwig, 26, 78
Wolbarst, Abraham, 172
Wolf, Elcan Isaac, 20, 157
Wolf, Lucian, 180
Wolfers, Dr., 60
Wolff, Abraham Emanuel, 103
Wolff, August Ferdinand von, 103
Wortis, Joseph, 110

Wulfing-Luer, Georges, 95
Wundt, Wilheml, 27, 58

Zakkai, Jochanan ben, 35
Zeissl, Professor, 67
Zeitschrift für Völkerpsychologie und
    Sprachwissenschaft, 27
Ziemssen, H. V., 95–96
Zionist movement, 239n.69; agenda for,
    105, 109; response to, 191; supporters of,
    100, 161
Zola, Emile: Nana, 69
Zollschan, Ignaz, 56, 108–9
Zweig, Arnold, 76, 194, 198; letters to,
    183, 191, 194–95. Works: Balance of
    German-Jewry (Insulted and Exiled),
    194–95, 196–97; Caliban, or Politics and
    Passion, 195–96